eedy'   Mum + Dad

Beginning

KENNETH BRANAGH

Beginning

Chatto & Windus
LONDON

Published in 1989 by
Chatto & Windus Ltd
30 Bedford Square
London WC1B 3SG

A CIP catalogue record for this book is available from the
British Library.

ISBN 0 7011 3388 0

Photoset in Linotron Baskerville by
Rowland Phototypesetting Ltd
Bury St Edmunds, Suffolk
Printed in Great Britain by
Mackays of Chatham plc, Chatham, Kent

Acknowledgements

Many thanks to my parents for their patience and help with the Belfast chapters; to Annie Wotton for her computer wizardry and her constant support; to Phyllida Law for the marvellous drawings; and to Jonathan Burnham for his expert and invaluable editorial advice.

For
Lizzie Branagh, who was there at the beginning of it all,
with love and gratitude

'I will tell you the beginning,
and if it please your ladyships you shall see the
end,
for the best is yet to do.'

AS YOU LIKE IT

Introduction

Beginning (bigi-nin), vbl. sb. ME. [f. as prec. + INGi.] 1.
The action or process of entering upon existence or upon
action, or of bringing into existence; commencing, orig-
ination. 2. The rudimentary stage; the earliest proceed-
ings.

As this book reveals, I have read a great number of actors' autobiog-
raphies. I've come to think of them as rather dangerous things. I'm
suspicious of talking about acting or 'life'. It seems that as soon as I
think I know something and try to describe it, it's gone. At twenty-
eight, the chances of really knowing something are slim, and the
possibility of losing what grasp you do have, great. So why write this?
Money.

In January 1988 the tiny office in my Camberwell flat was bursting
with the activities of the Renaissance Theatre Company. There was
a packed year of theatre work ahead, and little chance of earning
enough cash to remove the centre of operations from under my own
roof. I discussed the predicament with my literary agent. He and I
had both been approached by various publishers with the idea of my
writing some form of autobiography which would feature an account
of the formation of Renaissance. We decided to auction the idea, and
among the publishers who expressed an interest were Chatto &
Windus.

The deal was made, and a handsome advance was paid out. The
advance provided the funds to buy accommodation for the Company's offices, thus moving Renaissance out of my flat and bringing
me a little nearer sanity.

I had agreed to write 100,000 words. Quite what I was going to
write I wasn't sure, but I was hopeful that it would work out
somehow – a pattern that characterises much of the career described
in the pages that follow. It's an odd and difficult task to try and make
sense of one's life at twenty-eight. I've set out therefore to describe, as
far as I can understand it, the beginnings of a life and of a career.
When I read it back, this book seems merely to describe a professional journey, the arrival point of which is another beginning.

Looking back has been an instructive process for me, but for the ordinary reader, interested in actors and acting, I suspect that it will make a different kind of sense. I hope that there will be some value in the fact that this book has been written now, with all its imperfections on its head, and not in fifty years' time. It makes no claim to be a manual on acting, or a careers advice book, or a survey of the British Theatre today. It's the story of a particular talent, and how that talent was combined with a measure of ambition and some quite extraordinary professional good fortune. Above all, it describes a first stage, from which it seems too early to draw far-reaching conclusions.

This is simply what happened to me.

Home

ONE

'Mewling and puking'
AS YOU LIKE IT

The smell of pigs' feet boiling,
with nabs and ribs and noints,
Greeted all men-folk as they
rolled home from the joints.
Mother cut the soup-greens
whilst waiting for her sire.
Then bathed the children briskly
in a tub beside the fire.
That was Saturday night in York Street;
boyhood memories remained . . .
Saturday night in York Street
will never come again!

(From SATURDAY NIGHT IN YORK STREET, by
John Campbell)

Even in the 1930s, a Saturday night in Belfast's York Street was 'a quare oul do'.

The fighting and the swearing at chucking-out time were as savage and regular as the arrival of the peelers, who gathered up the familiar faces into a packed paddy wagon and took them straight to the police station. With equal regularity, the wives would arrive the next morning at the 'polis' to say their Sunday hellos to the station officer and to bail out their hungover husbands. The rancour of the previous evening would have mysteriously disappeared and the former enemies would walk home arm-in-arm with their wives as if the combat of the previous evening had been a strange dream. The daily intimacy and neighbourliness which characterised relationships in that world returned as if by magic, and they wended, by way of a drink, back to the Belfast legend that was York Street.

At the time it was more than just a street. It constituted an area right on the docks that included names like Ship Street, Nelson Street, Pilot Street and a small network of roads and alleys that collectively took their name from the main thoroughfare. The houses were battered, cramped terraces that sardined their inhabitants together for more years than the buildings can ever have been intended for. People rarely knew who owned them. Except in very few cases, it certainly wasn't the inhabitants. They paid their rent weekly – at least, that was the plan – to an agent. The mysterious landlord seldom ventured into this part of Belfast.

Rough it was, but the people who lived in and around York Street had a fierce pride in their area, and its nearness to the docks, Belfast's great heart. Everyone knew each other and York Street folk were famous in Ulster for an encyclopaedic knowledge of family affairs that stretched from street to street. This knowledge was often gained through blood ties. Large families were the norm and it was these little tribes and clans, Catholic and Protestant alike in rough segregation, that dominated the area. The Branaghs and the Harpers (my mother's family) grew up within streets of each other. Both were large Protestant families and both were ruled over by highly colourful patriarchs in the shape of my two grandfathers, who shared the same first-class York Street credentials of being universally known 'characters', hard drinking and hard up.

Alcoholism was an unfamiliar word in those days, but on a York Street drinking table Grandpa Branagh would have been in the middle and Grandpa Harper threatening the leaders. Neither of them actually found their way into the great caged Saturday night 'polis' wagon but I suspect this was only because they moved bars quickly enough.

'Speedy' Harper worked on the docks. He got his name from the pace at which he could empty cement boats, a frequent Belfast cargo. With just a sack over his head, he and his fellows ran up and down the gangplanks like ants, cement dust everywhere. The docks operated a highly discriminatory system for distributing work. There were the blue button men, the red button men and the casuals. When work was to be had, which was usually on a strictly daily basis, the stevedores would select first from the blue button men, then from the red, and then from the casuals. Much of the Saturday night bother arose from arguments about this exclusive preferential treatment. Blue and red buttons were handed down from father to son and buying or bribing your way in was very difficult. Once you were in, the difference was considerable, with a blue button man receiving as a daily wage what a casual might make for the week. In spite of being a beneficiary of this local corruption, Speedy Harper seemed little better off. With his colleagues, he had the usual dockers' breakfast – an hour in the pub between 10 and 11 – and if, with his customary skill, he had emptied a cement boat by 3 pm, then the blue button benefits found their way into the bar for the rest of the day. They disappeared very quickly, commemorated only by the ever-full slate which each bar ran, and to which every York Street man inevitably became indebted.

A fearsome man in the home, dogged by injuries at work (when he was in work), Speedy Harper's volatile, alcohol-infused personality must have shuddered at the arrival of yet another addition to his large family. Frances Harper, my mother, was born on 6 September 1930. A complication after the birth ensured that some twelve days later her no doubt exhausted mother died, at the age of thirty-eight. Frances had been her eleventh child.

For a while my mother escaped the aftermath of a tragedy which was all too familiar in York Street. Her elder sisters were too young to play any maternal role, so Frances was sent to a great Aunt Alice who lived in BallyMcCarret, East Belfast, and she remained there happily until she was six. Alice, very elderly, gave her, for a brief period, some sense of what having a mother and living in a small, reasonably comfortable house might have been like. The kind, dumpy old lady doted on her, bringing her a wonderful breakfast in bed every morning – a Jaffa orange with the top cut off, full of sugar, with a spoon stuck into it. Then Aunt Alice died, and my mother's unsettled childhood took another blow. Shaken by the double loss, she returned to Belfast and a family divided by death, with a father whose drinking had intensified, and who had little sense of responsibility about the family finances.

Ship Street was a long way from Aunt Alice's, and the early disorientation had a profound effect on the six-year-old girl. There had been other deaths, all sons – Willie-John, George, Martin, who had a fall in Speedy's beloved shipyard, and Andrew, who died tragically from eating an infected banana found on a rubbish tip. The family now consisted of Charlie and James, Kathleen, Rosie and Frances. Jeanie and Sarah, the oldest girls, had left already. There were two rooms, one up one down, with a stone floor, a wooden table and a scrubbed wooden settee. It looked a bit like a butcher's shop. The girls slept together in one bed and the boys shared their bed with Speedy (something that Charlie refused to do as soon as he was able – because of the drink that reeked from his father).

Frances attended the Mariners' Public Elementary School, earning a reputation as a tearaway. Perhaps not having a mother, living with a drunken father and a measure of fierce Harper pride were the cause. In any case she was too busy rebelling to notice a rather quieter boy in the class of sixty or more, but her future husband, William Branagh, must have noticed her.

'Pop' Branagh, my father's dad, was a 'handy man' – a phrase prevalent in the folklore of the time to describe York Street men who 'dabbled' for their income. Pop could be seen at the docks some mornings (as a casual) trying for a day's work on one of the boats. But his real love was horses, and for a time he had a little yard at the back of Nelson Street where he sold hay and oats, and repaired horse-carts and bits of saddlery. Sometimes he worked as a kind of agent, buying horses for Belfast delivery men who couldn't make the trips out to the local fairs. The kids were kept off school for these missions so that they could ride or lead one of the horses back to Belfast. It was on horseback that my father first saw the Fairs at Killreigh and Ballyclare, and caught a breath of the country which had a much stronger pull for him than the brashness of docklands Belfast.

Pop and Lizzie Branagh, with five children, had fewer mouths to feed than the Harpers, but for Pop the work was even more irregular and the call of the bar just as strong. Both my parents were introduced to pubs early on with the nightly crane round the door of the public house to scream 'Tell my Da his tea's ready'. Within shouting distance of each other's homes, both Bill and Frances were aware of the cruel hold that drink had on their fathers.

At Christmas, the Da's would leave at the very last minute for the market and come back late (drunk, of course) with a chicken and some vegetables under their arms. The women in each household performed miracles, Kathleen taking the mother's role at the Harpers' and Lizzie Branagh ensuring there was at least an apple and an orange in the Christmas stocking. If she'd managed to keep the money from Pop, there would be twelve new pennies for Annie, Walter, Tommy, Lilly and Bill. For my mother, Christmas and birthdays offered much the same prospect, with perhaps fewer pennies, and more time to envy the rare child in the area (perhaps in another blue button home) who had a 'proper' present. Her dream was always to have a bicycle, a wish granted by Speedy Harper in her

4

late teens when a second-hand boneshaker was offered. Her disappointment when she talks of it is palpable even now.

My father's quiet early education at Pilot Street Elementary School was interrupted by the war. He was nine years old, and both he and Annie were evacuated to Rosharkin, in the countryside near Belfast, amid much gas-mask-issuing excitement. The sense of childhood adventure was soon shattered when Bill was placed under the demonic authority of his country schoolmaster, Mr Eaton, a Celtic Murdstone. He was now separated from both his mother and father. Pop had gone to England to work as a miner in Melton Mowbray and Lizzie was bringing up Tommy, Walter and Lilly in Belfast, sixty miles from the terrified children.

My father lived in mortal dread of Mr Eaton, a man with a smouldering and unreasonable resentment against Belfast, the Belfast accent and Belfast schoolchildren. Picked on relentlessly by Eaton, this period was a very miserable one for my father, and I have often thought of him praying his child's heart out in that small Irish village, desperately wishing that the Austin car which drove the dragonish Eaton would crash and kill him. The evacuees' home was comfortless. Talking was forbidden, bed was at eight o'clock and it required the greatest daring to creep out of the bedrooms to hear Alvar Liddell's nine o'clock war bulletin.

Later, there were compensations. My grandmother was able to join them in Rosharkin after a year, bringing the rest of the children and renting at last their own two-roomed accommodation in the village. The family sent fervent but often hopeless prayers that Pop's registered money envelope would arrive from England. If the drink had devoured it that week then Bill was dispatched across the road to the landlord's to explain that the rent would not be paid and to beg for understanding. But they were in the country, which my father loved, and he earned a few extra pennies by collecting eggs for the local farmer who let him keep one from every batch. Indeed, the Branaghs' landlord grew so attached to this enterprising Belfast lad that he approached my grandmother about adopting him. At this point the Belfast authorities relaxed the evacuee regulations and the problem of whether my father should remain in Rosharkin or not was solved by the family's swift return to the city and a new two-up two-down in Nelson Street.

Pop returned from Melton Mowbray and the family were reunited for the last part of the war. Bill and Tommy, when not at the

Mariners' school, would continue to help their Dad with his general 'dealing'. On an old cart pulled by a horse which grew or shrank in size according to the varying success of Pop's ventures, they rode around York Street selling eggs or vegetables or whatever job-lot they'd managed to find. Herrings were a favourite. Pop would pick up a box on the fish quay and sell them round York Street for two bob a dozen. This, with the horse dealing, the saddlery and removal of fireplaces, continued to provide Pop with an erratic income in a Belfast relatively prosperous through the temporary boom provided by the munitions industry.

The street lore of this time was particularly rich and both my parents were beginning to enter fully into the York Street world of Ulster eccentrics. People like Jimmy Foster, who flitted from street to street and house to house as a twinkling handy man who was 'only temporary'. If he mended something, it was 'only temporary'. If he broke an appointment, it was 'only temporary'. Then there was 'Buck Alec', a knotty, sinewy fellow who, it was said, had been a Strong Man in the circus. If the peelers knew they were to deal with 'Buck Alec' on the Saturday night clear-up of the pubs, they laid on extra manpower.

They often had cause to speak to him. 'Buck Alec' kept a lion in a cage in his backyard in York Street. He took this with him round the Fairs in Ulster as a sideshow. Alec would leap fearlessly into the cage, take hold of the decrepit animal's mouth, open it and put his head inside. It was believed that Alec had pulled all its teeth. What everyone was sure of was the incessant roaring of the beast through the York Street night. Alec promised to do something. After a time calm was restored and residents breathed a sigh of relief until another uproar followed as the police station was inundated with people reporting their domestic cats stolen. 'Buck Alec', who could be as 'temporary' as Jimmy Foster, disappeared with the cat-eating cat in tow.

Apart from murmurings in 1935 and the usual Saturday night free-for-all, this period and through to the 1960s was relatively free from sectarian violence or other trouble of that kind. The ratio of Protestants to Catholics in York Street was two thirds to one third, and they worked, ate and played together in peace.

The chief trouble for my mother was her own schooling. Her rebellious streak was much in evidence. On one occasion her sister, Rose, who was in the same class, asked to be allowed to go to the toilet. The teacher refused and after a while, in the scrum of the packed classroom, Rose fainted. Indignant, my mother rose up to tear a strip off the teacher and immediately marched her mortified sister back home and then brought the dreaded Speedy to the school to put the fear of God into the teacher. That kind of Harper spunk made her unpopular with the staff and my mother's response was to refuse to care and to stop listening, a course she has been regretting for the rest of her life, and which she has repeatedly enjoined her own family not to do. She remains lively and intelligent, but haunted by the fact that her education was neglected. This has bred a sense of inferiority, and an inbuilt suspicion of the world and the blows it will inevitably inflict upon her and the family – which is not surprising in the light of troubled family history and of Speedy himself, who seemed dogged by misfortune. Protective coatings have developed to protect this vulnerability, which must be linked to the absence of her own ma, but traces of the rebel child are manifest in my mother's anarchic and irrepressible sense of fun – her giggling fits have punctuated family life for as long as I can remember.

Speedy had moved the family to North Anne Street, where they had four rooms. Like the Branaghs, they lived on barley soups and vegetable broths which lasted for three or four meals. There was shin beef or brisket once a week or once a fortnight. Rationing helped put my father off margarine for life, and egg powder haunts the entire tribe of my aunts and uncles. Speedy was drunk by degrees. The Harper girls preferred him to be paid weekly because then he was only drunk all weekend; if he was paid daily then he was drunk every night.

Late each evening it was the task of the girls to get this dead weight up the stairs, and from time to time they took a secret pleasure in letting him fall, stifling their giggles the next day when he murmured to himself about why the hell he was so black and blue. The temptation for some sort of revenge was great. He would frequently come home plastered and demand that my mother be brought downstairs to sing to him while he became darkly maudlin about his dead wife. Nearly forty years later I appeared in a television play by Graham Reid set in Belfast where just such a scene occurs. All of my mother's family vouched for the authenticity of the scene, one which must have been repeated all over York Street in those days.

The drink and the fags always had the first call on his money. When the girls wanted to decorate he put his foot down about wallpaper, saying it carried bed-bugs and insisted instead that the house should be red-leaded. When he was broke and had no cigarettes he made my mother search the streets for dog-ends. Woe betide her if she returned empty-handed. He insisted despite the shame it caused my mother, who desperately cajoled friends into joining the hunt until they too refused and she felt only the deep indignity of forcibly serving this drunken man's poverty-stricken addiction. She remembers the time and the shame with great force. It remains difficult for her to talk about, and only in recent years has she been able to share these tearful recollections with her own family.

Elsewhere in York Street at this time, papers were being delivered by William Branagh Junior, who was also finishing his education at the ripe old age of fourteen. As with all the York Street kids, the options were few. Mr Burgess, his headmaster at Mariners', wanted him to go on to higher education, but it was out of the question that 'young Willie', as his mother called him, should not start bringing some wage into the house. The obvious place was the textile mill. Burgess was appalled and did everything in his power to save this bright boy from such a fate. Nevertheless a starting wage at the mill for young Willie was £2 10 shillings and not to be ignored. Rescue came in the shape of Billy McMillan, who ran Dad's paper-round and who had a mate with a building business looking for an apprentice. Mr Burgess was delighted, Dad decided on doing his time as a joiner and Lizzie accepted the drop in wage that this inevitably meant. Twenty-three shillings and sixpence was his starting pay, of which one pound was handed into the house. By the Thursday of each week, through his bus fares and the two or three trips to the cinema which was the staple diet of the York Street youngster, Lizzie ended up paying a few bob back so that young Willie could have some sort of social life. But serving your time (if you could manage the immediate financial hardship) was a terrific start, and my father set to it with a will.

For my mother there was the mill, or nothing. She dreamed of getting away, of becoming a professional ballroom dancer. If that wasn't possible, then at least she would try to get to England, the next best thing. No, was the implacable reply from Speedy, not until she was twenty-one. The rest of her adolescence was spent in avoiding his wrath and, whenever she could, dancing. This was more difficult than it sounds. Apart from the cost of going to a dance, maybe borrowing shoes, painting your legs with stain to stand in for stockings, there was also Speedy. If an application to be 'let out' for the evening to go to a dance wasn't lodged at least two weeks before, then you were in trouble. And if there was any domestic work which needed doing, then you were simply required to stay in, regardless of what arrangements had been made.

My mother and father first met properly when they were both sixteen years old at a church youth club – a group of around twenty-four York Street kids, who went on day-trips together; many of them, over the years, married each other. Although the club was attached to the church, my parents both maintained only a nominal interest in formal religion, a reaction perhaps to the religious obsessions which gripped the province.

Dad came out of his time at nineteen and, yet again confounding the apparent rules of working-class opportunity, he was made a gang leader and put in charge of three of the men he'd been serving under for the previous five years. What's more, his boss had special assignments for him. New building systems and materials were developing and young Willie's firm had Irish franchises for important elements of these. He was sent off for a week's course to London and returned starry-eyed and shell-shocked from the first hotel he had ever stayed in, the Strand Palace, which must have seemed like wonderland in 1950 for the twenty-year-old from York Street.

He returned home and then went to the Republic (or the Free State, as it was referred to then) to implement these new skills and at last to earn some real money. He worked all over the south, each job lasting roughly six weeks. The wages arrived on Friday at the local post-office, and a fiver would go back to his mother who at last could be repaid for the sacrifices of his teens. She saved the money and tried to give it back to him when he came home at the weekends.

With plenty of overtime down south, the money was really very good, and meant that on the trips home both 'Pop' and Speedy, the future in-law, were able to benefit. By this time Frances and Bill were writing to each other regularly and seeing each other on his trips back. But their relationship didn't stop my mother sticking to her childhood promise of going to England. At twenty-one she pawned her coat in order to pay her way to Manchester where her elder sister, Jean, was living, and she acted as governess to two young Jewish children in a wealthy northern family. She made a great success of this, and despite pleas from the host family to stay, she was – as she always has been – Belfast to her very bones, and her homesickness

9

drew her back to Nelson Street and into the arms of my father.

They were now officially 'going together', something that must have been a comfort to her when she faced the latest of Speedy's peculiar dispensations. He had had an accident at the shipyard and lost a couple of fingers. He had put in a compensation claim that had taken over a year to be processed, and when it eventually came through no one was quite sure what the amount was, but there was talk of it being a vast amount. In fact, it was around £1500, which was a greater sum than the Harpers had ever seen before. All through the year-long wait, Speedy's slate had been running at the local bar. His credit was good. Everyone knew the claim was in. On the day he got his money he walked into the bar to pay off his slate and buy everyone a drink. His tab ran to nearly £500.

He gave my Aunt Rose £100, and he entrusted the rest to Kathleen, as she'd always managed the household miraculously. From her he received the balance in handouts from which he drank himself slowly to death. To my mother he gave ten pounds, saying that anything more would turn her head. It seems he thought his own was stable enough.

My parents married on 28 August 1954 at St Anne's Cathedral, Belfast. They'd paid for the wedding themselves, and for the reception (six shillings and sixpence a head). Mum wore a borrowed wedding dress and at the last minute, after endless cajoling and a final threat that he would never be spoken to again, Speedy came to give her away. He stayed as long as the photographs and then went off back to the pub. In the wedding pictures he is a haunted, wasted figure. My parents look radiant, handsome and happy.

Married life for the first two years was in one room above Pop and Lizzie's house-cum-shop. They squeezed in a dining-room suite and a bedroom suite and managed to find room for Bill junior, who arrived a year after their marriage. Pop doted on my mother and young Bill, and I'm sure my mother loved Pop far more than her own father. But like Speedy, Pop was often short of the readies. She discovered his own roguish method of acquiring them when he asked her, shortly after they moved in, 'Can I mind ten bob for you?' 'What do you want to do that for?' she asked innocently. Enter my father to catch his own dad red-handed and point out fiscal expedients to his new wife.

After two years of marriage and regular work for them both, Mum in the mill and Dad now working in Belfast as a joiner, they made the huge York Street leap of buying their own house. The semi-detached at £1350 in the Cavehill suburb seemed within their reach, but furnishing the place and bringing up baby was a strain. There were buses to catch everywhere and six pounds a month mortgage plus HP on some of the furnishings. After a while they had to sell their dream home. It was a terrible disappointment and they certainly suffered as a result of this 'fall'. And quite a fall it was. They'd been on the council waiting list for some time but the powers-that-be decided that a probationary period was also needed to see if they were suitable tenants. They were placed at the lowest end of the council's accommodation lists and were eventually housed in the Downview Bungalows estates.

These were pre-fabs, made with asbestos and designed to last for ten years. Some of them remained for forty. My parents had their first shock when they were required to have referees for the baker and the milkman. When trying to buy on HP they were told 'credit was not good in Downview Gardens'. My mother assumed naively that all the men on the estate were doing night work, since she saw them around during the day. In fact my father and one other man on the estate of sixty pre-fabs were the only ones in work. Everyone else was 'on the club'.

My mother finally decided something had to be done when strange male visitors would knock on the door and say that they'd been sent by 'a friend'. She kept sending them off until Dad found out that 55, Downview Bungalows (our address) was being confused with 55, Loughview Bungalows, part of the red light district. It was only this case, specially pleaded by my mother to an (at last) understanding council that persuaded them to rehouse the Branaghs one grade up at 96 Mountcollyer Street, N.15.

Just before that, on Saturday 10 December 1960, in the late afternoon, a second son was born, Kenneth Charles. It was about ten minutes to five and apparently I was just in time for the football results.

My first memories of Belfast begin just after the death of Speedy, who was already becoming a Harper family myth. My aunts had clubbed together to propagate the legend of a man who was hard-done-by, tough but fair, who loved his family to death, despite outward appearances, and whose one fatal flaw was drink. Over the years the family have granted Speedy a Santa Claus-like aura of benevolence. In all of the Harpers there was also a feeling of having been through something of tremendous significance, an impenetrable bond of pride in having survived upbringings of extreme hardship, and a father whose temperament was unpredictable and often cruel.

I never knew Speedy, and although Pop Branagh was not as dramatic (or tragic) a character, for me he was a real grandad – kind, warm, and sweet-natured. I loved him and Granny Branagh to death, and as an infant explorer, running amok in his front room workshop, I was introduced to the Aladdin's Cave that was Pop's factory of commercial ideas. As my father recalls with melancholy, 'He could have been a millionaire, but for the drink. When he did make money, he gave half of it away and drank the other half.'

My mother certainly vouches for his generosity, as she was the first to receive a crisp note after one of Pop's successful schemes. By this time one of his main ventures was removing old tiled fireplaces (then called 'Kitchenettes') and replacing them with wooden 1950s' models. He was still enlisting help from Dad, who provided the mantelpieces for this part of Pop's work.

Both Pop and Granny Branagh took a great interest in me and in Bill, who was five years older than I was. My mother now insists that I was always a difficult child. At the age of three I spoke but could be understood by no one but her. Aunt Kathleen was convinced I was German, and my mother believed I would never be able to speak properly.

The cause of this problem was my tonsils and adenoids, which were promptly removed amid death's-door rises in temperature. I emerged from this brush with death in a considerably calmer state than my family, and with my new vocal dexterity was able to scream the house down about my school dinners. The kitchens of the Grove Primary School were absolutely fine, I'm sure, but a mysterious and morbid dread of puddings and of being forced to eat them – as I was by a dragonish teacher called Mrs Robinson – left me a gibbering wreck.

With Mum and Dad both working, I had no choice. I appeared to comply, but as my weight dropped over the weeks, my parents knew something was up. I was rumbled when a pile of loose change was found in the pans of the boys' toilets. What I'd done was to tell the teachers that I was going home then hid in the loos, where I was so paralysed with guilt that I threw the dinner money down the toilet. I hadn't realised that the coins were not flushing away and I was soon exposed. Whether they felt they had a Freudian textbook case on their hands is unclear, but my folks certainly deemed the problem serious enough to write a note that excused me the horrors of custard, tapioca and bread and butter pudding, and thereby save themselves some money.

Pop and Lizzie came to the rescue and each dinnertime I walked to their house, which was near the Grove, and had their famous broth or 'champ' (mashed potatoes, spring onions and butter) or fish fingers and other treats. Chief among these was a threepenny bit which my Granny produced just before I headed back to school each day and which allowed me a fine selection from the penny tray at the local sweet shop.

As well as my daily visits, the family went to see my grandparents at least twice a week. Belfast seemed to be all about visiting your relatives. As my folks seemed to be related to one half of Belfast and to have been at school with the other half, visiting time was hectic. At my Granny's we were certain to see my Aunt Annie and maybe her kids, Eileen and Joss. On the walk down, or on the bus, we were bound to see Aunt Kathleen and Uncle Jim, Uncle Tommy or maybe his kids (my cousins) Scott and Jackie, or any number of neighbours – Wallace Moore, Peggy Beggs, Mary Page. There was a strong community life which already fascinated me.

I sat listening to these grown-ups as they monitored life in the area – who was marrying who, leaving who, abusing who, moving house, moving country – all of this discussed with continual reference to similar incidents in the past. Everything was linked to their fathers and uncles and aunts, and the daily gossip promoted floods of stories. The past was strongly alive in everyday discourse and was relished by all generations. The built-in Irish preoccupation with history, political and social, was at its most appealing in this context. It is true that the younger working-class generation wanted fridges, TVs, nicer dining-room suites, in short, wanted to better themselves, but never at the cost of rejecting their backgrounds. People like my mother embraced the stories and culture of my grandmother's generation and implicitly encouraged me to do so. It was no hardship. All the Irish, old, young, male and female, are natural storytellers who immortalise the Buck Alecs and Jimmy 'only temporary' Fosters.

The collective yarn session was a colourful occasion, but in the Branagh/Harper clan it did not extend to anyone believing they could 'perform' professionally. There were no actors or singers in the family and none could be remembered by my grandparents. It was hardly necessary. When the sexes got together (for our visits to grannies and aunts were almost always female affairs – the men did their gossip and reminiscing in the pub) it was entertainment of a high order.

These family nights or 'do's' often began informally, growing out of the normal daily visits, or they were arranged to celebrate the arrival of some distant relative from foreign parts. If it had just happened spontaneously then the kids had more chance of viewing the grown-ups and 'the crack' – the Irish word for the pleasure of company, conversation, arguments and songs. On the very rare occasions when I saw my grandmother involved she would sit with a glass of milk or lemonade in her hand and get very merrily weepy. A drink never passed her lips. Like my mother she had an almost pathological distrust of the stuff. There was no such suspicion felt by the rest of my relations, who could even persuade my mother to sip at a Snowball or a vodka and orange. Either drink would last her the entire evening.

While encouraging even greater wallowing in York Street folklore, these do's provided everybody with the chance of a 'turn', which seemed more or less compulsory. My first real impression of my parents comes from these evenings. My father, with a strong compact body, knotty, dark and handsome, had the same twinkling eyes as Pop, and I could already see he was a great 'kidder'. Often in these sessions, when his turn came, he would tell a few jokes or, very occasionally, be persuaded to sing. But singing was really my mother's forte. She always seemed to me to be very fashion-conscious and would sit in her latest pair of glasses – the frames seemed to change every week – and stare at the floor as she tore into her speciality. It was, and is, a funereal ditty called 'Marguerite' which was a great favourite among the rest of the family and for which, over the years, I have tried, but failed, to develop a taste. As the last bars of the song would fade, with more 'ee's' in it than I thought possible, 'I love you Mar-gah-reeeeeeete!', my Uncle Jim would go down on one knee in front of his delighted and embarrassed wife, and croon, 'I'll take you home again Kathleen, to where your heart will feel no pain'.

I watched all this with surprise and delight. I can't recall anyone getting drunk. There was never enough money for a great amount of booze, but there was tremendous merriment, people loving 'the crack', all jammed into somebody's tiny front room, squatting on the floor and perching on the ends of sofas. I wanted more than anything to join in, but entry to that élite came with age, or perhaps with the onset of a talent for performing.

In Mountcollyer Street I was developing my own network of relationships. I knew everyone of my own age in the street, and I'd see many of them in the local corner shop where we'd converge, doing 'messages' for our mothers. The shop was run by Harriet, who had been to school with my mother and was a fund of local knowledge.

The tiny terraced houses were three-up, three-down – an increase with every move. In 1981, on my first return trip to Belfast after eleven years, I went back to Mountcollyer Street and was astonished at how small the houses seemed. It took a while before I remembered that I was smaller then. The streets were tightly packed together and in the evenings, when it was time for our tea, my mum would simply stand on the front step and yell 'Ken!', 'Bill!' – I could hear her streets away. I wish I'd inherited her projection. When all the mothers were doing this at six o'clock in the evening, there was a strange Mountcollyer Street cacophony.

We played in huge groups. 'Raleigh-oh' was a sort of hide-and-seek game on a large scale, involving groups of hiders and seekers and spread across the whole area. We played football in the street too, and the number of broken window incidents improved my sprinting ability no end.

Religion seemed to have as little effect on my early life as it had had on my parents. My only feelings towards it were various forms of resentment. I was made to go to Sunday School, but that didn't seem so bad because at least they gave you prizes at the end of the year for good attendance. If you actually stopped to concentrate on what the teacher was saying, you were in trouble. I remember one dark Sunday when I had been transfixed by the information that when we died we arrived at a fork in the road. One long, straight road led to heaven, the other – narrow and winding – to hell. In my astonishment at this geographical gem, I had paid scant regard to which road was which. I spent a sleepless week certain that I would die early and would not remember which road to take. I cursed the church for not supplying me with some easy-to-read chart, a kind of Tube map for purgatory. The catechism was all very well, but I had enough to think about.

On Sunday evenings we were often sent as family representatives to the big church in town. Whenever I read about actors being fascinated by the ceremony and theatricality of the Catholic church, I remember my own repulsion at the far more sober Presbyterian version. I hated its ornateness, the oppressiveness of the buildings, the clothes the ministers wore, the smell, and to this day I dislike churches, which make me feel physically ill. Coventry Cathedral is the only place I've ever been where the building seems light enough to bear some relation to the joy that organised religion is alleged to provide. My innate aversion was confirmed early on by the bombastic threats of those fire-and-brimstone Belfast ministers, and they were the last push I needed to resist the demon of fear which religion seemed determined to establish in the province.

I'm not sure what set off my interest in the arts, but two events coincided when I was seven or eight that ignited some spark of inquiry. The first was my brother's tortuous rehearsal process for his 'joke' in the Grove School end-of-term concert. He was playing a blacked-up American minstrel (with a strong Belfast accent). There were weeks of agonised practice around the house and I remember thinking that it was a strangely painful activity to volunteer for. I was mad keen to see the results, but on the night I found that I was so transfixed by my brother's black York Street shoe-shine that the delivery of the gag escaped me.

It was around this time that I saw Burt Lancaster in the film *The Birdman of Alcatraz*. It is a gripping story about a convicted murderer who finds peace rearing birds in his prison cell. I was struck by how real it seemed. No one appeared to be 'acting'. Lancaster's own performance was tremendously powerful and affecting, and I was so engrossed that I studied the end-credits list so that I could check the names of the other actors and everyone else responsible for the movie.

It was the beginning of a habit that lasted throughout my youth. I started mentally logging all the unsung character actors – in *The Birdman of Alcatraz*, for instance, Telly Savalas, then relatively unknown, played the side-kick to Burt Lancaster. I began to wonder what 'continuity' was, and imagined it as the person who joined together all the bits of film. And who did 'lighting', which I always misread as 'lightning'? I must have noticed it first on a horror film. Very soon I became a fund of useless information and, if nothing else, I knew that the Westmore family seemed to provide the make-up artists for every Hollywood film and that Michael Ripper was almost guaranteed to play the innkeeper in a Hammer horror film.

I had my first trip to the theatre: a production of 'A Christmas Carol' at the Grove Theatre, which starred Joseph Tomelty, with whose daughter, Frances, I would later work. I was enthralled by the tale itself – which promoted a great love for Dickens – but also by the nature of the performance. They were there, actually in front of me, *being*. There was no other word for it. Magic.

My parents didn't share the same enthusiasm, as the arts did not play a big role in their life. They read voraciously, but only news-papers and magazines, and there were no books in the house: if people needed fiction or poetry it was there in everyday life, in gossip, conversation and storytelling. My folks did enjoy the sheer escapism of movies and there were family trips to the cinema, which I loved, to see *Chitty Chitty Bang Bang*, *The Great Escape* and the deliciously absurd *One Million Years B C*, which seemed ridiculous even to my nine-year-old sensibilities. I've had a soft spot for Raquel Welch ever since.

During the late 1960s the family finances continued to fluctuate. I was never aware of any real hardships, only that some Christmasses the stockings were fuller than others. I was always taught to be aware of 'the value of money', and never to abuse it or to put too much store by it. At dinner I was never allowed to leave an empty plate, because 'somebody in the Third World would be glad of that'.

We took a holiday every year: sixty-seven pounds at Butlin's, which was enough for full board for the four of us for the week. My dad remembers praying that we didn't ask for yet another ice-cream in the middle of the afternoon as he tried to eke out their allowance for the week. I made my own unconscious attempts at household economy. Just before one trip there had been a TV advertising campaign which boasted that everything in Butlin's was free. I put this to the test by leaving a camp-site sweet shop with a basket full of Smarties, only to be nabbed by an irate Redcoat who told my dad that he didn't believe my story.

Money remained scarce, and despite Dad's efforts to go solo in business, he hit a bad patch in which work in Belfast became difficult to find. A slightly better job came up in England, involving ceilings and partitions, and he decided to take it. From 1967 he flew back every third Friday on the Aldergrove standby and brought his youngest a tiny Matchbox car on each trip. By the time we left

Belfast in the Spring of 1970, I had an enormous collection of much-cherished vehicles.

His departure coincided with a resurgence of the Troubles. Tension was high all over the province. Confrontations of gangs and individuals in the local parks and streets were common. You'd be stopped by a bunch of youths, and pushed around, and asked if you were Catholic or Protestant. Sometimes it was impossible to guess what religion they were, so the right answer was a gamble. Often you'd get hit anyway. If you did answer correctly, they'd say you were lying.

Apart from religious trouble, there were the usual adventures of growing up. I went on my one and only inept shoplifting expedition and, although I wasn't caught, I was identified by the manic shopkeeper who, of course, knew my mother. Retribution was the usual clip round the ear, administered by my mother, Dad being away. Punishment was always short, sharp and harmless. It didn't always seem logical, however, and I learned when to keep my mouth shut.

I had my first lesson in this when sitting on the tiny wall in front of the house while my mother chatted with her neighbour, a daily event up and down the street. Most of the time, Dad was away working slavishly, but when he was home he would occasionally slip off to place a wee bet.

'Where is Mr Branagh then, Frances?'

'I'm not sure. I think he's on a message.'

'Sure he's at the bookies', Ma.'

'Oh, that's right, son. Thanks.'

We finished the conversation and went back into the house where the door closed and a fiercesome belt from Mum sent me flying across the hall.

'Don't tell your business to everyone.'

Point taken.

School life was Dickensian in its severity. I was once caned for running across some flower-beds during a chase in a playground game. I had been spotted and secretly reported, and was summoned to see the headmaster. I shall never forget the relish with which he slowly put books away, opened and closed drawers, while he calmly scolded me. Years later, the scene retains a Pinteresque menace. The preamble of quiet, deadly reprimand, delivered in a sepulchral drawl, was far more of a deterrent than the actual blow with the cane.

18

If I later wondered why school discipline seemed much more effective in Ireland, I had only to remember this Donald Pleasance look-alike and imagine him tearing the wings off flies.

My form teacher, Mr Gribben, upheld the tradition of grisly intimidation. He kept two gym shoes on his desk. He called them Dougal and Zebedee after the characters in the then popular children's TV series, *The Magic Roundabout*. If, for an offence, you received a whack on the bottom from Zebedee, you were fortunate. That was his left shoe, which he chose to wield with his weaker left hand. If you had been especially naughty (perhaps talking in class when you weren't supposed to), then you were hauled out to the front of the room and given a whack with Dougal and the full force of his right-handed wrath.

Academic discipline seemed equally harsh. A weekly maths and English composition test was savagely marked and the results tabled so that in the four rows of uncomfortable wooden form-desks people were regrouped on a weekly basis. Those children with the highest marks sat at the desk beside the teacher's table, and everyone else was graded accordingly, with the least successful at the bottom of the fourth row and furthest away from the teacher. A cruel system that did everything to confirm hopelessness and breed conceit.

My maths never allowed me to get to the top desk but I was always near enough to witness Amanda Watson, the object of my unrequited love, elbow to elbow with Edward Brown, the numerical genius. I prayed that when we grew up she might marry us both – although she had eyes for no one but him – and at least I could look at her.

With Mum working and bringing up two boys, and Dad away, it was a worrying time for them both. My mother was in charge while Dad was away but she could do nothing about the rising tide of street violence which, up to then, had not really affected us. Then, one evening, things came to a head. My brother was playing football a couple of hundred yards down the hill. I and a few friends were idling outside my house when we became aware of a strange buzzing, like an enormous swarm of bees in the distance. Then we heard the screams of my brother and his mates tearing up the hill towards us, yelling 'Get inside, get inside!' They were being followed by a dark, clamorous mass which revealed itself to be a crowd of wild-eyed Protestants from the Shankhill Road.

I ran inside to my mother, who stuffed me underneath the

dining-room table and tried to control my terror. The sound of yelling and pounding was horrendous. The mob was the width of the street and a couple of hundred thick. Bill, watching at the window, described how they were lifting the draining grates from the gutters and smashing them. With the broken pieces of wrought iron they smashed a single window in each of the Catholic houses. It was clearly understood that this was a primitive form of marking out the houses of undesirables, like the daubing of doors in times of plague. It meant, we know who you are and where you are, and if you don't move out, then next time we'll set the house on fire.

The great cloud of ugliness passed as quickly as it had come. The reaction of the street was just as swift and just as alarming. I peeked out of the front door to see women on every doorstep talking thirteen to the dozen while every able-bodied man was ripping up paving-stones and carrying them in wheelbarrows and makeshift trolleys to the top of the street, where a fierce-looking barricade was already being erected. The word 'vigilante' was flying around. I was still shaking. The next day there were troops in the street.

On my dad's next visit home it was clear that he was shaken and worried for his family. On a trip to his local pub he was warned as he was leaving to stay away, as the bar staff was Catholic. If he used the place again it could mean trouble. His defiant reaction was to go back in and order another pint.

In the strange intoxication of the time, I joined a local gang who were looting a nearby supermarket that had been bombed. I was so terrified after I'd dared to run into the stricken building that I grabbed whatever was to hand, in this case a family pack of Omo and a jar of Vim. In my innocence I took them back as trophies to my mother, who surpassed herself with the speed at which she knocked me sideways. She made me take them straight back, a nightmarish experience, as the cops were due to arrive at any moment. I made it with minutes to spare, and resolved that my criminal career was finished.

My parents had had enough. The first escape route was Canada, where my Aunt Rose and Uncle Billy had found sunshine and prosperity. But the Canadian authorities were not looking for joiners or mill workers, so the chance of an assisted passage was out. They simply did not have the money to emigrate. Then there was a changeover at work, when Dad's firm was sold lock, stock and barrel to a new company. Fortunately, the new owners wanted Dad to stay on and were prepared to offer him a house at a nominal rent. My thoughts flew immediately to my infant love life. There would be no more dawdling around Amanda Watson's house on the way home from school. The love of my life was not to be. I was in tears as my parents told me about the move, despite their promises of a garden and my own bed. At the end of an evening of sobs, I relented enough to ask:

'So where are we going?'

'Reading, son.'

My dad spoke as if he were talking of Shangri-la.

'Where's Reading?'

TWO

'What country, friends, is this?'
TWELFTH NIGHT

'The best way to see Reading is going through it on a train.'

That was Oscar Wilde's view, but then he had his own reasons for disliking the town of the 3 B's – Bulbs, Biscuits and Beer. Sutton Seeds, Huntley and Palmers' and the Courage Brewery were the three names that distinguished the town in those days. But as the Branaghs arrived, the M4 motorway's new extension was nearing completion, and Reading's second life as a commuter-filled adjunct to London was about to begin.

For me, the most disappointing aspect of Reading was the size of our back garden. Bedtimes in Belfast before the move had been imaginative flights of fancy which turned the new house into a kind of Disneyland castle with croquet lawns and tree-houses, and the chance to do everything I'd seen gangs of adventurous children do on the box. What we had instead was a rather small suburban semi-detached, not much bigger than the house in Mountcollyer Street, but with considerably more pretension. The back garden was the first I'd ever known, but playing football in it would be as dangerous for the windows as it had been in Belfast.

But my new school, Whiteknights County Primary, seemed a real improvement. From my first day at this green and pleasant establishment, I was aware of being a stranger in what seemed – to a Belfast boy used to fierce, grey discipline – like a very strange land. There were nice cheerful buildings, playing fields, even the classes had 'play' corners (I thought I'd read the sign wrong). All was cosily middle-class, quiet and nice. Mr Shanks, the headmaster, was everybody's favourite uncle and always smiling, and introduced me to the gentle lions of Mr Cortiss's class with a generous speech of welcome. The first question whispered to me, a startled white rabbit, by an inquisitive classmate during the maths lesson was, 'Are you any good at football?'

I was competent at it and, more importantly, passionate about the game. This kept me going during the early days when I had to repeat everything I said, in order to give them a chance with my Belfast accent. I was acutely aware of my speech at a school where it seemed to me everyone spoke like BBC newsreaders. The accent problem was already causing friction at home.

For my father, the move had been easy. He had been living in England part-time for three years and apart from a greater natural confidence he had already made the tiny adjustments in speech that allowed for instant understanding in a social context. For my mother, it was not so easy. There were endless arguments between her and my brother about her accent and our non-English status. For Bill, in middle adolescence, the culture shock was profound and the confusion immense. He was in daily fights at his secondary school and chose to deal with the disorientation by changing his accent almost immediately and completely. The suburban sound was like having a new member of the family and my mother's accent became a target for his own divided feelings. There were regular criticisms of what she said and how she said it, which reduced my mother to tears.

It was a traumatic period, for the whole family was undergoing an enforced change of personality. My mother, removed from the support network of sisters and cousins and made to feel almost ashamed of her speech, had a very painful time of it. The outgoing dancer and spunky fighter for family justice was rendered impotent by the isolation of English suburbia. The neighbours were fewer and quieter, community life, as she knew it, almost non-existent. The men were out and about in company most of the day, but my mother suffered from a loneliness and loss of confidence from which it took her years to recover. Her one salvation through this period was the arrival, in her fortieth year, of my sister Joyce.

The early 1970s were not a good time to be Irish in Reading. Many of the children at school had older brothers in the Army. Every death reported on the television news made me try to change even further; I longed just to blend in. After a year or so I'd managed to become English at school and remain Irish at home. It was a dreadfully uneasy compromise about which I suffered inordinate guilt. I instinctively wanted to remain the Belfast boy, but pressure at school was very strong. I was already conscious of being different from people who had 'friends round for the day', who had parties in their large houses, and who ate curries *at home*. I was hardly becoming a cod 'working-class hero', but the differences between me and them were plain.

For as long as I could, I kept up the double life, but my voice gradually took on the twang of suburbia. However I still sounded different, and was very careful when the subject of English casualties in Ulster came up at school. It was another stage in the painful process of learning when to keep my mouth shut.

Soldiers weren't the only people dying in the province. Shortly after our move, Pop Branagh passed away. It was the end of an era for my parents, as Pop had always exerted a strong influence over the family. He had had a long illness, but through it all he urged my parents to leave Belfast and make a new life. The old order and the old good-heartedness were over, he said. The gangsters were moving in and young families should move out before kids did more than looted the shops.

Pop would have approved of Whiteknights. Its taste for theatricals was encouraged by Beryl Levitt, my final form teacher and a great enthusiast for drama. She gave me my first break, boldly choosing me to play Dougal in a hotly-contested casting session for a Christmas production of *The Magic Roundabout*. The show was intended for infant schools and, in a thick brown blanket, with fringes to represent the canine hero, I remember thinking in old pro fashion that I was 'very good with the kids'.

A few weeks later, with a wilful precocity which has been annoying people ever since, I made my debut as an author. It was a five-minute piece for harvest festival. The central character was called Lord Ponsonby-Smythe, a young aristocrat who visits his farm labourers, discovers the extent of their poverty and the difficulty of their labour. Stricken with guilt at this economic and social imbalance, he replaces their tools and ups their wages. A very unlikely parable.

There was always football and music. A local group put on a production of *All the King's Men* by Richard Rodney Bennett in which I thought myself rather thrilling. I played the Royalist soldier with the slightly bigger musket *and* a pennant. Subtle touches, but they made all the difference. Imagine my surprise when Thames Junior Opera failed to renew my contract for the next production.

It was rather a shock for the Infant Phenomenon to hear that another domestic move was being planned. Unknown to us, our landlord had acquired planning permission for a supermarket at the back of our rented house which meant knocking it down to provide access for delivery trucks. Meantime the success of the M4 led to a vast rise in Reading property prices. My parents were in no position to buy, and so we were at the mercy of my dad's boss and landlord, who eventually offered us a dilapidated property to rent on the other side of Reading. The house was much bigger – three bedrooms – but was in a dismal state. Gas mantles, stone floors, leaky roof: a sort of luxury York Street. There was no alternative, and so a couple of months before I finished my primary education, we moved to Berkeley Avenue.

The consequences for me were serious. All Whiteknights' pupils went to Maiden Erleigh School, the cosy secondary complement to the idyllic primary school, where my brother was now happily installed. Moving house meant moving catchment areas and for me a different secondary school. We tried briefly and in vain to get round the council red tape so that I could stay with my new friends, but a place had already been assigned for me at a brand new school, the Meadway Comprehensive, which was opening in September 1972. It had 1200 kids and I would know no one among the 300 children who would make up the first year group. I was terrified.

The omens were not good. At the end of the summer holidays just before I was due to start I asked my dad to drive me past the school buildings. Meadway was to exist on two sites. The first- and second-year intake were housed in what had been the old Wilson secondary school, and my father showed me this imposing Victorian red brick affair. It was a shock after the cosy freshness of Whiteknights. It looked to me like the setting for an Edgar Allan Poe short story. We would remain here for two years before travelling a mile and a half to spend the rest of our schooldays in a spanking new building which the fourteen-year-olds and older students occupied. On the morning of my first day, I was much relieved to find others quite as nervous as myself. The camaraderie of shared terror united us quickly and before we were herded into the great assembly hall, I was breathing a few quiet sighs of relief.

I was assigned to form 1/3. I checked quickly. No seven-foot psychopaths, and the only really mean-looking creature was fat, smaller than me, and a girl. It was looking good. The teacher checking our names off smiled. I was safe. We were going to be O K.

Certainly the faces were rougher. The atmosphere was a little more like *The Blackboard Jungle* than at Whiteknights but certainly less Dotheboys Hall than the Grove Primary, Belfast. I made the fatal mistake of relaxing. Very quickly I was 'good company' in 1/3, and the attention accorded to my schoolboy funnies brought small playground audiences of a pleasing kind, and then its inevitable consequence – the attentions of the school bully.

'You're a divvy.' This was classroom slang for 'prat'. It was morning break. I felt a dig in the ribs from behind.

'You're a divvy, ain't you? What are you?' A small crowd was beginning to gather. They smelled blood. 'I said you're a divvy. What are you?'

Squirming. More breathless fear. Cornered now. Literally against the wall. My lapels were seized.

'What are you?'

Mumble.

'*What?*'

'A divvy.'

Hysterical sneering. Flashman laughter. The bell rang. Escape, thank Christ.

I wasn't bullied for long, but it affected me badly. I was also being terrorised by a boy of my own size who was an honest-to-goodness thug. I lived not in fear of him but of the confrontation. I'm sure I'd have stood a good chance in a fight, but it was the anticipation, the dread of the potential indignity, that ate into me. I began to play truant. Usually I'd skip the last lesson before lunch or the afternoon break in order to escape the horror of playground exposure. I was consumed with guilt and fear and would end up ringing my father at work, pumping misery money into a public phone box. I chose my father for these confessions, as I was terrified of what my mother would say. My father's schoolboy nightmares at Rosharkin bred understanding and sympathy, but my mother had put up with Speedy Harper, and after him school bullies must have seemed trivial.

Eventually the whole family were involved in my daily traumas. They knew the situation was getting out of hand when I tried to throw myself downstairs. I reckoned that one clean break meant a leg dramatically in plaster for a couple of school-free months, and the glamour of those signatures all over it. When I did go back, no one would pick on me if I developed the right kind of residual limp. I had everything worked out. My only problem now was that when I reached the top of the stairs on the appointed morning I could find none of the necessary courage. I finally bumped myself down the last few steps, banging rather noisily on my bottom and attempted to act out the rest of the scenario. My father rushed from the kitchen. I knew he was concerned and upset about the situation. The hall door opened.

'Dad . . . aagh . . . I . . . think . . . aagh . . .'

The groans were quiet but rather effective, I thought. If Marlon Brando could play a con-man cripple in that film with David Niven, why couldn't I?

'Dad . . . I think I've broken something . . . I don't think I can go to school . . . ooh.' (Thump. A final collapse.)

He laughed in my face.

Despite the absurdity of my private melodramas, I was genuinely upset by the situation. My avoidance technique was not working. Despite ridiculously circuitous routes through the school to avoid the bully, I was still regularly disappearing altogether when my nerve failed me. In desperation, my father paid a quiet visit to the headmaster and this made the situation worse. I was a marked man.

My release came in true British fashion when, after a month, the PE sessions developed into organised sports. I was good at rugby and my tormentor, of course, was a physical coward. I was strangely fearless in sport and took a dark pleasure in tackling the fiend as ferociously as possible. It did the trick – a wary respect was accorded me as, once again, sporting ability granted survivor status to the lucky few and condemned the physically weak to even greater misery.

I eventually became captain of the rugby and football teams, more, I suspect, for my innate sense of drama – I loved shouting theatrically butch encouragements to 'my lads' – than for any real sporting skill. I was a plodding workhorse, blessed with physical robustness.

Despite my elevation to Roy of the Rovers, the damage had been done, and it was cheerio to the giggling extrovert who'd been brought out of his Belfast shell. I kept my head down and my mouth shut. Meadway was essentially an excellent school, and, notwithstanding the odd psychopath, there were many genuinely friendly pupils and teachers. I kept my distance from them over the next three years and opted for an isolated adolescence. School holidays were spent alone. Mates did not visit. I was still frightened of the social conventions of my classmates; I simply didn't know what to do in an English house when your friends came round. So after school I simply went home and up to my room. I had £1.22½ per week from a paper-round I did in the mornings and I started to read.

It was a genuine surprise to me that I could buy a paperback for as little as 25p. When I found a children's author that I liked (Malcolm Saville was a great favourite), I would start collections. I loved seeing, for the first time in our house, a shelf with books on it. My father couldn't understand why I had to buy the things – after all you only read them once, and there were libraries for that sort of thing. It seemed a waste of money and certainly very foolish to buy two or three at a time.

But up in my attic bedroom hideaway I was building up a miniature library of my own. The more I read, the more I wanted to write. My imagination grew in proportion to my isolation, and I started to write letters. To everyone. My interest in television and film had never diminished and at that time I was enthralled – as I still am – by Morecambe and Wise. I wrote to them after a fascinating documentary called 'Fools Rush In', and asked for tickets to their show. I remember thinking it wasn't too cheeky, as I was sure I had read that the BBC gave such things away. I sent the letter. It was a small step for anyone else, but a giant leap for the Bard of Berkshire.

I think their reply was the first letter I'd ever had addressed to me as a proper grown-up. The name and address were typed, and in the corner, stamped in red, was the full glamorous seal on the whole event, the letters BBC. My brother was so flabbergasted and curious when he saw it on the mat, that he wouldn't let me open it until I told him who it was from. I protested excitedly, though I was desperate to open it. Quickly sibling tyranny won the day. Morecambe and Wise, I admitted. Curiosity turned to astonishment. My brother tore the envelope open to reveal a photograph of the two, with a message in their own handwriting on the back. 'Sorry. No tickets available. Our series is over. Many thanks for your letter. Morecambe and Wise.'

My brother gave me a quizzical look and then handed it over. He headed off to school while I took the reply back up to the nerve-centre of my literary operation. It was possible, these people *did* write back. I was excited beyond belief. Some sort of door had opened. I made a note to be sure in future to get to the postman first.

I've often thought I should check Equity records to see whether any members had asked for something to be done about me. I was certainly tormenting the actors – Dave Allen, Sally Thomsett, Gillian Blake – and anyone I admired on TV at that time. All sweetly wrote back, and my ambition grew.

My new status as a collector of books and man of letters allowed me to cast a critical eye over the literary world around me. I picked up the *Reading Evening Post* one night and looked at their books page. It was packed with reviews, but only one children's book was mentioned, and that review was written by an adult. I set to immediately, and a letter was dispatched to the editor complaining about the situation. I employed a favourite phrase of the time: we want book reviews '*by* kids, *for* kids'. I'm not sure whether the junior population of Reading would have agreed, but the letter worked its spell on the pape's features editor, June Sparey.

She ran a Saturday half-page section called 'Junior Post'. As it happened, they did receive children's books from time to time, and she took up my suggestion to pass them on to me to review. No money was involved but I could keep the books, and I could tell my father I'd found a way of saving money. She wrote back inviting me to mastermind something called 'Junior Bookshelf'. I had my name just below the title. Fame at last. I was thirteen.

Teenage empire-building extended to the BBC, where I wrote to the Head of Children's Programmes demanding my own junior chat show '*by* kids, *for* kids'. When he wrote back suggesting a meeting I realised that my gargantuan confidence actually went no further than my four bedroom walls. Once it came to implementing these schemes beyond the written word, I was helpless. It was not to be the first time in my adolescence that my imagination would reach beyond my capacities.

My parents had no illusions about my condition. Between the ages of twelve and fifteen I went into an odd form of retreat. I was aware of their concern because, apart from their own enquiries, they cajoled my brother and every visiting relative to try to discover why I stayed up in my room and didn't go out, or even have mates round. So insistent were their worries that even I began to wonder if there was something wrong with me.

I think I really did prefer my own company but had also built some subconscious once-bitten-twice-shy drama about myself and the world. If nothing else, the solitude was providing an obvious career choice: I would be a writer. Although I was having an unpleasant adolescent flirtation with the world of sub-editing and deadlines, journalism seemed the right road.

Ideally I saw myself cutting through all the court-reporting drudgery and heading straight for investigative TV journalism, and eventually to my own chat show. I also thought that I could probably cut the training down, or do without it altogether. I couldn't spell or type or use grammar correctly, but I was sure these were things that you could pick up. I knew that, journalism or not, the last thing I wanted was an ordinary job.

One rainy day in autumn, the drama teacher, Roger Lewis, came to watch the school football team. Something was up. Generally they looked down on all that butchness but Mr Lewis was clearly in trouble. He had planned a school production of *Oh! What a Lovely War* to play in the dinner hall at the end of the Christmas term, and had had a miserable response to his casting appeals. With tickets and advertising booked, he was now stuck. It didn't take much to persuade me to join in, although some of the other lads had to be persuaded that playing soldiers had great girl-pulling potential and could easily be as macho as their activities on the football field.

Roger Lewis was a director of enormous energy and the rehearsals were the most fun I'd ever had at Meadway, partly because I was nabbing parts like flies. The more image-conscious of the soccer team eventually dropped out and Roger himself, who'd had to take on several roles early on, shed some when he saw there was an eager show-off waiting in the wings.

It was still a huge cast. *Oh! What a Lovely War* is an ensemble piece with many scenes. I played the American arms dealer (Burt Lancaster in *Bird Man*), the Young British Soldier (Tom Courtenay in *King Rat*), the Old British Soldier (Robert Newton in *Treasure Island*) and the officer (Michael Caine in *Zulu*). Nothing I did had much to do with acting, but it was a great laugh.

I was astonished by the camaraderie such things could inspire, which was just as much fun as the playing itself. It was an extraordinary new club in which I felt completely at home. I loved the dressing-up. I loved things going wrong. I was completely stage-struck and just waiting for the magic words supplied by Roger: 'Have you ever thought of doing this professionally?'

I was sixteen years old and everything clicked at once. Not only had it taken me out of my old hermit self (I actually started seeing girls – my parents were relieved and delighted) but from that point on there was simply nothing else I could think of doing. Journalism was no longer an option. I was so much better at acting than I was at reviewing books, and the notion of acting for a living made work seem as if it wouldn't be work at all. In short, every dream-filled cliché danced through my head. Others in the cast of that lovely production felt changed, and talked about taking up acting. I knew I meant it.

I felt certain, but also terrified. How was I to go about it? Parents, drama school, money – I decided on a long, slow campaign on all fronts. The obvious thing was to stay on at school from sixteen to eighteen – it was impossible to think of leaving for London any earlier. And I needed the experience: more plays, more reading. I imagined that you had to be very bright to be an actor, and I felt thick. I knew I had to do something about it.

My dad was quietly appalled that I had decided to stay on. English, History and Sociology 'A' levels meant little to him when there was an opening in his own firm. It would mean another two years of his keeping me, but he finally agreed, and I showed willing by getting a weekend job in a supermarket, so that I wasn't forever 'minding ten bob' for him.

In the meantime, I started on my own secret theatrical education. I joined the Berkshire County Drama Library, and visited second-hand bookshops assembling a paperback collection of Shakespeare.

I scoured the bookshelves in Smith's and found that there was a magazine called *Plays and Players*, but that you had to be quick, because only one person in Reading seemed to buy it and I had to get to the shop to read the single copy before it disappeared.

But this covert operation was soon rumbled by the tortuous question-and-answer session of the Meadway 'careers interview'. Parents were invited to this momentous half-hour, and my father dutifully turned up to hear what Mrs Bell, the careers supremo, had to say. She took the initiative, and in the first ten minutes she referred to my academic record, my likely pass levels in future exams, and laid before me the employment riches available in Reading at the time. There were basically three choices: British Rail, the Prudential or the Army. I had to get it over with.

'I'm going to be an actor.'

The air suddenly turned chilly. I didn't look at my father but I felt his little jump of shock and then the deep, weary sigh. He'd obviously seen it coming, and here was the confirmation. His son was a homosexual.

Mrs Bell gave a puzzled smile. 'I'm not sure how much information we actually have on that particular career avenue.' She went to the tiny filing cabinet which housed the school's careers information. 'No, there's nothing. I don't think we've had that one before.' Pause. 'Are you sure about this?'

All the arguments were trotted out, my dad joining in as best he could. High unemployment, fierce competition, my own lack of experience, poor money.

'I want to be an actor.'

'What about something to fall back on?'

'Like what?'

'Banking.'

'I'm afraid I've made up my mind.'

Mrs Bell had done all she could, and I promised that I would go down to the careers department in the Civic Centre where they had more detailed information on the subject. Perhaps that would make me see sense. There had been no hard words in the interview, just an amused indulgence from Mrs Bell. I think she felt rather sorry for me – I'd clearly let school dramatics go straight to my head. My father looked as though he'd been punched, but smiled bravely and shook me by the hand as he left and went back to work.

I stayed in my room all that evening. I had no wish to be part of the conversation that was going on downstairs. My parents' bewilderment must have been immense. My father had only just been given the chance to run his own company, the place was thriving, and his only disappointment was that my brother, Bill, who had originally joined the firm, left it after a year to set up his own company. If I failed to succumb to the lure of this secure opening, it would be the end of Dad's dream of establishing a strong family business. To both my parents' credit, they remained patient over the following months and simply watched to see how I was pursuing entry into this strange, unfamiliar world while desperately hoping that I would grow out of it.

As promised, I went to the Civic Centre for detailed information. The assistant was almost as puzzled as Mrs Bell, and after half an hour one rather sad-looking sheet of A4 paper was placed before me. It was headed 'Advice to those interested in stage careers', the writing was on one side only, and it was dated 1968. I took a deep breath and consulted the oracle, which began 'An empty theatre is a lonely place. Behind the tinsel glitter of the curtain and the greasepaint, the theatre can be a hard, lonely world, especially for the actor.' You can imagine the rest.

Back to the bookshops. I found an old Foyles' Handbook called 'Making The Stage Your Career', which had Tom Courtenay as Faustus on the cover. Inside it mentioned Albert Finney and Peter O'Toole a lot, so I thought it must be all right. It was written by Denys Blakelock, who had been a teacher at RADA in the mid-fifties and had taught both of the above, as well as John Stride, Richard Briers, Sian Phillips, all referred to in the book. Even though it was slightly antiquated, it became my Bible. If his advice was good enough for them, it was good enough for me. He talked a great deal about drama school auditions but, for all my reading, I still knew so little about what plays to use, what speeches to read. I had to act in more plays.

I had read in the local paper about the Progress Theatre group. It was an amateur company and the building was within walking distance of my house. I wanted to join, but once again my confidence failed me. I was all right in private, in books, in dreams of glory, but still desperately reserved in real life. I rang them up, found out when they met, and promised that I would turn up. On the appointed night I walked to the little 100-seater theatre which was on the edge of the Reading University Campus. And then I froze. I stood under a tree and watched as people filed in and simply prayed that some kindly figure would walk across and say 'Hello, you must be the hugely talented youngster we've been expecting. I'll look after you and make sure you don't feel utterly ridiculous and stupid. Come with me.'

It didn't happen, I simply got cold and walked home. It was the second time that this had happened – the same summer, in 1977, I had auditioned (through Roger Lewis's encouragement) for the National Youth Theatre. When I heard that I had been given a place on their summer season, I withdrew immediately. Terror, sheer terror of living in London for the summer, terror of all the new people – I couldn't face it. I was beginning to wonder if I could ever be anything but a suburban Walter Mitty.

I tried Progress Theatre again, and this time God was on my side. Their newsletter had told me they were auditioning for *Who's Afraid of Virginia Woolf?* by Edward Albee, with a part for a young man that I could conceivably have played.

This time I actually attended the audition. I waited nearly an hour to say my first lines as Nick and experienced the sweaty-palmed anticipation of actors at read-throughs. Nearly twenty of us were sitting in a circle, a mixture of potential Marthas and Georges and Honeys, but very few Nicks. The other young auditionees were much older than me, and I thought that my youth might be an asset. Perhaps they needed some new blood.

Groups of four had taken it in turns to read different sections of the play, and I thought my bit was over far too quickly – there hadn't been time for them to be bowled over by my extensively researched and rehearsed American accent (Marlon Brando in *On the Water-front*).

I revelled in the words 'Some of you will be hearing from us' at the end of the session. This was proper theatre, brutal, tough, Warner Baxter in jodhpurs, the real thing. Then, of course, I recoiled when someone said 'Shall we all go to the pub?' My annoying Irish flush flushed, I mumbled my apologies and made my way back to the bedroom at Berkeley Avenue. This had now become a garret in Greenwich Village where I was hanging out, while making my name in New York. Jimmy Dean was on the next landing, and Marlon often stopped by for coffee and an intense discussion about Stanislavsky. To my utter astonishment, the director of *Virginia Woolf* had decided that she wanted me as Nick. And to my embarrassment, she rang my mother to discuss her one reservation. She had heard that I was not yet seventeen and explained that there were scenes of sophisticated sexual game-playing in the play, indeed a little actual mauling, and she wanted to know if my mother objected, if it would destroy some delicate psychological balance. My mother's surprising response was to say that she thought I'd be fine, and that if I wanted to be a professional, then I'd better get as much practice as possible.

I'd cracked it. Parental acceptance. Three cheers for York Street. My only disappointment was that the director changed her mind anyway and decided that having a son of my age herself, she would be too aware of corrupting me in rehearsals. I didn't care. I was established at Progress Theatre and was on the way to winning over my folks. They still thought most actors were unemployed homosexuals, but one thing at a time.

I did land a part in the next production, *The Drunkard, or Down With Demon Drink*, a Victorian temperance melodrama. I played William Dowton, a simple rustic. Simple was not a word you could use to describe my performance, which resembled Benny Hill crossed with a manic opera diva. The result was an overblown mummerset thicko in the great tradition of 'never knowingly underplayed'.

I also joined the Progress Youth Theatre, and with this and other school play rehearsals, I became a busy actor-about-town, running from one 'job' to another. During the school holidays I made my first trip to Stratford-upon-Avon. I hitched up the A34 with my tent on my back and pitched at a site just outside the town. I was in seventh heaven. After visiting all the Shakespeare landmarks, I had a drink in the actors' pub, 'The Dirty Duck', and went on to the theatre, where I stood entranced by the programme – *The Taming of the Shrew*, *The Tempest*, *Measure for Measure*, Michael Hordern, Jonathan Pryce, Ian Charleson, Juliet Stevenson, Alan Rickman, and more. The weather was lovely, and the whole trip was like a miraculous pilgrimage. Acting it was to be, and Stratford looked as if it was to be my Mecca.

And about this time I was given a wonderful present: hundreds of back copies of *Plays and Players*, *Theatre World* and *Encore*. They dated from the early fifties and were a real treasure trove. Each night in bed, before I went to sleep, I would read a copy from cover to cover with minute attention to every detail.

I was still scouring film and TV titles sequences, and I loved cross-referencing the spear-holders of the sixties to the stars of the seventies. I wanted to know who did everything – music, lights, direction. And I took untold pleasure in building up an encyclopaedic knowledge of post-war theatre, while theatrical biographies were giving me an insight into different eras. At this time – I was nearly 18 – I was reading *Early Stages* by Gielgud, *George* and *Emlyn* by Emlyn Williams, biographies of Irving and Garrick, and the criticism of James Agate. My appetite for theatrical history was voracious and the quest for it was sheer, unadulterated joy.

Part of the great quest was theatre-going itself. I had seen my first Shakespeare at the St George's Theatre, Tufnell Park, when I was fourteen. It was a hysterical schools' matinee of *Romeo and Juliet*, with David Collings as a thrilling Mercutio. Peter McEnery and Sarah Badel gave wonderful performances as the lovers. The whole production was rough and thrilling, completely dispelling the classroom image of Shakespeare as boring.

Now that I'd found my vocation, theatre-going was a wonderful adventure. I banished all social timidity in order to savour all the treats available, such as my first momentous visit to see *Hamlet*. There was a new production playing at the theatre in Oxford; I asked Jayne Thurgood, a girlfriend whom I was trying to impress, and we took the train from Reading. I was completely bowled over and so was my companion, which was a relief – it was not the most obvious evening's entertainment for a young surburban couple. It seemed unbelievably dramatic, dark and rich to look at, full of exciting lighting effects. The production had tremendous pace, and the acting was passionate and electric.

I cheered at the end as he came on. I'd read all about him: Cambridge, Birmingham Rep, understudying at the National Theatre, taking over from Jeremy Brett, Cassio in Olivier's *Othello*, Ivanov for Prospect, and now here he was, live – a completely thrilling Hamlet. I was watching Derek Jacobi.

With all this excitement my school work inevitably suffered. I had patient and understanding teachers who put up with me, mainly because I loved the work in class, however lax I was with homework and background reading. My subjects were all grist to the mill: history is the very stuff of drama, and Miss Sheppard, our history teacher, loved the theatre in it as much as I did. I loved the personalities – Parnell, Lloyd George, MacDonald, Churchill – and wanted to play them all. I enjoyed Mrs Nalpanis's sociology lessons, but it was English that I revelled in and I owe the most thanks for my release into the enjoyment of language to my English teacher, Stan Grue. An actor and director himself, all our lessons were infused with a Celtic relish for words. I fell for the poetry of Dylan Thomas, John Donne, and Shakespeare's sonnets, and for a whole range of modern poetry. We read countless plays: Wesker, Osborne, Shakespeare and Congreve; and our 'A' level course (chosen by Stan) contained far more plays than was prevalent in most syllabuses. Stan could do no wrong for me, and proved it by casting me as Toad in the Christmas school production of *Toad of Toad Hall*. It's one of the most enjoyable parts that I've ever played.

The only problem during this whole golden period was that I was neglecting my homework. The 'A' levels that I promised to provide as a safety net were looking very precarious. No amount of classroom zeal makes up for background reading and notes, and I was really banking on something else.

I'd quietly sent off for prospectuses from all the major drama schools and was putting the next phase of my secret plan into action. I secured auditions at the Central School of Speech and Drama and at the Royal Academy of Dramatic Art. The appointments were within days of each other in early January 1979, and were for admission in September of the same year, just a few months after I was due to leave school. I was required to produce two two-minute speeches, one from a modern play and one from Shakespeare. I knew I wanted the classical piece to be exciting, dramatic and above all, original. With a startling lack of imagination I decided on *Hamlet*. And from an interesting selection of modern pieces I chose the most familiar: a scene from Pinter's *The Caretaker*.

Friends were enlisted to take me through the speeches. Colin Wakefield, a colleague from the Progress Theatre, helped me on making the Shakespeare ('What a piece of work is a man') seem more natural, and Stan Grue tried to curtail the movements of my flailing arms, which always seemed to get stuck in the air at the wrong moment, and accompany dramatic lines with entirely inappropriate gestures. Pauline and Harry Grey, two really fine Progress Theatre actors, took me through the Pinter. Alone, I practised the piece opposite an empty chair, trying to summon up as much menace as possible.

Central was first. The school was housed in a collection of shambling, picturesque buildings just off the Finchley Road, at

Swiss Cottage. Despite preparing some interesting alternatives, I again played safe and presented the judging panel with two very familiar pieces – Edmund's 'bastard' speech from *King Lear* and yet another bit of *Hamlet*, with which I was obsessed. Derek Jacobi had a lot to answer for.

The Central School audition was so casual that I became worried, and took the judging panel's relaxed style for indifference. As I waited my turn in the student common room, nothing seemed to be going on. I don't know what I expected – maybe harlequins and people with leg-warmers doing ballet exercises, and someone rushing into the canteen shouting 'Let's do the show right here'. Instead all was calm and normal, and I did my audition with relative ease. Not a flicker on the faces of the panel, a polite thank you at the end, and no questions asked. Outside a dragonish grey-haired matron shrieked, with operatic grandeur 'You've been recalled' (rather like Edith Evans intoning 'A haaandbaaag?'), which meant that they wanted to see me again. I had got through to the next round, which would take place at some future date.

The experience had been fine, but it was its ordinariness that I resented. Why hadn't Olivier been passing through on his way to rehearsal? He'd gone to Central, hadn't he? I'd seen all those period Hollywood films where the hero walks up the steps to his club and passes a bearded figure on the way down to whom he says, 'Morning, Dickens'. Why couldn't that happen in life?

RADA was a very different affair and appealed strongly to my thwarted sense of glamour. The unprepossessing doors opened up onto a marbled hall full of busts and portraits, names I recognised, and great boards on the wall with lists of people that I'd heard of from the distant past. There was the sense of a real connection with theatrical tradition – the Vanburgh sisters, Maggie Albenesie, Gielgud – it was like breathing in ether. In retrospect the entrance hall was probably a little shabby even then, but it did smell of theatre and of actors and I loved it.

Richard O'Donoghue, the registrar, welcomed a group of about ten of us and promptly learned and remembered all our names. Very impressive. We then filed up to the common room, where I had an inordinately long wait because an eccentric Liverpudlian who was in before me had decided to build a castle. He was doing a piece from *Macbeth*, and wanted to create a setting for it by piling up chairs and tables in the audition room to give a sense of the 'pleasant seat'. By the time I got there the place looked like a furniture warehouse.

I have never been able to tell how auditions go. I simply did it and went back to wait in the common room with the rest of the applicants. We had all been gathered for about ten minutes when the phone rang. No one had explained quite what would happen and so one of the girls nervously picked up the receiver.

'Yes . . . right . . . I will.' Her hand went over the mouthpiece. 'Would the following people please go to see Mr O'Donoghue.' This was it. She started calling the names out. Seven, eight, nine. She'd finished. She hadn't mentioned mine.

They started to troop out and I sat there alone, stunned and not knowing what to do next. I had found what I had been looking for and had bollocksed it at the first hurdle. Total defeat. Then it dawned on me that I was still there. Could Mr Donoghue have made a mistake?

The phone rang again. I forced myself not to panic.

'Hello, Ken?'

'Yes?'

'Come down to the office, will you? Sorry to keep you waiting.'

Eureka. I was through the first round.

Every drama school has its own quirky auditioning system, and at RADA you returned on the afternoon of the same day if you had made a favourable impression with the first three examiners. There were four of these trios at work on auditions day, and the afternoon session was a repeat performance by the applicants so that the other nine judges could see the shortlisted students.

I had two hours to kill and decided on some lunch. I found a working men's café and sandwich bar on the corner of Goodge Street and Tottenham Court Road and sat down to gaze at the limited menu, plumping eventually for a hamburger. As I ate, I turned to the back of my well-thumbed copy of the RADA prospectus. There was a dizzyingly long and impressive list of theatrical luminaries, most of them former students. I knew that this was where I wanted to go.

I also realised with a stab of horror that I'd eaten the wrong lunch. My breath reeked of onion. I ransacked the local sweet shop for some strong mints but, despite risking dental suicide, I re-entered the famous portals sure that I smelled like a portable kebab stall.

If the toxic fumes exhaled by my afternoon Hamlet affected the judging panel, I was unaware of it. I simply couldn't see them. The venue had changed from one of the classrooms to the small George

Bernard Shaw Theatre, a friendly auditorium which, on that occasion, couldn't have been more intimidating. The panel was impressively lit from the back so that the poor, dazzled auditionee looked out at a gestapo-like line of silhouettes.

The figures asked me about my education, about my acting experience. I was in and out in fifteen minutes, and was told that they would be making decisions 'very soon'.

The whole experience had been agreeably formal and well stage-managed, and apart from the grim theatricality of the afternoon's debriefing, quite enjoyable. I got the train back to Reading. I prayed that I would get in.

The phone rang three days later. It was a Saturday evening at 7.30, and I was just about to set out for a party. My sister called me and said,

'I can't make it out, but there's someone called Jo Huttell on the phone for you.'

'What?'

'Hello, Kenneth. Hugh Cruttwell here.'

Jesus – the principal of RADA. His was the chief voice in the darkness. He was going to let me down gently.

'Now look, I'll be quite frank. All the others want to offer you a place here.'

This was too much. I sat down.

'The thing is, I'm not sure. I have to say the kind of acting you came up with the other day is ten-a-penny. I simply wasn't interested.'

'Oh.'

'So look. What I suggest, if you're willing and interested, is that you come back with a different audition speech and you and I will have a work session on it. How's that?'

'Fine.'

If he'd asked me to dance naked in Gower Street I'd have agreed.

'When is your recall for Central?'

'Thursday, sir. Thank you very much, sir.'

The spiritual forelock was being tugged to within an inch of its life.

'Well, why don't you come along here on Wednesday, say 10.30, OK? Good. See you then. Cheerio.'

I was breathless with excitement and terrified to boot. Another speech. What? And what was it he didn't like? Everything, it seemed, and yet he was prepared to give me another chance, *and* he had asked me about Central. I must be in with a shout. I went off to the party elated, had one drink, and was completely plastered.

Pauline and Harry Grey rallied magnificently to take me through the gentleman-caller speech from Tennessee Williams' *The Glass Menagerie*. I thought an American accent should impress him, the slow drawl of Jimmy Stewart in *Harvey*, which at least was a change from *Hamlet*. If it was a total disaster, I could at least use it for the recall at Central, the next day.

I took to Hugh Cruttwell at first sight – a sharpish face with the aspect of a wise old eagle, and a strong, wiry body. He was instantly commanding and completely honest. I started on the speech from *The Glass Menagerie* several times, but he stopped me continually, and made me go back to the beginning. His criticism was very direct – he was saying exactly what he thought, not to wound or play power games, but because it was patently true.

We started again, this time on *The Caretaker*. 'What you're doing is *demonstrating* to me what the character is doing. You're *indicating* what he is feeling. The execution is tremendously accomplished but the overall effect is soulless. I am not asking you to present me with a fully rounded character in a two-minute speech, but I want to see the potential of that character, not your actor's commentary on him. Try again.'

He urged me to abandon my carefully rehearsed moves around the vacant chair in which my invisible victim was sitting, and made me start the speech in a different physical position. He talked about the play and the character.

'Good. Now, you clearly know a great deal about this character, so you must trust me when I say that your actor's instinct is sufficiently developed for you not to have to "present" him. Abandon this point-making and allow, if you can, the character to play you. You'll be surprised at the results.'

I tried everything he suggested and my biggest surprise was drying stone dead after three sentences.

'Excellent. You were surprising yourself then. All that acting had been dropped, and you were discovering things in performance by being true to the character, not your idea of it. Naturally, things come out differently. It's an unfamiliar experience and that's why you dried. Well done, you've dropped all that acting.'

We carried on for another half an hour, and it was exhilarating. I found myself acting in a way I had never done before, and, as Hugh pointed out, I'd had a tiny glimpse of the difference between being a performer showing off and being an actor actually serving a character.

At the end of the session he said, with great precision, 'You've absolutely convinced me of your potential to work in the way I think is important for you. Good luck at Central, and let me know how you get on there.'

I still hadn't cracked it, or at least, I wasn't sure. It was now or never. 'I must say, sir, that even if they offered me a place I would far rather come here. I would really love to.'

He hadn't been fishing for this, but he was clearly pleased that I'd declared my preference. 'Thank you. I'll certainly let you know as soon as I can.'

It had been a wonderful morning, and it was proof, if ever I needed it, that acting was the career I wanted to follow. It had also shown me that there was a place to go where I could really learn, and a person who could really teach me. Acting now meant more than just showing off in school plays – a door had been opened on something far more interesting: the way you could submerge your personality fully into someone else's words, the way you could become an instrument, a vessel through which something else could channel and expand itself, take on colour and meaning. It was frightening to be faced with the truth of the tiny extent of one's knowledge, but hugely exciting at the same time.

On that one magnificent and humbling morning, acting stopped being simply another means of escape for the working-class Belfast boy adrift in English suburbia. It was no longer to do with aspirations to fame and having nice things said about you. An enormous area had suddenly opened up where the attempt to plumb the mystery of real acting offered a lifetime of attractively elusive satisfaction. A profound shift had taken place in my mind, and I was absolutely certain that RADA was the place, and Hugh was the man, to start me on this immense journey.

But he still hadn't offered me a place.

The next day, at the recall for the Central School, I was introduced to the acting profession in competition. We arrived at nine o'clock for a movement session. These sessions usually consist of an hour's worth of ballet-based, aerobic exercises which vary in difficulty. They are designed to improve and enhance an actor's body control, and in this case they were testing whether we had any body control at all. There were around forty of us, a very mixed crowd – and there were several deeply embarrassed males like myself, looking ridiculous in their football kit, and insisting on their heterosexuality with every uneasy pirouette. Then there was a whole selection of dazzling leotards and a few 'pros' who had sweatbands on every available area of exposed skin. We finished half an hour of rudimentary exercises and gathered back in the common room. The silver-haired matron appeared with a flourish. Her name was Miss Grey, and she was there to announce that half of our number were already 'out'.

We were in for quite a day. The next session was audition speeches. Split into groups of five, we were required to perform in front of our fellows as well as the judging panel, a particularly gruelling experience. One was aware of 'favourites' emerging during this process – auditionees whose talent and confidence seemed to shine through. I felt I performed well.

Then there was a ninety-minute wait, and Miss Grey appeared again. Another eight names were read out and people with whom one had quietly been making friends had to pack their bags and hold dignity intact while they made the long exit from the common room.

A nervous lunch was followed by a singing test. I was shown a book with a collection of show songs and asked to choose. There was only one I recognised. Conscious of a certain irony, I launched into 'Dream the Impossible Dream'. It was shaky, but reasonably in tune.

By this time it was late afternoon, and I went back to the common room where the numbers were about to be reduced by another six. One cold sweaty minute later I was through. I was relieved at the decision, but was becoming increasingly resentful of the selection process. This was one aspect of being an actor that I wasn't going to like. There was too much relish in our hostess's ceremony, and there had to be less humiliating ways of doing these things. But who was I to complain? They had a place and I wanted one. Or did I? At around six o'clock, after another nail-biting hour, I said aloud,

'I wish they'd let us go home.'

From my right a girl, who was visibly feeling the strain, turned round and snapped,

'Well, why don't you piss off then, and give us a better chance.'

I was taken aback. I'd hardly spoken to the girl all day and had certainly done nothing to annoy her. What I saw was the naked fear and aggression that tends to be one of the occupational hazards of being an actor. It was a result of succumbing to that helpless feeling of being a pawn in a game that someone else controls. I understood exactly how she felt, but I resolved to avoid that kind of reaction at all costs. It must never matter *that* much. When she was asked to leave at Miss Grey's final pronouncement, the girl's face turned to stone.

There were two of us left. It was 7 pm. We'd been there for ten hours and I was fed up. The principal asked us into his office and offered us both a place there and then. The other successful candidate was a lithe, red-lycred American girl who was shrieking with excitement. I smiled weakly. 'Thank you very much.'

Later, we said goodbye to each other at Swiss Cottage tube station.

'See you in September,' she shouted as the train doors closed. As I waved goodbye, I knew I wouldn't. Whatever the outcome of the session with Hugh, I knew Central, for all its undoubted prestige and excellence, wasn't the place for me. I had a gut feeling about the personality of the place as it then was, and made a simple, personal decision. The day seemed like a microcosm of the least appealing aspects of the theatre and was filled with everything that frightened me. The whole episode was comically capped by my being propositioned by one of the students, a flame-haired Scotsman in pink dungarees who threatened to celebrate my admission by taking me down to Piccadilly for 'a good time on the meat rack'. Suburban sensibilities suitably shocked, I headed for Paddington with relief.

That night I wrote to Central explaining my refusal of their kind offer, and then worked out what to do when Hugh Cruttwell rang to say that, much as he'd like to offer me a place, the course was filled. I got out the rest of the prospectuses. Bristol and Guildhall looked affordable. I prepared myself for the second round.

The next day Reading was covered in snow. There was a hard afternoon at school explaining why the latest history essay was not on time, and when I came home there was an envelope still on the mat, with the words *Royal Academy of Dramatic Art* set out in red letters across the bottom. My heart started pounding, and I stood for ten minutes just holding the letter. I finally opened it. My eyes swam, and I could read nothing while I searched for the magic words, '. . . and so I would like to offer you a place.' They were there.

My mother was asleep upstairs, and I didn't dare wake her. I couldn't stop jumping around, so I celebrated by taking the dog for a three hour walk in the snow. He didn't know what had hit him, and after ninety minutes he was whimpering to come home, but no chance – in my mind I was miles away at Stratford, the National Theatre, Hollywood, playing Macbeth, Hamlet, Hotspur. The dog was so exhausted that I had to carry him for the last half hour.

My parents were thrilled and deeply relieved. RADA was the one drama school they had heard of, and the 'Royal' tag seemed to bestow an acceptably conventional status on it. If I had got in to one of the more avant-garde schools, they would have been terrified. And RADA gave you a diploma – if I didn't make it as an actor I could perhaps teach.

When I re-examined the magic letter, I noted with alarm Hugh's request that I contact the local authority to apply for a grant covering fees and maintenance. The course did not offer a degree, and naturally, because it was an arty course, in a discipline which some felt could hardly be described as work, any award would be discretionary. I did some research. The Conservative-controlled Berkshire County Council had not made an award for a Drama course in four years. Bloody hell. I worked out some figures: they came to roughly £1,000 per term for seven terms, plus maintenance of £500 per term. £10,500 for the whole course, a sum my father could not possibly afford. Despite his pride in the very legitimate status of my RADA acceptance, he was in no position to pay for me. It was a grant or nothing. Hugh had already indicated that there were no scholarships available. I made my application and was informed that the funds available were severely limited.

It was hardly surprising. All available funds had to serve those wanting to study music, dance, sculpture and all fine art foundation courses, and this meant that although candidates had already been accepted at recognised and prestigious colleges, they were lumped together to compete with each other for money which they would have received automatically if they had chosen to go directly to University.

In my case, it meant that despite winning places at both Central and RADA, I would have to audition for Berkshire County Council, and they would decide my fate. It was my first brush with the absurd anomalies in attitudes to arts funding, and I felt real resentment. It wasn't that I didn't appreciate the luxury of individual subsidy, but I bitterly resisted the implicit assumption that the arts were always a borderline case.

I already had strong views about the application of my training.

The Government would not merely be sponsoring a private fantasy: I knew then, for instance, that I wanted to act in or take theatre to Belfast, which was then rapidly on its way to becoming a cultural wasteland. I also watched every piece of drama that came to Reading's Hexagon Theatre, and knew how powerfully good theatre could affect people. I dragged unwilling friends along, and saw their reaction to good work and to rubbish. I looked at the different audiences, and wondered about how they might change, how more people – people like my parents – could at least be offered the choice of becoming theatre-goers. I had firm convictions of the importance of popular art, and of its power to make life seem richer and better. I knew in my bones that drama need not be élitist in the way suggested by the council's attitude.

I was certain, even then, that it was necessary to take a long-term view. It seemed essential that a council, government, or any administrative body had to concede the notion of quality. If you wanted a great theatre, then you needed great writers, directors, designers and actors, and if you didn't encourage them, or allow them to be trained properly, then you reduced the possibilities of widening audience choice. Why should audiences take an expensive chance on any theatrical experience, if what they are usually offered is dreadful? I was – and am – convinced that greater quality can mean greater accessibility.

My half-formed adolescent views were part of an embryonic actor-militancy. I was attracted by the glamour of the theatre, but I was also proud of my parents and my background, and I wanted to do something of which they would be proud in turn. Imbued with the Protestant work ethic, I believed that work was a good thing, that one should make oneself useful and put something back into the world through whatever work one did. I felt that as an actor this was possible and the implication that any aspirant thespian was an effete, money-grabbing waster galled me.

The Council audition was set for May, and as a gesture towards my parents and teachers, who were all worried about me not getting the grant, I applied for University. Lots of actors had come up through University, so I thought I should at least go through the motions. It might give me that old favourite: something to fall back on. The Oxbridge route was suggested at first, and the theatrical alumni it boasted gave it great career kudos. Meadway Comprehensive, with a roll of 1500 and a sixth form of twelve, was obviously keen to boost its academic record, and if I could only be persuaded to stop acting a bit and do some work, I might just scrape in. But I was dead against it.

My one experience of Oxford had been on a visit with a girlfriend who knew people in one of the colleges. We sat in some ancient rooms at midnight, drinking port. Our host put a violin concerto by a little-known composer on the record player. The smooth-talking undergraduate next to me turned and spoke as if the effort might kill him. 'They're taking this at quite a lick, aren't they?'

I smiled and shifted nervously in my seat, moving an enormous working-class chip from one shoulder to the other, and thought that this definitely wasn't the place for me. I felt much the same on a visit to Cambridge, where the weight and complexity of traditional customs made a deep impression on me. If I had experienced a sense of cultural collision in moving from Belfast to Reading, then a potential jump from suburbia to the intricate élitism of Cambridge was even more terrifying. The prospect of London and drama school frightened me enough as it was.

I was given an interview at Manchester University which convinced me finally that academic life was not really the place for a frustrated actor – it was to be RADA or nothing.

At the Council audition I behaved like a sulky child, since I was outraged that they should demand proof of my abilities after I had been accepted by two major schools. But the Council had at least entrusted a recommendation to two drama professors from the borough, both of whom I knew. Alistair Conquer, a great friend of mine who had the ear of the examiners, reported afterwards that I had seemed rather peremptory. I rushed to the dictionary and my heart sank. They wouldn't announce their decision till July.

At that point I had to plunge myself into 'A' level revision, and I tried desperately to cram two years' homework into a month. My renewed efforts had been hastened by the terrible disappointed look in my father's face as he watched me across the dinner table, learning lines for Noah Claypole in *Oliver*. It was a school production and I'd agreed to do it, even though the performances were only eight weeks before my exams. 'Do you think you could pull it together for a couple of months, son? Stop all this theatre gallivanting and do some studying.'

There was a tired, reproachful note in his voice that got to me, and I was stricken with guilt and shame. I knew it was too late. I also knew that Noah Claypole was a delightful little cameo that was irresistible. I'd make it up to him. It happened again, however, when I was cast as Cassio in the Berkshire Shakespeare Players production of *Othello* at Reading's Abbey Ruins. At first my parents were pleased, as it was a successful production, in a magical setting with fine local actors. But the dangers became more real when the production transferred a month later – during exams – to the Cliveden Festival, where it played in the grounds of the famous house. I pleaded successfully to be allowed to do it, and they gave in. I think they knew I was an academic lost cause.

Much good the Cliveden experience did me. Fighting the main flightpath from Heathrow airport, I discovered the peculiar torture that open-air theatre can be. On our final matinee we clashed with the men's singles final at Wimbledon. There were twenty-five in the cast and seventeen in an auditorium which sat 1200. The ticket tearer was very deaf but still intent on watching Wimbledon on the bar-tent TV. The cacophony reached its heights in the fifth act, when the desultory audience of sleepy pensioners were treated to:

'It is the cause . . .'

'Fifteen love.'

'. . . It is the cause my soul . . .'

'Borg to serve –'

'. . . Let me not name it to you, you chaste stars . . .'

'Lovely backhand.'

'. . . It is the cause . . .'

'Extraordinary, he's cracked it!'

Othello carried on gamely as Desdemona was smothered and Borg won the third set. Othello had no choice. The cast had taken a vote, and given the interest evinced by the tiny audience, had decided to listen to the match as they worked.

July came, and with it the joyful news that the County Council would pay my fees and maintenance for the whole course at RADA. My fellow candidates had not fared so well: mine was the only drama award made that year. There had been many applicants, and the snob value of RADA's name had obviously done the trick.

The summer was devoted to earning money to supplement the grant, and I took a job as a hospital porter, working in the supplies depot of Reading's Battle hospital. Orders for equipment would come from the various wards and I would load up the trollies of goodies. I was in charge of shrouds and specimen bottles.

They gave me a day off every week and I used this to travel to London to look for accommodation. I was only just coming to terms with the place, and was still fighting a country boy's awe. It was such a relief to know that you could walk everywhere. In my previous visits to see plays I'd always taken the Tube for fear of getting lost. My terror of living in London had been the main reason for turning down the National Youth Theatre. It was still very intimidating, and seemed a place to be lonely in. But I had things to do. RADA had sent a list of required items for new students. Jazz shoes and dance tights rang alarm bells, but I went at it with a will and strode along dutifully to the leotard emporium in St Martin's Lane with my butchest grin and my lurex under my arm.

Sometimes on these trips I had company. David Longstaff, a long-standing chum from Progress, was hoping to go to University in London and we looked for a place to share. Our daily routine involved calls to ever-shadier accommodation agencies and a dive for the early edition of the *Evening Standard* after lunch. Scouring the paper for flats one day in a Tottenham Court Road pub, David made the fatal mistake of ringing home to see if his 'A' level results had arrived. They had. I followed suit, and both of us were disappointed. My results were bad. I cursed myself for all those plays I'd done, and felt remorse for the intense disappointment I knew would be felt by my teachers and my parents. I'd let them down, and here I was adrift in a pub on the Tottenham Court Road, a thick student actor with no place to live. Life was a bitch.

I left David drowning his sorrows, and walked around the corner to RADA where they sometimes had news of accommodation. The place smelled better than before and Summers, who ran the front door, was charm itself. Apart from having a name like a 1930s' butler, he was understanding of nervous new students. He gave me a telephone number, and I rang a number in Clapham.

'Hello, Angus Mackay?'

'Yeees.' It was the most actor-ish voice I'd ever heard.

'I'm a student from RADA. I believe you have two rooms to let.'

'My deaaar. Of course I do. When would you like to see them?'

'Would this afternoon be possible?'

'Of course. As soon as you like, though I'm not even up yet. There you see, your introduction to what actors really do.' A great hearty laugh. 'See you later.'

I felt as though I'd just spoken to a cross between Noel Coward and Basil Brush. Whether the rooms were right or not, this man had to be worth meeting.

When I arrived, the house – in Manchuria Road, Clapham – turned out to be a roomy terrace. Angus Mackay was tall and distinguished, with thinning silver-grey hair, and an old-fashioned theatrical line in persuasive charm. His conversation seemed enormously flamboyant, and was scattered with references to his late wife, Dorothy Reynolds, the co-author of *Salad Days*.

The house was the sort of theatrical Aladdin's Cave of which I had dreamed. He had even more back copies of *Plays and Players* than I did, and the walls were covered with playbills and prints of famous actors. The place was absolutely crammed with books: a formidable theatrical library and thousands of novels. We took to each other right away. I was his first lodger and the first person to share the house with him since his wife had died, three years before. The back bedroom and the little sitting-room were very comfortable, Angus's company was highly enjoyable, and it was all for twenty pounds a week. I had fallen on my feet.

I returned to Reading that night and gave my mother the good and the bad news. To my mother it all seemed bad. The 'A' level results gave me very little to fall back on, and my academic record was important to my parents, who felt that they had thrown away or had been denied their own educational opportunities. I had let them down and, what was more, now that I had found my own accommodation, another home, the last ties were being broken.

'Well, I hope this place isn't full of nancy boys.'

I left her scowling over the washing up, but I was certain that I was right to move to London. My days as a hospital porter came to an end, and the big day arrived. I left home on a Sunday. Mum had been ironing for days, and I had more pressed shirts than I knew what to do with.

We'd never been a family to demonstrate emotion. We weren't unloving, just reserved. I went for a drink with my father, his custom on a Sunday lunchtime. I came back to find my mother doing the sprouts. I made all the usual protestation about coming back at the weekends, that London was so near, then gave her a hug. I was fine – my emotions were well in control.

I went into the living-room. My dad was sitting there quietly. I noticed an envelope on the mantelpiece, and walked over to it: it was addressed to me. I opened it, and inside was a pink 'good luck' card of absurd sentimentality, a kind that only my mum can choose. After the treacly verse, she had written 'We are both very proud of you son. Here is something to help you on your way.' There was a hundred pounds in cash. I was speechless. Their generosity was extra-ordinary. I turned to my father who had naturally averted his eyes. The words wouldn't come, and I could barely see him. My eyes were brimming with tears.

THREE

'Learn of the wise, and perpend'
AS YOU LIKE IT

It was the Sunday evening before my first day at RADA, and I was nervous and lonely, but somehow ready for anything. I'd occupied myself making the first tentative explorations of Angus Mackay's marvellous house, which looked more and more like a miniature theatre museum. I marched down to Clapham South Tube station to get my three-month season ticket. I had dinner with Angus that night, and a roast leg of lamb made me feel considerably less lonely. I'd already started to torment Angus with questions about the theatre and actors, and the nerve-wracked evening passed quickly and enjoyably.

The next morning all the first day horrors I'd imagined gradually disappeared. I didn't sleep in, there wasn't a delay on the Tube, but yes, horror of horrors, I was the first one there. John Alderman, a huge ex-policeman of Karloffian menace, who shared the reception job with Summers, showed me how to clock in. They were very strict about lateness at RADA.

That done, there was my first appearance in dance tights to accomplish. I entered the men's locker-room trying to look confident about where my locker was, gave a few nonchalant, warm-but-strong smiles to a few of the older students who were already there, and then went down the wrong aisle three times.

The first class was Movement, in room ten, directly opposite the locker-room across a short stretch of landing. I changed as quickly as I could and rushed across into the empty class. I was in room ten and ready to go at 9.45. The class started at 10. I was completely alone and hoping that life would eventually cure me of pathological punctuality. At 9.50, with my paranoia reaching new heights in walked Glen Wyand, tugging at his tights.

'Jesus, how do you walk in these things?'

A tall, tanned West-coast American in his mid-twenties, Glen was kind and generous and about as laid-back as you could be without actually stopping. The sound of that soft, velvety voice, apparently devoid of all worry, relaxed me instantly. We began to share mock macho complaints about what this training would do to us.

The room started to fill up with equally uncomfortable but smiling young men and a smaller number of girls who performed the usual trick of convincing you that they had all been professional dancers. Just before 10, Ruth Eva Ronen entered, a movement teacher of enormous precision and metronomic discipline. Neat, in dark blue leotard and always beautifully groomed, she looked like someone's favourite aunt, but the reality was a sergeant-major of the dance floor. Her technique was a sweet smile as she walked round the room, while she pushed students' legs further up in the air or along the bar or round their necks. After an hour of what I came to think of as gestapo aerobics, I was aching all over and consulting the timetable. Christ. Movement every morning. Still, all part of creating the perfect machine for acting.

We then had our first voice class, with instructions about what was to be prepared, speeches and exercises. And then on to music rudiments, where my grasp of reading the stave could hardly have been more rudimentary.

Lunch at RADA was a very cheery affair, and took place in a heavily subsidised canteen right at the top of the narrow building in Gower Street that was ginghamed, bright and airy. Here was where we first shared Movement miseries and consoled ourselves with some of Mrs P's spotted dick. I'd grown to like desserts by then, and Mrs P, who ran the canteen, could make a mean pud.

The afternoon brought the first spot of real acting, with our introduction to Wedekind's *Spring Awakening*. We'd been split up into two groups and I was rather miffed because the other lot were working on Chekhov's *The Wood Demon*. We did have an excellent director in Jane Howell, but even she was unable to lift the unremitting gloom of this view of troubled adolescence. I was given a long speech by a character called Hans who seemed to spend most of the play in the toilet masturbating (I don't know what impression I'd made at the reading!). Hans gets very carried away during this speech – I took his example, and by the end of the first week I'd have been audible in the back row of the Coliseum.

'Remember, he's in a toilet on his own, not wishing to be heard,' said Jane in hushed tones.

'Ah.'

Having got through the first day, I poured out my impressions to

Angus that night: yes, there were some marvellous actors, it seemed; no, I didn't think I had a second career as a dancer; yes, I loved the building, old-fashioned, wood everywhere, sweaty, a bit frayed at the edges, but a real place for work. Things were going on, the place was full of activity. I was a convert on day one.

As the days and weeks of the first term went by, RADA completely took over my life. The institution was all-embracing. Classes ran from 10 to 6, and in the evenings there were rehearsals, tutorials, singing classes. We often worked on Saturday mornings, and most evenings throughout the term there were productions to watch in one of the Academy's two theatres, performed by the finals students. The place seemed to take up all one's waking hours, which was fine by me, as it not only satisfied my voracious appetite for learning but it made leaving home a relatively painless experience. By the time I got round to noticing the first term was over I was already a Londoner.

I made some good friends, sometimes in unusual circumstances. During our first week we all awaited the arrival of a mysterious student, John Marshall, who was late starting term because of a delay in his flight from Canada. He still hadn't arrived when we began our first 'group project' session. There appeared to be a teacher running it, for the curly-haired, compact lumberjack-type before us was asking plenty of questions. After fifty minutes I rumbled him.

'You're not a teacher.'

'No, I'm John Marshall. I start today.'

There was a general moan from the assembled group who'd spent all that time being well-behaved, and this was my introduction to the mild-mannered Scotsman with the manner of a teacher who was to become John Sessions. This incident provided me with a marvellous stick with which to beat John who had come to RADA at twenty-six with two degrees and a feeling that he was already too old. Activating John's age-neurosis became a RADA sport. He and I formed a student threesome with Mark Hadfield, another actor in our term, and together we went to see practically everything the London theatre had to offer.

RADA's location in central London was an enormous boon. We could walk to every West End theatre, the National Theatre, the RSC in pre-Barbican days, and not only were there student stand-by tickets offered by the theatres themselves, but RADA was often given complimentary seats for struggling shows. Student arrogance knew no bounds when it came to savage criticism of plays and performances.

As the term wore on my faults were catalogued in gruesome detail. I suppose this process might be described as the 'breaking down' process, prior to the 'building up' of a technically competent actor. At the end of the first term I was not so much broken down as broken up. Ruth Eva and her colleagues had convinced me that I couldn't walk, stand or sit. If that really were the case, I sensed limitations in my future work.

The voice teachers were particularly hard on me. At one notable voice class I gave what I thought was a splendidly heroic Hotspur. It was a speech from *Henry IV Part I*, which begins 'My liege I did deny no prisoners'. I'd read about the character's famous 'thickness of speech', which was sometimes interpreted with a Geordie accent, and sometimes (as by Olivier) with a stutter. With my customary originality I went for the latter. A splendid frustrated bark on the line, 'For he made me mmmmMAD.'

It had worked like a treat. You could hear a pin drop. Robert Palmer, a splendid teacher with a voice that was made for sexy chocolate commercials, was effusive. 'Marvellous, absolutely super, tremendous grasp of that. A couple of reservations.'

Here it was. The iron fist in the velvet glove. 'Horrendously stiff jaw there, Ken. That'll lose you all vocal flexibility if you're not careful. You've got to work on that sibilant 's'. Also those dark 'l's are letting you down badly. Don't want to be just a regional actor, do we? The hollow back really is a problem. It's affecting your rib control and contributing to that annoying sailor's roll you've developed. I think also if you can even out those vowel sounds, you'll do yourself a favour. Can't have kings sounding like peasants, can we? OK. Let's have the next speech.'

Exit quivering student.

To be fair to Robert and his fellow voice teacher, Geoffrey Connor, there was never any attempt to 'standardise'. Their points were always specific, and there was no attempt to produce the legendary 'RADA voice'. There was however an insistence on silly-sounding phrases like 'thick, rich, dark, round, brown sound', which you had to say as if you were seducing someone. I can't think of a less likely line for the job.

Weekend trips back to Reading became increasingly infrequent. When I did go home, I was always astonished to see that my parents had grown older. While I was living at home, time had stood still, but now I noticed the deeper lines in my mother's face, and the grey in my dad's hair. My sister, Joyce, was now a young woman and no longer a child, and my brother had married and had children. Mum and Dad asked me about life in London, but I told them little, as all they really wanted to know was whether I was 'all right' – eating well, and getting enough sleep. As far as Mum was concerned, if my bowels had moved, then all was well with the world.

Life in London was becoming frantic, with homework – preparing speeches and reading plays – taking up more and more time. Life at Angus's was also delightfully engrossing, with his actor friends coming round to dinner to be plagued with questions from the gauche lodger. I had also abandoned my Reading girlfriend with a callousness that amazes me even now. I'd known Sandy for a couple of years and had been seeing her regularly for about nine months. She was delightful, both understanding and supportive, but not the right person for the young actor obsessed with independence.

'I'm just too busy . . . it'll never work out . . . it's better this way.'

What was that I was saying about it must never matter that much?

The student Burbage had taken over with a vengeance. *Richard III* was on the menu and I had several scenes to act as the crookback. I'd seen Olivier in the famous film and could do a wicked impersonation. This of course was not quite what was required for the wooing scene with Lady Anne. We'd been rehearsing the scene in different pairs for weeks. On the day we presented our work to Jane Howell, I was inspired. Flying. The first time since I'd arrived that I thought I was *doing* it. It seemed effortless, brilliant acting, and I was also thrilled by the girl playing Lady Anne. We neared the end of this wonderfully constructed scene.

ANNE   Didst thou not kill this king?
GLOUCESTER   I grant ye.
ANNE   Dost grant me, hedgehog? Then, God
                grant me too
            Thou mayst be damned for that wicked
                deed!
            O, he was gentle, mild and virtuous!
GLOUCESTER The better for the King of Heaven,
                that hath him.

56

ANNE	He is in heaven, where thou shalt never come.
GLOUCESTER	Let him thank me that holp to send him thither,
	For he was fitter for that place than earth.
ANNE	And thou unfit for any place but hell.
GLOUCESTER	Yes, one place else, if you will hear me name it.
ANNE	Some dungeon.
GLOUCESTER	Your bed-chamber.

Electric. I could feel people all around completely gripped. The scene ended. I looked at this gorgeous creature who had been part of my triumph. I knew what she must be thinking.

'Well?' I said.

She seemed puzzled. Then she asked, 'Are you always going to play it like a Dalek?'

Well, actors are never the best judges of their own work, but it hardly mattered. I was in love. It felt like the real thing, and was in fact a relationship that would last for several years.

The penny was slowly beginning to drop about 'performing', about the need to create each part or speech, and not simply slot in some carefully remembered voice or mannerism from another actor. Not that I am against nicking things. I do it all the time – from life, or from other actors. It's just that a really good actor will put such borrowings into his own soil and make it his own.

Hugh Cruttwell continued with illuminating definitions of where my faults lay. 'You want to produce great acting. There are three major ingredients: passion, poetry and humour. You often have the humour, though not necessarily of the right sort. You have great access to passion, but you seldom find the heart of the poetry. For this you must surrender yourself much more to the part. Not indulge, but give away your technical awareness to a large extent. Not advice to give to every actor, but certainly to you.'

It was sinking in, but it was also painful. I spent my entire RADA career haunted by the voice of Hugh saying 'not true, don't believe it'. Not that his judgement was infallible, simply that I agreed absolutely with him over the severity of the changes necessary to convert the school show-off into an honest actor. He and I never argued. And as he tactfully pointed out, my acting never seemed vulgar or ungenerous. It was just that for certain roles, i.e. the ones I wanted to play, the performer in me had to be clamped down.

Hugh's great gift was to say out loud what I knew myself. It didn't matter if ninety-nine per cent of your audience, critics and colleagues raved about your performance, if a single voice rumbled it as a cheat, as not true, for all its flashiness and technical accomplishment, then you really had to own up and do something about it. Hamlet was right:

> Now, this overdone, or come tardy off, though it makes the unskilful laugh, cannot but make the judicious grieve; the censure of the which one must in your allowance o'er-weigh a whole theatre of others.

These words continue to haunt me. I have always suffered from original guilt. About everything. I don't know whether it's a peculiar part of the Irish inheritance, but it's a powerful and motivating force in me, and my acting has never been free from its grip. The first two terms at RADA let me see that I was gifted in particular ways – good at sight-reading, good at accents, quick in most ways – but that this was not always a help. Being betrayed into superficial performances by these accomplishments was a continual danger.

If I fell into this trap it was never conscious, but the consequent guilt and misery were massive. I knew that it was an acceptance of second best, and an abuse of the advantages I had been given, and I had no choice but to get better and truer by working as hard as I possibly could. This ridiculous extremism has been a major factor in the inner drive that has accompanied my work and career ever since. I find myself unreasonably suspicious of praise; in fact, I am so seldom satisfied with my own work that I become instantly alarmed when other people express their approval. This acts as a kind of puritanical insurance policy against possible failure, and means, of course, that I have rarely enjoyed any true success that I have had.

In the meantime, and before this masochism became too well-established, there was work to do. In any case, things were kept under control by another Irish legacy, that of philosophical acceptance. A drink in the hand and the familiar mantra, 'Ah, fuck it.'

Appropriately, *Fears and Miseries* – Brecht's play set in the Third Reich – was the production that absorbed me during my second term. This picked up on my modest success in *Spring Awakening*, and continued my interesting line of manic Aryans. With thick blond hair and an even thicker German accent I became, for a time, the Anton Diffring of RADA.

Type-casting of this kind did not protect me from improvisation and 'experimental' work. Although RADA subscribed to no specific school of acting, Hugh Cruttwell's policy was to expose the students to as many different techniques and directors as possible. One day I found myself walking blindfold up the Tottenham Court Road, attempting to persuade my 'partner' to cross from the other side. I forget what this was supposed to teach us, but I did learn that artificial sensory deprivation and major thoroughfares do not mix. During the more extreme of these exercises John Sessions, by far the most easily embarrassed student, would hide in the nearest coffee bar until we had all 'found our centres'.

We were also required to visit the Zoo once a week and study an animal, which we would later present in closely observed physical detail to various teachers. This was designed to test students' powers of observation as well as their dexterity. I have to confess to a less than committed attitude to this class, which was run by a soft, pixified lady in beaming middle age who appeared to be visiting Gower Street from Pluto. At the end of each class – in which we might have to be an animal or imagine ourselves a ball of mercury, or a tree, or a Mars Bar – she would stop us and then hold a mystical pause. Slowly she would point her finger at each student in turn. She spoke as if in a trance. 'You had it . . . you had it . . . you didn't have it . . . you had it . . .'

There were often variations.

'You had it for a bit, then you lost it . . . you didn't look like getting it . . .'

Needless to say I never had it or if I did, I certainly didn't know what 'it' was. I sometimes thought that perhaps I'd had it and not known what to do with it. Certainly if I ever did get it, she never saw it.

I don't think she'd ever forgiven me for being a crocodile. I'd chosen this creature because it hardly moved, and afforded me a good view of the rest of the class as I lay on the ground, hooded eyes half-closed, the all-seeing scourge of the jungle. I have never realised my crocodile professionally, although I have of course worked with several.

The world opened up for me at the end of the second term when I stopped playing Germans and was cast as Shakespeare's Pericles. I was remarkable in jeans and white T-shirt. All the cast were dressed alike and my mother said I looked the oldest, at about twelve. She was allowed to see this studio production because the school's policy was to have public audiences invited from the second term onwards.

We all relished the chance to practise in front of real live people from an early stage. I wish I could say that it improved my performance but I remained chronically overparted from beginning to end – the role was simply too much for me to take on at that time and at that age. The reconciliation scene between Pericles and Marina is one of the most moving in all the plays. I fell into a trap here that Gielgud has described eloquently: I did the whole thing awash with tears, genuinely and deeply moved by it, but almost incomprehensible to the audience who strained to hear a barely audible actor emoting to no particular effect.

I was learning rather swiftly about love. My Lady Anne – a girl called Wendy Seagram, who was in the same year – really was the one for me. I left Angus in Clapham with some sadness, but I had no choice, the primrose path was leading me inexorably to Willesden and to the arms of my beloved. We moved in together at the start of the third term. My brother had already broken the taboo about cohabitation, and so my parents accepted me living in sin without a murmur. I think secretly they thought it would ensure that I ate properly.

I certainly entered on full domestic life with a vengeance. There was a regular Saturday visit to Waitrose on the Kilburn High Road, and we bought a 'slo-cooker', which would be left on in the morning when we left for college and would produce something hot and tasty when we arrived back late at night. Favourite and cheapest was liver casserole. (Tray of liver – very cheap – pour over a can of tomatoes and anything else you fancy. Cook forever. Then drink something very strong like Retsina when you're eating it. You won't be able to taste it, but it must be doing you good.)

Our flat had everything we could possibly want but heat. There was a huge window the length of one side of the main room, and a gorgeous tree outside: the room was filled with light and the view was green. In the winter it was different – the tree was bare and the windows iced up on the inside, and there was the horror of making the morning dash from the warm duvet to the tiny kitchen to put the kettle on and then rush back before something got frostbite. However many liver casseroles I consumed, the two-roomed love-nest in

Willesden Green was not good for my circulation. At least it was cheap.

The journey on the number 8 bus each morning, or on the Jubilee and Bakerloo lines to Euston Square, was never enough to warm me up. That happened during movement class, not because of the activity, as I was often a shameless malingerer behind teacher's back, but I did get hot under the collar. Our accompanist was a sweet man, but had a limited repertoire of tunes. I have nothing against Andrew Lloyd Webber, but nearly three years of 'Close Every Door To Me' accompanying what seemed to me impossible movements against a wall was more than I could take. I'm unable to hear the tune now without wanting to put my leg up on the nearest table, bend over, and hope that Ruth Eva doesn't come and double me up even further.

Doubling up was quite another problem. 'Corpsing' – laughing on stage when you're not supposed to – had already become a hazard. I don't know why it happened to me, but I had been doing it since I'd started acting. People say it's a form of hysterics, which I'm sure is true.

At RADA the first of a long series of tickings-off came my way, and similar reprimands have been dogging me ever since, to my eternal shame. They usually begin 'I wouldn't have expected it of you,' or, 'You really have let yourself down'. Sometimes it's an irate fellow actor who thinks that they are the object of your mirth. With me, almost always, there's no particular reason, but it's as if some puff of laughing gas had been sent through my system. It can happen at any time. Later in my career, I once corpsed myself in a one-man show, which must be some sort of record. Nothing had happened, I was just struck by the thought that what I was doing must seem absolutely ridiculous, and so I was off. I then amused myself further by attempting desperately to convert the smiles into 'acting'. Not a chance; once begun, a corpse is a lost cause.

I'm much better these days. The tickings-off and the shame have worked, as has the memory of the excruciating pain when you know that you've let down an audience or a fellow actor. I used to shuffle backstage, head down, aware that the word 'amateur' was written in neon lights across my forehead.

At RADA several people pointed out that in my case I didn't have much to laugh about. They were probably referring to my singing. We had a lesson one evening a week in which the teacher, Daryl

Moulton, coached me in classical songs and encouraged a flamboyant, italianate delivery. We worked in the canteen where I was encouraged to stand on the tables and belt it out as if I was at La Scala. I loved it. But only in the canteen.

At the end of each term, on a grim Saturday morning, we had to sing solo in front of the other twenty-two members of the class and all the staff. It was a terrifying experience for nearly everyone, but RADA, quite rightly, insisted on it as absolutely necessary to improve the equipment of a versatile modern actor. Hugh demanded a certain seriousness for these occasions, even though the atmosphere was fraught with the hysterics of frightened student actors. Our group was very supportive, and each time one of us got through it the cheering could be heard in Gower Street.

I managed the first two of these occasions with relative ease. At the end of the fourth term I was given Purcell's 'Music For A While' to sing. Daryl insisted on my progressing from the Cole Porter ballads I loved to this extremely taxing song. I practised hard and felt much the same as I had always done when I entered the packed classroom for the session. When it was my turn I went to the front. The introduction was played, and I sang the first phrase. I faltered, and with that stumble an uncontrollable fear and sickness rose up in me. I was about to cry. So I stopped and walked to the piano, picked up the music from my astonished teacher and turned to the huge group of staff and students. You could hear a pin drop. 'I . . . I'm sorry . . . I can't do this . . .'

I walked to the door and tried to get out. It was stuck. For what seemed like an eternity I waited and prayed for the earth to swallow me up. The door finally opened, and I ran down the stairs and out into Gower Street. The tears were pouring down my face, but I was also furious with myself for having given in to my first horrendous bout of stage-fright. I walked round the block replaying the humiliation. After half an hour I realised that I had no choice but to go back. I was scheduled to sing two other voluntary pieces after the compulsory ones. One was a duet with Mark Hadfield, and I couldn't let him down as well. But voluntary? What had I been thinking of?

There was a break before the next session and during the coffee I arrived back to squirm in the puzzled sympathy of my fellow students. The session started. I got back on the horse, as it were, and stood in front of all those people feeling more stupid than I had done

62

before in my life. The singing was fine – that wasn't the problem. It was confidence, and it had been a shock to find out how fragile mine was. I was determined not to be neurotic about it but it did sabotage my performing for a while. I came out of the depression by resolving one day to be in a professional musical in which I sang the most difficult song imaginable. I'm still working on that one.

A rather more visible fear presented itself on our school's tour of the *Merchant of Venice* – violence. The North London comprehensives we played in made Meadway look like a holiday camp. For the first time I confronted an audience who talked loudly all the way through the play, who heckled and threw things. It probably resembled the crowd's response in Shakespeare's playhouse. When their attention was engaged, at whatever volume, it was exhilarating, but it was also a salutary experience of the barriers that separate Shakespeare and the theatre in general from a truly popular audience.

The barriers are high, but not insurmountable. It depends on how you do it. You have to be good for a start: my Salerio and Prince of Arragon were not creations to win over these urban adolescents. I played Arragon as Don Corleone and threw in dark glasses to complete the effect. I didn't go as far as putting cotton wool in my mouth like Brando, but the accent was impenetrable enough as it was. Another fine addition to my gallery of 'mystics'.

The fourth term brought me the Edmund Grey prize for high comedy. I was Sir Joseph Wittol, a fop, in Congreve's first play, *The Old Bachelor*. Rather than 'high', this performance can best be described as 'orbital'. Orange wig, white face, silly costume. Nothing could stop me. Certainly not good taste, and if the abuse of good taste is the spirit of restoration comedy, then I was marvellous.

'Yes, you certainly get full value from that one, Ken.'

Hugh chose his words carefully. I could think what I liked.

'Maybe we'll move you onto something a little more demanding.'

Demanding or impossible?

Old men. I knew it – a life destined for character parts. This was a classic student fear. If drama school condemned you to wigs and funny walks, then so would the outside world. It was no good if potential employers saw you as a ninety-year-old fop – we were young actors and wanted young parts.

Feelings about casting ran high at RADA, but it must be the same everywhere. Midway through the training I, and everyone else, became extremely rancid about the whole process. Why is *he* playing so-and-so when I'm the right person for the part? She *always* gets the femme fatales . . . he can't even *read* Shakespeare. None of this was particularly malicious, and we were a friendly team, but the claustrophobic, enclosed society had its disadvantages.

The part of Chebutykin, the melancholy, middle-aged doctor in Chekhov's *Three Sisters*, was not without its problems. We rehearsed for seven weeks with a director determined to rehearse as Stanislavsky might have done. In this case, the application of the famous method was a little shaky. To be fair, the director was dealing with a pretty stroppy cast. Things had not started well when she announced on the first day that we would not be using the translation we had been given. Some of the actors had learned the parts and weren't at all pleased to have a new version to learn.

She also insisted that we 'headlined', or described each line that our character spoke. For instance, if Chebutykin said in the text 'Hello, Natasha', the headline would be 'The doctor greets Natasha warmly'. Then a subtext had to be written: 'The Doctor appears to be greeting Natasha warmly, but in fact only slightly covers up his annoyance with her, whilst appearing to be polite for the others.' As this was done for every single sentence of dialogue, rehearsals entailed writing a short novel which was then questioned by the director, who wanted subtextual rewrites every time you discovered something new.

I'm certain that in the right hands this demanding variation on the method can work superbly well. Unfortunately I was twenty trying to play sixty and wanting to learn how to manage this feat, bar half a bag of Homepride over the barnet. I ended up looking like a cross between a demented Brigham Young and an anaemic Abraham Lincoln.

In desperation I did ask for help. I found the address from *Who's Who* in the RADA library and a letter was duly dispatched to Sir Laurence Olivier. Not only had Sir Laurence directed a famous stage version of the play, but he had also made a film version in which he played the Doctor. I wrote asking for information about anything that might have inspired him – books, films, paintings – anything that I could look at or read to help me with the part. The writing of the letter was partly a sort of exorcism of the dilemma, and I posted it with little hope of a reply.

A week later, to my great surprise, the following reply arrived at RADA.

LAURENCE OLIVIER

K. Branagh, Esq.   10th February 1981
R.A.D.A.,
62 Gower Street,
London W.C.1.

Dear Mr. Branagh:

I think it is really fairly clear the sort of man Chebutykin is in the Three Sisters. Like Hotspur, Mercutio, etc., he is the plain man in all of Chekhov's plays.

I am afraid I really cannot guide you in a purely literary way in a matter which is entirely at the disposal of your own thoughts and workings out. I don't think you can go very wrong, basically, as the author has it all there for you.

If I were you, I should have a bash at it and hope for the best – which I certainly wish you.

Yours sincerely,
Etc.

I don't know that the advice helped me one jot, but the thought that the great man had given it a moment's consideration was enough to send me roaring into the next rehearsal, headlines ablaze – 'Chebutykin goes mad', 'Chebutykin picks his nose', 'Chebutykin walks down front and gets into a much better position than the director has given him' – anything to annoy Miss Moscow Arts. Chebutykin came and went in a whirl of mediocrity.

Contact with the theatrical gods intensified. It was RADA's seventy-fifth anniversary, and Hugh announced a visit by the Queen and Prince Philip to mark the occasion. They would go on a tour of the Academy, and there would be a small concert in their honour, a miscellany of items that charted the progress of students through the Academy.

Hugh asked for volunteers who might like to do some Shakespeare or any other solo work. John Sessions and I went to see him, as John had already been developing his one-man shows and wanted to do a three minute solo improvisation.

Hugh laughed. 'Oh no. Oh no, no. no.' (More laughter) 'It's simply not possible, John. Your language is quite unacceptable. I have no objections, but there could be a national incident. I don't know what you'll come out with, and I simply can't take the risk.'

There was room, however, for the extremely boring and conventional student who came up with the least original idea.

'Could I do a bit of Hamlet?'

Although I was by no means Hugh's favourite student, I think he admired my doggedness and enthusiasm, and I was allowed to perform the 'rogue and peasant slave' soliloquy. We rehearsed it in detail with Hugh asking me first to colour particular lines and words and then encouraging me to forget all point-making and let the speech surprise me. It was yielding good results, and at the end of our second session he said, 'Yes, that's really coming alone. Now look, John Gielgud, the President of the Academy, is coming in on Monday to discuss arrangements for the royal visit, as he'll be showing them round. Perhaps we'll get him to listen to your speech. What do you think?'

I heard myself say, 'That would be terrific,' but my feet had left the ground. Gielgud had been one of my heroes since I had first begun to read about the theatre. My next reaction was the worst possible. I went back to the speech on my own in the following days and worked it to death. The margin was full of 'brilliant' ideas, and I stayed late at college to work on breathing and voice. If you were going to do a speech from *Hamlet* for the Hamlet of the century, then you had to be prepared. I ended up over-prepared.

On the day, I waited nervously in RADA's Studio 1. Hugh was due to bring him in at three o'clock. The door opened on the dot. My legs turned to jelly. There he was in the flesh.

'I hear we're going to see a bit of your Hamlet.' That voice. Oh, my God. I began.

And that's about as much as you can say for my performance on that frightened afternoon. My voice had gone up an octave with nerves. I was as tense and tight as a drum. It was terrible, terrible acting.

As I finished I saw Gielgud wipe away a tear. There is absolutely no doubt in my mind that he was moved by seeing a young actor struggling in utter desperation with a part that he had made his own. He must have felt sorry for me. I felt pretty sorry for myself. I knew I'd muffed it. Trying too hard, I was straining and shouting and my delivery was wildly exaggerated. I simply wasn't very good. Gielgud knew it, and Hugh knew it, but I shall never forget the kindness in his tone as he came up to me and put a hand on my shoulder to give the following advice:

'Well done. There are some good things there, but you're really trying too hard. Don't over-colour the early section. You can be much straighter. Give yourself a breather in the middle. Don't stress "I *am* pigeon livered" when "pigeon livered" is much more juicy . . .'

He went on to give me some more specific notes which I failed to take in because I was hypnotised by the humility of the man. He spoke to me not as a teacher but as one professional to another. He was completely beguiling. He left as quickly as he'd arrived and I sat down half depressed at my failure genuinely to impress a god of English theatre, and half exhilarated by his presence and kindness.

The concert was a week later. All the Academy's students and staff were there, along with hundreds of former students and associates, including Ralph Richardson and Peggy Ashcroft. The adrenalin flowed but was under control, and I tried to remember everything Gielgud had said, telling myself that I would never do anything quite like it again and simply to enjoy it.

> Oh what a rogue and peasant slave am I.
> Is it not monstrous, that this player here
> But in a fiction, in a dream of passion,
> Could force his soul so to his whole conceit
> That from her working all his visage wanned?

I did enjoy it, and the speech was a hundred times better. At least I'd satisfied a certain personal pride. Afterwards we lined up on stage while the Queen and Prince Philip went down the cast. The Queen asked me how I managed to remember all those lines. I didn't know. Gielgud followed and said, to my delight, 'Oh, that's much better. Very good. You took all my notes.'

I could have kissed him. I'm sure he forgot the whole episode the moment he left the building, but his remark made all the difference in the world to me.

A few days' insufferable arrogance was soon cured by the latest wrist-slapping events in the RADA timetable. I had made enough of an impression with my student Hamlet to be cast in Peter Weiss's play, *Marat/Sade*, as 'a mad animal'. What impression was I giving?

Further indignity was provided by the Standard English Test. This informal exam tested our command of BBC English, or Received Pronunciation (RP). It took the form of an audition speech which we performed to a panel of staff and then an interview with the same, remaining in RP. Quite a challenge for anyone with a strong regional accent, but necessary.

The point was made early on about the lack of imagination among employers. If you walked into an interview speaking RP, they were prepared to believe you could play a cockney or a Scot. If it was the other way round, they were unlikely to give you the benefit of the doubt.

I expected to sail through. I may not have developed the honeyed tones of a Gielgud, but I thought my suburban twang was neutral enough for the panel. Not so, I was failed.

I'm sure I would have failed in any case, but the test was much more than a speech exam. It came just before our final terms, and it was a chance to be reminded of quite how much work there was left to do. The panel returned to my jaw, my back, my walk, my 'l's, my 's's. I took the test again, was given a weak pass and decided to forget about Gielgud, Olivier and all, and just concentrate on learning to speak properly. A rather humbler young man approached the last two terms.

Finals offered our group of twenty-three twelve productions over two terms, during which each of us should have at least one 'showcase' part. Having been through my run of juveniles, old men, stormtroopers and then, in Edward Bond's *The Sea*, getting a chance to revive my simple rustic, I was clear about what I would like to play. At the beginning of the fifth term Hugh had asked us about what we wanted to play. He promised nothing. He had his own ideas about what was appropriate, but he was ready to listen to anyone who was passionate about a particular play or part.

After this announcement I found myself in Sidoli's, an Italian coffee bar and bacon-roll emporium just around the corner from RADA. The music of lunchtime orders rang round the steaming shop, and I sat down and wrote a letter to Hugh explaining why I wanted to play Hamlet.

There were obvious reasons for the pushy drama student to wish to play the part, but playing it ensured nothing. If I imagined for a moment that it would be guaranteed to impress the casting directors and agents, I had my Gielgud experience to warn me. Getting the part didn't mean you would be good in it.

Nor did I relish the idea of potential envy or critical rejection on the scale which Hamlet induces. What I wanted was to say 'Fuck it' to all that, that the really important thing was having a go at the part, especially at the age of twenty, regardless of the consequences. I'd read everything I could – Gielgud's wonderful description of playing Hamlet in *Stage Directions*; Richard Sterne's account of the same actor directing Richard Burton in the role; Albert Finney's comment that you should play it at twenty or forty, and I was also very impressed by Tyrone Guthrie's *A Life in the Theatre*.

Guthrie's advice to young actors was to do as many of the great roles as you could as early as possible, so there would be more chance of getting them right later on. He cited Benedick, Romeo, Henry V and Hamlet as parts it would be ideal to play before the age of twenty-five. Of course he was writing about a different theatre, but I believed in the principle.

I wanted one day to be a great Hamlet. Not a particularly unusual dream for a young actor. The crassness of my continual mistakes in performance made the advice of Guthrie and others even more potent. A lifetime already seemed a short span to get anywhere near the heart of great acting. I wanted to play Hamlet as many times as possible, so that each time I played it I would get better in the role, and would get closer to the truth of the character.

I had no divine right to a so-called classical career – I could as easily see a fulfilled acting life in situation comedy, or children's theatre, if I was destined to work at all. I also felt that nothing should be ruled out. It was important to be prepared for anything – for washing dishes, selling newspapers, doing Kissograms, being enormously successful, or not working at all.

I said much of this in my letter to Hugh, and put my case as eloquently as I could. The worst he could say was no.

The plays and casting for term six was announced, with no *Hamlet* on offer. There was always the next term, and it was still a great season of plays in which people really did get their own bite of the cherry. *Time and the Conways* by J. B. Priestley, Dusty Hughes's *Commitments*, *The Maid's Tragedy*, a new improvised play – *Dance of Death*, *No Orchids for Miss Blandish* – adapted from the James Hadley Chase novel, and a great musical, *Lady Be Good*. I hadn't fared badly. One old man, one gangster, one servant, one waiter – a quiet line of parts, perhaps *Hamlet* wasn't out of the question for next term.

The lighter work-load gave me time to attend to my troubled emotional life. Things were going very wrong in Willesden Green and every problem associated with living and working day after day with the same person made itself felt. Wendy moved out, and then I moved out, unable to face the place alone.

I ended up paying double the rent for a deeply poky bedsit in Ealing. One very small room, a broken hot plate, wallpaper that needed a volume control, and it was also freezing. Everything was on a meter and because my Dickensian landlady forgot to empty the bloody things, I lived literally in a twilight world. Most of the time she feigned deafness about these things. She didn't like climbing the stairs, but she was as quick as lightning when the front door opened late at night and she popped her head round the door to check whether you had a 'friend' with you or not.

This was the lowest ebb of my time at RADA. I hated the place in Ealing so much that I went back there at the last possible moment each evening, which meant that I drank and spent more during the evening, and that the journey took longer because the trains were scarcer late at night. My few belongings sat round me in boxes. There was nowhere to put them. I was utterly miserable, and each day Wendy and I faced each other across the class experiencing the horrors of a troubled relationship between two fellow students. On one occasion a director in our improvisation class set up a situation in which two lovers were splitting up and had to decide how to divide up the belongings in their shared flat. He chose Wendy and I to act it out. It was agony, and ended with Wendy bursting into tears and running out of the room.

Moving out of the Willesden flat seemed to help, and once we started to spend less time together we began to miss each other. Gradually the dust settled, and the relationship began to improve. In the meantime, I was able to indulge my moments of despair as Buffo Cole, the character I was playing in *Commitments*. Dusty Hughes's play was an examination of the trendy left-wing fringe in the mid-seventies, a mixture of media people and artists involved in an unsettling flirtation with radical political organisations. Buffo was a sort of refugee from the Blunt/Burgess school of Oxbridge leftists, adrift in disillusioned middle age. My career as a cranky character actor made this the perfect part: dark wig, wild eyebrows, moustache, cherubic expression and a flushed alcoholic complexion. It was an example of the amusing extremes to which a young actor is forced by the absurdities of casting for a drama school finals session. Of course, if I'd left RADA in the early fifties, and was in rep, then I might well have been playing such a role professionally.

Chameleon tendencies continued in *The Maid's Tragedy*. England was in the grip of Adam Ant fever and this look, the director felt, was exactly right for this piece. The result was a parade of costumes and make-up that resembled a gay bordello, and it was also very funny. Sometimes unintentionally. Needless to say, I succumbed to hysterics on one occasion when I was confronted with the latest green-haired, gelled, Red-Indianed student. My ever-growing shame was compounded by a reprimand from a fellow actor whom I very much admired, Douglas Hodge. The poor chap was trying to play a king while facing a lot of shaking students looking upstage towards him in ridiculous costumes, laughing uncontrollably. I was a despicable ring-leader.

'You might have to play a king one day, see how you like it.'

I was learning my lesson painfully.

I brought off a rather convincing Al Pacino impersonation in my next role as Eddie Schultz in *No Orchids for Miss Blandish*. I think I may have been the only one who saw the performance as a tribute to Pacino's role in *The Godfather*, but it created enough interest to draw a letter from an agent asking if I would go and see her. I was wildly excited when the magic envelope sat in the 'B' pigeon hole of RADA's mail rack. It would have been noticed by everyone – these things went round college like wildfire. I savoured the triumph and made an appointment.

The agent was a nice woman but ferociously busy, and the office was full of ringing telephones. I was terrified in advance, and the meeting did nothing to reduce my fear or sense of intimidation. A polite exchange took place, but I had the feeling that she was most definitely doing me a favour in offering to take me on. Of course she was doing me a favour, but I suspected it would have been cleverer of her to have perhaps made me feel more wanted. A delicate relationship at the best of times, I sensed that this particular combination might not be productive.

Still, I was in no position to be choosy. I accepted her vague proposal to 'keep in touch', and assumed that if she saw me being marvellous in something instead of just promising, then we had a deal. A very prestigious agent, but scary all the same.

RADA had provided a talk by a practising agent to give us advice about what to expect when the magic envelope arrived. I recalled that she had said to remember that an agent was your employee, and that finally it was you who had to call the shots. Good advice, I thought, but it was far from what I felt capable of doing with my first option, for whatever one's level of experience, one had to feel comfortable with one's agent. It had to be someone who was almost a family figure, someone who could be charming and tough, and produce the best deal for you without giving offence. Someone who would do more than just answer inquiries about you, but who, especially for unknown drama school graduates, would initiate possibilities for work.

The ideal person was someone, I imagined, a little like our wise counsellor. Her name was Patricia Marmont, but she hadn't seen my work, not unless you counted my Spanish waiter in *Lady Be Good*, and I couldn't be sure whether I'd impressed. I felt very much the secret song-and-dance man. One *could* be spotted in the chorus, I'd seen *42nd Street*. I was third line, second from the left in the hotel number. My heel-kicking could easily have caught someone's eye, and I know my voice stood out in the chorus. Eyes and teeth, love. People must have noticed me.

It was a Saturday morning in July, and the last night of the musical. I went straight for the hall noticeboard, eyes darting down the list. *Hippolytus, A Flea in her Ear, The White Devil, . . . Hamlet*. Eureka! Yours truly as the Prince. Thank Christ for that. I sat down and wrote to Pat Marmont immediately.

It was one of a hundred and fifty letters I wrote that summer. I also had my pictures done so that a 10 × 8 print could hang in the rogues' gallery of the RADA bar to impress visiting directors. I remember the first photographer, trying hard to relax me, a classically nervous student.

'Smile. I'm sure you're going to get lots of work. I think you'll be typecast as a policeman. Lots of parts there.'

Jesus. PC Hamlet. Thank you very much.

I had my pictures redone by a lovely photographer called John Fletcher, who was very encouraging and able to relax me with great ease by pushing a large glass of wine into my hand. Actors are often remarkably ill-at-ease as themselves in front of a camera and need a photographer who can make them feel comfortable.

I chose the right print, which gave me a look that had a balance of qualities – funny but sad, intelligent but wacky, kind but firm. I thought there was an expression in my face which said 'I'm a brilliant, warm, modest actor. Not dull, but no trouble either. Cast me as anything. I'm a chameleon genius.'

Postcards of this unique expression were sent to every repertory theatre in the country with my RADA CV, plus interesting personal touches that could mark my missive out from the rest of the bunch. Phrases like 'I particularly love Plymouth and want to work in the theatre there, having spent a happy childhood holiday in a village really quite near.' Or, 'My Celtic origins have always drawn me to a career in Cardiff.' Or, most desperately, 'I love being near the sea, I bet Southwold is lovely to work in.'

The worst excesses were vetted by John Sessions and the other students in my year who were all doing the same thing. I saved my major personal approaches for the theatres in Reading and Belfast. Not a sausage. Certainly not an audition. My photograph was sent right back to RADA, often with the CV, at best with a photocopied letter saying 'We'll put you on file'. After five months of letter-writing I left RADA without a single audition or interview in prospect, despite some professional good fortune which came my way during that *Hamlet* summer.

I spent the first part of the holiday working as a caretaker in St Martin's School of Art in Charing Cross Road. Apart from the income, it gave me something to do while Wendy was appearing with the National Youth Theatre. We were now very settled and happy and spent as much time together as possible. On one weekend we travelled down to Reading where I had promised to check on my parents' house, as they were away on holiday. Everything was safe and we took a walk around the town while I explained scenes of my former dramatic triumphs in the town whose theatre was rejecting me so cruelly.

Unusually, that week I had not bought a copy of *The Stage*. It had brought me little in the way of luck. Job adverts were nearly always for Equity members, and the rare exceptions yielded little. One week the National Theatre of Brent advertised for a new member, and the same night I wrote and recorded a song with my guitar and cassette recorder. I took the Tube to the address given that evening, CV, picture, and song in hand – such was my enthusiasm and ingenuity. All to no avail. Even though I'd returned to live in Willesden Green, in the borough of Brent, my credentials were not good enough. The song remains a favourite, a sort of cowboy-yodel number that celebrated northwest London, and I sang it in a demented Jim Reeves croon:

Sunriiiise on the Hiiigh Rooooad,
Willesden Haieeeaigh Road,
Kilburn looks good to me today
For you can see so faine
On that Jubilee laiiine
To Willesden Haiiigh Road.

They still didn't want me. I couldn't work it out.

I was nursing these slights on that fateful Saturday when we wandered into Reading's Town Library and looked at *The Stage* in the reading room. I soon wandered off, bored, until a scream from Wendy brought me back to an advert that did not require an Equity member.

BBC Play for Today.
Filming Belfast, Oct/Nov '81.
Requires Actor, 16–24
with authentic working-class
Belfast accent.

There was a number to ring but I resisted, as I knew this ad would draw thousands of bogus Belfast backgrounds, and I'd have no chance. Anyway, *Hamlet* played from 24–28 October, the dates would never work out, RADA would never release me. I really wasn't going to bother, but Wendy was having none of it. I was left in Reading while she returned to the National Youth Theatre threatening a definite parting if I didn't ring the number. On the Monday morning, I tried the number again and again, but it was engaged. I kept going, and eventually got through.

'Hello, Paul Seed.'

'Yes, hello. My name's Kenneth Branagh.'

It just worked. Paul Seed was suspicious of the accent but I reassured him that York Street was inches below the surface. He said he'd consider me if I sent him a CV and picture. No problem, I said, except that I had no CV and no picture – they were in London. I dragged my friend, David Longstaff out of his bed and we drove to

RADA where I took my one 10×8 photograph off the wall, hastily typed out a new CV and rushed round to TV Centre where the production office was. It was all done within six hours of the call. We arrived back in Reading breathless at 5. At 5.30 the phone rang, and I was offered an interview the following afternoon.

Paul Seed, the director, was in his early thirties. A former actor, this was his first TV directing job. He explained the plot, which focused on a divided Protestant family, the mother dying of cancer, the father drunk. The son Billy was rebelling against his father while attempting, with his sisters, to hold the family together. It sounded very powerful. Paul asked me to look over a section of the play and then read it. I knew it was fine writing and I knew I was right for the part. I felt it had gone well, but as usual I left the interview knowing nothing.

They rang again the next day. Would I come in on Friday to read with some people who might be playing Billy's best mate? They wanted to put couples together. I was very near. Paul had told me that their searches for actors had been extensive even before they'd placed the ad in *The Stage*. Billy was one of the leading roles and pivotal to the success of the piece. They'd even auditioned in Belfast schools to find the right raw quality, but the part also needed a competent acting technique, and it meant they might have to go with someone like me.

Before the second interview my parents arrived back from holiday. They were dismayed at my news, for, like many people on the mainland, and despite their connections, they saw Belfast as a dangerous war zone. They were praying for me not to get the part. My mother didn't hold out much hope, however. She had had one of her famous 'feelings', which were usually connected with births or deaths but were now directed towards my career. 'You'll get the bloody thing. I know it.'

No mention had been made about dates yet. I'd told the BBC about the RADA *Hamlet*, but it hadn't put them off.

Friday came and in the foyer at TV Centre, I met Column Convey, a pal from RADA with a similar Irish background.

'Are you here for what I think you're here for?'

'Ay, I'm up for the mate.'

'But you are my mate.'

'I know. We're laughing.'

It wasn't that easy, but we were the only people they appeared to be seeing for all their talk of putting couples together. We read the scenes for Paul Seed and Chris Parr, one of the producers. They had obviously discussed what to do if they liked us. The reading had gone well. Chris spoke.

'That's terrific. Look, we'd really like you to play these parts. Although the Equity question is difficult we think we can produce cards for you because of the special circumstances. We really have seen an awful lot of people and you boys are the ones for the job. The real problem is you, Ken.' Oh no. 'Dates. We need to start in Belfast the week you open *Hamlet*. I'm afraid I have to ask the terrible question: will you give up playing in *Hamlet*?'

I let out a sigh. I knew it, you can't have your cake and eat it in this world. I thought long and hard but the answer was clear – I couldn't give *Hamlet* up. I tried to explain. I wasn't sure that I would ever play Hamlet again, but perhaps there would be another TV play, and if I reneged on Hugh, what if an extraordinary film came up while I was doing the TV play? Would I then drop the play? I was genuinely sorry to have wasted their time but it seemed, even at that tense moment, that it was no good starting a career by sacrificing something that meant so much. Hugh had taken a great risk by casting me and I would never have those conditions to enjoy again, that rare freedom from critics and from life-or-death notices.

Chris Parr shook his head. 'I understand what you're saying and I respect it, but we'll have to go away and think again.'

I walked out of TV Centre with Column, who commiserated but clearly thought I was nuts. He had left RADA the term before and knew what it was like to be in the race for a job. I'd thrown away an opportunity that might never occur again.

That evening I sat down with a Chinese take-away in a new Willesden Green flat. I had my trusty copy of *Hamlet* by my side and a volume of *Teach Yourself Conjuring*. If I could work out an act I might be able to get myself an Equity card as a cabaret artist. The Catch 22 of Equity was infuriating: no card without a job, no job without a card, and I'd just thrown away both. I was considering whether to invest in a performing dove when the phone rang. It was Paul Seed.

'All right, you little shit.' He was laughing. 'We'll rehearse the first week in London, then go to Belfast.'

'What?'

'You've got the job. But only on condition that you'll rehearse during the day when you're playing Hamlet, and that Hugh releases you for a month after that to rehearse and record in Belfast. And that you give us one day out of *Hamlet* rehearsals for a bit of filming that we can't move.'

'What about Equity?'

'We'll do our best. So what do you say, you grand bastard?'

I was laughing now. 'OK, love. I'll talk to my advisors.'

I thanked him profusely and returned to my celebration chow mein. It was Friday night in Willesden Green. I had a job (nearly) and on Monday I started rehearsals for my first Hamlet. You really are a jammy so-and-so, I thought. When things go well, I have always tried to stop myself from getting cocky by putting achievements down to good luck rather than to appropriate talents, and if things go badly, then there is a neat excuse lined up to explain it all.

Hugh excused me from *A Flea in her Ear*, but insisted that I return to RADA after *Too Late to Talk to Billy*, the TV play, for the last three weeks of term during which I would be playing a very small part in *The White Devil*.

Although the Equity negotiations would be tricky, I started rehearsals for *Hamlet* in great elation at my good fortune. Graham Reid's script for *Too Late to Talk to Billy* was marvellous and rather than envy, I received nothing but support from the other students. Except for one. For a terrible first week of *Hamlet* rehearsals I imagined that I was back in my first term at Meadway.

To describe what happened as bullying would not be accurate, but my reaction was much the same. The actor in question was a good one with an aggressive, powerfully intimidating presence which had been more or less kept under control during the training. Now, for some reason, an undercurrent of menace made itself felt. From the first day he seemed to undercut my contributions, and, more worryingly, he became violent in his manner throughout rehearsals, or so it seemed to me. I know I was not alone in finding him frightening.

I succeeded, I hope, in betraying none of my fears, but inside I was devastated. I dreaded going to rehearsals with the same intensity that I had dreaded going to school. I even found myself ringing my father with the same babyish complaints. I spoke to Colin Wakefield, who spent a day with me trying to talk me out of this strange psychological intimidation. I was terrified, and I couldn't sleep. One night, after a particularly tense rehearsal, I walked the length of Marylebone Road in the rain crying my eyes out. All I wanted to do was run away.

I felt the performance was suffering terribly, and I was full of self-disgust at the weakness in my character which had allowed this to happen. I watched every minute tick away in rehearsals and prayed for them to end quickly, and I also felt that yer man knew exactly what he was doing and that it was a super-subtle but conscious decision to intimidate. Just because I'm paranoid doesn't mean people *aren't* watching me.

If there were advantages to the situation, I suppose that the combination of fear and my self-loathing at not being able to deal with it were sterling Hamletian qualities. I scarcely worried about the part itself. I worked hard, but for me the whole experience was about getting through rehearsals. There was an excellent director, Malcolm McKay, and it was a fine production – pacy, real and exciting. If it taught me anything, it was that I was unable to work easily in an atmosphere of tension or dangerous animosity. Anything that was good in my performance could have been achieved just as well and even better under conditions where a crazed ego wasn't ruling the roost.

The performance in general received a good response from the RADA audience. All the voice teachers thought that I was the quickest Hamlet ever. (Although Richard Briers claims that prize.) Too quick, they said. Hugh's response was frank and uncompromising: 'Yes, Ken. Lot of work to do. Two fundamental points. First, comedy and humour. There is a difference. You give us comedy in Hamlet. What he has is a deep-seated melancholia producing a black, bleak humour. You give us a sort of gratuitous clowning. Secondly, passion. Hamlet is a haunted man, shaken to his very soul by the deep repulsion about his mother's marriage and horror at the arrival of his father's ghost. You give us a sort of lively irritability.'

I was philosophical: I intended to play it several times. I did learn a great deal and, if nothing else, several bits of personal 'business' from this Hamlet went into my later one. And into everything that followed went a determination never to succumb to fear like that again. What a waste of time.

The first two days' rehearsal for the *Billy* play were spent in a daze. We opened *Hamlet* on a Wednesday evening and the next morning, St Crispin's Day, I started my first professional job. The BBC rehearsal studios in West London introduced me to the aircraft hangars in which the BBC rehearse their dramas. It was a short bus ride away from Willesden Green and seemed like Hollywood to the then temporary member of Equity.

In their infinite wisdom the Union had decided that I deserved a card because I had trained at a recognised Drama school and was one of the few people appropriate for the part. But, on the other hand, they felt this kind of queue-jumping should not be allowed and as soon as the job was over my card should expire, as presumably then – in my three remaining weeks at RADA – I might be taking the bread out of the mouths of needier members. Thank you, gentlemen.

It was tricky balancing two jobs at the same time, especially when the first day's rehearsal for the *Billy* play coincided with my second ever performance as Hamlet. I worked hard through that day, in a smoky atmosphere, high on adrenalin. Paul was kindness itself and there was an excellent cast, mostly young, led by James Ellis, a brilliant and entertaining storyteller.

At 5.30 I had the luxury of a car, courtesy of the BBC, to take me to Gower Street. But no amount of cosseting could change the fact it was difficult to play Hamlet and very difficult to concentrate on two demanding experiences at once. My head was full of the day's events. I talked too much, I didn't rest, and the second performance was a disaster. Such was my wayward concentration that I comically invoked the name of the cigarettes I'd been surrounded by all day:

> My tables. Meet it is I set it down
> That one may smile and smile
> And be a villain. At least I am sure
> It may be so with Dunhill.

It was unmistakable, and there was more to follow. There was a price to pay for telly fame.

Pat Marmont managed to see *Hamlet* on a non-disaster night. I went to see her just before going to Belfast. An elegant and very attractive woman, she charmed me straight away by saying that I must go and see other agents. But there were no other agents to see – she was the only one that had actually written to me. She stressed her love of the theatre and the belief that people should put something back into it, so if I wanted to make an exclusive screen career, she probably wasn't the one for me.

There was nothing pushy in her manner. Her quiet confidence was inspiring and beneath the pussycat that was subtly wooing me, she was clearly made of stern stuff. I was won over. She told me to think about it in Belfast and then talk again. She was pleased but not over-impressed with the TV job and, like Gielgud, she spoke to me as an equal, which I liked. I would think about it in Belfast, but my instinct told me it was a clear choice. I sensed a quick temper. We would clearly have our rows, but we thought the same way about the theatre. A former actress herself and an indisputable pro, she made my mind up. The problem was solved.

I felt apprehensive on my return to Belfast. Of course our relations would persuade us of the 'normality' in the province. Aunt Kathleen and my mother spoke on the phone each week, people could shop and go swimming and take the kids to school and do other everyday things with relative ease, but the news reports were frightening and with short hair and an English accent, I was warned about being taken for an off-duty soldier. I was ready to be very careful indeed. As we approached Aldergrove airport I was struck by the silliest and simplest of thoughts. The place really was the Emerald Isle. The grass was greener than green. Peaceful and calm, an ironic, moving characteristic of that troubled land.

The BBC minibus dropped me on the Shore Road and there on the corner was my Uncle Jim to welcome me home with the firmest handshake an uncle could have. A shipyard man all his life, Jim was a strapping figure of Lawrentian masculinity, all muscle and honesty. He took me round the corner to the small terraced house he shared with my Aunt Kathleen and I sat down to the first of the enormous 'feeds' I was due during those four, calorific Ulster weeks.

Like all families that have done without, good food and its plentiful supply was much enjoyed by all the Branaghs and Harpers in modern Belfast. They all shared the common belief that any member of the family under thirty needed feeding up. As a result, meals were an obstacle course of carbohydrate. Ulster has a terrible record of heart disease, and it is inextricably linked to the horrors of the fat-based diet. Too many 'Ulster frys' must have put many an Irishman into his grave.

Over that month I gained a stone. Lunchtime at rehearsals meant a bowl of stew and a pint; at tea-time, a huge plate of tatties and mince was washed down with a pint of milk and followed by trifle. On a Saturday night it was the works – black pudding, tattie farls, soda bread, fried eggs, steak, tomatoes, bacon and mushrooms. Of course one could always have refused these treats, but I was an

Irishman, and my appetite for the food, the drink and 'the crack' were unquenchable.

A true Irishman in spirit maybe, but in practice the split feelings induced by an adolescence on the mainland made for an uneasy time in Belfast. There were two brilliant child actresses in the *Billy* play. After the read-through on the first day, they heard me speaking in my English accent for the first time.

'What's happened to your accent? What's *wrong* with you, mister?'

As kids do, they had gone right to the heart of this strange situation: an Irishman in Ireland who lives in England and speaks English, but who is making a living as an Irishman. I was working in a world which my Irish relatives didn't understand, and I felt ashamed of opening my English mouth in the street or in the pubs. When you spoke of your background, people sometimes looked suspicious, as if you were merely covering up for some betrayal. I became aware of what Olivia Manning described as the Anglo-Irish sense of 'belonging nowhere'. I felt desperate to belong, but on this first trip back it was not to be. I had very divided feelings. Although the place ignited my Irishness – a love of drinking, of storytelling, of the crack, and although I loved many aspects of Belfast, it was very clear that this was no longer my home. My instinctive need for roots was provided more surely by the acting profession itself. This uneasiness about Ireland would remain for some years to come, and would only be exorcised when I could come to terms with my own guilt over this split in my personality.

My first experience of TV work was made easier by the presence of a committed, excellent team working together and believing in the play. There was a sense of something quite young and original going on. Paul Seed was unjaded, Jimmy Ellis was full of high spirits and BBC Northern Ireland was taking pride in this new drive to establish a first-class drama output. The play was about a family, and a family feeling was created among the team, complete with squabbles and fallings out, but held together by tremendous affection. Watching this convinced Graham Reid of the potential to write the full trilogy that he felt the material deserved.

I learnt about TV acting as I went along, one major omission from RADA's training. Screen acting is sometimes described as 'doing less' – using less voice, cutting out large theatrical gestures, keeping the body and face much more still. In reality, the process is much more subtle and complicated. It needs a supreme technical awareness on the part of the actor, who should know exactly where to place his concentration, how to pace himself for short bursts of intense emotion, when to let go. All of this must be invisible, and if you give anything away, the camera picks it up. I was struck by the immense difficulty of presenting the truth of a character or a scene for the camera. It isn't enough just to feel it, you must know what the truth of the scene and the character is, but you must also know how to convey it.

It is not a question of cold, technical acting, which is often effective in conveying the superficial truth of a character, but of acting where appearance and reality merge into one, where the actor sounds and looks like a real person, and not a performer. At this level, the audience is unaware of any artifice or conscious technique. Acting like this can be seen in a 'personality' performance, where a star gives a portrayal which is essentially an extension of their own screen persona. David Niven, for instance, who was a fine performer, nevertheless remained David Niven the movie star for almost all his film work, and distinctions from character to character seemed less important than his ability to present a truthful naturalism through his very particular screen personality. Character performers can do the same thing with the help of make-up and costume, transforming themselves from film to film. In both cases the magic can work its spell and arrest you in your living room or in the cinema. It is rare, and I love it both on TV and on film.

Billy made me realise that good screen acting depends on collaborative effort. I took in everything. I studied the way the cameras were moving; I questioned Paul about his camera script; I tried to find out all I could about the actual mechanics of TV. I didn't want to fight the technical elements of the medium, but to embrace them so that they wouldn't get in the way of the best acting.

At the end of five days' recording I felt that I'd just begun to warm up. Filming was over and there was nothing to do but pack up and head back for London. I couldn't do any of it again. In any case, the BBC Ulster studio doubles as a cattle shed for half the year and the cows were clamouring for the space.

I came back from Belfast with my instinctive love for my homeland revived. I'd enjoyed meeting the dozens of cousins and aunts and uncles that were on my visiting rounds, and I'd particularly loved talking to my only remaining grandparent, Lizzie, who at eighty years old remained strong and steadfast, humorous and full of stories. I was enjoying the treat of hearing someone who was very much my senior talking to me as if I were a neighbour gossip. It was lovely also to hear her version of my parents' youth, particularly my father's.

Back at RADA I was set to play a villainous servant in *The White Devil*, and decided that this was a part which would rid me of some of my mousy suburban attitudes. I paid great attention to costume and make-up. I'd come across some glossy photo books covering the work of Glasgow Citizens' Theatre – visually very extravagant, flamboyant and camp, the company was an inspiration to me, and I got myself up in long greasy dark wig, painted cheekbones (the first and last I've ever had), earrings and lots of black velvet. On the first night, I walked on stage, with fellow students Craig Crosbie as the other servant and Ian Targett as our master, Lodovico.

There was a great rush of music and we tore down the rake of the black and silver set, Craig and I pulling Ian behind us and flinging him down on to the apron. He starts the play off with an angry cry at his fate.

'Lodovico – Banished?'

Whereon I leaned against a pillar looking sexy, shifted a hip and took an age to say (while fiddling with my nails and looking off into the distance), 'It grieved me much to hear the sentence.'

It came out in a lurid, sensuous whine that was both gross and exciting, exactly right for Webster's universe, or so it seemed to me. The scene finished. We came off stage. Ian and Craig turned to me.

'What were you doing?'

'What do you mean?'

'All that terrible Kenneth Williams meets Liberace stuff.'

Maybe I was going to play policemen after all.

The final performance of *The White Devil*, on my last day at RADA, coincided with my twenty-first birthday. I was bought many a drink that night. I sat clutching a confirmation letter from Equity telling me that I was no longer a member. The *Billy* play already seemed like a dream. No one from our term had obtained work in advance of leaving, although many had agents. Pat had nothing for me at that time.

Where were my ambitions? Did I want to be a classical actor? Not really, I just wanted to work. I was excited about leaving – seven terms had been quite long enough. I had no interviews to go to but I was prepared to work at anything else in the interim to make money.

My dad had some manual work coming up that I was ready to do. There was the caretaking or the selling. Anything was fine till the first chance to work arrived. I would read and write and not be beaten by lack of activity.

As someone keenly self-motivated (there are other words for it, I know) I rather relished the gladiatorial aspect of getting a job as an actor. Not the competition with other actors, but the struggle with myself and with the job. If they wanted a short-sighted, hairy basketball player for a film, I was determined to find the stilts, the glasses and the moustache and then persuade them I was the man for the part.

I'd have done pretty much whatever came along: panto, rep, telly, radio, Shakespeare, comedy, whatever. I'd have cleaned floors, made sandwiches, delivered papers – anything to make a quick buck until professional acting work *did* come along.

I remembered a remarkable conversation I'd had two years earlier. In the flush of my enthusiasm at winning a place at RADA I had written to Derek Jacobi. The Hamlet hero of my youth, he was reviving the role at the Old Vic. I asked if I might speak to him, and to my surprise he agreed. In his dressing-room at the great theatre I asked lots of impertinent questions.

'Do you think of yourself as a classical actor?'

'No,' he said with great emphasis. 'I'm just an actor pure and simple. I have to make a living. I have to be prepared to do anything. Not just Shakespeare. Actors are still just beggars, really.'

I'm sure he believes, as I do, in the positive and creative role of the actor, but he was brutally realistic about the economic and professional restrictions, the almost total dependence on others and on the need for new jobs coming in at frequent intervals. I knew the early stages of everyone's career were different, but I hadn't forgotten what he had said and I attempted to be similarly realistic.

I prepared to leave the famous halls in Gower Street. I hovered at the door of the bar to put my coat on. It was snowing heavily outside. I wondered what sort of an omen that might be. As I knotted my scarf I noticed the bright green poster that had hung on the wall there all through my last term. It was a play that had been on at Greenwich, and there had been good reports of it and some talk of it transferring to the West End.

I looked again.

Another Country. Good title. Must try and catch that. I pulled up my collar against the snow, took a last lingering look at the front of the Vanbrugh Theatre and headed off into the London winter.

Work

FOUR

It was January 1982, I wasn't working on anything else but I'd delayed signing on, and I was now sharing a tiny room in a rather seedy Willesden rooming house. There was one payphone in the hall and an enormous family of Asians upstairs who were clearly involved in the north-west London underworld. Strange boxes were delivered in the middle of the night. I never saw the same faces twice. I had no objections to any of this, except that they ran their business empire from the hall payphone which, of course, was my crucial link to the world of showbiz.

I thought of taking it up with one of the fellows, but chose a moment when the burliest, six-foot, moustached mafioso type I've ever seen was coming down the stairs. Of course he needed free access to the phone. I saw no harm in it, I indicated as much when my voice squeaked out 'Lovely day' and I pressed myself against the wall to let him pass. I could see he was a man who put small children in sandwiches and toasted them. The phone was his. No problem. I could ring Pat myself.

'Hello Pat.'

'Hello darling. What's going on on that bloody number? It's always engaged and when I do get through it's a man grunting "no drop tonight" in a funny accent.'

'I'll explain when I see you.'

'Very well, darling. Now, listen . . .'

She explained about *Another Country*, and I thought immediately of that poster in the RADA bar. Pat had some clients in the play, which was indeed transferring to the West End if they could achieve some key pieces of recasting. They had already auditioned extensively but were prepared to waive the Equity bar at this stage to try and find the right folk. It was the same problem as before. They needed reasonably experienced actors who could look seventeen and who were appropriate for the parts. She'd arranged a meeting for three days hence with the author, Julian Mitchell and the casting director,

Celestia Fox. This was a sort of first round. I was about to put the phone down when I remembered.

'What's it about, Pat?'

It turned out to be a highly funny and dramatic fictional account of Guy Burgess's schooldays and the emotional genesis of his life as a spy. There was no script available, and I was immediately depressed. The upper middle classes I had encountered all had an innate assurance and arrogance that both annoyed and intimidated me. One thing was for sure, I didn't have it. I had confidence on occasion, but that social ease and casual command didn't come naturally to me.

I felt certain that public school changed people profoundly. I found it very difficult to imagine what being a boarder must have been like. I found a book called *The Public School Phenomenon* and set to work. Even if I felt instinctively wrong and phoney, I would certainly give it a go. I fished out an old striped blazer that I had worn to parties when I was sixteen. If I could carry that off, and polish up the accent a bit, I could sneak in.

Julian Mitchell opened the door of his Knightsbridge house. He gave a great laugh. 'Ah, I see you've worn the jacket. Well, you're bound to get the part.'

He seemed enormously warm and funny, but there was my plot in ruins before I'd even begun. How could I have been so crass? Celestia asked me briefly about RADA and then gave me the script. There was a brief scene they wanted me to read, featuring a character called Barclay, the head of house, who is under stress because of a suicide in the school. As I read it over quietly the front door bell rang twice. They were obviously seeing hundreds of people. Oh God. Well, here goes. Remember 1930s' English, Ralph Richardson in *The Q Planes*.

Before I came to the end of the first sentence, Julian stopped me. 'Are you putting on a voice?'

Was I putting on a voice? Is the Pope a Catholic? Yes, yes, yes. I was putting on a stupid, ridiculous voice that was redolent of my Lord Ponsonby-Smythe at Whiteknights. I dropped all Leslie Howardisms and read the scene straight.

'That's better. Thank you.'

Better, but still fucking hopeless. I decided that I'd never get to play upper class parts. It would be coppers, coppers, coppers all the way. I went home furious with myself. Fuck this, I thought. If I do get a second chance, bugger all this residual class chippiness that's confusing me. Just read it as truthfully as possible. I hadn't been to public school. So what? I hadn't studied at Wittenberg, but I'd played Hamlet. What was I going to do if Macbeth came along? Kill some reigning monarch so that I felt I had the experience for the part?

A second round had been arranged which Robert Fox, the producer, would attend with Stuart Burge, the director. It was to be held at the Whitehall Theatre the following Wednesday but on the day before Pat had arranged another audition, which, this time, was with the Royal Shakespeare Company.

Near the beginning of each year the RSC casts for its long Stratford season, and often the small parts are taken by RADA graduates from the previous year. The Company were in a position to give an Equity card with the job and sometimes the debuts happen in marvellous parts – Anton Lesser, for example, made his professional début just after leaving drama school as Gloucester in Terry Hands' production of *Henry VI Part III*.

Several members of our term had been granted auditions for play-as-cast contracts which involved doing just that, as well as understudying. This must often have provided a wonderful chance to watch and occasionally perform. During my years of RSC theatregoing I had followed the fortunes of the small part players, looking out for promotion where it occurred and trying to imagine what the workload must be like.

Joyce Nettles, the RSC's casting director at that time, had seen my student Hamlet. She was in an impossibly busy job and I am astonished that she ever found the time to catch the show. We'd had a brief meeting before Christmas in which she had tested me about my feelings towards the Company – whether I was their type, and whether I would be prepared to go to Stratford for a season. Naturally I answered each question with an eager 'yes', and smiled my face off.

The audition day arrived. I was first on after lunch. I waited in the empty Floral Street rehearsal studio, an enormous, echoing wooden warehouse, with huge, open spaces yawning at me as I sat in the little partitioned corner that served as green room and canteen. Then the first director appeared. Barry Kyle came in clutching a prawn salad sandwich and three bags. A cheerful shambles, he was carrying so many things that he shook hands with his left hand. The others followed. Adrian Noble was courteous and formal, with flyaway brown hair and a wispy goatee beard which convinced me that he should change his brown leather jacket for a tunic in order to complete the look of a dashing Renaissance man. Then came Ron Daniels, crisply dressed in a black leather jacket, with a neat shirt and tie. His hair was very carefully groomed, and he made a strong contrast with the charmingly dishevelled look of Barry and Adrian. I have developed an enormous affection for Ron, but on that day his usual nerves made him behave like an SS General. He looked at me through narrowed eyes, head held slightly back, as if he were highly suspicious.

Then Terry Hands appeared, dressed entirely in black, and received my handshake with an unsmiling nod. He wasn't particularly unfriendly, just eccentric. I half expected Peter O'Toole to walk in, and for everyone to launch into a scene from *Night of the Generals*.

Barry, Adrian and Ron sat behind a long trestle table, and were joined by Joyce. Terry sat to the side, with his back against the wall, very much on his own, and not speaking at all during the interview. Adrian and Barry were really very friendly, and asked about parts at RADA and the audition for *Another Country*. Ron continued with his comic intimidation technique, shifting in his black leather jacket and moving the steel-rimmed spectacles further down his nose. Still the same penetrating, slightly suspicious look.

I went into Hotspur, and then, as the comic piece, I produced Lord Foppington from Vanbrugh's *The Relapse*, a marvellous speech to do at an audition because it needs such attack – you're really forced to produce energy, if nothing else. There were smiles from Adrian and Barry, a laugh from Joyce, a tell-tale movement of the curled upper lip from Ron and in the corner Terry remained impassive, as if he was in the middle of a mantra. I was enjoying this. Ron spoke, feigning disdain and trying to suggest I might have cheated.

'Have you played that part before?'

'Well . . . no . . . I did play a fop at RADA. Sir Joseph Wittol, who I suppose is a sort of second cousin to Foppington . . . but . . .'

'Oh, I see. And you played it like that?'

'Well no . . . I . . .'

'Thank you.' He looked round at the others as if to say, 'What did I tell you? I rest my case.'

Joyce came to the rescue. 'Can we see a bit of your Hamlet?'

The others nodded. Can't be bad, I thought – three speeches. I gave them 'Rogue and Peasant Slave' from my greatest hits album, and as they say, went for it.

As the chorus of 'We'll be in touch' started up I thought that at least I'd given full value. I looked round and said cheerio as I left the room. I'd grown rather fond of this group. Joyce had played my mother to good effect, and even on my exit, Ron was still producing a very charming Goebbels-meets-Clouseau manner. The smiles of Barry and Adrian had reached Noel Edmonds proportions and there, in the corner, was Terry the black Buddha, still staring into the middle distance and waiting for the latest casting advice from Olympus.

My first RSC audition. What larks, Pip.

Next morning was the second round for *Another Country*. Just before I went in I was asked to look at the scenes featuring Barclay, the character I'd read at the first audition. I obliged, and when I entered the auditorium was taken aback to be asked to read Judd, a part that I hadn't even looked at. I shook hands with Rupert Everett, who would be playing the part of Bennett, the Burgess character, and climbed onto the set. I relied on sight-reading and discovered the scene as I went along. Rupert judged his reading beautifully. He could easily have bulldozed me, having played the part of Bennett already to huge success; alternatively, he could simply not have bothered. Instead, he played the scene with me so that I could start to understand it as we went along.

It was marvellous writing. I hadn't seen the rest of the play but if Judd had only this scene it was still a terrific part. He was a natural rebel of tremendous intelligence, with a colourful temperament and a lacerating wit. Judd was the school outsider, and an example of the heroic, committed English Communist of the 1930s, extravagantly indignant at the hypocrisy of the English public school and of English politics. Inspiring, hugely funny, warm and passionate, Judd was a brilliant creation.

I somehow assumed that because it was being put on in the West End, the leading roles must be for grown-ups, for adult actors. Surely a part this good couldn't be entrusted to an unknown, and yet Judd was only a schoolboy. I didn't know what was going on. We finished the scene, everyone was very kind, and I went back to Willesden to recover from the excitement of the last two days.

Miraculously that afternoon the drug-dealers of NW6 appeared to be having a tea break, and Pat Marmont got straight through to my number. The RSC were offering play-as-cast and, wait for it, Robert Fox wanted me for *Another Country*. The catch was Equity. Rehearsals for *Another Country* began in three weeks' time which was not long enough to allow me to secure my card, but it would be too long to keep the RSC waiting.

So began a couple of nightmarish weeks where the question of my membership remained uncertain. The whole job might fall through, and I would have then lost the chance of a job and a definite card at Stratford. My first obligation was to Robert – I'd seen him first, and if the reading was anything to go by then the part was a great deal more stretching than anything the RSC would offer at such an early stage.

Pat appraised both parties of the situation, and they were understanding. The RSC suggested that in the meantime I should meet Howard Davies, who was directing the first play of the season and who had not been present at the original audition. I admired Howard's work enormously and found the man a delight, polite but still informal. More to the point, he also felt he might have something specific to offer me.

True to his word he rang Pat and offered me an excellent juvenile role, but he did stress that the RSC couldn't hold on forever. Meanwhile the wheels at Equity were turning very slowly. Eventually the dispute went to arbitration and Robert Fox reiterated the point that they'd seen literally hundreds of people, and if he couldn't at least have his first choice then there was no point in taking such a huge commercial risk on a new play with no stars. This must have clinched it.

At the eleventh hour they relented. Yes, I could do it. Pat let the RSC know. They had very patiently kept their offer open but were very understanding of the situation. That done, Pat filled me in on the terms of my first engagement: £150 per week for six months.

The longest I'd ever been in anything was two weeks. I had no idea how I'd deal with a much longer run, but guessed it would depend on the character I was playing. I was still in the dark to a certain extent— I had a job and a salary but still hadn't been given the play to read. It arrived on the Saturday before Monday's first rehearsal, 1 February 1982. I read it with growing amazement: not only was the play riveting but the part of Judd was demanding and very long. I finished the play and sat in a state of shock. I simply couldn't believe my luck. Although I'd read very well at the audition and had sensed that I might get the part, I had completely underestimated the scale of the opportunity. As a first professional role in the theatre, it was an unbelievable break. Christ.

I started to learn it that afternoon. Eight of the strong cast of twelve had been in the play before, and with only three weeks to rehearse I would have to work quickly to catch up. To help break the ice for the new boys, Julian Mitchell had arranged a drinks party early on the Sunday evening for us to get to know each other. Riddled with nerves, I arrived at South Kensington station an hour early and wandered around in the freezing cold for an hour and a quarter and mused whether I could ring in sick. But there was no turning back, it was all part of the job.

I was one of the first to arrive and took a large slurp of white wine to calm me down. Then, with an uncharacteristic punctuality, in bounced David Parfitt. Bounced rather than walked, for one of the trademarks of the most optimistic person I have ever known is to travel with a marked spring in his step.

This Peter Pan figure with the toothsome grin was already part of my youth. In the course of cataloguing British Equity members through my days of adolescent TV watching, I had grown up with David. The familiar trampolining movement had been one of the chief pleasures of *And Mother Makes Three*, a situation comedy in which the young Roscius had played Wendy Craig's son. The beaming smile which lit up when his name appeared in the jaunty end-titles sequence was a memorable pleasure, and series after series brought David into my living-room.

Although a veteran of stage and screen he still looked (and looks) very young. He claimed to be twenty-four but though he looked about eight, I suspected his real age to be nearer forty-seven. He played Menzies in *Another Country*, and we struck up an instant rapport, the start of a friendship which would be an important one for me.

It was a very lively group. Rehearsals began in a draughty warehouse building in Old Street. A quick reading of the first scene took place round a table, then we went into the blocking or setting of the physical moves. I tried my first line, binoculars in hand, staring out of the 'study window'.

'What's this? What's this? Three o'clock from bushy-topped tree.'

The director, Stuart Burge, stopped me. His style was amiably offbeat.

'Er . . . (scratch, scratch) . . . I think we need . . . (scratch) . . . I think we need more suspense on that line.'

Suspense. Right, will do. I tried again.

'No, still not quite right. Never mind, let's move on.'

The rest of the day and the week were spent blocking and learning the lines. The only drama was the predictable one of being ticked off for corpsing. Rupert was quite as bad as me when it came to giggling and the tea-party scene which took place between Rupert, David Parfitt, Piers Flint-Shipman and I, was too much. David William, the one senior member of the cast, and an inveterate giggler himself, feigned rage and turned on us all.

'Just STOP. This really is boring. Balls-achingly boring.' Silence and stifled whimpers followed.

In the second week we rehearsed on the stage of the Royal Court Theatre, where more detailed work began. Stuart Burge kept up his stance of distracted eccentricity, but he was in fact as sharp as a knife and very stubborn. He let nothing go and wasn't afraid of using abstract directions to get what he wanted.

'Rupert, there's marvellous detail in all that. But I do think overall in that scene you must convey ecstasy about your new love, and certainly about your own secure future. You must be more golden.'

'Golden?'

I was relieved that Rupert was given the tough ones, too.

'Oh, and Ken.'

'Yes?'

'More suspense.'

Rupert and I seldom talked about the parts we were playing, and our acting relationship was almost entirely instinctive. Rupert, like myself, seemed to prefer to get on and do it, and to put an idea into practice instead of describing it. We had a quiet and wary respect for each other which acknowledged our different backgrounds and characters, but I shall never forget his kindness during those rehearsals. It would have been very easy to be resentful of a newcomer arriving to throw the rhythm of his role. He had already had a huge success as Bennett and nearly all his scenes were with Judd, but he positively welcomed the chance to change and rework the scenes to allow for my slightly different interpretation of Judd.

The whole experience of these rehearsals was a very gentle

introduction to the harsh world of commercial theatre. Robert Fox kept a low profile but offered words of encouragement at the right moments. He was clearly excellent at his job, and he introduced me to my first press interviews, he was present at all significant run-throughs of the play and acted as an occasional go-between between the director and cast.

'I think Stuart feels that on that first line there could be a little more . . .'

'Suspense?'

'That's it.'

If the first line remained dodgy, the rest of the character was shaping up well. Judd was a deliciously meaty role – intellectual, yet capable of real feeling and humour, a great soul in embryo. He was a man who really might have gone onto become something extraordinary. Julian Mitchell had the character of Judd based on two men, both dead. The first was Esmond Romilly, who married Jessica Mitford and who provided the anarchic streak in Judd and the second, John Cornford, the poet, who died on his twenty-first birthday while fighting in the Spanish Civil War.

Cornford provided the intensely lonely and romantic side to the character. Judd is a visionary capable of a knowing sadness far beyond his years, a quality which the play suggests he shared with the young Bennett. Both are outsiders, and both have an uncomfortably prophetic awareness of their probable futures; both, in the course of the play, rebel against their prospective fates, Bennett selfishly, and Judd, by trying to change the system. Through Judd's anger and irony Julian Mitchell presents a memorable picture of genuine goodness, an altruism and hope of a kind that was uniquely possible in the 1930s. The total effect was most moving.

I seemed to spend most of my real life moving house, and the most recent move was a mile or two from Willesden to Harlesden, an even less salubrious part of north-west London. Wendy had joined the Royal Shakespeare Company and was moving to Stratford. I swapped one underworld for another. Evan Carruthers, my landlord, was a car dealer. He looked like an ex-RAF fighter pilot, with a twirly moustache, distinguished, greying hair and a kind, military manner. He had a professional shiftiness which offered much to enjoy. He stayed up very late each night and never rose before lunchtime. The curtains of his room were permanently drawn and he chain-smoked Gauloises.

Evan advertised weekly in *Exchange and Mart*, sometimes under different names. Part of his work was quick escapes, and he'd sold plenty of 'dogs' in his time. Each week I was an unwilling party to his attempts to pull more wool over more eyes. He used a secret mixture in dodgy engines which kept them sounding sweet until the punter got home.

I would know when he'd been up to his tricks when he mysteriously disappeared and I had to deal with irate customers at the front door. Some of this was dangerous, as invariably the 'big bruvver' would have been called in, but Evan kept cheerful about all this. He'd been involved on the edges of petty crime for thirty years, and belonged spiritually to the Soho of the fifties, shifting a motor for someone. The real appetite had gone, but he kept his hand in.

I'm sure he wasn't short of a bob or two, but I suspect it must have been kept under a floorboard in that funny old flat. I certainly had to be on my toes in this house: apart from complaining punters, there was Roger, Evan's business partner, and a visit from him and his boys was like the arrival of the Kray brothers. I often thought I'd arrive home to find Evan in a wooden box.

Still, it did take my mind off West End nerves, but these had pretty much disappeared as the part began to take over. It was one of those rare experiences where the more you put in through research and reading, the more you got out, and I was already an expert on fellow travellers, the Spanish Civil War, the English public school system of the thirties, Romilly and Cornford, and it all helped towards drawing the emotional graph for Judd. By the time I got to the first preview I thought I had built up a convincing tragic hero, an earnest, misunderstood romantic. There was a light side to him, but I knew it was important to present his seriousness and weight.

The audience laughed themselves stupid. I was outraged. I was playing Hamlet, not Lancelot Gobbo. By the end of the first half I calmed down and realised that this was what Julian had intended. The more seriously I took it the more they laughed, until the play started to twist and the truth of Judd's earnest rebellion became clear. It also began to dawn on me that Judd knew he seemed funny and, up to a point and with certain people, enjoyed it. I took this and a million other bits of information into the second preview and hoped I wouldn't be so surprised if they giggled. It was much better.

Better still was the shock as the dressing-room door opened afterwards and Albert Finney walked in. His company, Memorial

Films, had money in the production and he was taking a very personal interest. He's a big man in every sense and he was so warm and encouraging that when he'd gone I ran all the way to Green Park tube station and rang my mother in a breathless shriek.

'Albert Finney! Albert Finney, Mum! He was in tonight and he came round to say well done.'

'Very nice, son. What would I have seen him in?'

The preview days went by with friends from RADA visiting and Stuart calling us in each afternoon for comments and advice on the show. By now I was taking the initiative.

'I think I should go for more suspense on that first line, Stuart.'

'Good idea, Ken. I'll leave it with you.'

The day before we opened I rolled up for the afternoon session to be greeted, to my great surprise, by a hug from Mr Finney.

'Congratulations, you've won the Bancroft Gold Medal.' I was absolutely thrilled. It was the top RADA prize for the outstanding student of the year, and my joy was intensified because I knew the folks would be thrilled, and the whole thing would help the management for *Another Country* to flog their unknown actor playing Judd.

It was a week of giddy pride for Mum. The week before, *Too Late to Talk to Billy* had been shown on BBC. The response had been tremendous, especially in Belfast. This was a huge relief to my father who had read the script before I'd done it and had dismissed it grumpily. Despite having left Northern Ireland, he didn't care for anything that showed the old country in a bad light. And the truth of the matter was that the script touched too many raw nerves in both my parents' experiences. Indeed when my Uncle Charlie witnessed James Ellis's bravura performance as the drunken father, he said, 'That was Speedy Harper, that was my father.'

On reading the play I think my father expected a gloomy re-enactment of all that was bad about the Belfast he was brought up in, but what he found was a story in which the Troubles were for once in the background, and in which the humour and warmth and passion in working-class family life was made accessible to everyone, and not just to people living in Ulster. The province became fiercely proud of the *Billy* plays because they appealed to families everywhere. The RADA award coming on top of this five-minute fame caused my father to write to me, the first time he had ever done so, to express his pride.

He was largely on my thoughts the next day when I prepared for the first night of *Another Country*, 2 March 1982. He had always told me to face nerves on a full stomach. We were called late that afternoon and before we went to the theatre I lunched alone on a large steak in a tacky Berni Inn in the Strand. I was remarkably calm.

The fact was that I was enjoying myself, I'd had four weeks of being a professional actor and I loved it. In a way, the importance of the evening's events affected me little, and in fact I had so little sense of the 'occasion' that it was only late in the afternoon that I thought about buying first night presents.

Panic set in and I ended up rushing round Soho buying the most inappropriate and stupid cuddly toys. So un-West-Endy was I that it was only at 6.30 that it struck me that I should need some drink to offer round afterwards. Wine, where was I to get wine? What was I thinking of? Champagne. That's what it should be. Shouldn't it? I was rescued by one of the two dressers who worked on the show, and once the curtain had gone up, he whizzed round Soho for bubbly and plastic cups.

The performance was that of a typical Press night, and the atmosphere was tense with friends willing us on, but it was a good tight show and Rupert, driving the piece, was in marvellous form. I didn't know what to expect after the show. I went to my dressing-room, changed as quickly as I could and waited for a knock at the door. Robert Fox and Celestia were there first with large hugs and well dones, but after they left, the place flooded. Two schoolfriends appeared whom I hadn't seen for years, Hugh Cruttwell was there, and so were my parents. My mum and brother were in tears, and I knew my father had enjoyed it because he employed an adjective he reserved for moments of greatness, 'Tremendous, son.'

He clutched my hand firmly, but then, like the rest of the family, took a step back when anyone entered the room. It had taken a great deal of persuasion to get my mother to come at all, as she was terrified of 'letting me down', but I plied them with champagne and told them to stop tugging their forelocks whenever people came in.

It was a great pleasure that evening to see my mother get tiddly. The champagne and excitement had gone straight to her head, and by the time Joan Plowright and Albert Finney had been and gone the intoxication was complete. Finney had been marvellously entertaining. The family had stood agog as he put his arm round my giggling mother, champagne and cigar in hand.

'Your young lad,' he said, sending up some northern actor laddie, 'has just got off the bus, as we say in the business. But . . .' – Dad's jaw was on the floor at this point with anticipation – 'he's not half bad.'

Later, as we walked to my parents' car in Berwick Street, there was general agreement that Mr Finney was a good sort, that Julian Mitchell was very nice, that Robert Fox looked just like his brother, and all kinds of giddy instant recollections. They all piled in, Bill, Sally, Joyce, Mum and Dad. My father spoke.

'We'll never forget tonight, son. Thanks very much.'

Wendy had arrived as the last visitors left my dressing-room. An RSC rehearsal had meant that she had missed the whole thing. This was not her fault at all, but she was very upset, and it seemed inauspicious that we should not be together on such a momentous occasion. With a long, enforced separation ahead of us, I felt that there were problems to come. We stood forlornly in a wet Soho watching my dad's car drive off. No official party had been arranged and I wasn't sure where the other actors had gone. It was midnight, and I had no idea how you were supposed to celebrate a West End first night – my chief worry had been whether my parents would enjoy it or not, and my chief pleasure had been watching their delighted faces afterwards. I wouldn't have known where to celebrate even if I'd known how, but we opted for a Chinese meal and took a minicab back to Harlesden. I was in bed by one o'clock. I wondered if Noel Coward ate take-away on his first nights.

The show was a great success with the critics. The play and company were both praised, with Rupert and I singled out for special mentions. There had been worry about whether the show could run without stars, but it looked as if these fears would be proved groundless.

Six months seemed like a very long time, and I had decided to take the long run business very seriously. As I'd read in all the best biographies, I rose late and had a good healthy breakfast of cereal, toast, bacon and eggs. I then took a walk, and had a sleep in the afternoon – very important this. A light meal at around four to allow plenty of time for digestion before the evening performance, and I would arrive at the theatre at 6.30, read my mail, say a few hellos, then lie on my back to do some breathing exercises. All very virtuous, all very boring and all destined to last three weeks.

A number of factors came together to rock the paragon of virtue. I arrived home one night to find that Roger, Evan's crooked landlord, had decided to redecorate the flat. One of his 'boys' was already on the job, and this highly unprepossessing type claimed to have his own decorating system which would take 'as long as it takes – OK, Mister?' Neanderthal man could have shown this one a few tips in DIY. He had started in my room, had moved nothing and had stripped one wall of paper, leaving the scraps all over my bed and covering my books. He had then got bored and moved on to another room. It was chaos.

I got out as quickly as I could, and as a stopgap, Julian Mitchell said I could use his house in Knightsbridge. This was not without its complications. I was feeling guilty because the corpsing in *Another Country* was getting a little out of hand, and I was doing very little to stop things. Although Julian lived in the country, I was terrified that he might come up and catch us, and then I was convinced I would be marched out of the house and out of the play.

There had been various sticky moments – girly pictures in the copy of *Das Kapital* that my character read throughout the play, spiders in the sandwiches during the tea scene, and apple-pie beds in the dorm scene. On a particularly wild matinee, halfway into the run, with about seventeen people out front, a decision was made to try the antique gramophone that sat on the set. Not only did it work but it completely drowned the dialogue. The first half ended with one of the staider characters in the piece coming on in a kilt.

It was all very amusing to us, and we flattered ourselves that these little private jokes could not possibly offend anyone in the audience, who would assume that they were part of the play. Unless, of course, the author was in the audience, as he was that Wednesday afternoon.

I have never seen fury as white and as hot as Julian's on that afternoon. It seemed highly appropriate that we should be in a play about schoolboys, and Julian's fiery lecture invoked the familiar adjectives: 'pathetic', 'arrogant', 'stupid', 'amateur'.

This hysterical corpsing was partly induced by the unusual demands of a long run on inexperienced actors. After three months I began to go a little stir crazy. Much as I loved the play, I began to pray for the safety curtain to stick so that the second half would be cancelled and we could all go home.

At the same time, after a marvellous start, I felt my own perform- ance to be set on automatic pilot. It grew wooden and heavy and my concentration wavered in performance until I dried desperately in the middle of one show and had to walk off while Rupert saved the day with an ad lib – 'I think Judd must have a headache or something'. This produced a terrible stage-fright for the next two weeks where all acting stopped as remembering took over. I would stare glassy-eyed at my fellow actors, thinking of my next speech, and waiting for their lips to stop moving so I would know when to speak. I think we all went through such a phase, but particular visits would perk us up. Gielgud came to a matinée and saw me after-wards. 'Very good. Didn't I see you at RADA?' A gent.

Sitting in bed one day, I pulled out the script and started to read it again. I felt compelled to do this, not just because of my reaction to the long run but because my lack of freshness was letting the side down. In the last few performances Rupert Everett had been produc-ing astonishing acting, and in the last scene between Judd and Bennett I really had a sense of him soaring away on a flight of great acting. It was a high voltage scene and demanded that I try to keep up with him.

I looked at the lines and started making new notes in the margin about what I thought Judd meant. It worked: it not only cured my stage-fright by giving me something new to think about but it really did rejuvenate the performance. Towards the end of the six months Rupert and I sometimes really did catch light together and it was exhilarating to play the scenes with him. He can be an electrifying actor.

Most of my colleagues shared my resistance to the supposedly conventional daytime life of a West End actor and towards the end of the run we decided to mount a lunchtime production. Gogol's *Gamblers* really marks the beginning of my involvement with inde-pendent production, and it was significant because it produced all the usual problems – the performances were for charity, we had no venue, no money and no organisation. We were simply a small company of actors learning this as we went along, naive but wildly enthusiastic.

Julian Mitchell provided a new translation for the piece, on condition that he could direct it. The Upstream Theatre Club became the venue and we tried to cast it in order to give the understudies and people with smaller parts in *Another Country* a decent opportunity. We found props and furniture ourselves, de-signed the set between the ten of us and let David Parfitt (who else?) work out a 'deal' with the venue. It was hard, often shambolic, amateur work but it was great, adventurous fun. There was great co-operation from everyone, except on the issue of my performance where I was allowed to get away with a third-rate Charles Laughton. I was playing Captain Cropper, a gambling shark, and my ever understated make-up talents were devoted to creating an impression of that particular beast. You can imagine the results.

The performances of *Gamblers* took place at the end of the run. Robert Fox now wanted to extend the run by at least another six months. We were asked to stay on, and there was great loyalty to Robert, Stuart and Julian but, in the end, the rigours of eight shows a week outweighed any considerations of security or finance. Julian and Robert were gracious, but obviously very miffed, and I was certain I would never work again, as I was leaving the show with nothing in view.

The day after my departure was confirmed with Robert, Pat rang to say that a book was on its way to me, *The Boy in the Bush* by D. H. Lawrence and Mollie Skinner. I was a great Lawrence buff, as I'd started reading his letters in a moment of emotional crisis and had been hooked on the man and his work ever since. I had heard of this novel which Lawrence had recast for Mollie Skinner during his journey through Australia in the early 1920s. Channel Four were planning to make a four-part serial of the book and was I interested in the central part of Jack Grant, the book's central figure?

It was a wonderful read. Jack Grant is in disgrace after being sent down from public school, and is packed off to Australia to stay with relatives. The new country starts to make a man of him, and he learns to love and to fight. Lawrence had infused this conventional adventure story with great psychological detail, particularly in the character of Jack, and the book had tremendous atmosphere. The sounds and smells of Australia were powerfully evoked, and there was a great deal of very provocative Lawrentian discourse on the subject of marriage.

It would make a very arresting and offbeat film that combined action with some rather interesting philosophy, Jack Grant would be in every scene, and the series would be shot in Australia over a period of three months. It sounded like an ideal opportunity. But this was August, and it wasn't scheduled to start until April. They weren't absolutely sure that they had the money and the project was put on ice. This still left me without work.

Another novel came to the rescue: *To the Lighthouse*, which was to be made into a two-hour television film. I had read no Virginia Woolf, and with an actor's typical lack of shame I decided, after a quick glance, that the whole thing would be too much to read before the interview, so I scoured the text instead for the name Charles Tansley, the character I was up for. I filled in the rest of my knowledge by buying the appropriate 'O' Level 'Study Notes' for the novel – these small volumes provide helpful short précis of character and plot for the poorly read actor.

Colin Gregg, director, and Simone Reynolds, the casting director, both kept straight faces as I bullshitted my way through the audition.

'Of course, I've always loved Woolf. She's a marvellous writer, and Tansley is absolutely my favourite in all the books, really.'

No shame. They let me take a script away and asked that I come back to do a reading. It had been quite beautifully adapted by Hugh Stoddard – it read like a Chekhov play, and Tansley was a wonderful, cravenly ambitious, snotty little loser. A small man, depressive, vulnerable, and with an enormous chip about his background. I began to wonder what sort of vibes I gave off at interviews.

By the time it came to the second interview I knew that half the cast of *Another Country* were up for parts in the film and that the rest of Equity weren't far behind. I read well and, more than that, I got on very well with the director. Colin Gregg, a resolutely independent film maker, is fascinated by actors and by the process of acting, and really quizzed me about why I'd made particular decisions about the character. It was a very enjoyable meeting but as I left the room I walked past a line of potential Tansleys. I knew it was a part that a dozen young actors could play, in different ways but equally well.

The RSC rang again. They were halfway through their Stratford season and someone had fallen ill. Would I be interested in another juvenile role? I would, but before I had to consider being swallowed up by the RSC machine, Colin Gregg called to say that he would like me to play Tansley. It began shooting on the Monday after the final Saturday performance of *Another Country*. The gods were obviously stringing me along – all this good luck, he whom the gods would destroy, they first make cocky.

Another Country ended its first run with a manic matinée and a spectacularly good Saturday evening performance. There was a quick meal at Kettner's in Soho for the entire cast, and then I was off.

I left early as I'd already begun to loathe goodbyes of this kind. It stemmed from cowardice, as it was painful to bid farewell to people who, as in this case, had become like brothers. I knew we would all meet again in this small business, but it never felt like it at the time.

The next morning I was on my way to Penzance, where *To the Lighthouse* was being filmed. It made a change from the drive to Stratford which I'd made every Saturday night for six months to see Wendy. The pressure on our precious Sundays was immense, as there was great tension involved in making this one day as perfect as possible. Apart from being in the same business, we had ceased to have any shared life together, and it was very hard spending our limited time simply catching up with each other. I was now off to Penzance for five weeks, and would be unable to get to Stratford at all. The perils of long-distance relationships in the acting profession were already upon me.

I was lonely at this time but thrilled by the work. I was on my way to meet several heroes: Rosemary Harris, who had been a definitive Yelena to Redgrave in Olivier's famous production of *Uncle Vanya*; Michael Gough, whom I'd first noticed as the First Murderer in Olivier's film of *Richard III*; T. P. McKenna, Suzanne Bertish, Pippa Guard, Lynsey Baxter, all really good actors.

It never follows that this will automatically produce a happy experience, but in this case it did, as it was a blissfully happy five weeks where cast and crew mixed with abandon. There seemed to be a different huge restaurant booked every night, there were parties and Sunday trips to the sea, and in the middle of it some very good work was being done.

I continued my crash course in film technique. On my first day I introduced the character's walk in long shot. Tansley is out on a cliff stroll with Mrs Ramsay, played by Rosemary Harris. I'd read what Alec Guinness had said about finding a character's walk and how important this was; I knew Tansley was tense, repressed and splenetic, and that the walk had to reflect this. After the first take, Colin Gregg asked, 'Why are you playing it like Charlie Chaplin?' He wasn't trying to raise a laugh. Colin's great gift was for seeing what actors offered up in quite literal terms. If it wasn't truthful, he would say so, and his method was as simple and honest as that. I soon stopped acting and calmed down.

Michael Gough was a delight, and like Rosemary, he'd worked with everyone. I would torment him at the dinner table for stories, and asked him about his career and ambitions. I couldn't resist asking him about the Olivier *Richard III*.

'Yes, talking of ambition, I nearly didn't get that.'

'How did it happen?'

'Well, I'd been out of work for a while and was pretty rancid about it. There was all this talk about *Richard III* and gossip about the casting. It seemed as though it would be full of stars and when I heard that Richard Attenborough and John Mills were lined up to play the two murderers I was enraged. I started moaning about it at parties and complaining to my agent and generally making a stink. Anyway, late one night the phone rings. I was in bed, and it was midnight. I say "Hello". Then this sinister voice says,

"Well, you've been stirring it, haven't you?"

"What?" says I, not knowing who the hell it is.

"A right little shit."

"Who is this?"

"It's Larry."

"Oh Christ. Oh Larry, I'm so . . . I mean . . . I'm . . ."

"Which one?"

"What?"

"Which one of the bloody murderers do you want to play?"

I wasn't sure how I should take this. I jumped in. "Whichever one's got the most lines."

"Fair enough. You start Monday week." Then he laughed. "And I hope that's the last bloody trouble we get from you." ' Olivier kept to his word and even broke up the filming of the scene over several days so that Michael, who was really very hard up, could earn some more cash.

Green I was, but I had been introduced to the notion of 'waiting'. In July, a month or so before the filming of *To the Lighthouse*, I had met briefly with Miloš Forman, the director, and his producer, Saul Zaentz. They were making the movie version of Peter Schaffer's play *Amadeus*. I, along with the rest of the acting world, was up for the part of Mozart. Maggie Cartier, the casting director, had alerted Pat Marmont to the opportunity.

The brief for the role was Mozart as small, bright, childlike and charming. Bright and charming I could manage, childlike I would busk, but small was tricky. They reckoned Mozart at around five foot four. At five foot nine and a half I'd always been too short for the tall parts and too big for the small ones, so I bought a pair of flat-soled plimsolls and tried to walk with my knees permanently bent.

I was so childlike at the first interview that I could barely put a sentence together, and I even attempted a version of the cackling laugh that Schaffer gives Mozart in the play. It was a complete performance.

A week later I heard that I was now through to the next round of readings, to be held at the Connaught Hotel when Mr Forman was in London. A date was set for a fortnight ahead and I went to work, with a thick biography of Mozart, a Sony Walkman playing the music, and another read of Schaffer's play. I'd been told that the film script was considerably different but in that helpful way of film companies paranoid about secrecy they sent only selected pages so that I could prepare for the reading.

These sessions took place over five days and I was Tuesday's Mozart. I arrived at 10 and was shown up to Mr Forman's suite. He was standing at the window eating a sandwich from a tray which would come and go all through the day for the nervous auditionees. He had dark hair swept back, wore glasses, appeared permanently preoccupied and had the charming accented English which is the prerequisite of the International Film Genius.

During the course of that day we got on very well. Actors and actresses would appear for Mozart's wife or teachers or neighbours, and after their read-through would depart. There was often a gap while we waited for the next one and we would talk about the play, acting, his home in Czechoslovakia – everything. I was reading well. The part is a marvellous one for any young actor and I attacked it with relish. Forman made comments on each reading – too funny, too sad, too mad, whatever. I was enjoying it, as he seemed to be considering me seriously, and I was also enjoying acting with the idols of my *Plays and Players* youth, all of whom seemed to be turning up for the audition. Such is the lure of the big American movie for the English acting profession, that I was reading scenes with really marvellous actors.

Next morning they rang to ask me to come back for the Friday readings. Either I was being used as a Mozart dogsbody or they were very interested. They also wanted to be clear about my availability for the filming in early 1983, and Pat told them of the possibility of the Australian job, but they thought it could fit. 'Only checking' they said, covering themselves. The second day was even better, as I was beginning to see what Forman wanted from the character. I tried desperately to relax but I was getting so excited now that in our interim chats I could barely restrain myself from crying out, 'Tell me, tell me I've got the part, please.'

On the following Monday the news came back that they were very interested indeed, and there would be a screen-test as soon as Forman was back in London.

Three weeks later I was at a small studio in Cricklewood, dressed up in a wig and period jacket, once again playing Mozart for the day. I had gathered that a shortlist of four had been established, and I was told that I was favourite. I don't know what they told the others. Once more a British acting roll-of-honour arrived, and superb actors strutted their stuff for Mr Forman's video. He seemed far more distant now, and I tried to seem less friendly, as if I wasn't desperately hoping for the job. He was clearly concentrating more now that he was actually at work.

I was still on form. There was only one funny moment when a mad English actress who was screen-testing for Mozart's wife succumbed to the fear of losing the role. Forman had shouted 'Cut' and then thanked the actress for having completed the scene.

'No, no, no, no. I want to do it again. *Please*, Mr Forman. I can emote more. *I can emote more.*' A great deal of emoting went into this plea, which was accompanied by arms thrown around the neck of the besieged director. We tried again and I played the scene with someone who appeared to be in the grip of a nervous breakdown and was having an epileptic fit. There was little I could do but throw my lines in whenever I could. Her arms were flailing around in demented fashion and I'm sure the sobs could have been heard in the street. It may have been emoting, but it certainly wasn't acting.

Pat rang that night. She could barely contain her own excitement. 'Darling, you are *so* near. It's accent now. They've never been sure whether to cast Americans throughout or English throughout or do a mix. They wondered if you were capable of a sort of mid-Atlantic accent, take the Englishness off it, maybe taking James Mason's voice as a model.'

I was outraged. I'd been to see them endlessly, I'd acted it every conceivable way except on my head, and now they thought that because it was a great part in a huge American movie I would compromise my voice, my very personality.

'And when do they want this new accent prepared for?' I said as sniffily as I knew how.

'Tomorrow.'

'Done.'

That night 'cahn't' became 'cehnt', 'class' became 'cless', and the James Mason of Harlesden was born. Pat had neglected to tell me that these thoughts about accent were provisional and that Maggie Cartier was simply marking my card for the next day. I tested the water with the even more distracted Miloś Forman.

'I wondered if you'd had any thoughts about accents?'

Oh no. He'd smelled a rat. He didn't like actors doing anything but act. No suggestions.

'No, no, no. Don't you worry about accents. We'll sort that out some other time. Please don't worry.'

Oh God, I'd made him irritable. It was clearer and clearer that he wanted puppet actors, folk who seemed so natural for the parts that he could pull all the strings. He didn't want troublesome input or actor cleverness. Either my accent was right and natural or it wasn't. I went on with the screen-test, and Pat rang later the same day.

'The phone call came, darling. The part is ninety per cent yours.'

'Wonderful.'

'Hold on, darling. Look, they're going back to New York tomorrow and next week they have to go through the same process there in order to satisfy Equity, but they are so keen on you it's not true. They simply have to go through the motions with the others.'

I now entered the never-never land of 'you'll know very soon'. A fortnight passed. 'They've found no one in New York. They've got to do the last stage in LA before they get back to us. It's still very hot.'

A month passed. 'Now they've got that time-consuming thing of going through all the tapes of actors' tests. I'm sure it'll work out.'

Two months passed. 'Pat, don't you think we should check on this?'

'OK, darling.' She rang Maggie Cartier. The last time she had spoken to them I had remained their number one choice. By now *To the Lighthouse* had come and gone and I had completed a second *Billy* play. It was December, and nearly six months after the first meeting. I'd had enough practising my Oscar-acceptance speech, and asked Pat to send a telex to America demanding that they declare their degree of interest. The reply came back the same day.

'Acknowledging your cable STOP Plan has changed STOP Now casting American actors STOP'.

Pat prevented me from sending my proffered reply: 'Thanks for the wait STOP Good luck with the film STOP Why don't you stick it up your ass and don't STOP'.

I took Pat's advice and decided that it would be nice to work again. Another part came up almost immediately in Julian Mitchell's new play, *Francis*, a dramatic reconstruction of the life of Francis of Assisi. We staged a reading of the piece at the Queen's Theatre with myself reading Francis and the rest of the cast made up from the second cast of *Another Country*.

The politics of the piece seemed particularly meaty and relevant. Robert Fox and Albert Finney were there and afterwards Julian rang me to say that he felt the play would be given a production, but that it might take a year to organise. When it was ready would I play it? I had been forgiven for leaving *Another Country* early, and I answered with a firm yes.

We were both in a good mood. We both had nominations for the SWET awards, Julian for 'Best Play', and myself for 'Best Newcomer' along with Rupert, whom I was sure would win. On this occasion, I won, and Rupert picked up two awards elsewhere for his performance. I was both pleased and very shocked – my instinctive fear of being carried away by any success that might later blow up in my face told me to play the whole thing down. It was also meaningless and unpleasant to have a television camera shoved up your nose to record your reaction, although I was able to enjoy celebrating with my parents, who were genuinely thrilled, and did not share my complicated response to winning awards.

The following day the producers of *Boy in the Bush* shook themselves out of their lethargy and decided in the wake of my award that now was the time to sign up the award-winning newcomer while he was hot. And so my name went on the dotted line and I knew that on 7 April I would be flying 12,000 miles away at the tender age of twenty-two.

The rest of the profession seemed not to be taking the lead from these far-sighted folk, and the expected avalanche of offers did not appear. I spent a whole afternoon reading for every character in Terence Rattigan's *While the Sun Shines*, for a season at the Royal Exchange Manchester. 'We don't think it's quite his thing,' was the reply that came back. Too common, love – that was my trouble. If there'd been a policeman in the play I'd have been laughing.

Short of carrying the award with me to interviews, I could see no way of actually organising work that might fall neatly before the trip to

Australia. I had plenty to occupy me, but it was the money I was after. I had to learn to ride before I left London, as Jack Grant spent much of the story on horseback. At the interview when I had been asked about riding experience I came out with the usual actor waffle: 'Oh yes, born in the saddle . . . I mean my grandad made them . . . I haven't actually . . . I'm sure that with sufficient . . . I love horses . . .'

Lies, lies, lies. I was terrified of the bloody things, but I was determined to crack it. Alas, English riding schools aren't necessarily the best place to learn, and I think they saw me coming. It's hard to gain confidence or improve as a rider if you don't have a decent horse, and I was sure that when my car appeared in the driveway, most schools rang the knacker's yard and brought some poor beast back from death's door. My horses always combined the following remarkable attributes: aggression, disobedience and extreme old age, so it was impossible to expect them to do anything that might tally with the image I had of myself galloping one-handed through the bush.

All I needed was to look as though I could ride, but I was up against impossible odds. If I pretended to be a normal learner than I was reprimanded for wanting to get on too quickly and told to abide by the 6,000,000 Pony Club rules of training which would take several lifetimes to complete. If I revealed myself as an actor desperate to learn quickly for a part then out came a great squeak of embarrassment followed by silence, and then, 'Are you famous?'

'No.' I tried to be as firm as I could and would start asking more questions about instant galloping. It was no use.

'What would I have seen you in?'

'Hardly anything.' Time was ticking by. I needed to be a brilliant horseman, but it was no use. I could hear them thinking.

'Ah . . . were you in that Hovis commercial?'

'No.'

'The one with the paper-boy who . . .'

'No.'

'He visits his grandad and . . .'

'No.'

'Yes, you were. I bet it was you, you're just shy.'

'Really, I've never done a Hovis commercial. I'm just an unknown actor. I've hardly done any telly at all.'

'That's what they all say. Well, I bet it was you in that one where there's a human cabbage in the saucepan and . . .'

In the midst of my equine depression the RSC rang again. They were obviously fed up with being turned down. Pat said that they were now asking, with no particular end in mind, what part Dame Branagh would deign to consider if she were to come to the RSC at all? I asked Pat to point out that I had never actually turned them down, that other jobs I had been committed to had come off. Still, I knew the part I'd like to try, as I'd been working on it since drama school. It was a young man's role, and the play was littered with references to his youth. They hadn't done it for a bit. Why shouldn't I ask. I was only twenty-three and I hadn't done any professional Shakespeare, but surely that made it all the more exciting? Have a go, love. They could only laugh in my face.

'Pat, tell them I'd like to play Henry V.'

She informed me later that day that the laughter had been deafening. Ah well.

At last, after three interviews, I got another job. It was a couple of episodes in a series called *Maybury*, about a psychiatrist played by Patrick Stewart. The format was described to me. 'Pat's there every week being the problem-solver, and every episode we have a guest nutter – your character is so bananas that he has to have two shows.' A complicated creature indeed – Robert Clyde Moffat was the fictional ego of the author, Douglas Watkinson, and this was the story of Douglas's highly dramatic attempts to come to terms with epilepsy. His adolescence had been plagued with 'the falling sickness', and marked out as 'odd', his life interrupted by a series of embarrassing fits, he had developed something called the epileptic personality, which took the form of a pathological unwillingness to accept his condition. There was great heart in the writing, and it read as if Douglas was exorcising some demon. In the process he had produced a wonderfully showy part.

The phenomenon of what one might coldly describe as 'disability acting' is a strange one. For this role I had to research and produce epileptic fits and various other clinically detailed symptoms and manifestations of his condition. Once an actor does a very physical role like this, accurately portrayed, I've noticed a disproportionately favourable response – people seem extraordinarily impressed. The fact is that when there is a very specific thing to reproduce like an epileptic fit, then the tangible details are available in text-books. A degree of physical dexterity is required to bring them off in performance, but the details are often surprisingly easy to reproduce.

I could feel this strange, enhanced status being accorded me in the rehearsals. This virtuoso part was fascinating to play but I knew that I had been just as good in parts that weren't as showy and hardly been noticed. When I watch acting, it's the latter I prefer. I love theatricality, I love detail about real physical conditions, but for me a great naturalistic performance in a quiet part can be just as exciting as seeing someone in heavy make-up with a physical contortion very clearly 'acting'.

The risks are different. With virtuoso histrionics you can be accused of going over the top, but at least you'll be noticed. I think it's much braver to eschew spurious theatricality and be as truthful as possible, not worry about the notices and hope that the multitudes will see that even though you're simply walking, talking and sitting (which of course anyone can do), a great deal of work and thought and research has gone into it. These are crude distinctions, but when this reality *and* theatrically can combine, the results are riveting.

All the great actors have done it, but two favourite examples of mine are by Michael Bryant and Anthony Hopkins. I came upon Bryant's performance quite unexpectedly, in an episode of the TV wartime escape drama, *Colditz*. Bryant played a prisoner who was attempting to escape by feigning madness in order to be repatriated. The Germans smell a rat when they see him behaving oddly and a particular soldier is asked to keep an eye on him. The German has a brother who had gone mad and he is considered an expert, and the episode develops the relationship between Bryant's character and the German. Throughout the series Bryant shows quite brilliantly the descent from feigned 'acting' madness into the real thing, with great theatricality, but utter conviction, and it is heart-breaking to see the character, with his last glimmer of sanity, wave goodbye to the real world. It's a performance which has always haunted me and I've noticed that whenever I've mentioned this performance to actors, almost without fail, they've mentioned it as being in their own 'top tens'.

In *Pravda* Tony Hopkins produced a physical eccentricity which seemed to be the perfect manifestation of a convincing inner drive and tortured ugliness that was caught magnificently in his portrayal of a ruthless newspaper magnate. An absolutely riveting combination.

My attempts to scale such heights were looking a little bleak. I'd finished my very raw performance in *Maybury* and the weeks were rushing by towards my departure for Australia. A third *Billy* play was now planned for August of '83, and it suddenly struck me that since leaving *Another Country* a year before, I had done nothing but screen work. If I wanted to work in the theatre (for which I had been trained), then I had better do a bit of conscious planning. The classics were what I fancied doing but I had no faith in parts just presenting themselves out of the blue. Leicester were doing the two parts of *Henry IV*, I auditioned for Hal and didn't get past the first round. I decided that I would have to do something myself.

In a state of desperation about my riding skills, I'd taken a riding holiday, which meant that you could be on terrible horses all day instead of just three times a week. At the end of two days I was no better as a rider but I did have a bottom that shone. I'd also found a classical piece to do.

I had taken with me Tennyson's *Maud* which he referred to as a 'monodrama'. Its subtitle was 'The Madness'. The word 'monodrama' had appealed immediately to my actor's instinct for one-man show or audition material, but I didn't read it until the riding holiday. There were 1400 lines of often very complex verse, the most famous lines of which began 'Come into the garden, Maud', a refrain I'd heard in the languid Edwardian musical arrangement. This treatment seemed rather incongruous in the context of the whole piece, for *The Madness*, as I preferred to call it, was a full-blooded, passionate, poetic tour de force. I also felt that it was meant to be acted, and not just read aloud. It would be a hell of a job to learn and a very tricky piece to present, but there was a great narrative hook which I was sure would keep people interested for an hour and twenty minutes.

I knew I had money coming in through the Australian job and the third *Billy* play, but I needed to find somewhere to do the piece. I would finance it myself. But before I found a venue, I decided to find the director, and Colin Wakefield was the obvious choice. He had made a late decision to become an actor and had left Reading at the same time as me to train at the Webber-Douglas Academy. He had worked steadily as an actor, we still kept in touch and I knew he was very keen to direct. He'd known my work since I was sixteen, and he was scrupulously honest – no flannels, no 'Darling, you were marvellous'. I decided to charm the pants off him and entertain in style.

We ended up in a rather dowdy trattoria in Southampton Row. He didn't know the piece but after the prawn cocktail he would certainly consider it. By the time we'd finished the spaghetti alle vongole it was a 'very exciting idea', and in the middle of the zabaglione we shook hands. This was the Wednesday night before the Saturday I was due to leave for Australia. Although I was very keen about the project, my old timidity held me back when it came to dealing with the world about it. I knew I wanted a venue but I was terrified of picking up the phone. What would I say? What sort of deal would it be? Who looked after the money business?

Time was running out, and I had no choice. On the Thursday I rang the Upstream Theatre Club, who knew me through *Gamblers*, and on the Friday at four I was sitting in the crypt talking to the vicar, David Wickert, and his assistant, Anne Hopkinson discussing rents. I was terrified but determined to go on with it. They had only two spare weeks available for their theatre: I could have it from 6 September (my mother's birthday, a good omen) for a fortnight. I would have to pay for everything – the printing of tickets, programmes, lights, the whole production costs, set, and so on. In return I had a 150-seat theatre rent-free and we split the income (after overheads had been deducted) fifty-fifty.

I didn't know if it was a good deal, but then I wouldn't have known a good deal if it had stood up and punched me in the face. I didn't care. I had nervously got through my first professional negotiation as a manager and I had a deal – a theatre and a run for *The Madness*. I was ecstatic. I rang Colin. He knew the theatre, had acted there and was delighted. We would communicate by cassette when I was in Australia to discuss the production, and I would spend any spare time I had learning the text.

Pat Marmont was out when I rang, so I left the details with Rose, her brilliant assistant. I was rather relieved that I didn't have to explain why I was mounting this independent venture – there would be none of the usual ten per cent commission and I was rather afraid that she might ditch me for going it alone. Anyway, cross that one later. After a year away, I would be back in the theatre with a huge, frightening classical challenge that would teach me more in a fortnight than months of hanging round for the next telly. If Australia turned out to be a disaster I had this delicious agony to look forward to. One step ahead. That's the way.

The next evening I shared a tearful goodbye with Wendy. After prolonged separation, another three months at the other side of the world was particularly painful. But there was nothing to say – it was part of the job.

My brother drove me, a tear-stained wreck, to the airport on a gloomy Saturday evening. He shook my hand as he left me at Passport Control, and gave me – with typical Irish sentimentality – a horseshoe that he and his wife, Sally, had brought me as a goodbye present. I was as butch and brusque over the farewell as I could manage to be, and, as I strode off purposefully towards the departure lounge, I started to dramatise the whole situation to myself. This was an important turning-point in my life, I told myself, there was no going back, chin-chin, old man – any old rubbish to help me deal with the intense loneliness. Turning up the dramatic volume, I marched down the long airport corridor and on, like some great hero, towards the brave new world that lay ahead.

FIVE

'Upon the rack of this tough world'
KING LEAR

It was the first time I had flown Club Class, and I celebrated the new luxury by eating and drinking anything that came my way. By the time we left Bahrain I was sozzled and had developed an allergy to dry roasted peanuts. I was desperately trying to remember something I'd read about how to avoid jet lag, and sensed I hadn't made the right start. I perked up on the last stage of the leg between Singapore and Sydney, and as we flew over Sydney harbour the sun was shining and I caught my breath at the first sight of the majestic Harbour Bridge. As I looked down I saw the Opera House to the left of the bridge, and the two structures made an eerie, beautiful combination in the early morning light. There was something strong, comforting and honest about the Bridge, and the Opera House was flamboyant, stylish and fun. It all looked wonderful.

I had momentary doubts just before we disembarked. A hairy man wearing a mask sprayed the entire cabin with fly spray, and I wondered what this ritual was supposed to represent. I was convinced it was a charade. The Australians basically believed everyone else had bad breath and this was a large can of Gold Spot.

The producer and director met me from the plane and I was driven through Sydney, which seemed a curious mixture of English bungalowed suburbia and American-looking shop fronts and malls. We drove over the Bridge and had an even better view of the Opera House. I found the combination awe-inspiring, if nothing else because they seemed to be screaming out, 'Yes, you really are here.'

We roared over the crest of a hill and the Pacific was stretched out before us, roaring a great, happy-go-lucky 'Hi!' We drove right down to the front and arrived at my hotel, the Manly Pacific International, right on the beach and facing the magnificent azure-blue ocean. Dickie Bamber, the associate producer, suggested that I go to bed and ring him whenever I woke. I'd slept only fitfully during the twenty-three-hour flight. The hotel was new and fancy and had everything the seasoned international traveller might want, except home. It was all too much for me, so I rang Wendy. Monday morning in Australia, it was Sunday evening in London, and the disorientation turned me into a snivelling wreck. Three months, I'd never last.

On the first day I was introduced to a bewilderingly large crew at the ABC's French's Forest Studios. Channel Four and an Independent British company were making the series with the Australian Broadcasting Company, and all the production people were ABC staff. On that first morning I met the make-up and hair artists, and had the first of an endless series of costume fittings. In the process of Jack Grant's transition from callow English youth to butch Australian bushy I would need a large number of costumes and varying degrees of tan. I had tried to help out in England by having sun-bed treatments in order to warm up my milky Irish complexion. The normal happened. I either remained deadly pale or I switched the control up and I emerged like a small strawberry. Mad dogs and Irishmen weren't meant to go in the sun. For *The Boy in the Bush*, it could all come out of a tin. The excellent wardrobe department had already produced a marvellous pair of leather riding boots which seemed to me half the battle in convincing myself that I could ride like John Wayne.

The producers had insisted on a two-week acclimatisation period, which was intended to allow me to deal with jet lag but also to give me time to familiarise myself with my horse. As I had yet to become familiar with any horse, I was glad of the time, and lessons started straight away. I was to be taught by a wrangler, Graham Ware, whose farm was an hour's drive from Sydney. We pulled up at the quiet house and were greeted by the man himself. Small, knotty and apparently made of leather, Graham shook my hand with the bone-crunching firmness that I'd come to expect from the real boys in the bush and said, 'Hez yah roidun?'

Graham's accent wasn't impenetrable, it just took a little getting used to, and I think I was so beguiled by his appearance that at first I didn't concentrate. Stocky, with a gap-toothed grin, he walked at an angle, leaning forward with a pronounced roll of his slightly bandy legs. We walked to the corral.

'Oim pootn yoo on Dollah, Kin. 'E's a rockin' horse ter roid.'

I mounted, and to my great surprise Graham clicked his fingers and set the horse off on a cantering circle. No warm-ups, no walks, and no preparation. I was delighted, and I bounced around like a

bag of beans. Graham watched me through narrowed eyes. He looked like a character John Carradine would have played in a gangster film. We got on like a house on fire. He saw immediately that I had lots of work to do if I was to fulfil my riding commitments in the series, and he introduced me to the much simpler and more relaxed 'cowboy' riding style that the Australians use. It had none of the British Pony Club stiffness, although it was a little harder on the horse. But it was Graham's horse, Dollar, that made all the difference to my confidence: after weary riding-school nags I was on a highly trained, responsive, good-natured beast that was used to dealing with incompetence. Within a week I was transformed and very, very cocky.

The evenings would still catch me unawares with stabs of home-sickness and, of course, there was Sunday. The Irish Protestant in me had always hated Sundays, and this first Sunday in Sydney was particularly miserable, and it was pouring with rain. However it also provided a farce. Jon Blake, the actor who played my bosom buddy in the film, was concerned about our riding, and we decided to visit a friend of his who lived just outside Sydney and who had horses we could ride for the morning. We pressed ahead, in spite of the rain, and got to a farmhouse that was littered with people who were asleep, drunk or stoned. There had been a wild party the night before, and if the human inhabitants were anything to go by, the horses would be on the ceiling.

In the middle of our visit the police raided the place and I found myself running across the backyard in the rain, hoping I wouldn't celebrate my first week in Sydney by getting arrested. Jon was mortified, but I could have forgiven him anything, for like the rest of the crew and cast he had a professional welcoming instinct which is common to Australians and to the Irish. The number of kind invitations to welcoming dinners that I received in those first two difficult weeks was rather moving. And deeply un-English.

That night Alfie Bell, a Pommie actor who lives in Australia, who was to play the mysterious Dr Rackett in the series, insisted that I come to Sunday dinner with some friends of his, including our director, Ken Hannam. I whimpered something about wanting to be on my own.

'Rubbish. I'm coming to get you now.'

I've never been so warmly looked after. Ten days in and I wasn't sure that I would ever want to go back home.

Filming started. Jack's story was shot out of sequence, which was very tricky. The callow youth who arrives at the outback farm of his distant relations develops considerably over the four episodes, and his clothes and appearance change as he becomes used to farm life, wins the respect of the natives, and falls for the local girl, played by the great Australian star, Sigrid Thornton. As the story progresses, Jack becomes a miner, and later a gold prospector with two wives. We would sometimes shoot scenes with the weathered, rough Jack in the morning, and then return to the younger Jack in the afternoon, which would mean a change of stubble, hair, make-up and costume. This was particularly difficult as I was in practically every shot and my film-acting education really began here. There is really no substitute for practice, and being in front of the lens all day every day for three months was a great crash course. Ken Hannam's direction was patient and thorough. He was determined to capture the special atmosphere of this piece, and not just allow it to become a cowboy romp. He used faces as landscapes, and there were many close-ups to reveal Jack's internal isolation, and indeed to explore the complexity of the other characters.

Each day after shooting, at around six or seven in the evening, the entire crew would watch rushes of the previous day's work. This was a very brave thing to do, especially for the actors, and directors often banish actors from these sessions as dreadful damage can be done to a performance if an actor's hysterical subjectivity is brought to bear. The Australian actors took these sessions in their stride and were very grateful for the opportunity to monitor the filming, particularly as the story was spread over several years, and it was always a very jolly occasion with people cracking open a tube (a can of beer – I was becoming steeped in the culture). This daily process cured me forever of obsessive worry about my own appearance – gosh, do I really look that awful? This feeling is a waste of time, and after a couple of days of seeing myself on film, I was so used to the uninspiring features which, short of plastic surgery, were with me for the rest of my days, that I stopped worrying. I found myself able to look at the character objectively and use the sessions as a useful tool for looking at the character and seeing how the different aspects of the part fitted together. If some quality or other was missing then a discussion with the director would mean that you could be sure to include it at some other point.

It was still early days and the material looked good. We were shooting three and a half minutes of film every day and the spirit among the crew was good. Roger Lanser, the brilliant camera operator, who became a close friend, shared the crew's relief. They'd been working on a series with a particularly demanding director who seemed to share little of Ken Hannam's concern for detail in the acting or for the atmosphere of the piece. He was glad at last to be working on something of real quality. I asked him who the director had been.

'His name is Rob "Rocket" Stewart.'

'Rocket?'

'Yeh. Because he works so fast.'

'Christ, save us from that.'

It was clear after a week that something was wrong. The atmosphere on set remained very positive but there were rumblings in the administrative corridor. Each night after rushes I would have a shower and then make my way to the car, and as I passed the producers' office I would hear noisy arguments about the rushes. Poor Ken Hannam.

The problem was more serious than I thought, and at the end of the second week's shooting gossip was rife. On the Friday night Dickie Bamber picked me up at location and drove me back to the studios.

'Don't worry, Ken. There's a bit of confusion over what we're all after. Mr Warren' – this was the series producer – 'is coming over at the weekend and we're all going to have a chat to sort it out. Nothing to worry about.'

It sounded ominous, but I decided to give Dickie the benefit of the doubt. I knew there had been talk of there being a lack of 'production value', in other words, there had not been enough footage of landscapes or our marvellous sets, anything that showed where the money had been spent. The first two weeks had been spent in concentrating on character work, but I felt sure that production value would come later in the schedule.

I decided not to worry. I had enough to do, with lines to learn and a new flat to move to. It had been suggested that I might be better off financially if I moved – I would be given the money it would have cost to keep me at the hotel (a contractual arrangement) and if I found a flat that was cheaper I could keep the difference. I found an extraordinary place overlooking the ocean. It was perched on a rocky outcrop of Queenscliff and the main room had miles of window and 180-degree views of the Pacific.

I'd begun to change into costume at 6.30 on the following Monday morning when one of the wardrobe girls came in.

'Haven't you heard? No shooting today. Ken's been sacked.'

Moments later the gang of four producers descended on me with all sorts of explanations for their action. I was panicked and wanted to know what was going to happen to him, to me, and to the production.

I protested weakly on Ken's behalf. It was completely hopeless. I had no idea what to do. 'I'll need to ring my agent,' I said, and it threw them.

'Oh, I don't think there's any need for that . . .'

It was no use, I was on a very high horse. 'I'm afraid there is. I signed to be in a show that Ken was directing. The situation has changed, and I need to review my position.'

I didn't know what I was talking about but it was clearly alarming them. I was growing up quickly.

'Now come on, Ken, just calm down . . .' Calm down? I hadn't realised that I'd heated up. I decided to listen. 'No look, we're going to have to stop shooting for a week while we get this thing sorted out. Obviously we have some thoughts about a new director. If you have any ideas we'd be glad to hear them.'

Cobblers. They already knew who they wanted. I had a very uncomfortable feeling.

'Perhaps over the next few days if you fancy spending a little time at the Barrier Reef, we'd be very happy to send you up there.'

'No. Absolutely not. I don't need to salve my conscience.' I had no idea where my bottle had come from.

'Well, of course we don't mean it like that. Just think about it and please don't do anything rash. You've got an international career to think about.'

This was the stuff of which Hollywood legends are made – hirings and firings and tough-talking executives. I loved reading about it but I didn't like being in the middle of it. The cast got together later the same day, and the Australians put forward suggestions for alternative directors. We all knew what was coming and we all knew we would have no choice but to accept it or be out of a job. Pat Marmont was sympathetic and advised caution but felt there was no choice but to stay, however frightened I felt about being in a vulnerable position, and however much I feared the return of old dreads from the days of *Hamlet* at RADA.

The next day the expected news was announced. We were all called together and told that our new director was to be a marvellous and sensitive director called Robert Stewart. Perhaps some of us had worked with him before? There was an audible groan.

I suddenly felt as I had done in the first term at Meadway, and through those awful *Hamlet* rehearsals – terrified, intimidated, and small. Well, bugger it. This time I would not be bullied. I started to fume and marched into the producers' office. Only one was there.

'I'd like to see you all. Now, please.'

'Well Ken . . .'

'*Now.*' My God. I was starting to frighten myself. They filed in. 'Two things. Firstly, don't give me any sweet talk about this fellow's reputation. I know exactly what it is, and if I get any trouble from him, and if there is any attempt to interfere with my work, then I'm on the next plane home. Understand?'

'Now, come on.'

'Don't think I'm joking.'

I tried to control my body, which was shaking all over. They were not going to treat me like a child. Until then I had been all sweetness and light. Mr Pro. Now they would see what I was made of.

'Second, I want a car.'

'A car?'

'A car. Good morning, gentlemen.'

God knows why I had asked for a car. They sent cabs for me every morning, but as they drove on the left in Sydney it felt like home, and I fancied the independence outside work. The car arrived by lunchtime of the same day. I had taken no pleasure in blowing my top. Afterwards, I was wracked with guilt, certain that I had done the wrong thing and finally (actor to the very core) I was worried they wouldn't like me any more. The toughening-up process had only just begun.

Three days later a new read-through was called so that our second leader could tell us his view of the piece. 'Rocket' was about six foot two, blond and well-built, and looked like the original Medallion Man. His shirt, when it was on, was undone to the navel, his legs were permanently spread while he performed ad hoc exercises, and his handshake was so strong I thought I would faint. His opening remarks laid out the kind of relationship that was ahead:

'G'day, Ken. Now look here, mate. Old D. H. Lawrence was a funny bastard, wasn't he? Well look, I'm not interested in all this motivation shit. I think we wanna just shoot some film, have a few tubes, fuck a few women and fuck off home. What do you say?'

I couldn't believe my ears. He knew how provocative he was being and this was clearly meant to test what an arty Pom I really was, but I suppressed the queeny outrage in me and decided to credit him with being nervous. I would give him the benefit of the doubt.

The first week proved quite how wrong I'd been. Rocket's hero was Sam Peckinpah. If Rocket had been making *A Room with a View*, Maggie Smith and Judi Dench would have been blown up in the first ten minutes. Alas, Lawrence's delicate tale had far too much cowboy in it for Rocket to resist the 'rip, shit and bust' adventure style. This was fine up to a point, but there was much more in the story and I took it upon myself to defend atmosphere and character. It was difficult.

Week one. 'Ken, what do you look like with your shirt off?'

'What?'

'The girls, Ken, the girls. All this fucking chat's boring the ass off me. We've got to get the girls interested. Whip your shirt off, get a bit of tan and oil on there, we'll be laughing.'

That was what I feared.

Week two. Shooting had gone up to eleven minutes of film a day. 'And . . . Cut! OK, moving on, next set up.'

'Hold on, hold on, we've only done it once. I'd like another go.'

'Fuck me, Ken. It's dialogue. We need to get on to the fucking action.'

Too much for me. I could butch it up with the best of them but I hadn't come to make *The Dirty Dozen*. He was walking away. I exploded.

'*The dialogue is interesting, you Philistine git.*'

Pause.

'OK, the fucking Queen of the May gets another take.'

I was so angry by this time that acting went out of the window. Next day I tried a new tack: humour. In all truth, Rocket, who to my annoyance I was growing increasingly fond of, was highly risible. His macho-ness was so exaggerated that you expected him to open cans of beer with his teeth. I'm sure he'd tried it. Bully though he appeared to be, he was very conscious of his image among the crew. He didn't mind being thought a bastard, as long as he was a big butch bastard. The mickey-taking did the trick, and I was the only one with sufficient professional status and power enough to challenge him.

It was a rather dangerous game. After all, he really was a big bloke. In the end I took to him because he cured me of whatever weakness had made me susceptible to intimidation in the past. At last I had begun to stand up for myself. Twelve thousand miles from home, in a situation from which I couldn't run away, I had developed new muscles that I feared I didn't have. I hoped it wasn't producing a stroppiness that would plague producers and directors ever more, but it certainly meant that I would not be walked over in the future.

Except possibly by marsupials. Rocket pitched me into the ring with a one-eyed, one-armed, arthritic kangaroo called Smokey.

We filmed Jack Grant's kangaroo fight at an antipodean extravaganza called Nature Wonderland. If Smokey was an example of Australian wildlife, then the wonder was that any wildlife survived at all. I wrestled with this decrepit beast, but Rocket still wasn't satisfied. He found an animal sanctuary nearby which housed a crazed 'roo'. This was obviously going to be more dramatic. We went into the compound and exited one minute later minus a camera and with Roger Lanser in shock, having been attacked by the meanest marsupial I've ever seen.

Because of the original stoppage over Ken Hannam's sacking, the filming had been delayed by several weeks. The limited rehearsal time for *The Madness* had been further reduced and Colin tried to guard against it with trans-continental tapes in which he described how the set would work in the Waterloo Road. I sat listening to the tapes in Bulahdelah, a one-horse town almost in the middle of nowhere, trying desperately to learn the lines between takes of sheep-shearing and logging.

The job ended in a flurry of intense social life. I really had made some good friendships, and at the party on my last day, Graham Ware pulled a cart full of presents onto the lawn at French's Forest and finished me off. I was still awash with tears the next day as I left Sydney, where I had been made so welcome. I would even miss Rocket. Maybe he could come and help Colin with *The Madness*. Exploding Tennyson. That would be new.

As I weepily settled down into the long flight, I felt that I had – rather like Jack Grant – matured a little in Australia. I'd dealt with being away, being bullied, working on a film and had experienced a care and concern from friends that allowed me to see once again that professional problems should be seen in a wider perspective. Frightened though I was by the prospect of *The Madness*, I felt certain that it was the right thing to be doing while I was in this more realistic frame of mind.

I returned to emotional madness. The inevitable effects of a four-month separation wreaked havoc on Wendy and me. After three and a half years of a more or less steady involvement, we decided to go our separate ways. It happened in the first week after my return from Australia – Wendy instigated the break, and I played the wounded martyr, but we both knew it was for the best.

Much more therapeutic was the feeling that I was a real actor once more. I returned on a Saturday from Australia and on the following Monday morning I was walking along the Waterloo Road at 9.30 with a take-away tea and a bacon roll in my hand. This is what I always did when going to rehearsal at RADA, and it felt proper, it was what you did. One never got the same sensation arriving for a television production.

Rehearsals for *The Madness* were tough. A one-man show is a delicate affair. One performer plus one director can equal boredom, and puts great pressure on both of them to provide enough energy to keep rehearsals flowing. *The Madness* had particular demands: it's a high-voltage piece, which combines an atmosphere of Edgar Allan Poe gloom with something of the romantic intensity of *Romeo and Juliet*. It was difficult to rehearse for long hours in any piece of this kind under such conditions, but the delays on *The Boy in the Bush* had left only one week before I was due to fly to Belfast for *Billy III*. We did our best in the seven days, and the rest of the rehearsals were held on Saturdays and Sundays over the following month. I would fly back from Belfast on a Friday night learning the rest of the text in the aeroplane, and the next day we would try to cram a week's work into one day.

The combination of an unusually tough work-load and my own depressed emotional condition made it a rather bleak time for me. The recurring Hamlet in me was much comforted by Alec McCowen's *Personal Mark*, which gives an account of his work on the one-man show *St Mark's Gospel*. The comfort it offered to someone engaged in the same lonely process where self doubt was the name of the game was immense.

Colin Wakefield's patience was extraordinary. In the latter stages of rehearsal when we were attempting a run-through I would often stop speaking and just give up in utter despair. Very quietly, without bullying, he would make me pick it up and carry on, ignoring the fact that I was on the verge of tears with exhaustion and a sense of my own impending failure.

I did wonder seriously about who would come and see it. Colin and I were learning fast about independent production. When rehearsal fatigue overtook us, we would be on the phone pumping in coins and trying to persuade *Time Out* and *Ms London* to give us a mention. We had no press agent, and had no real idea of how to secure publicity.

Back in Belfast during the week being the Ulster James Dean, the cast of *Billy III* were plagued with requests to hear my lines. This was the latest drama: would I be able to remember it? Any spare time was spent filling envelopes with leaflets for the show and sending them off to journalists, friends, anyone. We were twisting arms all over the place. I had already had the artwork for the poster done by the design department of *The Boy in the Bush*. Incidental music for the show had been cajoled from Kate Edgar, an excellent musician who was a friend of Colin Wakefield, and Colin had also managed to obtain the services of Kate Burnett, a highly talented designer who produced a set that could allow a dramatic, poetic monologue to come to interesting stage life. The piece changed locations from the Narrator's house, to the moor, to the manor where Maud lived, to the woods where the father had died, to France, to the sea. The overall effect was achieved by the simplest of means – a naked wooden stage dripping with blood-red paint and a selection of dramatic scaffolding poles, cut and placed to form a miniature wood at the back of the set. When it was properly lit, it ignited the imagination in a powerful way that managed not to conflict with the text.

When *Billy III* was finished I had confirmation that Julian Mitchell's play, *Francis* would go ahead that Autumn at the Greenwich Theatre, and that I would be playing the lead. Rehearsals were due to start a week after *The Madness* closed. I was back to the theatre with a vengeance.

I had yet to complete a run-through of *The Madness* without drying or being overcome by the panic and fear, and wanting to run away. The single preview was on the Tuesday night, and we opened on the Wednesday. All sorts of chums and associates were dragged in to the dress rehearsal on the Monday. Several of them fell fast asleep, which was a disaster for me as I could see every single person in the tiny auditorium. I didn't dry, but I did do a little Tennysonian paraphrasing.

Pat Marmont came to the preview. 'Brilliant, darling, but too quick. It's so dense you must give us a chance.'

It was what Colin had been saying all along, but fear prevented me from taking his advice. The quicker I went the less chance I had to be scared and also the less chance the audience had to be bored rigid. But I decided I would try.

With unswerving loyalty Pat also came to the first night, and I was undoubtedly slower and better. It was nice to have a fuller house than before, although disconcerting to see the three or four critics who had turned up, scribbling noisily in my many significant pauses. Colin was very pleased with the performance. A great party of his friends were in and we trooped off afterwards for supper in Covent Garden. People had enjoyed it, and if nothing else, they felt as if they had been at an event. Wherever else would they see eighty obscure minutes of a Tennyson poem performed on stage by an actor?

There were no notices the next day, and the bookings for the remaining performances were dismal. Colin and I continued a rallying-round of persuasion, David Parfitt helped us, and even lent a hand by selling programmes. These few days really were tough. Colin had seen the show so many times that he really deserved a break. I told him not to bother coming in on the Friday and Saturday nights. It left me even more lonely. Before the show there was only the stage manager to talk to, an unemployed actor who was doing it for the prospect of a profit share which I'd promised to him and to Colin and Kate. Not much chance of that.

On the Saturday night, things reached rock bottom. The show started with twelve paying customers in the 150-seat auditorium, of which six were my family. I might as well have been doing it in the front room. I spent eighty minutes acting my face off and being permanently on the edge of breaking out of it and saying, 'This is ridiculous, let's all go home.' That Sunday, with no girlfriend, no audience and a new room in Brentford to get depressed in, I was a sorry sight.

On the Monday morning a notice appeared in *The Times*: 'The most exciting young actor in years.' And at lunchtime the *Evening Standard* also ran a review – 'Dazzling, virtuoso performance.'

I rang the theatre. The phone hadn't stopped ringing, we were sold out from Wednesday onwards, and Monday and Tuesday had really perked up. Several actors who were in shows had rung to ask would I do a midnight matinée, so that they could see it? In a moment of real madness I agreed. There would be two shows on the last Saturday, one at 8 pm and one at 11 pm. My God, what a difference a day makes.

My confidence was transformed and the performance began to grow. Many people I admired came: Ronald Eyre, Jimmy Ellis, Edward Petherbridge and his wife, Emily Richard, lots of young actors and, to my delight, Alec McCowen, whom I was able to thank in person for the comfort his book had provided. Even Mary Wilson, the former Prime Minister's wife, and a Tennyson devotee, made an appearance. She endeared herself to me for ever by bringing round to the dressing-room a volume of her poetry which she had signed.

'I hoped you might like it.'

I thanked her profusely and when she had gone looked at the inscription. 'To John Branagh, Congratulations on your perform-ance.' I'd clearly made a great impression.

That week of packed performances also brought Joyce Nettles and Genista McIntosh, another high-powered RSC colleague. They'd been threatened by Pat Marmont who sat through the show a remarkable four times, and I was told that the RSC might 'be in touch'.

The last performance on Saturday produced a wonderful standing ovation from a lot of fellow actors, mostly friends, who were amazed that I was still on my feet and who were mostly high as kites on having finished their own two shows that day. It made a great celebratory end to my first fully independent venture. Many lessons were learned, and over the last day or two David Parfitt and I chewed the cud over how to make the administrative side work efficiently, and how to work independent ventures of this kind so that they actually paid people like Colin Wakefield and Kate Burnett who had both heavily subsidised it with their talents. It was the first of many such discussions.

A brief holiday followed – three fascinating days in Rome, and then a research trip to Assisi where I was able to examine the way of life of modern Franciscan monks. I also spent a day with David William, an actor from *Another Country* who was to direct *Francis*. He had seen *The Madness* and wanted to pass on a few comments that might be useful to take on into *Francis*. Like Hugh Cruttwell, David's precision with words and desire to present the truth on stage was inspiring. We discussed how an actor presenting the visionary quality of a man such as Francis must be able to show the character's remoteness from real life at certain moments. It was a form of spiritual isolation, the ability to see 'some other where', a quality that any actor playing Hamlet must give to these lines:

> There is a special providence in the fall of a sparrow
> If it be now, tis not to come. If it be not to come
> It will be now. If it be not now, yet it will come.
> The readiness is all.

David William believed I *could* present this sense of vision and spiritual gravitas but that at present I was much happier in the emotions of the here and now. At the same time it was important to present Francis's spiritual qualities without the performance seeming ponderous or dull. Francis was neither of these things, and his faith was a practical one. He was an exciting charismatic leader but he was still set apart. The part was a tall order but very exciting, and the play contained all these possibilities, but with David there to describe all the different aspects in such an illuminating way, I felt confident of learning a huge amount in the four-week rehearsal period.

I came back from Italy inspired and also convinced that holidays abroad alone when you were recovering from a broken heart were not a good idea. It was better to call a mate, get pissed and have a good moan. I did plenty of that when I got back.

Rehearsals started, and by the end of the first week we had 'blocked' the whole play. By the beginning of the second week I had learned the part. (*The Madness* had done no harm to my retentive memory.) David encouraged me to develop a 'spiritual vocabulary', an extreme receptivity to the man and the ideas in the play. It was very un-modern and very unfamiliar to me. The play dealt with profound themes, and I felt if I could get to grips with the imaginative demands of the part, I could draw new qualities from my acting.

There was a brilliant team effort over those four weeks. Frederick Treves was producing a superb performance as Cardinal Ugolino, Francis's chief adversary, a part he conveyed with real compassion and intelligence. At the final run-through, in the British Legion Hall at Putney, his acting was as fine as any I have seen. From an audience that included wardrobe and stage management personnel, and the artistic director, Alan Strachan, there was a unanimous response. Tears poured down their faces and the response from everyone there gave the impression that they felt they had witnessed something very special.

Introduction to the theatre part 74: new plays need time. Julian's piece was in good shape when we began rehearsal, and it was fine when we moved it to the stage. After only one performance in front of an audience it was seen by the critics, who savaged it. The play would have benefited enormously from a week of previews, which gave the actors a chance to work on the text and also to adapt the set and costumes to fit the needs of the play. There was no time to learn from a single preview. The rough edges threw into sharp relief elements of medievalism which a modern audience can find boring and difficult. I believe this obscured an excellent production of a fine play.

At the time I was certain that I had produced the best work of my career and that the high sights we had set ourselves had been met. I was in a tiny minority, but, for the first and only time, I was completely unaffected and unworried by the reviews. I knew the work was honest and real and powerful, and the difficulty lay in conveying this, but there was still no denying that it wasn't going to catch on. The first night faces told the story. All the ecstatic fan mail in the world – and there was a great deal – could not salvage the show, which played to rapidly dwindling audiences and finished its Greenwich run a week earlier than planned.

I have two glorious memories of the first night. One was the sight of my grandmother in tears in the foyer. She had been persuaded to brave the terrors of aeroplanes at the age of eighty so that she could see her grandson on stage for the first time. She had been deeply moved by the play and only came out of her post-show reverie to giggle wildly at the mention of my nakedness. At one point, when Francis rejects his father's wealth, he takes all his clothes off in the village square in order to make his point. My granny found this scene hysterical, as did my fellow actors, who were playing villagers and peasants, and, facing upstage, couldn't be heard hissing, 'Christ, I've seen more meat on a dirty fork.'

Nor shall I forget the marvellous diplomacy of Robert Fox, who had been keeping an eye on the play with a view to transferring it if it worked. He came into the dressing-room and gave me a great hug accompanied by an awe-struck, 'Extraordinary . . . absolutely extraordinary.'

We looked at each other and his face forbade further comment. He looked as though either his life had been changed or that he was so appalled that he couldn't bring himself to speak. He said one more 'Extraordinary', and then left. I loved him for it. He was in an impossible position, and going round after the show is a ghastly business at the best of times. Now I could choose to believe that the whole thing was 'extraordinary . . . crap' or 'extraordinary . . . brilliance'. I went for the latter and have never troubled Robert for his real choice. The sadness produced by the notices in the subsequent weeks was alleviated by the company spirit, which was high to the point of danger, and corpsing had to be kept under strict control.

Something was definitely afoot at the RSC. Ron Daniels came to see *Francis*, and a trip to see other work was a rare event for a busy RSC director. He stayed behind afterwards and was kind about the play, but he still acted as though he were in a World War II film. This time, I thought, he thinks he's in the French Resistance – he spoke almost in a whisper and kept looking over his shoulder, and I was sure his parting line would be a wink and then 'Ze blue moon eatz ze lazee dog in zee evening,' or some other code phrase. He wanted to meet to chat about . . . something, he wouldn't say what. We would have to go somewhere very quiet – I half expected that he'd want me to wear a trench-coat and stand under a clock with a carnation. The next day his secretary rang to say that there was a table booked at Joe Allen's. Short of putting an ad in *The Stage*, I couldn't think of a more effective way of alerting the entire acting profession to our plans. Still, I was sure there would be method in his madness.

We were on the pudding when I thought it was time to prize Ron out of his Peter Lorre impersonation.

'So what actually was it that you wanted to talk about, Ron?'

'*Henry V.*' Yippee. Ron went on. 'I passionately believe that this play must be done. I passionately want to do it, and I passionately believe that you should play Henry.'

His intensity was convincing. All that passion. 'Well, that's great, Ron.'

'Ah. It's not quite that easy.'

Here we go.

Ron explained the complexities of the RSC's planning system. There were more considerations than individual ambitions for particular plays.

'But you do passionately want to do this, Ron?'

'Passionately.'

Well, that must be a help. 'What do you see in the play?'

'Mud.'

I checked the wine. No, it was OK, we were still on the first bottle. 'Mud?'

Ron explained about the earthy, filthy approach he wanted. Sounded fine to me. 'When will you know?'

The eyes narrowed again. The chances of pinning Ron down like this were small. We finished the meal and agreed to keep in touch, but quite how I was going to keep in touch with him, short of sending a weekly telegram declaring my interest in the part, I wasn't sure. I asked Pat if she knew what was going on in the RSC planning department. 'God knows, darling.'

A fortnight later she rang to say that Barry and Adrian would like to see me. Yes, they were confident of offering me a line of parts, but they needed to chat. I was filming Edward Bond's play, *Derek* for Thames TV during the day, but they gave me the afternoon off to make my first visit to the great airport lounge that is the Barbican Centre. I waited in the RSC's casting office where Siobhan, the casting assistant, tiptoed over to me and spoke in hushed tones that suggested she thought I might hit her. 'Ron has asked me to say that he's sorry he won't be directing *Henry V*, but there is another play he passionately wants to direct and the two couldn't work out.'

Gosh, I thought, all that passion in one man. He'll explode.

Barry Kyle and Adrian Noble, the two senior RSC directors, were equally passionate, so they said, about my joining the Company. They were as pleasant as they had been before and I had no reason to disbelieve them. Ron, it turned out, was directing *Hamlet* and passionately wanted me to play Laertes. Before I became worn out with passionate pleas, Barry explained that he was directing *Love's Labour's Lost*, and thought that I might be very good as the King of Navarre. I was encouraged by the fact that he was interested but didn't feel it passionately.

The real crux of the talk and the offer was Adrian's production of *Henry V*. It was definitely going to be done at Stratford in the following year and Adrian – rather than Ron – was going to direct it. He was interested in me but had not – bar my original audition – seen me in the classics. Perhaps I could go away and prepare a piece of *Henry V* to come back and work on. I offered to do it there and then.

They took me at my word, Adrian suggested 'Once more unto the breach', and we walked down onto the vast Barbican stage. I put down the book and started. I knew the speech by heart and was so excited that I decided to go for it, regardless. Empty theatres have always thrilled me – the fantastic response with which you can imbue your imaginary audiences can sometimes be more rewarding than the real thing.

Barry and Adrian made helpful comments and I did the speech half a dozen different ways.

'Terrific. We'll be in touch with your agent.'

I suppose that that meant I was through, but I wasn't sure. I didn't dare hope. As I was leaving the stage door, a friend who was in the company rushed up to me. 'Well done, that was great.'

'What was?'

'Your audition.'

'How do you know?'

'The tannoy and the video monitor were both on. We were all in the green room having a bite between shows and cheering you on.'

'Bloody 'ell.'

'I'm sure you've got it.'

He was right. Two days later the offer was confirmed: the three

Shakespearian plays, and a part in a new play which Barry was directing which was still at an early stage. The contract was for the sixty weeks of the Stratford and Newcastle season, with an implicit understanding that if, as was usual, the shows transferred to London, then I would stay with them for another nine months. Two years' employment. I hoped I'd made the right choice. *Henry V* opened the Stratford season, and if it was a disaster, I'd either be kicked out or have to suffer it for two years. At twenty-three, I was the youngest Henry ever to play at Stratford. What chance did I stand? It was exactly what I wanted and it was frightening, but there was no turning back.

SIX

Ever since that first camping trip to Stratford in 1978, I had felt destined to join the RSC. *The Wars of the Roses* in the early sixties, the work of Peter Brook, and the Trevor Nunn seasons in the mid-seventies all seemed to indicate an extraordinarily versatile and skilful company, and it became my ideal. The variety and quality of the work were consistent, and it was full of immensely talented people – Trevor Nunn, Terry Hands, Adrian Noble, Barry Kyle – with whom I was longing to work. I felt very privileged to enter the RSC at such a level, and I was determined to be a model member of the Company. I bought my copies of the Arden Shakespeare and set to work, hoping that a successful first season would lead to a long relationship with the company that I felt was my natural home. In the meantime, *Henry V* demanded attention.

Adrian Noble and I sat on either side of a rusty gas-heater in a freezing dance studio near the Barbican; at the other end of the desk were the Assistant Director, A. J. Quinn, and the Assistant Stage Manager, Ian Barber. This was how the luxurious ten-week rehearsal period for *Henry V* began and in the first ten days it was really just the four of us. The lengthy preparation period was in part because *The Merchant of Venice* would open directly after *Henry V* and several key actors were in both productions. *Henry V* was to be the prestigious opening show of the 1984 season.

The wonderful advantage of that first week or so was to be able to establish my fundamental instincts about the character. Shakespeare's Henry V has been described as a jingoistic warlord, a brigand, and a thug. Despite the huge success of Laurence Olivier's film, made in the forties, the character continues to create great uneasiness in the minds of modern actors, directors, critics and academics, and we had a particular media spotlight focused on this production. It had already been labelled a 'post-Falklands' version of the play, and there was suspicion from both sides of the political spectrum that the production would set out to condemn the war in a

136

crude way or, conversely, to celebrate it with all the jingoism that the piece can offer.

Adrian and I discussed this problem in great detail, as much would depend on the portrayal of the central character. Studying the part at RADA I had been struck by the sense of Hamletian doubt that runs through the part. Henry was haunted, I felt, not just by his father and their troubled relationship, but also by the ghost of Richard II, whom he invokes at the end of the famous 'Upon the King' soliloquy. This seemed to me to reveal a massively guilty man who was quite terrified, and the speech was not a perfunctory plea from a pious zealot certain of his own victory, but expressed the anguished fear of a young man whose mistake would cost thousands of lives.

HENRY   Oh God of battles, steel my soldiers' hearts;
Possess them not with fear; take from them now
The sense of reckoning if the opposed numbers
Pluck their hearts from them.
    Not today O Lord!
O not today, think not upon the fault
My father made in compassing the crown!
I Richard's body have interred new
And on it have bestowed more contrite tears
Than from it issued forced drops of blood.
Five hundred poor I have in yearly pay,
Who twice a day their withered hands hold up
Toward heaven, to pardon blood; and I have built
Two chantries, where the sad and solemn priests
Sing still for Richard's soul. More will I do;
Though all that I can do is nothing worth,

<pre>
                    Since that my penitence comes after all,
                    Imploring pardon.
GLOUCESTER   My liege!
HENRY   My brother Gloucester's voice! Ay!
                I know thy errand, I will go with thee:
                The day, my friends, and all things stay
                    for me.
</pre>

It was clear from these early discussions that Henry's genuine humility in relation to God would be a cornerstone of my interpretation. I wanted to infuse 'and all things' with the dark dread of a man who would expect to go to hell and for whom the place was an absolutely real concept. Right from the start he attempts to make everyone genuinely aware of the same thing, of his vision of 'how to war'. Despite political and war-mongering intrigue, despite irresistible pressure from the Church and from the nobles, he insists on fighting an honourable campaign. I wanted the first speech to Canterbury to put this man of God very explicitly on the spot with an injunction directed at the wily archbishops.

<pre>
          And pray take heed how you impawn our person,
          How you awake our sleeping sword of war:
          We charge you in the name of God take heed;
          For never two such kingdoms did contend
          Without much fall of blood; whose guiltless drops
          Are every one a woe, a sore complaint
          'Gainst him whose wrongs gives edge unto the swords
          That make such waste in brief mortality.
          Under this conjuration speak, my lord
          For we will hear, note, and believe in heart
          That what you speak is in your conscience washed
          As pure as sin with baptism.
</pre>

I wanted to produce a moral gravitas that would arrest the clerics and the court with its weight. When my Henry used words like 'sin' and 'baptism' and 'conscience', I wanted the audience to feel that these were real and practical concepts which were deeply felt. It seemed the only way to make the audience care, and thus to make them genuinely question this man's actions. It also created dramatic conflict: the archbishops are faced not with a warlord who simply wishes a plan for invasion to be given the Church's approval, but

138

with someone who is asking real questions and underlining their own sense of responsibility. Such a Henry could put everyone on edge, and start to make the story more than just a *Boys' Own* adventure tale, but leave the audience thinking 'What happens next?', 'Will they go to France?'

We felt that the play had to be shaken out of its superficial militaristic pageantry, and given new force. The large numbers involved make it an expensive play to put on, but I was sure there were other reasons for *Henry V* being performed so seldom – even the RSC only does it every ten or so years. Poor productions of the play which portray Henry and the English as thugs have failed to win audiences over, and critics have condemned the play's political standpoint.

All this was healthily challenged by Adrian. He didn't want Henry to be a saint throughout the play, and neither did I, but I was determined to examine and expand what David William had described during rehearsals for *Francis* as 'a spiritual vocabulary'. It is an area of Henry's personality which is viewed with suspicion by critics, but the richness of the text told me to believe in Henry's concept of honour. He is a man with a close understanding of what war involves, and an intense, visionary appreciation of its consequences. He is a killer, a brilliant politician, but much of this is in embryo and is subject to change during the course of the play. Above all, he is a complicated, doubting, dangerous young professional – neither straightforwardly good nor consciously evil.

Adrian and I both agreed that we should not try to explain this man but rather explore all these paradoxes and contradictions, with an awareness of his historical and social context. We wanted to be faithful to the complex inner debate that Shakespeare conducts on the subject of war, and as we discussed the play it seemed less like a historical pageant and more like a highly complicated and ambiguous discourse on the nature of leadership.

After a fortnight the new Company started to assemble. Brian Blessed, who was to play Henry's warlord uncle, Exeter, was a very striking figure, and his capacity for enthusiasm and encouragement seemed boundless. Ian McDiarmid was playing both the Chorus in *Henry V* and Shylock in *The Merchant of Venice*, and seemed a shy and reserved man, but was really leading the company from the front. He would turn out to be one of the most significant influences on my Stratford season. By the seventh week we had run each half of the play several times and I had finally learned the part. I had deliberately set out to delay this process for as long as possible in order to take advantage of the rehearsal period, and to remain responsive and adaptable.

Although Adrian worked very methodically and was moving towards a very particular conception of the play, ideas and approaches changed daily, and it was important not to become locked into certain ways of saying the lines too early on.

There was also a great deal of technical work to accomplish, and it was a great pleasure to work with the legendary Cis Berry, the RSC's voice supremo. With her assistant, David Carey, one could work specifically on difficult speeches and passages that required the special attention of voice and speech experts. Cis did not come from the 'red leather, yellow leather' school of speech training, but she did have her own idiosyncratic methods, which sometimes involved running round the auditorium singing 'Once more unto the breach', or standing on my head bicycling while reciting the St Crispin's Day speech. There was rather more dry technical advice, but the idea was always to keep the words fresh, however silly you might feel. Words and thoughts and actions must always be linked to provide the correct clarity and tone of sound. I could have spent ten weeks just doing this. The Stratford auditorium sat 1500 people. I remember from my own experience of watching shows from the balcony that projection could be a problem, and I had to be on top of it.

And I had to be on top of the part. I had already been through the usual selection of actor tools – I'd read every biography of Henry V I could get my hands on, and had been wooed in and out of a number of absurd ideas. I discovered in one book that Henry, who had been fighting from the age of twelve, had received a facial wound which had left an enormous scar running from the corner of his mouth to one ear. The effect, the historian wrote, was to make Henry seem as though he was smiling all the time. A very sinister disguise for this most mysterious monarch. Ha, ha. The idea fired me immediately: a marvellous make-up job would ensure that the audience were aware of the king's savage past and would allow the critics to hail my extraordinary new interpretation. A few home experiments allowed me to see that my aspirations to be the Lon Chaney of the classical stage were doomed. I looked as though someone had driven a Reliant Robin across my cheek and appeared about as sinister as Shirley Temple.

140

If the visuals were to remain straight then the internals would have to provide the character's fascination. Work on this was proceeding slowly. I was remarkably diligent. Each evening I would record details of that day's rehearsal on a small tape recorder and, in the act of speaking it, I would attempt to make clearer sense of the part. Henry was a young man, and so was I. He was faced with an enormous responsibility. I didn't have to run the country and invade France, but I did have to control Brian Blessed and open the Stratford season. I was sure I could convey a certain sense of responsibility. With Adrian's expert guidance, I could analyse the text in great detail, and although it was difficult to convey everything he revealed to me straight away, I was getting there.

The major problems by the eighth week, with all this experience swilling away in my acting tank, were two elusive areas of Henry's experience. The first was war, and I tried to do something about this by reading Clausewitz, Sassoon, historical documents about the combat detail at Agincourt. I was very slowly beginning to picture the horrors of a hand-to-hand medieval combat. It was quite easy to get a graphic impression of what fighting could be like from people in the company. Sebastian Shaw, for instance, had been in the RAF during the Second World War, and his account of the terror of a 'night raid' was a chilling highlight of one of several fascinating rehearsal discussions.

But it was much more difficult to get my imagination around Henry's royal status, the isolation of his role as spiritual and military leader. Quite simply, what was it *like* being a king? As with war there was plenty of written material, but there was no one to talk to, no one with whom I could exchange ideas. In a welter of indulgent frustration I would bore my friends at the numerous suppers that accompanied my last weeks in London before the move to Stratford. Very early one morning, after a spectacularly verbose evening, my dinner party host rang me to say that he felt something might be done about my problem.

A week later I was motoring up the long gravel drive to Kensington Palace. After a week of meetings, I had been vetted and through several contacts had been given an introduction to the Prince of Wales. Getting the afternoon off rehearsal had been rather tricky, but I decided to abandon the notion of toothache and come clean with Adrian. A director of the *Royal* Shakespeare Company could hardly refuse such a request, and I swore him to secrecy. The heir to the throne did not wish to be plagued by the membership of Equity, all requesting advice on regal roles. I felt several bonds of allegiance: firstly to the chum who had helped organise it, to his friend, and, of course, to the Prince himself, who I felt must be fed up with continual minor betrayals.

My grubby green car came to a halt by the security hut, and the policeman waved me through. My God, they really did expect me. I walked to the front door without being ambushed by three hundred security guards and when the door opened the footman greeted me with, 'Mr Branagh?'

I waited downstairs in a room filled with Royal Wedding memorabilia. The footman who brought me a cup of tea explained that the trays, pictures and mugs were all gifts sent by members of the public, and that this was one way of using them. I wondered with alarm what exactly I was going to ask the heir to the throne, but the time for panicking was over, and I was shown upstairs and into the Prince's drawing-room where he shook my hand warmly, smiled and said, 'I really have no idea how I can help you, but please sit down, and let's have a chat.'

I felt an instant rapport. I had never encountered such an extraordinary and genuine humility. It would be all right.

'Well, sir, I know it seems rather strange. I'm not intending my Henry V to be an impersonation of you, but I simply wanted to explain some of my feelings about the character, particularly his role as king. They're not necessarily highly academic or intellectual observations, but as you're in a unique position to comment, I'd love to run them past you, and if you have anything to say about them I'd be most grateful. You don't *have* to say anything.'

I began Henry's spiritual checklist. It seemed to me that royalty involved the suppression of many facets of one's character. In Henry this meant (as has been proven by many productions) that the sense of humour which I felt belonged to the man was often missing, as was his latent violence, in fact, all the normal extremes of human behaviour which in ordinary mortals find their own balance but which in a pressurised monarch could emerge with even greater force. I wanted my Henry to display these unexpected qualities with tremendous intensity, and I felt that Shakespeare's text encouraged this view. Prince Charles concurred: yes, there was a tremendous pressure and temptation to be at times either very silly or very violent. As with most people, these impulses were resisted but the underlying pressure was greater than most people would ever experience.

Henry's isolation was another fascinating area. Through the course of the play a number of betrayals take place: his 'bed-fellow', Lord Scroop, is discovered leading an assassination attempt; his former mentor, Falstaff, dies; and later still he is required to order the execution of another former drinking companion, Bardolph. His loneliness is intense and his hurt at the various betrayals and losses is very acute. I asked Prince Charles whether the various newspaper betrayals of events, dramatic and mundane, had changed him. Yes, it had, profoundly. And it had, as I suspected was true of Henry, produced an extraordinary melancholy. It was a sadness that could either produce bitterness or a more useful but painful wisdom, and Prince Charles had clearly developed the latter. He bore the inevitable bruises of his position with great courage, and although, sitting opposite him, I could detect the haunted look of responsibility, the very fact that he was speaking to me was an indication of his continuing desire to give people the benefit of the doubt.

Loneliness, however, was unavoidable. Henry makes one desperate attempt in the play to be like other men. During the famous night-time sequence, he walks among his men in disguise. The experience is extremely unsatisfactory: he wants to be one of them, but he can't be; he wants them to understand his position but they resist it. Had Prince Charles ever felt like doing the same? Yes, while he was at Cambridge he'd attempted to do the same thing, but the results were disastrous. By the end of the night-time sequence in *Henry V*, the young king's only comfort is the very certainty of his lifelong isolation. The young Hal had at least the taste of the Boar's Head life, but when he became king there could be no such contact with an ordinary existence.

There is little solace to be found in such remoteness. I believed that Henry's only real comfort could be his faith, and Prince Charles was in total agreement. Some kind of belief in God was the only practical way of living from day to day, it was the only way to deal with his position. This confirmed what I felt I should try to convey in Henry. I didn't wish to present Henry as a tortured martyr, but I did feel strongly that a complex psychological portrait had been set up by Shakespeare which included guilt, doubt and self-questioning. Prince Charles's comments were immensely helpful and I had the impression that he shared with Shakespeare's Henry a desire to strike a delicate balance between responsibility and compassion.

I left Kensington Palace on that grey March afternoon in considerably more awe than when I'd entered. My blind actor's ambition had emboldened me to undertake the meeting, but by the time I left I was aware of having met a quite remarkable man. He did not possess the same political power as Henry but his influence was considerable, his humility genuine and his desire to lead an honourable life was most striking. The taint of politics made Henry a much darker figure than Charles, but my abiding impression was that leadership could incorporate the finer spiritual attributes that, I felt, lay at the root of Henry's character. I had no desire to beg an audience's forgiveness for a man who had invaded another country on dubious pretexts and with enormous loss of life. They had to make up their own minds about the fascinating, enraging conflict between the ruthless killer and the Christian king. I continued to read about war and politics, but Prince Charles had enormously increased my understanding of many aspects of the role.

I had decided that I would live outside Stratford, for when I had visited the town during the 1982 season I had felt that the heavy workload of the actors and the presence of a whole army of tourists had created a kind of midsummer madness. I couldn't work *and* live in the same claustrophobic atmosphere. Alcester was about eight miles outside Stratford, and I found an idyllic country cottage with lots of room for visitors to come and restore my sanity. There was a large garden running down to a river and almost everything about the cottage and my life seemed lovely.

The first bleak Sunday evening brought its share of fear and loneliness, as I imagined myself ruining my career with a terrible performance as Henry, and living a lonely, loveless life. It was the first morning in Australia all over again. The seventh cavalry arrived that night in the form of a phone call from the actor Richard Easton, who was building a strong performance as the Constable of France in *Henry V*. He was giving a small dinner party at his flat in Stratford for a limited number of the new boys, and Boeuf Bourguignon-ed hospitality has never been so welcome. I drank too much red wine, told too many stupid stories, but went to bed in a pleasant oblivion. When I woke the cottage was already warmer and the first day's rehearsal in Stratford seemed slightly less intimidating.

This was our last week before technical rehearsals and at first my chief worry was about Adrian Noble. I have never seen anyone consume so many indigestion tablets – if digestive disorders are any guide to artistic ability then Adrian was a genius. When he wasn't correcting his stomach he was rubbing his eyes. He wore contact lenses and when he was wrestling with an idea his fingers would be pressed so violently into his eyes that I was terrified that the lenses would slip round the other side of the sockets.

The week was full of exciting new experiences. We were rehearsing in the 'Conference Hall', a huge room which had housed the original Stratford theatre that had burned down earlier in the century, and it was here, sixty years before, that Sebastian Shaw, our King of France, had played Romeo. The atmosphere was thick with ghosts and living memories of its illustrious past. Here for the first time, full of the excitement of Stratford and the adrenalin of the forthcoming opening, I tasted what the great speeches in the play could produce. Slowly the production was beginning to take off. I had been so engrossed in my own role that all the other elements of production had escaped my notice. I was aware, through costume fittings and drawings, that Bob Crowley was producing a brilliantly simple set, but not until the end of that first Stratford week did the whole thing start to come together.

The next big excitement was the arrival of the band. We rehearsed the musical cues out of sequence, and I remember with a thrill the sensation of hearing the end of one of my speeches accompanied by a great brass section:

> Cheerly to sea,
> Tarah, crash, boom, da dah.
> The signs of war advance.
> Badah, badum, beWAAAAH. (I nearly fainted)
> No King of England if not King of France.
> WAAAAAAAAAAHH WAAAAAAAAHH!!

Blimey, I thought, I wish I was watching this.

On the following Monday we began the technical rehearsal. We were falling behind schedule, as the rehearsal of lighting, sound and costume changes was a time-consuming affair. By the morning of the first preview on Thursday we had still not finished, and there was a grave danger of not having a dress rehearsal at all. This terrified me, as it was so long since we had 'teched' the first scenes that we were all in danger of forgetting everything. Adrian seemed to accept this as

145

part of the process but my mounting terror made me throw a mini-wobbly. In a slightly shrill, hysterical falsetto I demanded the chance to run the part before facing an audience. Adrian breathed a heavy sigh. I wasn't the first queeny actor he'd run across. At three o'clock that afternoon we started our first dress rehearsal of the play. At 7.30 we did it again for the paying public. I went through the first performance in a daze. The first time you play a large classical role your energies are completely absorbed in how to get on and off the stage, where your costumes are, and how you can manage to drink a cup of tea during the first half. Remembering and acting the lines seem to come a poor second. Rehearsal room revelations, psychological detail, conversations with prospective monarchs are all out of the window while the old pro inside you is screaming, 'How do I get *off*, love?'

All was fine until we'd won the Battle of Agincourt. I was wandering o'er the battlefield looking suitably moved and about to go into the scene with Fluellen and Williams where Henry sets up a complicated plot involving the exchange of gloves and lasting several pages. This works very well if you are in possession of the gloves. Mine were supposed to be tucked into my belt, but weren't there. My crash course in Shakespearian paraphrase began there and then.

> Fluellen, . . . as I do remember me,
> I bethinkst myself that I did have some gloves
> For which it was my full intent
> That thou should'st with them work.
> But see alas they are not here,
> Nor know I when'st they be.

By this stage every actor at the Battle of Agincourt was regarding their monarch with new amazement. From off-stage the noise of scurrying stage management drifted onto the battlefield. There was no stopping me now – I'd have to get us out of this.

> Good Fluellen, although the gloves I do desire
> Be not here i' the field.
> My mind does't tell me of another pair
> That thou shoulds't find
> Were'st thou to look elsewhere.
> Be busy about this errand
> And return again I absolutely prithee.

146

Siòn Probert, who was playing Fluellen, had turned green. What was I talking about? This wasn't what he'd rehearsed. He ran off-stage and as I continued through the thick, interminable pause, marching around the battlefield, being (if it were possible) even more moved, I saw his arms waving up and down in the wings, and the Stage Manager whispering frantically, 'I haven't got any more fucking gloves.'

The moments passed and by this stage I had mourned individually over each of the Agincourt dead, and the shuddering shoulders of the English army told me that concentration was at an end. The air of perplexity coming off the audience was palpable. At last Sion ran back on carrying what looked like two motor-cycle gauntlets, and yelled,

> I have found thine gloves, my liege.

A moment before I had spotted the original pair lying amongst the dead bodies. I had just snatched them up ready to carry on with the scene when the mad Welshman rushed on. Now the audience really were confused.

> Well done, good fellow.
> Thou does't thy office fairly.
> But I have found another pair
> Which suiteth me more goodly.

Before I could wrench myself back onto the text I heard an audible 'Fuck me' from under Sion's breath. He clearly thought I'd done this on purpose. The rest of the show was performed on sheer adrenalin. The age that the gloves incident had seemed to take was clearly exaggerated by actually being part of it, but by the time I walked out of the theatre and to my car I was sure that the audience had not noticed.

I'd got through it, which was a huge relief, and Adrian was pleased. There was lots of work to do next day, but the reaction had been good and we'd got away with the one major embarrassment. As I opened the car door another vehicle drove past and the window was wound down. 'Superb, absolutely superb.'

That was nice. There, I knew we'd got away with it. They called again.

'Loved the gloves!'

As the previews continued I began to put my rehearsal ideas into practice and stopped worrying about whether the crown was on straight. On the Saturday afternoon before the preview matinée performance Adrian came into my dressing-room for his daily progress assessment. By this stage his eyes had been rubbed so hard the contact lenses must have been in his nostrils. God knows what his stomach was like – I kept a packet of Rennies on the dressing-room table just in case. We had our first real argument.

'Look, Ken . . . I think that er . . . I mean, the er . . . performance is certainly developing enormously er . . . but I do think that you must try less hard to er . . .'

'What?'

'. . . be liked.'

I was enraged. 'What do you mean?'

'Well, I think that um . . . specifically . . .'

'What? What is it?'

'I think you should cut your hair.'

'*What?*'

It turned out that my blond mop, on top of a glorious red and blue costume, was fighting the 'Dirty Harry' that we were trying to present. I was apparently looking too glamorous, although I found it very hard to believe that a short-assed, fat-faced Irishman could possibly give this impression. Still, I decided to be flattered and compromised my matinée idol look by applying my trusty Max Factor black pancake and that wonder of the world of modern coiffure, hair gel. The first application made me look like Al Jolson crossed with Jack the Ripper. Adrian intervened. 'I think you've taken me rather too literally, Ken.' A Henry that looked like the Boston Strangler wasn't going to work either. We did crack this look, but it took several performances. I have never really been any good at stage make-up. Before the photo-call for *Henry V* I made the fatal mistake of listening to a fellow actor who had watched part of the dress rehearsal from the gods. 'You're so fair, lovey. We can't see your eyes. You've got to fill in your eyebrows and use more mascara.' Never listen to advice like that. Always take a look from out front at other people first. As a result of all this I am now haunted by pictures of that production where I look like Joan Collins *and* Groucho Marx.

The audience reaction to the previews was mixed. Some people wanted their warrior king in red, white and blue with no inner doubts, while others wanted the play to come firmly down on the anti-war ticket. Very few could ignore the emotional impact of our production which, if nothing else, was distinguished by the sight of Branagh looking all of twelve in the title role.

The days during the last previews had been occupied with the usual process of persuading my mother to attend the opening. Both she and my father were very intimidated by the 'Royal Shake-spearian Company' (as my father called it), but the major problem for Mother was the meal afterwards. As it was a special occasion I suggested we eat in the very grown-up Box Tree restaurant next to the theatre: there would be Mum and Dad and the rest of the family, David Parfitt and his girlfriend, Sue, Alistair Conquer and his wife.

'I can't have anything with sauces, son. I'd better not come, I'd let you down.'

I went into my familiar routine. 'You don't have to *have* anything with sauces.'

'I'll never be able to read the menu.'

'*I'll* read the menu.' I couldn't remember if it was in French, but I spoke even less than my mother, so we both had a problem. 'I'm sure they'll do you something plain.'

'Sure, that'd be embarrassing.'

'Do you want to bloody eat or not?'

'Don't shout at me, I'm not coming now.'

'I'm not shouting and yes, you are coming.'

Christ knows how many conversations it took before we established that my mother would come, but only if she wasn't forced to speak to anyone, and only if I sat next to her at dinner. The annoying thing was that I knew she would talk to *everyone*, enjoy herself hugely and be the star of the evening. At least it took my mind off the merry monarch.

It wasn't until months later that I realised, because people told me, quite how much tension had been flying round the Memorial Theatre on the night of the opening. Everyone was terrified that I would cock it up. There were over a hundred members of the press in the audience, and adrenalin was high. The RSC had taken a great risk, and were extremely tense, but fortunately I was insulated by my obsession with the part and with domestic catering arrangements. I was nervous, but it was a first night that I rather enjoyed. I don't think I was especially good, but somehow I didn't expect to be, the important thing was to get through it. I felt sure the production was rooted in the right soil and having planted myself, I assumed that it would take the full two years for the performance to fully grow. There were so many things to develop: my voice and speech, all the different aspects of the role, and I hoped that the critics would give me the benefit of the doubt.

The response from the packed Stratford auditorium was very enthusiastic, and backstage there was the usual hysteria. Adrian walked backwards into my dressing-room partly because he was drunk, but mostly, I'm sure, because his contact lenses had disappeared into his bloodstream. His internal organs were confused, but he was delighted, and within seconds it was a re-run of *Another Country*. The dressing-room was full of family and friends who were visibly relieved because, although it was Shakespeare, they had actually understood it. My dad offered the usual qualification. 'Mind you, son, we wouldn't know.'

In the restaurant my mother was presented with a plaice in some mysterious sauce which I managed to scrape off before she left the table. Although I enjoyed the meal, I probably expended more energy on the post-show domestics than on the actual performance. 'Twas ever thus. The next day I did not rise at 6 am to buy the newspapers but allowed Pat Marmont to choose the nicest remarks and read them to me. The reviews were obviously mixed but the general consensus seemed to be that this was a rich production, sometimes controversial, which would only get better as time went on. Some critics thought I was over-parted, and some thought I over-acted, but several thought I was good, and I convinced myself that we had got away with it so that I could relax and start enjoying the season.

I had built in a rather clever tactic to relieve me of possible post-opening depression. I had twelve days off (the one holiday I would have that year) while *The Merchant of Venice* opened and before *Golden Girls* started rehearsal, and very generously, the RSC gave me permission to fulfil a yearning that I had had for some time. I checked on all the flights, allowed a day or two for delays, and celebrated my first Stratford opening by holidaying for six whole days in Australia. It seemed mad to everyone but for me it was the perfect way to put such an intense experience into perspective. The tonic of seeing friends and the brevity of my stay removed jet lag almost completely. Most of my Australian friends had only the faintest idea of what the Royal Shakespeare Company was, and by the time I returned I had the very healthy sensation that I'd just done a rather nice little play in the provinces which would be seen by few folk and was nothing to get hot and bothered about. By the time I finished at the RSC, I realised that I needed a trip to Australia every ten days.

On my return, there were plenty of things to keep me occupied. Kensington Palace had asked me to provide four seats for a performance of *Henry V* for Prince Charles and his guests. While I was about it, I booked three seats directly behind for my parents and sister who I knew would be thrilled if the great visit actually came to pass. I had sent the tickets off and was sworn to secrecy, but on the day before the magic date I was worried that I had heard nothing, and I decided to check with the House Manager. Perhaps security had been in touch with him. I asked him rather gingerly, 'I think we may have some VIPs coming tomorrow night. I wondered if you had heard anything?'

'Anyone in particular? The Prime Minister? The Queen?'

'Not exactly.' They clearly thought I was mad. Never mind. Early the next morning the phone rang and the shrieking voice of the House Manager announced, 'He's coming, he's coming. Oh God, oh God, the theatre's not clean. What'll we do?'

My parents informed me that the reactions of the audience when their Royal Highnesses took their seats were an entertainment in themselves. The visit was entirely private, so the surprise was great for everyone, and the news spread like wildfire front and backstage. At the beginning of the second half the stalls audience were waiting down at the front, staring up at the balcony to get a view of the Royal return, and in the upper balcony, people had crowded down to the front to do the same thing. Instead, they were faced with my mum and dad who seemed to take all this attention in their stride. Charles and Diana returned and the place was an uproar of cheering and whistling. One of the first speeches in the second half was Henry's 'Upon the King' soliloquy which deals, among other things, with the lack of privacy in royal life. From the audience that had just robbed Prince Charles of this very thing there was an almost audible shudder. The penetration of Shakespeare's lines was chilling.

I spoke to the Prince and his wife afterwards. He seemed much moved by the evening and said as much in a letter which he wrote some weeks later. Not only did he feel a very personal connection with the story, but both he and Princess Diana were both fascinated by the process of acting, by what you actually *feel* when you're being angry, sad, or whatever. It was a satisfying and all too brief conversation that confirmed our rapport and intensified my admiration for the man who was about to fight his way through the ten thousand-strong crowd that had gathered outside the theatre since news of the visit had swept round Stratford.

Golden Girls was a new play by Louise Page, which no one in the Company seemed to know very much about. The first actors conversations concerning such a project were always about what part we were playing, and jocular-modest was the dominant tone in these exchanges.

'So what are you playing?' I would ask.

'Well, the characters aren't fully developed yet. All I know is I'm playing the lead. What about you?'

'Well, actually I think *I'm* playing the lead.'

I asked around. Jimmy Yuill, Josette Simon, Polly James, Kate Bufferey. They were all playing the lead, and that made nine of us in total. I didn't know what the story was but it was supposed to be about athletics – clearly it concerned a nine-headed monster who'd been chosen to run for England.

The first day's rehearsal arrived and there was no script. It did make an appearance in unfinished bits which we all took away to digest, and for the rest of the day the Stratford phone lines were red hot. After the initial scouring of the text to assess the quantity of a character's lines, there were several irate telephone calls to Barry – it'll have to change, I'm not playing this. The usual stuff. Then there were the demure casual calls from folks who had enormous parts, saying, this is really very good, I'm so glad she sees me like this. I came very low in the lines count, but I could hardly complain after *Henry V*. I was looking forward to finding out about athletics and working with a group of really strong actresses. The play turned out to be the story of a British women's relay team and their Olympic adventures, and the plot was full of drug scandals, blackmail, and love affairs. The rehearsal period had begun and all of us got on with the often indulgent process of researching the part.

In this case, it meant athletics training. Jimmy Yuill and I were the male athletes, he the strangely named 'Laces', a trainer, and I, if you can believe it, a 100-metre sprint champion. The play was to be performed in Stratford's smaller theatre, the Other Place, and with seating for only 250 and the audience too close for comfort, vanity

152

insisted that we get ourselves into a sufficiently impressive physical condition. Like myself, Jimmy enjoyed a pint and, unlike myself, smoked himself stupid. For both of us, measures had to be drastic. While the girls pursued sprint training, Jimmy and I enlisted the help of Brian Blessed, the Company's fitness fanatic, who agreed to take us through a training programme that would leave us looking like the young Olympians we needed to be. Cramped together in the front room of Brian's Stratford cottage, Jimmy and I wheezed our way through interminable press-ups and sit-ups and pull-ups and definitely no let-ups. Brian simply smiled all the way through these pre-rehearsal and lunchtime agonies.

A favourite torture was the end-of-work-out run. Brian's cottage was close to Stratford racecourse and strapping weights to our ankles and wrists he would send us off through the spring mud to run twice round the circuit. After these runs we would arrive back at Brian's cottage, me exhausted and panting, and Jimmy a hospital case, and despite the hot bath and sweet tea which Brian would provide, nothing could make us recover sufficiently to do anything other than fall fast asleep during any rehearsal that followed. From then on we decided that living the part had to stop and acting ought to take over. Arnold Schwarzenegger had nothing to fear from us.

Rehearsals were difficult. I felt very sorry for Barry Kyle, who made me aware for the first time of the pressures of the RSC timetable on its directors. On the Saturday before rehearsals started he had just finished a production and immediately after *Golden Girls* opened he would begin work in London on another. For Barry and for almost all his fellow directors, this was a familiar schedule. Although he worked like a Trojan he was quite clearly exhausted, and the behaviour of the cast didn't help matters. Louise's re-writes were arriving very slowly, and everyone was desperately throwing their weight around and implying that they might leave at any moment. The actors felt betrayed, Louise felt persecuted, and Barry, I'm sure, felt both; this combination of circumstances had contributed to exacerbating the already difficult task of bringing a new play to life. It was my first experience of an overtly combative rehearsal period, and although there was no malice in the air, there were very strong differences of opinion.

I wish that Barry and I had had a difference of opinion about my accent. In my attempts to give definition to what seemed an under-written part, I decided to use a Geordie brogue. I thought that the success of the many athletes from Gateshead would make this sound familiar, realistic and topical, and I convinced myself and Barry that I had a good ear for these things. It wasn't always totally under my control. In the night-time sequence of *Henry V* I had used a Welsh accent in order to underline the king's disguise. We had several real Welshmen in the Company, I did the research and became a real dyed-in-the-leek Welshman, although, as one reviewer pointed out, 'In the night-time sequence Mr Branagh is effortlessly a Geordie.'

It seemed that all I had to do was think I was playing my athlete Welsh and it would come out as the Gateshead hero. Sometimes, in truth, it did, but more often than not the accent would arrive at Gateshead via New Delhi and Australia. Well, athletics is an international language.

With only days to go we received the last scenes of the play, and many of us were still confused by the convolutions of the plot. I still don't know whether the leading athlete had taken the drugs or not, or whether the 'drug' was actually a placebo. Fortunately by the time we reached this point in the play my character was cracking up and it was quite conceivable that he had no idea what was going on. The breakdown I had to act was a tricky affair: I found it quite impossible to give the necessary emotional weight and retain any intelligibility in the accent – it veered all over the place – you either had Hamlet in tears, or what sounded like an inexplicable Peter Sellers mumbling 'Goodness gracious me.'

With confidence in our work at its lowest ebb we started to preview, and with the divine logic that operates in such cases, we realised immediately that we had a hit on our hands. Barry had provided an ingenious production that miraculously conveyed the smell and feel of a real athletics stadium, all in the confines of that tiny tin hut. The relay race finale, complete with strobe lighting and *musique concrète*, was a real theatrical coup. Audiences came away as excited as if they'd been to an Olympic meeting. In the course of our self-indulgent rehearsals we had lost all sense of the play's values, and while our reaction to the play's success was still tempered by these feelings, we were mightily relieved that it was a success and that we could work away at it as we played it through the year. I had learned a valuable lesson about not getting bogged down in rehearsal, and that it was essential to be as honest about the play as possible. It had also left me genuinely worried about the welfare, spiritual and artistic, of Barry in particular and the RSC directorate in general. I thought, quite simply, that they must all be knackered, and that good work was difficult under such conditions.

With *Henry V* and *Golden Girls* now both in the Stratford repertoire I was performing three or four nights a week. When *Golden Girls* opened, there was one day free before rehearsals started for *Hamlet*, and I had barely caught my breath from seeing Tony Sher's dazzling Richard III the night before when I found myself back in the Conference Hall with the five other *Hamlet* principals discussing our preliminary thoughts with Ron Daniels. This was the beginning of two or three days of advance rehearsal before the main six week block, and after that there would be a whole month of previews – a comparatively luxurious preparation time.

Roger Rees had returned to the RSC to play Hamlet, and it was his first major role with the Company since his huge success as Nicholas Nickleby. Brian Blessed was Claudius, Frank Middlemas was Polonius, and Frances Barber and Nicholas Farrell, who had both received great acclaim in that season's production of *Camille*, were joining the *Hamlet* company to play Ophelia and Horatio. The final member of this group was Virginia McKenna, who was joining the RSC to play Gertrude. I was particularly glad of Brian Blessed's presence in the group. A large man in every sense, he concealed a tremendous warmth and tranquillity under a surface gruffness and apparent coarseness designed to keep people at arm's length. He is totally without malice, and his outrageous humour would be a marvellous counterbalance as we set to work on this forbidding and complex tragedy.

It was a pleasantly informal way to start work on this great play. A director, sometimes faced with a full RSC company of perhaps thirty actors, can often feel that a lecture is required on the first day, a talk which will give a detailed analysis of the approach he or she is going to take. Often brilliant, this technique can be very dangerous, and I have seen it take up the whole of the day, when, however dazzling the analysis, the company tend to be more worried about costumes and sets and other apparently mundane matters. Ideas can also become too easily fixed at an early stage if rehearsals are forced to fit in with a rigidly preconceived idea of the play. Preparatory work and a view of the play is absolutely necessary but, as with actors, the degree of flexibility required is enormous.

This small group took all pressure away and it was one of the luxuries of RSC resources that this overtime session could take place.

Our first talks threw up some fascinating issues. At first we all listened dutifully to Ron, who talked with great passion (what else?) about the three levels of the play. I wasn't quite sure which levels they were or if there were only three but it seemed a useful way to start talking about it. Brian Blessed was determined to be less rarefied, he'd come to the RSC very humble about his relationship to the classics, and he was a mature, successful actor who still wanted very much to learn. He was always asking, in a very direct way, 'What are the rules of Shakespeare?' A big one that.

On our first morning he offered his first thoughts on Claudius. Up to this point everyone had been very timid in the face of Ron's intellect. Brian started to develop some of Ron's ideas about the character, but quickly reverted to a rather more dynamic and instinctive approach.

'The thing is Ron, I believe that . . . basically, when you look at this man and, you know, begin to wonder what makes him tick . . .'

'Yes?'

Brian was clearly burning to say it. He shot a quick glance at Virginia who sat beaming at him with her English rose fragility. He decided to plunge in.

'Well, the thing is . . . he just wants to fuck her.' I clenched my buttocks on Virginia's behalf. Although Virginia is not at all prudish, this was her first day at the RSC and her first experience of Brian's rehearsal style. I adored Brian, but I sensed this was perhaps not the best opening line, however true it might be about Claudius. 'He just can't keep his bloody hands off her. In the palace, in the garden, in the bloody kitchen. He's wild for her, she's in his blood and every time he sees her he wants to give her one.'

It seemed that Brian had finished. I looked for relief on Virginia's face. I thought we were over the worst.

'And the thing is . . .' – oh, Christ – 'she fucking *loves* it.'

I was ready to leap up and catch Virginia when she fell off her chair. Brian was unstoppable. 'Old Hamlet couldn't get it up. She hasn't had a decent fuck in years and here comes this bloke, her brother-in-law, who is a fucking stud and she cannot resist. She's just the same, she wants it every hour of the bloody day.'

By this time Ron Daniels had broken into a cold sweat. Brian's monologue had come out with his familiar all-embracing energy. This would not be a weak Claudius. Brian finally rounded off his character assessment. 'I mean, that's got to be it. A great big unstoppable plonker . . . I mean I think that's part of it . . .' He looked around amiably asking for agreement. 'I mean, I don't know what you feel, Virginia?'

· 'I think it's time for a cup of tea.'

Well done, Ron. It was a helpful break, and it helped to forge a very strong friendship between Brian and Virginia who, incidentally, were united in their advocacy of animals' rights. Brian's approach has its advantages.

The following Monday was the first full day's rehearsal with the entire company, and it revealed the curious advantages and disadvantages of the great RSC machine. Before us we had detailed costume designs, a set model, and an explanation from Ron about how everything would work. I was very happy with my Laertes costume but I couldn't help wondering whether this was the most effective production process. A part of me looked at the costume and thought, 'So that's how I have to play it.' Actors want it both ways: they'd like enough time to come up with ideas for costumes and props, but at the same time they resent providing the input for a director who has not arrived with sufficient ideas. The RSC had a huge staff, an enormous number of productions, and it simply wasn't practical or economic to make lots of last-minute decisions about production details. Advance work had to be done and that preparation could be constricting for the actors, who had to accept that certain decisions had already been made.

When I was playing Hamlet at RADA, the director was quoted as saying to the actor playing Claudius, who was rehearsing the Laertes plotting scene, 'We've really just got to get on with this as quickly as possible. All this stuff with Claudius and Laertes is where the audience are simply waiting for Hamlet to come back on again.' Well, not exactly, but I know what he means.

My Laertes, of course, would be different. The great idea arrived in week two: Laertes was mad. It was as simple as that, and I couldn't understand why no one had spotted it before. Nearly four hundred years of Shakespearian acting had gone by, and it was my revelation which would change the accepted view of Laertes.

It took three weeks of foaming, twitching and yelling to realise that this might perhaps not work. The play does deal with madness to a great extent, but so many of the other characters are so much madder, that poor old Laertes gets left behind. Nevertheless the flirtation with this idea did yield positive results. I wasn't mad but I did manage to get in cross, annoyed, perplexed and 'Blimey, all my family are dead – I'd better kill Hamlet'. This led me to the great discovery for the previews: Laertes was thick, as the proverbial plank, and that's why he was unstable, frightened, aggressive and finally vulnerable. He was a little man surrounded by great men and events that were way beyond his comprehension. With my typical leanings to excess, for a week or so Laertes resembled the Peter Sellers character in *Being There*.

Ron went along with all this, and showed remarkable patience, as did Virginia and Brian who never knew what was going to hit them when Laertes returned from Paris. For a while Frances Barber thought we should change parts: she could revenge her father and I could go and drown in the weeping brook. Silliness fell away as previews started. Roger was producing quite brilliant things as Hamlet and in its early stages the production had great clarity of narrative and tremendous commitment from the cast. My continuing experience of playing Henry was enormously helpful, it had increased my vocal power and my new confidence in playing the role was so marked that I had a few days of delayed shock and anxiety at the thought of how rough the performance must have been when we opened. Thank God we can't feel everything at once.

Hamlet opened to a divided press who ran the usual gamut of opinions about the production and performances. I had some good mentions and received further careers advice. 'Mr Branagh cannot speak the verse. He is a resolutely modern actor.' I rather liked the second bit. Traditional *and* contemporary, that's what I long to be.

Love's Labour's Lost started rehearsal before *Hamlet* had finished previewing – such was the increasingly frenetic pace of the Stratford season. The day began at 10, six days a week, and there would be rehearsal until 5.30, and at 7.30 most of the Company on any one night would have a show to do. At this stage my nights off – the nights *The Merchant of Venice* was playing – were increasingly rare. But not as rare as a visit from Trevor Nunn, with Terry Hands, the joint artistic director of the RSC.

The great day came in the middle of the season. The entire Company gathered in the Conference Hall. It was the first time I'd seen this man whose work I so admired, and I was desperate for him to see *Henry V*. Terry Hands had already made a visit and had been most kind and encouraging about the performance. I learnt a great deal from Trevor's performance that day. He is unquestionably a star. He sat leaning forward in his chair, speaking quietly in that warm, honeyed voice, and within five minutes the entire Company were leaning forward and straining to hear him. The impression was of a room of worshippers. Everyone was afraid to move in case they missed something in Trevor's address which took on more and more the feel of a quiet religious chant.

He spoke of this as a 'confessional'. He was well aware of his absence from the Company and knew that many of us felt hurt. Things would change. The whole speech was completely beguiling. He seemed, as they say, a regular guy. He talked of his hopes for the Company, his plans for the new musical *Les Miserables*, which he hoped very much would include some of us, and as far as his failure to see the work at Stratford was concerned, he was determined to put that right. His triumphant finale was pitched to the mesmerised audience in a tone of quiet, Martin Luther King intensity. Trevor 'had a dream', and that dream appeared to be to see all the Stratford shows within a fortnight. I imagine that subsequently he woke up and found other things to do. The next time I saw Trevor was twelve months later. Still dreaming, I presume.

The idealism I had felt on joining the RSC had been severely eroded, and many other actors felt the same way. Part of the problem was that the system raised expectations which were sure to be disappointed – the tone and substance of a Terry Hands speech, right at the beginning of the season in a London Company meeting, was built on the premise that we were one big family. This notion seemed to be the legacy of an RSC philosophy which began in the early sixties, based on the experience of a small, close-knit group of actors and other artists who came under very personal control and concern from the then artistic director, Peter Hall. It was an ideal situation in many ways: there was just the one Stratford theatre, and there was a much smaller number of productions played for a much shorter season. The tradition of artistic paternalism that Trevor and Terry wanted to continue was much easier in those days. Things were more manageable, and actors' commitments would be for periods of months, not years. When I joined the RSC there were four permanent theatres, a fifth about to start building and a sixth in preparation.

The physical growth of the Company reflected its success, and the highlights of this amazing development were the stuff of my student reading. However, the Company philosophy did not seem to have developed in the same way over the last ten years. It simply wasn't possible for Terry or Trevor to lead the Company in the way they had done – it was too big, it was dispersed geographically, creating major logistical problems, and laid a huge burden on the directors themselves. The system had become highly pressurised and enormous, and it struck me as wrong to encourage actors to expect an old-fashioned paternalism from joint artistic directors who did not have time to implement this.

Disenchanted RSC stalwarts talked with regret of the old days when you could talk to Trevor at any time about anything: the part, the play, or the rent you were paying on your cottage. The acting company seemed to require qualities from its leadership that could not be supplied. The directorship, by the same token, felt aggrieved, I think, at the lack of understanding on the part of the actors. In response to all this confusion the actors weren't exactly in a state of revolution, but they were, for better or worse during this time of intense change in the Company, beginning to assert themselves. At times it seemed closer to school with the actors as the stroppy sixth-formers and the directors as the misunderstood teachers, and both sides could assume these roles with depressing ease.

Next on the agenda was *Love's Labour's Lost* and, once again, Barry Kyle was being stretched to the limit. He did a magnificent job with a collection of increasingly argumentative actors, among whom I was chief. By this stage I had lost all perspective of the genuine advantages and luxuries that the RSC enjoyed, and I seemed to notice only the negative elements. My best interests were for the quality of the work, but the atmosphere resembled the claustrophobic self-obsessed world of drama school at its worst. Instead of assessing the quality of the excellent designs for *Love's Labour's Lost* I became exercised by the fact that everything had been decided beforehand. I did *not* want to wear a red waistcoat as the King of Navarre. To the management I must have seemed like a spoiled child.

This foot-stomping was partly induced by the particular atmosphere in Stratford at the end of the season. Like the directors, we too were absolutely knackered. The world began and ended in this strange, isolated town. There was no single person to talk to about the way things were, so we fought it out among ourselves. God knows what we expected of an artistic director: a nanny/psychiatric nurse/estate agent/mega-talent, that was all.

Love's Labour's Lost was warmly reviewed. It had the benefit of a wonderful Berowne from Roger Rees and a very strong group of women. I was way over the top as the King of Navarre – 'Benny Hill', said one fan, which was fair enough. I became very depressed by the whole thing, a feeling that was shared by many others in the company, although the reviews and the response of the audiences were very good. Many of us felt we could do much better. It wasn't just an end-of-season disillusionment, but it was a mixture of anger and sadness at our mutual complicity with a dangerous smugness that was developing in the Company. Somehow this big machine wasn't working.

All these confused reactions were poured into a one-act play called *Tell Me Honestly* which I wrote for the Company's innovative fringe season in Newcastle, and had its première in March, 1985.

David Parfitt, a Geordie himself, was in Newcastle and helped me with the show, and with the London transfers. We were building a small library of information about printing and posters, budgets and publicity, and we were gaining real satisfaction from this degree of connection to the work. It was referred to as an in-house satire, as I had based what loose structure there was on the end-of-year interviews that each actor had with Terry Hands. The piece was never meant to be malicious or accusatory, but I wanted to find through comedy a way of pointing out what seemed to be going wrong. The blame, such as it was, for Company uneasiness lay with everyone, but not everyone saw the joke. Luckily, this did not prevent the play from transferring to London or from transferring yet again for a limited season to the Donmar Warehouse Theatre. The very act of writing, directing and producing the piece with my fellow actors was in itself a way of understanding what it was we were rebelling against.

Tell Me Honestly described the desire, encouraged by the Company, to be more involved on every level and the frustration felt at not being able to achieve this in co-operation with the management. Many company members felt that they could offer more to the Company than just their basic skills as actors, but the system could not cope with their needs. My appetite for involvement, for real participation, was far stronger than any ambition simply to stay with the Company in order to play leading roles.

The Company management was perplexed by my attitude. Why couldn't I just shut up? Why couldn't we all just shut up and stop being ungrateful? This antagonism emerged in a protracted pay dispute distinguished by unreasonableness on both sides, with the RSC threatening to take *Henry V* out of the repertoire, making me certain that I was being singled out for special punishment. I threatened to resign, and finally the Company made an application to a special Trust Fund in order to find the nominal extra sum.

The whole episode depressed me no end. During the long months of this dispute the prospect of my leaving the Company at the end of the Newcastle season was both real and terrifying. I was not a fully established actor, and I was afraid that this new bolshiness would haunt me and stop me working ever again. My parents and friends begged me to give in, and I tortured myself about whether it was right to persist. In the end, when I got what I wanted, there was no sense of victory at all. Terry Hands' last minute farcical intervention over the Trust Fund was the final straw. I felt I was working for a Company that didn't really need me, and that if it weren't for the interruption it would have caused to the London performance schedules, I would have been out on my ear. To my great disappointment no single director had intervened in the dispute. I felt abandoned and it was clear that we were not agreed on the expectations of what the Company wanted from me and what I wanted from it.

The opportunist in me simply got on with things. I had the chance to play *Henry V* in London in a marvellous production, and it might establish me so that I would have enough weight to put my money where my grumbling mouth was. Through that Barbican season I was already planning a production of *Romeo and Juliet* in which I would play Romeo. I would have to direct it as well, as I was very interested in the play as a whole, and I would use the production to experiment with the size of company and working methods that my experience was telling me was necessary – an attempt to return, if you like, to the model of the early RSC. *When* I could do this was quite another matter.

Thanks to the RSC's regular employ I was able to meet a monthly mortgage payment, buy a flat, and protect myself forever from the north-west London underworld. I went dutifully through the Barbican season causing as little trouble as possible and observing the strange phenomenon of the RSC's London transfers. After the London first night of *Henry V* I compared the notices with those of the Stratford opening: despite the decidedly mixed tone of the original reviews the new set welcomed this as the 'acclaimed production'. They talked of it having already garnered 'raves'. In truth the production had grown enormously and my own performance was immeasurably improved. We played 139 performances in total, and only after 120 performances and fourteen months did I feel that I was actually beginning to embody the role in the fullest way. The quest to conquer Henry had been very difficult but very exhilarating, and like Hamlet, I wanted to return to it as soon as possible.

There were no improvements in my Laertes or King of Navarre – a good performance gets better, a bad performance gets worse. Laertes had been mad and then thick, now he was just boring. Against all my better judgement the King of Navarre did end up rather too often being a return to my gratuitous clowning.

Corpsing had not improved, and I let myself down repeatedly. A clutch of angry reprimands used to hound me out of the Barbican:

'I think it's *disgusting*!'

'It's *not* what we're here for.'

'Young man, it is simply not good enough, and neither are you.'

It was getting harder to laugh.

On performance 138 of *Henry V* at the Barbican the word went round: 'he' was in. I wondered who 'he' was? The Shah of Iran? Ronald Reagan? Donald Duck? No, Trevor. Trevor was in. I wasn't sure why. I knew that some of the Company had written to *Jim'll Fix It* asking to meet him, and perhaps this was his response. Well, my time was nearly up at the RSC and he wasn't going to get away with catching the penultimate performance of a show that had opened the previous Stratford season. No, not without a piece of my mind. I wasn't going to be 'Trev'd', the famous charm would not work with yours truly. No way.

Dressing Room One, Barbican. Two minutes after curtain down. I'm just taking a shirt off when there's a knock at the door – right, here I go. I turned round to vent my spleen, but I could no longer see or hear. I had been enveloped in Trevor's hair and beard and deafeningly loud in my right ear was an enormous vowel sound which turned out to be, 'Huuuuuuuuuuuuuuuuuugely enjoyable.'

I tried to speak, but it was impossible. Eventually he let go of my hand, and stared intently at me as if I was a long lost brother. If it were possible he got more 'ooooo's into the next repetition: 'Really . . . huuuuuuuuuuuuuuuuuuuuuuugely enjoyable.'

I didn't dare speak. Despite the innocuous remark he looked as though he was going to cry. Oh. Hello. Here comes the big one. He was pumping my hand now as if he were leaving for the Front, definitely on the edge of a breakdown. The subtext was 'I'm worthless. I'm no one, but I will just try and say these things to you, a genius.' The body language was pure Uriah Heep. Martin Luther King returned for the closing lines. 'May I just say (pause. I thought he was going to fall over.) . . . may I just say that it is my very great ambition to work . . . with you (he started to move backwards) . . . really . . . (one hand on the door) . . . I really mean that . . . (fingers waving was all I could see) . . . Byeeee!!' The whole thing had taken a minute and a half.

Yes, I'd been 'Trev'd.'

In September 1985 I gave my last Laertes at the Barbican and took my leave of the Company. I felt some sadness but was certain of the wisdom of the move. Just before leaving, Terry Hands took me to lunch. He'd been to see *Tell Me Honestly* and I think had taken genuine note of all the actor-power that had manifested itself in this Company. He was also very perceptive about my performance of Henry V, and identified half a dozen things that would be tremendously useful to take into my next attempt at the role. There was no doubting the man's talent, and I regretted not having worked with him. He asked me straight out when I would like to rejoin the Company and what I would like to do.

'Direct and play in *Romeo and Juliet* with a company of my own choosing.'

He replied, 'Let me give you one piece of advice: don't. Firstly it'll ruin your own acting. Secondly, it'll never work. Ian McKellen's tried running actors' companies three times and still hasn't got it right. Thirdly, why don't you do it with us?'

'What?'

'We will give you your own company within the RSC, and you will have absolute choice over designers and directors, even stage management. What do you say?'

I tried not to look too shocked. 'Well, this is amazing, Terry. We must talk about it.'

I left the lunch table and never heard another word from Terry on the subject. If this was to be anything more than fantasy, I would have to do it on my own.

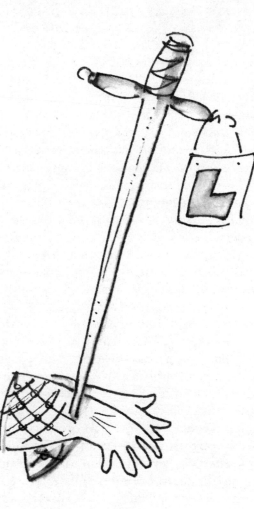

SEVEN

'O, brave new world'
THE TEMPEST

It seemed that I was not able to function well in large institutions. The RSC had given me marvellous opportunities, for which I was very grateful, and yet I left the Company with feelings of great frustration. I had enjoyed the excitements of rehearsals with Adrian, Barry and Ron, and the blaze of acting energy manifest in the fringe season had been exhilarating. However I felt that the size and merciless timetable of productions was working strongly against a consistently high quality in the work, and the burgeoning bureaucracy created tensions and fears among the members of the Company that were far from healthy. I had wanted so much to be a part of the RSC, but I was becoming increasingly unhappy, and decided to leave behind the impotent rage that had eaten me up for the last part of my time there.

There was no point in continuing to fight that system. I would go it alone. I knew the play I wanted to do. I had the energy and I had the passion, but what I didn't have was the money or the courage. On entering the big wide world I realised how much of my griping had been bolstered by being professionally secure; once the protection of the institution was gone so was most of my bottle. It would take something else to convert my natural cowardice and desire to work into a resolve sufficiently strong to achieve something.

In any case after all that raging, I needed something easier to do. Something quite different from the broader sense of responsibility that I felt at the RSC. I was also tired. I lacked the bravery of the McDiarmids. D. H. Lawrence came to the rescue. It was the centenary of his birth and Central Television had commissioned Alan Plater to write a ninety-minute television film about his early life.

I read the script and rediscovered my love for Lawrence the man. *Coming Through* covered the period up to his elopement with Frieda Weekley at the age of twenty-seven. This was the Lawrence I loved: young, passionate, brutally honest, intensely romantic and unafraid of the feminine side of his nature. In simple terms it was the story of a

166

bright lower-middle-class boy who had to come to terms with a talent that would cause him to leave his background, and his bewilderment and excitement at falling deeply and passionately in love with a married woman. I knew this period of Lawrence's life intimately. His letters are wonderfully honest and his literary work during this period reflects his emotional development. An immense amount of written material is available to flesh out the marvellous portrait provided by Alan, and for the first time in ages I could steep myself totally in a part. There was no worrying about designs or verse-speaking or the abuse of resources; I was simply being paid very well to play a part on film which offered me every opportunity for research into a subject which I loved.

During the two months of preparation for the part I lost two stone – I was determined to lose the look of a cubist cherub and produce the gaunt Lawrentian cheeks. It worked, and I looked as ill as Young Bert. I read everything that Lawrence wrote during this period, and I visited Eastwood where Lawrence lived and I explored the houses that his family had occupied. I went to the British Sound Archive and listened to recordings of Frieda Weekley talking about 'Lorenzo'. Contemporary accounts of Lawrence were invaluable: girl-friends, teachers, and colleagues all had impressions of the man which were often quite different from the image of the tortured intellectual. 'Bert', as they all called him, was wonderfully sunny, a great mimic, and marvellous company. I wanted, as Alan Plater did, to present *this* rather than the vituperative woman-hater.

The director, Peter Barber-Fleming, was highly sympathetic to this approach, which made the whole experience delightful. The cast included Alison Steadman, Norman Rodway, and Helen Mirren as Frieda. The scenes between the two lovers were quite beautifully written, and the final result was a very moving and informative film, of which I was very proud. We'd spent six weeks filming it, Peter had spent six months working on it. There was one showing, late at night on ITV, and it has never been heard of since.

TV was obviously what I was destined for. Two weeks after the Lawrence finished I began work on Ibsen's *Ghosts*, with a small cast made up of heroes: Judi Dench as Mrs Alving, Michael Gambon as Pastor Manders, Freddie Jones and Natasha Richardson, and they were all terrible gigglers. The rehearsals seemed to go in waves of intense creative work, followed by debilitating fits of giggles, usually initiated by Gambon or Dench who were always able to stop laughing long before me. Ibsen can be melodramatic at the best of times, but *Ghosts* had more than its fair share of semi-comic curtain lines. After a morning of going mad from syphilis it didn't take much to turn me into a hysterical wreck.

Judi's delight in this laughter seemed to be bound up in her greatness as an actress. She seemed able to embrace every emotion whole-heartedly. There is an amazing, child-like quality in her acting which allows her to cry or laugh with the full abandon of a child. She assumes nothing, doubts herself constantly, but without indulgence, and seemed often genuinely pained at what she regarded as her inadequacy for the part. Although she could be strong and commanding in life, she retains great humility and vulnerability. In a part that offered her marvellous scope for her extraordinary gifts I experienced great acting at first-hand.

Then there was Gambon. If it were possible, Michael is actually wickeder than Judi, a deadpan teddy-bear who is merciless in twinkling at other people while keeping a straight face himself. During the recording, Elijah Mojinsky, the director, wanted us to perform a short dinner sequence. A silent thirty second piece that showed the desolate supper in the Alving household. They would not be recording sound, but the later cut version would be accompanied by music and would be used to suggest the passage of time. All he wanted was for Natasha, as the maid, to serve each of us in turn while a tracking camera took a close up of each gloomy Ibsen face. Michael was served first while on his close-up. The difficulties of concentration for this scene that Ibsen hadn't written were considerable. It was the end of a long recording day. We were all tired. Tough.

'Action' was called, and we solemnly began our desultory improvised dialogue. Natasha began, leaning over Gambon.

'Would the Pastor like some potatoes?'

Gambon replied. 'Yes, I'll have eleven please.'

The face remained impassive. Then as the camera passed him he bent double over his soup and when he looked up at me the tears were rolling down his face. Judi's close-up was next and although the shot revealed only head and shoulders I could see that her hands were white, gripping the table-cloth for dear life. Once the camera passed her she threw her hands up to her face and stuffed a serviette in her mouth. By the time the camera reached me I was watching two Titans of the English theatre in silent convulsions. I was helpless and it was too late. I could no more have produced a straight face than

168

swim the Channel. They tried for several minutes drying my eyes and asking Judi and Michael to turn round. It was no use, every time the magic word 'Action' was called I could hear the tell-tale whimpers from Dench and Gambon and then I was lost. After five minutes the Floor Manager said, 'It's absolutely no use. Mr Branagh, the director has asked me to tell you that you must get down from the table and leave the studio. Goodnight.'

The air had turned chill. I started the long walk across the studio like the naughty dog in a Lassie film. This was it, the end of my career. We all met in the make-up room, Dench, Richardson, Gambon and me swathed in shame. The next day we were very good *indeed*.

I still felt compelled to be more than just an actor, and I felt almost guilty at the fun I had in making *Coming Through* and *Ghosts*. For some time I had had an idea about an Irish topic that I wanted to write about, and the experiment of *Tell Me Honestly* had encouraged me to write again. With Puritan zeal at its height I spent the evenings after rehearsals for *Ghosts* in the kitchen of my Camberwell flat writing the first draft of *Public Enemy*. A collection of different ideas had come together, and the play was an attempt to focus on several issues: the effects of long-term unemployment, the influence of the media, organised crime, religious fervour, the psychology of killers. All of this was channelled into a narrative concerning a Belfast lad with a Jimmy Cagney fixation. I knew it wasn't *King Lear*, but it was my first attempt at a serious bit of writing. I showed it to a few friends, confirmed for myself the amount of work required for a second draft and despatched it to my bottom drawer.

By the end of 1985 I was exhausted, and the New Year began with a month in Australia, for a holiday on which I intended to write. This time I set out to write an autobiographical love story for television, and once again it was banished to the bottom drawer. I obviously couldn't keep still. I felt guilty at working and guilty at not working. The problem was not the work itself, it was the nature of the work: I felt sure I should be doing something else and didn't have the courage to make the break. I wanted to form a company which tapped the imagination and energy of the actors involved, a company which placed the actors in a central position. If the actors wanted to direct or to write, then they would be encouraged to do this, and it need not be at the expense of full-time writers and directors. It would be a practical re-alignment of the collaborative process between writer, actor and director that would step up the contribution of the performer. I wanted to work on Shakespeare, but I wanted it to be accessible. There *was* an audience for Shakespeare – whether it was Newcastle, Belfast or Reading, and not just for people who knew about RSC. I knew it wouldn't be possible to do everything straight away and I didn't really have any master plan. I just knew that I wasn't doing the right thing.

The offers of freelance work came in with gratifying regularity. I completed *Billy IV* and even tried my hand at situation comedy, but I was still avoiding the real task that I saw in front of me and which David Parfitt and I talked about incessantly. The courage would still not come, and there were other temptations. Alan Plater's strong recommendation secured me an interview for the leading male in the BBC's *Fortunes of War*, their latest classic serial. Based on Olivia Manning's sextet of novels, there were locations in Yugoslavia, Greece and Egypt, Alan's adaptation was superb, the character of Guy Pringle intriguing, and the foreign travel very enticing. Stuff running a company.

I read all the novels, and went to the interview as Guy Pringle: bulky, teddy-bearish and distracted. Thank God the director, Jimmy Cellan-Jones, was taken in. It was early April, 1986, and after the lunchtime meeting he offered me the part there and then. I would start filming in September and continue for nine months. It was a great relief, and I already felt guilty about the delay it would mean to starting a company, but it meant money and possibly the kind of fame that would attract people to the shows that I was planning for the future. Anyway it was a bloody marvellous part.

I began to edge nearer to the kind of real involvement with the theatre that I needed; my writing continued its secret progress, and I flexed more directorial muscles. *John Sessions at the Eleventh Hour* was the latest of John's extraordinary one-man shows. David and I were producing and overseeing the bar, programmes and box office with another production company. I also directed, which was compara- tively easy. John is a comic genius, but at that stage a little undisciplined in his approach to his material. I prevented him from assuming too much of his audience by playing the thick fourth former to John's PhD. The combination worked well and we thought seriously about planning another venture.

Moving from discipline to discipline, I enjoyed the learning process but was still restless. Now the film world beckoned. Clare

Peploe, the wife of Bernardo Bertolucci, was to direct a picture called *High Season*, a comedy thriller set on the island of Rhodes which took a light-hearted look at the clash between tourism and ancient culture in modern Greece. The script had had quite a history, and at one point Jack Nicholson had been lined up to play my part. I found it amusing to think that he and I could be up for the same role. Rik Mayall had been another star they had in mind, but eventually they had to use lesser mortals and so I was engaged to play the suburban James Bond character who stumbles his way through the story.

In prospect it seemed very exciting. Seven weeks on the island of Rhodes, living and filming in the village of Lindos. The script had its heart in the right place although it still seemed a little disjointed. I was sure this could all be sorted out and in any case, my part was funny. The people were nice – Jacqueline Bisset, James Fox, Irene Pappas, Sebastian Shaw and Robert Stephens – but there was no question that I was doing it for the money and for 'the crack'. The mercenary coward in full flow. But it didn't stop me moaning.

I'm hopeless in the sun. Why don't I ever realise? I'm a winter person. I had lots of time to kill, and the leisure nearly drove me mad. My ingratitude knew no bounds. The movie was an honest attempt to produce a charming light comedy, but there was a certain cheerful amateurism abroad which I found frustrating. Yes, I suppose I could have read *War and Peace*, but I've never had that kind of discipline. Instead I let my self-loathing and rage fire me in another way.

I sat down in my Lindos villa with a copy of *Romeo and Juliet*. I kept one with me most of the time, and I already had ideas for cuts in the text. Earlier in the year I'd made secret visits to the Shakespeare Centre in Stratford and read every prompt copy for each Stratford production since 1947, making copious notes and nicking everything that worked. I was convinced I could do the play with eleven actors. Hanging around in the Mediterranean sun I worked out which parts could be doubled and tried to construct a rough budget, basing my calculations on the time available between the end of the movie and the start of *Fortunes of War*. There were seven weeks exactly: three and a half weeks' rehearsal, three and a half weeks' playing. I made allowances for set and lighting and theatre rental, totted up the sums and worked out that we could do it for around £15,000. Good, *High Season* would pay for *Romeo and Juliet*.

The communication gods decided to plague me. From the tiny

telephone box in the post office at Lindos I rang David Parfitt to put the scheme to him, and after two days and numerous attempts I got through. He was free, and he would do it. We were off. The first problem was the venue. David rang the various fringe theatres we fancied – most were booked, or not interested in a show for which some queeny actor was going to be the director. Especially not a cocky little shit like me. It was obvious that I couldn't direct the operation from a Greek telephone box, and that I would somehow have to get back to London. This was an elaborate procedure: there were sufficient gaps in my filming schedule, but the production company was understandably reluctant to let me disappear in case disasters occurred in filming or indeed on my flights. I behaved appallingly and managed to make three trips home, on one occasion simply ignoring the orders of the producer who, very sweetly, didn't take me to court. They knew I was mad keen to do *Romeo and Juliet*, and not even the difficulties of obtaining a holiday charter flight could deter me. These return trips could only be booked from London, but I cajoled and bribed my way into getting hold of the magic tickets. The show had to go on.

On the first trip back I got nowhere. All the problems of the venture raised their head, and very few of the solutions. David had received resistance from almost every theatre owner – it was all very short notice and everyone needed to talk it through. This was no use to me, as I was on the tourist special back to Rhodes on Monday morning. Then Peter James, artistic director of the Lyric Theatre, Hammersmith, expressed interest. The 110-seat Studio theatre was available for our dates, but Peter most definitely wanted to talk to me first. Like a gent, he was prepared to come at the crack of dawn on Monday morning so that I could get to Gatwick for the eleven o'clock flight.

Peter set out all the sensible arguments against the venture: he was very happy to see the Studio used at a time when it would normally be closed but he was also genuinely concerned for me. Three and a half weeks was not a long time to rehearse the first Shakespeare you'd ever directed, and playing in it as well would compound the problem. Did I know what I was taking on? This would be my first appearance on stage since finishing as Henry V. There was likely to be a very close scrutiny of me in a part which I had never played before. I myself knew how much the great parts benefited from a period of playing in, and because of the limited run, we could give

172

ourselves only one preview before the performance would be judged by the national press. I still wanted to do it.

I put my reasons as cogently as I could. The first and very necessary one was my passion for the play and the part. My reading had taught me that Romeo had always been a difficult part. Some of the greatest poetry in the play is given to Juliet and to Mercutio, and Romeo can often seem very limp. Conveying his virility and youthful energy as well as the gradual access to true poetic feeling is a difficult process. Both the leading roles provided an eternal problem: they require technical accomplishment and maturity of a kind that is rare in actors who are the right age to play them. I felt that there was probably a possibility that over the next couple of years I might be asked to play the part somewhere, but it seemed to me that with every month and year that passed I would have less chance of conveying Romeo's very youth. I might act it better but I would feel it less, and I wanted to take a risk on my own rawness. The apparent impetuousness that characterised the mounting of the production had in itself the kind of energy that Romeo would need.

Rehearsal time was short, but I had seen six-week rehearsal periods yield two weeks' work. The discipline which was needed to get through the play in three and a half weeks galvanised rather than depressed me. I ran through my insurance policies. I had already made contact with Hugh Cruttwell, who had agreed to join the production as an artistic consultant, and he would be there to monitor my performance and to offer regular comments about the production. Russell Jackson, from the Shakespeare Institute in Stratford, agreed to act as text advisor. Both men were available to the cast at all times on a private basis, so that despite the lack of time there was a back-up system comparable with that of a large company.

As I explained finally to Peter, I hoped that all this would free me sufficiently so that I could attack the directing of the whole play, which was my chief motivation. I wanted as young a production as possible: a young Lord and Lady Capulet, a younger nurse. I wanted to implement cuts that really could create, with the appropriately fiery playing, the 'two hours' traffic of our stage', rather than the usual acting time of over three hours. I'd often seen productions of the play drag, and wanted to create the effect of fate *rushing* the lives of these two people to their tragic ends.

I was doing it for a new kind of audience, an audience that I felt would respond to such a gesture. I received letters from people who had seen me on television and who wrote of their desire to take a risk on Shakespeare, or even on just going to the theatre. They would talk of their feelings of intimidation, and there were accounts of deadly evenings at productions which had confirmed their worst fears. I wanted to reach a large group of potential Shakespeare-lovers, beyond the obvious range of RSC die-hards, and I knew that although we couldn't do everything in a limited London run, and although it might be rough and raw, at least it would be different, cheaper, and, I believe, never boring.

The financial side of independent production is fraught, since so many things are being attempted at once. We were clearly in no position to seek subsidy, but this was fair enough given the circumstances of the production. We wanted seat prices to be low enough to be available to a greater audience, and yet we were dependent on box office revenue. The actors would all be paid £100 a week, on top of which we had to pay National Insurance, and there were fees for design, publicity, lighting, and printing. With a sell-out run, I would still lose nearly £7,000 of the £15,000 that the show would cost. I invested the cash gladly and David Parfitt worked for nothing during the remaining weeks of my Greek tragedy until rehearsals began. I was still utterly determined to do it and Peter James shook my hand and smiled. If nothing else, he was convinced that I couldn't be stopped.

Back in Lindos I worked very hard on the text of the play. Now that the deal was done, I was terrified, as there was no turning back, and I worried about everything – the directing, the acting, and the producing, and when I finished worrying about that I started worrying about the money. I wasn't in a position to be a one-man Arts Council. Pat Marmont rang up with a rescue plan: Pat O'Connor was directing a film *A Month in the Country*, based on a beautiful novel by J. L. Carr. I'd met Pat O'Connor earlier in the spring, when he'd indicated that he would like me to play the part of Moon in the piece. Since then the money had fallen through and I'd given up on the project, but now it was back on, only it was filming right across the *Romeo and Juliet* playing dates. They'd worked out a way of compressing my scenes into two weeks of shooting, and it would begin the morning after *Romeo and Juliet* opened. They would provide a car to get me back to the theatre in the evening, but would I be prepared to take on that kind of work-load?

174

I asked Pat what the money was like. She told me, and I thought of the budget for *Romeo and Juliet*. 'Tell them I'll ride to the set on a bike, just send the cheque.'

I managed two more trips back to London over weekends, and with days to go managed to cast the entire piece. I was so grateful to the actors who bothered to come to the interviews that I seemed to spend the time apologising for the lack of time and for the fact that I was directing. Many people turned us down, but we did produce an exciting cast – a refreshing mixture of people I'd worked with, people I admired and people I didn't know.

When rehearsals did start, their brevity was a positive advantage for the terrified novice director. There wasn't time to argue about silly things, lots of homework had to be done in advance, lines had to be learned early and things got on with, and the pace helped me. I didn't have to provide half-hour lectures after each scene, and I used a form of actors' shorthand to make many of my points. The cast didn't expect a highly intellectual approach, although the presence of Hugh and Russell ensured that this was available.

The pressure was immense. I would stay up late at night or arrive very early in order to do my director's homework, and at lunchtimes there would be meetings about design or costume. There were also fight rehearsals and publicity to do in the evenings, usually in the form of interviews. That done, there would be a trip to David's flat, where we talked about VAT, budget expenses, publicity and box office. Because of the short run in a tiny theatre we were already a hot ticket, and we eventually sold out even before we opened. That was a worry – what if it was dreadful?

Several critics thought it was, and the Branagh-bashing that I'd expected took place to a certain extent, but there were some good reviews, especially for the other actors, which delighted me. However none of this bore any particular relation to the quality of the work itself – I had my own clear opinions about what we had achieved but it did seem very important that we weren't publicly dismissed if we were to develop this company idea further. I was thrilled now to give opportunities to people who were clearly destined to be important actors: Samantha Bond as Juliet was singled out for taking the play's greatest role with such tremendous conviction. Andrew Jarvis, as Capulet, gave a highly charismatic and dynamic reading, and both these actors have gone on to produce really marvellous work in the classics. Simon Shepherd, Mark

Hadfield, Anne Carroll, and all the cast provided very exciting things. As part of the very necessary seedbed for this kind of work I regarded the production as a total success.

Gielgud has described the process of 'catching up' that is involved when an actor is both playing a role and directing. This is far less of a problem if you've played the part before, but in creating my Romeo for the first time I really had set myself an enormous task. But not impossible. With the help of Hugh and Russell and audience feedback I felt certain that by the third week I was far from letting Samantha or any of the others down.

The 6 am drive to location for filming was tough. Pat O'Connor and Colin Firth, who played the leading role in *A Month in the Country*, made the filming itself most fulfilling. Colin is a supremely generous actor and he was very kind when it came to allowing my shots to be taken first in order to let me get to the theatre at the end of the day. There were some very hairy journeys, and I'm not sure who it took most out of: Romeo, arriving pale and wan, or the anxious cast of clockwatchers who thought that Juliet was going to have to *scream* 'Wherefore art thou, Romeo?' But this nerve-wracked schedule seemed the only thing capable of producing the kind of work I believed in and calming my die-hard Protestant worries about getting into debt.

Lots of actors came to see the show, and Peter James remarked that there was a marked difference in the rest of the audience, which he identified as predominantly young and new to Shakespeare. Several people walked out, and an equal number regaled me in the bar afterwards with their disappointments in the production, but lots of people loved it. I was most impressed when Terry Hands paid us a visit, and stayed behind to talk. He was very generous about the production, although he did say that it lacked a context, some identifiable place or country within which the feud in the play would have extra weight. The play could, for instance, be set in Israel with the Montagues and Capulets as Jews and Arabs, or in Belfast with a Protestant/Catholic conflict – an analogy that had already crossed my mind. I explained to Terry that this seemed to me not context but distraction. The feud in the play was a domestic one, not a religious one, and in altering this, you disguise a central issue in the play. In this production, and in any others I might tackle, I wanted to see whether fine performances from excellent acting imaginations could actually provide as much illumination for a play as a single dominating design or production concept. I had no particular antagonism to strong directorial ideas, but I wanted the actors' contribution to seem more than just a facet of the production.

For hundreds of years, for good and ill, the actor has been acknowledged as the chief vessel through which the play is understood. In recent times the emphasis has moved dangerously far from this principle. The kind of theatre which had emerged in the late forties and early fifties, and which had been pre-eminent ever since, had produced excellent results, but, in my brief experience, one of its chief failings was a frequent underestimation of the role of the actor. This change stemmed from a healthy suspicion of a star system often ruled by destructive egotism, of everything that had helped the theatre to stagnate in the way that it had. It seemed to me that things had moved too far, and that it was time to re-establish proper balance in regard to the actor's part in the process of putting on a play. Not every actor wanted the situation to change, and the director-as-guru mentality was convenient for the masochistic tendencies in some and, for others, it often provided a convenient shift in responsibility. The greater degreee of responsibility that my work was beginning to advocate was a potential threat to both kinds of actor, and, of course, there might be many who believed that everything was designed for the greater glory of Kenneth Branagh.

Terry inevitably suspected a degree of fickleness. His own experience told him that the rigours of mounting this production would have taken a heavy toll on me, and he said as much after the show.

'Well, have you got this out of your system now? When are you going to come back and join us?'

He knew it was a lost cause. I had my own masochistic tendencies. Despite the remarkable privilege, it seemed too easy to waltz back into a glorious organisation which I knew perpetuated conditions that I felt militated against a sustained quality of work. Striving in the commercial world simply to become rich and famous was also not an option – clocking up money and parts, manically cashing in on the temporary kudos I had received. No. I was *compelled* to pursue the idea of a semi-permanent company, and to attempt a balance between running the company and managing what was also selfishly important to me, a successful freelance career. In a way, the one was impossible without the other. If I believed in the potential of this work I wanted it to be seen by a lot of people. For this kind of work to be truly popular the public would need to know who I was, I would have no qualms about extensive press coverage, and I had to build as far as I could on my commercial possibilities. It was unrealistic to think that you could eventually reach large numbers of people in the theatre if they hadn't seen you on television or on film.

I came to the end of *Romeo and Juliet* and realised that when *Fortunes of War* was completed, nearly a year from then, I might have this commercial credit. If I was to capitalise on what *Romeo and Juliet* had taught me, and if I was to attempt a semi-permanent footing for this company, then now was the time to act. I had plays that I was keen to direct, there were actors I wanted to work with, and there was an increasing network of contacts within the theatrical establishment that made it simpler to deal with the practical realities of finding theatres. David and I had found a way of working that divided responsibility clearly and with complete trust, and I knew that together there would be sufficiently strenuous scrutiny of our plans to make them both realistic and possible. I needed to make a commitment to continue putting (quite literally) my money where my mouth was, and would have to deal with the fear and doubt that would constantly attend. I certainly did not feel sure of the success of such a venture, but, by the time my feet touched the tarmac in Yugoslavia for the first day's filming of *Fortunes of War*, I knew I had no choice but to go ahead.

Adventure

EIGHT

'Company, at what expense?'
HAMLET

After the excitement of London theatricals, it was not surprising to find Ljubljana a little dull. The place itself seemed strangely devoid of character, and our hotel, the east European version of a Holiday Inn, carried all the same scars of modern comfortlessness. But Ljubljana was certainly a convincing backdrop to our show, which was proceeding well under the jaunty and enthusiastic leadership of Jimmy Cellan-Jones. I had quickly built up a rapport with the leading actress, Emma Thompson. The heart of the series was the story of the marriage between Harriet and Guy Pringle, a young, stumbling union full of misunderstandings and anxieties set against huge international events which gave greater intensity to the domestic difficulties. Emma's understanding of the role of Harriet Pringle was complete, and it was enormously enjoyable to work with her.

Emma's character was on screen much more than mine, so Yugoslavia provided me with valuable time to think about the

formation of a company. David and I had already left practical plans in motion. Peter James had a copy of *Public Enemy* which he was reading with a view to a possible co-production the following year. During the whole period of *Romeo and Juliet* he had been particularly impressed by David's administrative acumen and much encouraged by the new and large audiences that we seemed capable of drawing, and I hoped that these things might encourage him to take a risk with the play.

I was asking other people to take risks. Earlier that summer I had visited Chichester to see *The Relapse*, in which John Sessions was appearing. Lord Foppington, my old audition character, was being played by Richard Briers. Although the production was in some ways uneven, it confirmed to me what a superb actor Richard Briers could be. With remarkable good taste, Richard and his family came to see *Romeo and Juliet*, we chatted in the bar afterwards and, as he was leaving, I accosted him with an idea that had struck me with extraordinary force as I sat in the stalls at Chichester. The next Shakespeare that I wanted to direct was *Twelfth Night*, but there would be no point in attempting a production unless a piece of anchor casting were achieved. In the Vanbrugh Richard seemed to be an actor bursting to explore a great role. I grabbed him on the stairs.

'I hope to do another Shakespeare next year. Wondered if you were in the market?'

He looked rather surprised. I had obviously had too many pints – this was hardly the place for job offers. 'Oh! Fire away.'

'Well, I want to do *Twelfth Night*, and I'd love you to consider playing Malvolio.'

'Blimey! You serious?'

'Yes. I'll tell you what, if you'll seriously consider it then we'll talk about it when I come back from Yugoslavia. I don't know yet where or how we're going to do it, but it will happen.'

'You're on.'

I could tell that Richard had meant what he said. He'd admired *Romeo and Juliet* and I felt sure that if we could come up with the practical details, then he would play the role. So far, so good.

John Sessions had spent his Chichester season and beyond producing the first draft of a massively ambitious one-man show about Napoleon. It was to contain immense amounts of factual detail about Napoleon's life, which would be presented through the medium of

John's comic genius. The characters in Napoleon's life were to be 'played' by the enormous gallery of actors and politicians that John could mimic with such savage accuracy. He wanted the show to be 'total' theatre, a combination of high and low culture that was visually exciting, fast and intellectually stimulating. John's aim was to convey the shape of this fascinating life, but above all, he wanted to entertain. He also wanted me to direct it, and it seemed that yet another piece for a potential first season was falling into place.

As I Guy Pringled my way through Yugoslavia (which was standing in for Romania) I kept in constant touch with David Parfitt about all these developments. I also bored my fellow actors rigid with the preliminary working-out of my ideas for the company's first season. Emma showed immense patience with the Garrick of Eastern Europe, who would spend time between takes saying, 'And what if we did . . . ?' Or, '*I* know a marvellous play . . .' Or, 'Have you ever seen . . . ?'

I was particularly prone to plan-making on the days off when the actors would get together for a trip. It was on one such trip that the final part of an opening season began to take shape. We'd 'gone over the wall' from Yugoslavia into Italy and had spent the day in Trieste trying to find out where James Joyce had lived, and searching for pasta to relieve us of the Yugoslav obsession with Schnitzels. It was tea-time in the main square, and Richard Clifford and I were sipping a cocktail while waiting for the bus back to the camp. 'Don't you think,' I said, 'that it would be incredibly useful for really fine actors who've played in the great Shakespearian plays to direct young actors in the same roles? I don't just necessarily mean stars. Nor do I mean a sort of piecemeal experiment. But if you had a real season where these novice directors could have the comfort of each other and where the conditions were controlled enough to reduce their worries over the technical aspects, don't you think one could make great developments in one's acting?'

Richard nodded. There was no stopping me now. I was well into my stride and well into my third Martini. 'A season that could develop new Shakespearian actors and directors, and which would consequently have a special quality. And it wouldn't be done in London, in a glare of publicity, but it would be protected and performed, at least to begin with, in a place that's deprived of such work. Then there's a risk for both parties . . .'

Richard tried to chip in with his approval but I was already miles away thinking of people, places and plays. It really was possible, I thought.

Over the following weeks in Yugoslavia I developed the idea. There were senior actors I knew or had some contact with whom I was sure would at least listen to me. One that I knew slightly and admired hugely was Anthony Hopkins. After endless drunken evenings, Emma persuaded me that I should stop talking and simply write to him with my idea that he should direct me in a role that I suspected would never necessarily be mine, Macbeth. I wrote to him and he wrote back. Yes, he was interested and he would talk, and he agreed with my thoughts about the state of things in the theatre. Bloody hell. If this went on I really was going to have to form a company.

The Yugoslavian leg ended and *Fortunes of War* took up residence in the old Ealing studios newly acquired by the BBC. Tim Harvey, the designer, had produced a magnificent interior for the Athenée Palace Hotel, which gave a perfect impression of old Romania. I liked and admired Tim very much, and something told me that we would work together again.

Now that there was the semblance of over a year's work in prospect, David Parfitt and I attempted to face the financial realities of producing such a vast amount of work. We made preparations to visit the Arts Council and the British Council and developed our own ideas for luring 'angels' to finance the various ventures. Peter James had agreed to do *Public Enemy*. It would cost £50,000, we would have to provide £25,000 and any profit would be split down the middle. A date was set for an opening in July, 1987. After this we would present *Napoleon* somewhere, this time financed by John and myself.

Christmas 1987 was the playing period for *Twelfth Night*, but where we did it and how was up for grabs. Financially it would be affected for good or ill by the success of the previous shows, but we weren't in any position to hang around. Richard Briers needed to know soon if it was on, before committing himself to an unknown company. At the beginning of 1988 I had decided we would attempt a Shakespeare season of four plays, all directed by actors. We were talking about eighteen months' work built on promises, passions and hopes. We had no definite finance, only one confirmed venue, two actors (me and John Sessions), a lot of bull-shitting to do and no name.

At least, we did have a name, but it took some getting used to. I liked it, but David wasn't keen – he wanted to call the company 'Compendium', which reminded me of the boxes of assorted board games that you get at Christmas. While in Yugoslavia I had woken up in the middle of the night, some time after the Trieste adventure, with a name that I was certain about. It seemed to reflect our youthfulness and express some sense of rebirth that was going on in the British theatre. I wrote it down on my Holiday Inn easy-by-the-bed notebook and looked again in the morning. It still seemed good. Later that morning in a break, I made my umpteenth trip up the rather useless tower which constituted the one tourist attraction in Ljubljana. I tried it out on Richard Clifford who, in company with Ronald Pickup, was fighting the Ljub-jub blues.

'What about "Renaissance"?'

'Brilliant,' they said.

Done.

Judi Dench sent me a birthday card. I hadn't seen her since *Ghosts* but wasn't surprised to be a beneficiary of her famous ability to remember everything. She'd been in my thoughts, and fate was lending a hand. Everything about the way Judi had rehearsed as an actress for the Ibsen had convinced me that she could direct. She questioned not only the motivations of her own character but of all the other parts, and at all times wanted to know how the play was shaping up as a whole. We'd had chats about the instinctive feeling actors had that they could do just as well as the director, and we had also agreed that fear would always defeat such feelings. Not any more. I got in touch with Judi straight away and suggested lunch.

Behind the scenes things were moving swiftly. John Adams, who had directed me at RADA, was leaving his job as artistic director of the Octagon Theatre, Bolton, and was in a strong position to land the job of running the Birmingham Repertory Theatre. As part of his pitch to the board he wanted an artistic package to present, and he approached me in late '86 to join him as an associate director. I refused, but I did tell him about plans for the Shakespeare season. By this stage I was also talking to Geraldine McEwan and Derek Jacobi and although nothing was certain, John appreciated that this could be a strong part of his package. As part of my desire for controlled conditions, I very much wanted to use the Birmingham Rep Studio where the productions could have the right kind of simplicity to calm our novice directors. It would also be cheaper. John and I struck a deal where he could include Renaissance as part of his already impressive plan for the sadly neglected Rep Studio, and he guaranteed that if he got the job we would at least have a venue and a sympathetic landlord. Money did not come into it. Our season would be an expensive business and with all John's good intentions it would not be possible for Birmingham to help finance it. But at least, in prospect, we had a theatre, and the perfect spot from which to launch a tour which might or might not end up in London.

The plan was to rehearse and open all the plays consecutively in Birmingham, where they would remain in repertory for a short season before touring to Belfast, Dublin, Bath, Brighton, Manchester, Newcastle and Leeds, before a final – and we hoped, triumphant – three-month season in London.

Judi was shocked but delighted when I put the offer to her. She confessed with a shiver that only two weeks earlier she had admitted to herself for the first time that she felt able and wanted to direct. Which play, I wondered? I asked the question, and then, by an extraordinary coincidence, we both said at the same time, '*Much Ado About Nothing.*'

But Judi wasn't going to agree straight away. The prospect was still full of terrors, and her own humility made her quail at the prospect of actually auditioning or giving orders to actors. And anyway what was this new company, Renaissance? She was having to put all her faith in me. What if the money fell through? What if the previous productions were all terrible? How would that affect the reputation of these Titans? She knew I meant what I said, but I was still only twenty-six and a stranger in a strange land. She was impressed, excited and terrified. It had been a lovely lunch, and she said she would think about it.

I approached Anthony Hopkins with the idea of his directing *Macbeth*, and he agreed immediately. He was passionately opposed to bad directors and felt it was about time that actors had a go, and he recalled a particularly unhappy production of this play at the National Theatre, where everything seemed to have gone wrong, even the costumes. At our breakfast meeting he was still venting volcanic Welsh spleen. 'I looked like a fucking armadillo.'

It was taking a while to gather this group. I was very much in awe of them and would spend several days staring at the telephone, trying to find the courage to ring up and present these schemes, which I knew to be subject to all sorts of circumstances.

It was particularly odd to be facing Derek Jacobi across the lunch table. One of my original acting heroes, he had also encouraged me early on, and here I was attempting to offer him a job. The play I had in mind was *Richard II*. A brilliant young actor I knew was desperate to play the part and I remembered that Derek had done it on television. I wanted to bring another strong young leading actor into the company and I felt the combination of him and Derek would work well and give the casting more balance. Although realistic about commercial considerations, I did not want Renaissance to be the 'Kenneth-Branagh-gets-all-the-big-parts Company'. I remembered a conversation I'd heard in relation to Ian McKellen and the Actors' Company:

'Isn't it marvellous about Ian McKellen and the Actors' Company. This week he's playing Hamlet, and last week he was in something where he just played the footman.'

'What was the play called?'

'*The Footman.*'

A little cruel, I think, but it reveals the difficulty of balance when a leading actor and personality is the driving force behind such an enterprise. Often the personality is the factor which makes the theatre decide to take the shows, and the matter becomes purely commercial. If the personality then plays a very small part in a production, it can both confuse and disappoint the audience, and it can even upset the balance of the play, an accusation levelled at Olivier when he took the small role of a butler in a play during the latter stages of his reign at the National Theatre.

Derek did not jump at my idea. He felt that *Richard II* was far too demanding a role for the sort of young actor I was thinking of, and, an important consideration in this case, it was not a 'company' play – the women's parts were poor and there was a lot of standing around for the other men. Although I felt strongly that this rarely performed piece should be seen in the provinces, I took his point about the potential tensions it could create. What, then? Was there a Shakespeare that he did feel strongly about? There was, but he would only direct it if I played the title role. It was the play that he knew best of all, and the play that he had most to say about.

'You must be able to guess,' he said.

'No.'

'*Hamlet.*'

Christ. I really hadn't bargained on that one. I wanted to play the part again but somehow hadn't imagined it coming up so soon. Was

I ready, and were these the right circumstances? Would I be in awe of Derek to the point where I would be merely impersonating him? I thought about these things for all of three minutes before shaking Derek's hand and saying, 'Great idea. Let's do it.'

Anything to get him into Renaissance. It was Christmas '86, and according to our plans *Hamlet* wouldn't start rehearsing until April '88. I could worry about it then.

Before flying to Egypt in early '87 for the next leg of *Fortunes of War*, I had a few days in which to net Geraldine McEwan as the last of this potential quartet. The wife of Hugh Cruttwell, Geraldine, I knew, was able to convey a tremendous delicacy and lightness which seemed appropriate for the play that I wanted to include in our season, *As You Like It*. It was the only Shakespearian comedy that Geraldine had not appeared in, and Rosalind was one of the few Shakespearian heroines that she had not played. The piece had always fascinated her and, like Judi, it seemed that this association with a particular play was meant to be. Although Geraldine appeared the quietest and shyest of the four actors I had approached, she was also the one who accepted the challenge both immediately and whole-heartedly.

I left for Egypt knowing that I had their interest and provisional commitment, but many other things had to fall into place before it could all work out. And I had no idea how we were going to pay for it all.

Egypt was a revelation. Through the hallowed portals of the Cairo Hilton, the Giza Ramada and the Luxor Movenpick, we had a very privileged view of the land of the pharaohs, and an army of seventy BBC technicians and cast followed the Pringles on their travels. I visited the Valley of the Kings, and felt impressively solitary as I walked down the narrow steps to the eerie tomb of Tutankhamun. About halfway down the mysterious stairwell, I heard a familiar voice declaring theatrically,

'And so Larry told Zeffirelli to get lost . . .'

It was Robert Stephens, a member of the cast, telling an anecdote to a confused Egyptian guide. And there were many other incongruities as we balanced work with tourism – I shall long remember the sight of Alan Bennett bouncing along on a camel en route to Saqquara, the Peter O'Toole of Blackburn.

Work provided a combination of some marvellous acting scenes as well as the chance to actually climb, in the line of duty, one of the great Pyramids at Giza. Best of all, I had a week off in the middle. Any sensible thespian would have done some exploring, instead I rushed back to West London where there was a chance of a venue for *Napoleon* and *Twelfth Night*. The Riverside Studios were available if we could do the right deal. In five manic days, David and I booked in both shows and managed to convince Richard Briers that performing at this unconventional venue would not destroy his reputation. I told him in any case that this was the Titanic Theatre Company. If he went down, he would take us all with him.

John Adams now looked closer to getting the job at Birmingham and this allowed us to start committing all these details to paper. With my accountant we worked out a scheme for raising the first £25,000 for *Public Enemy* which would allow a punter some chance of a return on an investment of £500. Also in a moment of madness we persuaded the artistic director of Riverside to give us a weekend festival called 'Renaissance Nights' to play when *Napoleon* was on. This was yet another one of my aims for the Company: the promotion of new writing and acting. 'Renaissance Nights' was an opportunity for the Company to read and perform full length and one-act plays along the lines of the festival work I'd done while at the RSC. Although it was going to be our first full season, I was convinced of the need for this volume of work: we had to arrive with a vengeance, and I wanted to be sure that there would always be something new to do, so that the mistakes we would inevitably make could be rectified at another stage. At the end of that cold January week, I flew back to steaming Alexandria with deals done for our first three shows, venues confirmed and the 1988 Shakespeare season several steps nearer to being realised.

Malcolm McKay was to direct *Public Enemy*, and he made it my task on the second Egyptian leg of *Fortunes of War* to do a second draft. This was completed on my return but while we were in Giza I was helped by having the play read by both Alan Bennett and Emma Thompson. Alan was very encouraging, and made lots of specific suggestions, particularly about characters' names and their particular tastes, and Emma challenged the political content of the play.

The central character of Tommy Black – which Peter James wanted me to play and which I had written with myself in mind – had particular requirements. The piece opened with a complete re-creation of the famous 'Yankee Doodle Dandy' dance routine from the James Cagney film of the same name. Cagney had performed it in short sequences for the film camera, and I would have to do this difficult and unfamiliar routine in one burst. At Christmas I had met up with Julie Fell, an assistant choreographer on the West End Show *Me and My Girl*. She'd been recommended by Emma, who'd been in the show, and Gillian Gregory, the choreographer, who helped to take me through my initial paces. Despite the fact that it was a complicated tap dance, Gillian and Julie were convinced I could do it. I learnt the basics of the number in early January and in breaks from filming on the Pyramids found myself practising taps and jumps and twirls much to the bemusement of the Arab extras.

Back in England push was rapidly coming to shove. John Adams had got the job as Artistic Director at Birmingham. We confirmed dates with him, and we now had a full season starting in June '87 with *Public Enemy* and finishing in October '88, at the end of the Shakespeare season. We now had obligations and commitments to several people, but we still had no money. Between Egypt and Athens there was a fortnight in which to finance everything *and* get confirmations from Hopkins, Dench, and Jacobi, who now had a problem with availability.

Stage One. The Arts Council. David and I nervously entered the impressive building in Piccadilly, and waited patiently in a corridor until we were shown into an office and were introduced to two very amiable women. We explained our programme for the first season, but there was a problem in that we had not consulted them in advance, before certain commitments and decisions had been made. They made it clear that this was not how they operated, and that official procedures did not allow for any great flexibility on their part, in spite of the high quality of our programme and personnel. The answer was a firm 'no'.

We decided that going it alone need not turn us into capitalist monsters. The financial principles of the company were based on keeping afloat, and not on making a profit – David and I took no management salary, and any profit we did make would be shared out among actors and production staff whenever possible, as indeed happened after *Twelfth Night* and after the successful London Shakespeare season. It was a reasonably simple and honest approach, and general company accounts have always been available to anyone working for Renaissance. David and I were both disappointed that the Arts Council were not prepared to back us, but we wanted to stick to our original conception of Renaissance. How the outside world would view our enforced freelance status remained to be seen; for the moment, we had to get on with plans for the season, and there was much to be consolidated.

Phone calls to Judi, who was in the middle of rehearsals for *Antony and Cleopatra*, revealed a much greater fear of the project than I had suspected – she would still not commit herself. Hopkins was also now undecided. The night before I left for Athens I was rushing up and down the Euston Road from meetings, first with my accountant and then with John Adams, trying to find a phone box that worked. When I got through to Judi, and pleaded for a decision about *Much Ado* before planning a press conference, she was still unsure. The rain was pouring down and David Parfitt was outside getting drenched searching for more coins and clutching a soggy prototype of the investors' letter with which we hoped to lure the first moneys. The Lyric Hammersmith were insisting that we have a press launch soon in order to give *Public Enemy* a chance. I was about to go away for a month. Everything was getting too close for comfort. I told Judi I'd come and see her.

My bags were packed ready to rush to the airport, but I squeezed in some time to cajole Judi over the lunch table at the National. It felt like Joe Allen's all over again, with familiar faces walking past, smiling, saying hello, and 'Wonder what they're up to?' written all over their faces. Judi was now in previews for *Antony and Cleopatra*, and she had been thinking about *Much Ado* for four months. After a difficult few performances, she had thought about the work in progress and decided that she knew what was wrong, and put her thoughts to Sir Peter Hall, who accepted them gratefully. They were real directorial points, and she had had the courage of her convictions. A day or two later she had asked Sir Peter whether she should direct *Much Ado*. 'Of course,' was his answer.

And now, at last, I had mine. Judi is famous for what one might describe as creative vacillation, but I was glad that she had thought so long about it because I knew that once committed, she would devote herself heart and soul to the job.

Derek's availability was now certain. He was so convinced by the idea of *Hamlet*, and of directing the boy who had thrilled to his performance in the same role ten years before, that he had gone out of his way to make the American engagement for his West End hit, *Breaking the Code*, fit into our schedules. Geraldine was also confirmed. My only lingering doubts concerned Tony Hopkins, whose confidence about the project was shaky. None of them were doing it for the money, which was minimal. When another brick was placed in the wall, I would pass on the information to David who was rapidly producing a press release so that the whole impressive season might create the right bums-on-seats interest for *Public Enemy*, which would be in rehearsal with frightening speed.

A glorious Greek spring made the final foreign location for *Fortunes of War* sheer bliss. We filmed at the Acropolis and other ancient sites, and there were marvellous day trips. We even went to Delphi where we heard the first cuckoo of spring, but not even the oracle to whom I silently prayed could tell me whether the whole Renaissance thing was going to work out. Our commitments were firmer than ever. An art gallery had been booked for late April in order to hold a press launch, and David was now using a fax machine to send copies of possible letterheads and Company logos. Across the dinner table of the InterContinental, Athens, these roughs would be discussed and voted on by the cast and crew. We decided on a simple classical design by Shaun Webb, who was to become an integral member of the Renaissance Company.

We were gradually building up a strong team. Our stage manager for *Public Enemy* had worked on *Romeo and Juliet*, as had other members of the production staff, and, although David and I still took no salary (there was no account to take it from), we did realise that we needed some help. A secretary/assistant/Person Friday was chronically necessary, as the paperwork, which was increasing daily, was too much for the two of us alone. Loot from *Fortunes of War* paid for office equipment and the salary of just such a person. We were very fortunate to net Marilyn Eardley, who had worked closely with us on *Romeo and Juliet* when she was at the Lyric. We also searched for premises, but had no money to pay rent. There was no choice: the room in my flat, which I had always ear-marked as a study for the time when I would become a great man of letters, was converted into the Renaissance nerve centre over a weekend of frantic activity. The following Monday, with borrowed filing cabinet, desk and type-writer, Marilyn took possession and I said goodbye for a possible eighteen months to any possibility of escape from Renaissance. We had an office, headed notepaper, a full season's programme, and *still* no money. Pushing our luck wasn't in it.

We drew up a list of prospective investors which included friends, colleagues, actors and directors who might be sympathetic to financing the first show. The deal reduced itself to a simple flutter, but needed pages of accompanying text in order to explain everything to our and their accountants for tax purposes. A week before the press launch, we sent off over a hundred of these original requests. By now we were back at Ealing finishing off *Fortunes of War* and with deadlines expiring all round, Emma Thompson, David Parfitt and myself were on the floor in my dressing-room between takes stuffing envelopes with pleading letters. Emma took her own invitation, walked next door, wrote a cheque and brought it straight back. Money in the bank. We were off.

So was Tony Hopkins. With a week to go before our public launch he decided that now was not the time to commit to such a new and frightening experience. I was pretty frightened of him and had no intention of trying to persuade him out of it. There was some sense of relief: three plays seemed easier than four, and the balance of *Hamlet*, *Much Ado* and *As You Like It* felt right.

With the press conference almost upon us we'd attracted around £12,000 from friends and family, and there was no turning back. The *Fortunes of War* production gave me the day off in order to worry myself stupid and I walked into the Covent Garden Gallery in trepidation. Peter Thompson, the press representative we'd first met on *Another Country* and who had worked with us on *Romeo and Juliet*, had produced a marvellously impressive turn-out. The place was packed with journalists. We'd also managed to coerce Judi Dench, Geraldine McEwan, Richard Briers, Derek Jacobi, John Adams, Peter James and everybody's mum and dad. The logo was unveiled, the letterheads were there to read, there were information packs and later on there was me standing on a table, feeling very silly, but trying to explain in a short speech the idea behind the whole thing. If nothing else, the assembled members of the press had to admit that we had produced a very weighty programme of work. In fact one of the many questions I answered afterwards was whether I was trying to provide something for everyone.

The answer was yes – the appeal was intended to be very broad. We wanted to present popular art. Not poor art or thin art or even 'arty' art, but popular art that would expand the mind and the senses and really entertain. Fuelled by the passion and commitment that we felt to each particular project.

We got through it, and the press coverage was certainly impressive enough to create interest in investment for the *Public Enemy* account. However as the rehearsal date neared we were still short, and I was happy to dig into my own pocket to make up the slight difference, but it was a worrying precedent not to have a full subscription for the first production, and it would put more pressure on the need for *Public Enemy* to be successful in order to produce more finance for *Twelfth Night* and the Shakespeare season. Without Arts Council or private money, those productions would remain dreams, and our imaginations had already outstripped the financial realities. The budget for the Shakespeare season was based on reasonable estimates for sets, costume and lighting and the attempt to pay everyone at least £200 per week made a depressing equation with potential box-office revenue. Our decision to stay in the 150-seat Studio meant that seat prices and the actual volume of tickets sold could not possibly recover the overall budget which was standing at a frightening £250,000. Assuming that we could possibly raise this, which seemed almost impossible, it was becoming clear that we would have to tour the shows to much bigger theatres in order to recover the deficit of even a sold-out run.

What had we started? My involvement with Renaissance meant that I was unable to do any freelance work in order to subsidise it. I knew that we had to complete the season at all costs, and kept in my mind a last resort of selling the flat and then, perhaps, borrowing the rest. One thing at a time. Perhaps *Public Enemy* would be a huge success – West End transfer, film rights, who knows?

If directing and acting is difficult, then writing and performing in a new play is even more taxing. Although the second draft had made great strides, the piece required constant work. In a six-week rehearsal period, I spent evenings and weekends on rewrites, and then came in at 8.30 every morning to practise dancing for an hour and a half. There was also the part itself, which was immensely tough: part schizophrenic, highly energised, dangerous and very hard to place. And then there was the work-load of future Renaissance plans. I really was at full stretch and became irritable with the director, despite excellent help from him on both text and performance. I was also assisted by Hugh Cruttwell, who had agreed to continue his unpaid role as artistic consultant. I was and am still far too close to it to judge how good or bad the play and production were, but I also had to confess to being hoisted by my own petard in having written a great vehicle for myself. To give the play a real chance I really should have cast someone else in the central role, but there was some really fine acting, particularly from Ethna Roddy, an actress straight out of the Webber-Douglas Academy to whom we were able to give an Equity card. A week of previews revealed, as *Francis* had done, the need for time, but audiences were loving what was being variously described as a thriller, a modern melodrama, a political play and a star vehicle.

The critics, on the whole, dismissed it, and audiences dropped as the wave of indifference took hold. There seemed no attempt to see the piece as a serious play. I came in for an inevitable bashing over my presumption in having both written and performed in the play, and then there were others who indulged what they saw as my act of folly. The general feeling from the press was one of disappointment in a Company about which there had been high hopes. None of it really mattered; the Company remained happy and *Public Enemy* improved as time went on, but it was a blow to know that these first knocks would threaten the financial viability of the rest of our season. I responded to this by grabbing whatever freelance work I could. During the run I managed a week on a television adaptation of O'Neill's *Strange Interlude* with Glenda Jackson, and managed to land the part of Thomas Mendip in Christopher Fry's *The Lady's not for Burning*, which I could sandwich in between *Napoleon* and *Twelfth Night*. None of this was very good for my health or my private life, both of which were suffering. I felt out of control – it was as if I believed my enormous work-load gave me licence to behave exactly as I wanted. I would tell lies to all and sundry in order to explain absences which I deemed necessary because 'I was so tired'; I ate and drank immoderately, and didn't give a moment's thought to anyone but myself. I was unreliable to work with, and felt pretty miserable.

I had little enough time to worry about these things. The morning after the opening of *Public Enemy* I started to rehearse Napoleon with John Sessions, and realised that as much energy is required from the director as from the performer in rehearsals for a one-man show. John was kindness itself and worked around my erratic fatigue but all work and little play made Ken a very dull boy indeed. I didn't look at a newspaper, I never dreamed of asking after anyone's welfare – not while there was even more pressure on this show to succeed. Tension was increased by the necessary publicity for the show generated brilliantly by Peter Thompson and which centred inevitably on me. The imminent screening of *Fortunes of War* and the release of *A Month in the Country* meant that I was particularly hot property, and I was besieged. I was also attracting various sorts of nutters who badgered me for advice, money and jobs – understandable, but impossible for me to deal with in the circumstances, and quite often I wanted to avoid even answering the phone.

During the final stages of *Napoleon* rehearsals I received repeated messages from the Riverside box-office to call a stranger named Stephen Evans. I didn't bother – there was no information about what he wanted and I suspected the worst. In an unguarded moment going to the loo, the vague reception staff told me there was a phone call for me. For some reason I thought it was my agent and so picked up the phone. An intelligent, gravelly voice rumbled down the phone, 'Ah, got you at last. My name's Stephen Evans and I think I can help you.'

Oh Christ, I knew it was going to be another nutcase.

'I've read about you and your Company, and I think that I might have access to certain funds that might make your life easier.' Oh, really. I see, a City gangster who's trying to off-load some Panamanian slush-fund. Why do I talk to these people? 'Obviously, it would be good if we could talk. What about Monday morning? Say eleven o'clock?'

Yes, yes, yes. Anything just get him off the bloody phone. I put down the receiver and didn't give it another moment's thought.

At about five to eleven on the following Monday morning I was escaping from the Riverside auditorium where a disastrous technical rehearsal was in progress. The only thing in my mind was a coffee, which meant waiting for a quarter of an hour while the Coffee Bar assistant worked out whether they sold any of the stuff. Waiting at the counter with increasing frustration, I was joined in the queue by an attractive forty-year-old man of medium build who leant across the counter and attempted to communicate with the space cadet assistant. 'Hello, I've got an appointment with Kenneth Branagh.'

Bloody hell, I'd been nabbed. I introduced myself and made profuse apologies, although I was in no mood to talk even to this fairly innocuous looking customer. With deadly rudeness I passed Stephen on to David Parfitt and returned to the nightmare rehearsal where I really was needed. During the course of the next half hour I saw them wander in to have a look at the set being painted, but my mind couldn't have been further away. In another break I managed to shake his hand distractedly, and apologised for not having had a proper chat.

At lunch, David explained that the man to whom I had been so rude had agreed to find the £60,000 that we would need to finance *Twelfth Night*. I was now even more convinced of the Panamanian slush-fund, but David insisted that he seemed absolutely genuine and would send the first cheque in the following week. Understandably and ungraciously, I was suspicious, and remained so until my first proper meeting with Stephen when he visited *Napoleon* with his wife, Lyn. This time I was a pathetic Uriah Heep, grovelling with shame at my earlier behaviour. He chose not to remind me of that but instead enthused about the show, which was a tremendous tour-de-force for John.

It had not been easy. Technically, *Napoleon* was massively ambitious. There were over 150 lighting and sound cues, smoke, snow – you name it and we tried to do it, and all with one stage manager and one director, who were both working on *Public Enemy* up to the Saturday before Monday's technical rehearsal at Riverside. The technical week was a disaster, and the first preview was the most appallingly jinxed performance of anything I've ever been involved with. Nothing went right. There was no choice but to cancel the second preview and for me to get my act together. John remained remarkably calm. The day's break worked and on Saturday night we played to a full and appreciative house who showed us how the evening could take off if John's talent was supported by a reliable production.

By the time Stephen Evans saw it, John was hugely impressive and the show fulfilled all the Renaissance creeds of life-enhancing populism – at least that was my story and I was sticking to it. Stephen and I developed an instant rapport: he was a shrewd businessman, something of a maverick, a stockbroker with a strong freelance strain who was also genuinely interested in the arts. He had already dabbled in what he described as 'helping' opera and dance organisations, but none of them had satisfied his desire for greater involvement. He didn't want to interfere artistically, but he was seeking a realistic collaboration between the worlds of commerce and art. I told him of our plans and decided on the spur of the moment to outline a totally outrageous proposal which I felt could capitalise on what I hoped would be a triumphantly successful Shakespeare season. I had no facts or figures with which to support this idea, but I had my usual combination of vision and cheek, and two bottles of Lambrusco. I wanted the Renaissance Company to feed into other mediums. I felt that one shouldn't be limited by conventional patterns of work, or by the methods of other companies; healthy ambition, in this instance, should not limit itself. In any case, he asked for it.

'So what will you do after the Shakespeares?'

Pause. Here we go. 'I want to make a film of *Henry V*.' I checked his face. The colour hadn't drained, and he was still looking me in the eye. 'I will direct and play the leading role.'

He still hadn't flinched.

'Have you directed a film before?'

'No.'

'How many films have you acted in?'

'Two.'

A longer pause. He still hadn't backed down. 'Do you think it's possible for you to do it?'

The longest pause. 'Absolutely . . .' – another brief pause as I looked him in the eye and raised my glass '. . . with your help.'

His face broke into a smile and we clinked glasses. There was a lot of talk about, and the film was a distant prospect, but we were in business.

The reviews for John's *Napoleon* were marvellous, and made the job of organising 'Renaissance Nights' slightly less daunting. It fell to David to do a Herculean job in arranging favours left, right and centre for actor friends to perform what turned out to be a very wide selection of new work. I had pushed off to Leeds where I was having a delightful time on the Fry play and trying to cast *Twelfth Night* over the phone. The pace was increasing by the day. Stephen Evans' entry onto the scene was hotly followed by Howard Panter, a West End producer, who wished to transfer *Napoleon* for a limited season. The Albery Theatre looked as though it would be available, and Stephen and Howard combined to produce a financial deal that made a six-week season possible. Mounting it in the West End would mean a two-day absence from *Twelfth Night* rehearsals for me, but I was beginning to get used to this kind of manic scheduling. The effects of all this were beginning to show: when my mother saw me at a performance of *Napoleon* in the West End, she let out a gasp of horror at the spotty, scruffy, stubbly tramp before her.

As I had suspected, the presence of Richard Briers in the production attracted a very strong team of actors. Rehearsing the play gave me great pleasure, and my instinct that a production set in the winter, with snow covering a mysterious Victorian garden, would bring out the brooding melancholy of the play seemed to be justified. It is undoubtedly a comedy, but the dark undertow of rejection and loneliness and cruelty experienced by many of the characters was beautifully brought out by the cast. At the centre of this production was a definitive Malvolio from Richard, who proved that a great comic actor can be a great tragic actor. There was fine work from all the cast, but this was a very special performance, funny and, in the end, deeply moving. Hugh Cruttwell had advised me and had ensured that my instincts about the play were translated early into a production that attempted to reach as many people as possible. I took my parents as a touchstone, and they loved it.

This production was also the first occasion on which our Royal Patron could be present. I had had the gall to invite Prince Charles to become Patron, making my initial approach in a letter typed from a hotel bedroom in Egypt. The long and delicate process of Royal assent had given us his acceptance just before the press launch, and we were delighted that despite a frantic schedule he could attend a Royal Gala Preview of *Twelfth Night*. This was the first of a number of occasions on which David and I mercilessly dropped Stephen in it. The idea had seemed brilliant at the time, a wonderful way of benefiting one of the Prince's Trust's charities, an element of our work that we wanted to develop. But selling 350 seats at £50 a ticket is easier said than done, however worthy the cause, and especially if you are still a relatively unknown theatre company. Stephen came to the rescue by blackmailing and cajoling numerous City colleagues into attending what turned out to be an uproariously enjoyable evening.

The Prince was on fine form and left everyone in the building aglow. He had effortlessly made meaningful contact with anyone he met, and the euphoria of having encountered a genuine star was felt by everyone in the Company. We all went on to have a very late night indeed at a marvellous party provided by Stephen Evans, with not a slush-fund in sight. The excesses of the Royal Gala meant that the following evening's press performance was performed in an atmosphere that was relatively free of the hysteria normally associated with such events. I don't know if hangovers are the perfect cure for press night nerves, but it certainly worked in this case: the performance went smoothly, and after a week of previews was developing beautifully. The press reception was unanimous – straight raves. I couldn't believe it, they were the best notices I'd seen for anything and suddenly, despite the shaky start, we were the Company who could do no wrong.

Both Judi Dench and Geraldine McEwan saw the show and loved it, and it was a great relief to know that these risk-taking directors had seen a successful production. Derek Jacobi was already in America, where *Breaking the Code* was a huge success on Broadway. The busy lives of this trio had meant that casting the Shakespeare season was almost more difficult than my InterContinental Company negotiations with David. We had had one meeting in July which they were all able to attend, and since then Derek had seen as many actors as he could before leaving for America. Now it was Judi and Geraldine's turn. David and I co-ordinated reactions between the three directors over the telephone to New York. When Geraldine and Judi plumped for someone, a photograph would wing its way across the Atlantic for Derek's approval – his Horatio had to be someone else's Don Pedro, and it needed give and take all round. Time was short, and pressure increased when Thames Television took up the option to film *Twelfth Night* for television. The Renaissance cup was running over, and it became very important to keep things in control and to guard against the very dangerous increases in scale that we had always tried to avoid.

The financing of the Shakespeare season progressed with relative ease, with Stephen Evans and Howard Panter combining under David's direction to make the quarter million gamble possible. I made a quick trip to New York with Jenny Tiramani, our designer, and spent a week with Derek working on *Hamlet*. On my return to England I went up to Birmingham to discuss programming with John Adams – when to have matinées? How many performances? How much rehearsal time? We also agreed that Renaissance could be the subject of a television documentary, with a camera crew filming various stages of our work over the year ahead. This, with the success of *Twelfth Night*, was generating enormous interest.

I managed one quick break in Scotland before Christmas and then spent three days in Los Angeles in January '88 promoting *Fortunes of War*, a visit which allowed Emma Thompson and I to fulfil a lifelong ambition and visit Disneyland. Both of us were nearly sick on 'The Matterhorn', but we thrilled to the new 'Star Tours' ride, which was a mechanical but completely convincing trip on a space ship straight out of *Star Wars*. We emerged like wide-eyed six-year-olds, yelping through our candy floss, and heading for 'Pirates of the Caribbean', 'Wild West Land', and as many rides as we could fit in.

Emma and I were now established as a couple. It was a real pleasure to work together on her television show, *Thompson*, on our return to England. I thought it brilliantly original and innovative television. There was an excellent cast, and it was great fun to do.

Meantime, I approached the 1 February rehearsal date with trepidation, but also with some relief. After endless organising, it seemed that for a time I would go back to being simply an actor, and I had three marvellous parts – Benedick, Touchstone and Hamlet. These were thrilling opportunities, but difficult ones, too, and the old fears returned. Once again, I found it very hard to enjoy my professional achievement, and I was already torturing myself with visions of potential disaster. I decided to follow Olivier's advice, have a bash and hope for the best.

NINE

'Go travel for a while'
PERICLES

We were all feeling very nervous about the Shakespeare season, and throughout the casting sessions Geraldine and Judi had been modest and hesitant, with everyone straining to be nice to each other. It was a pleasant fault, but Judi saw the need for an ice-breaker, and once the Company had been finalised she had the inspired idea of holding a Company party in her country home, a beautiful Elizabethan house in Surrey, on the Sunday before rehearsals started. It was a chance for this young group to actually see each other once before embarking on nine months' work together. Riotous company photographs were taken, large quantities of champagne were consumed, and I ended up playing football in Judi's garden, with my godson, Calum Yuill.

The party had relaxed everyone but the following Monday morning, which started with rehearsals for *Much Ado*, was still a very tense occasion. Judi was visibly frightened, and grabbed me at once, telling me to stick close. It was plain that she wasn't keen to give a directorial lecture, and she declared immediately that she didn't have 'a concept' of the play. What she did have was a very clear idea of how the play might look, and convictions about certain aspects of *Much Ado* which she felt were important. Throughout our discussions she had been very humble about her own ideas, all of which were strong, and on this first morning she was touchingly vulnerable as she spoke to us about the dark side of *Much Ado*, about its strange treatment of sex, and its often sinister quality, which was an aspect she wanted to underline. She also stressed the lightness of touch which the play demanded. During the first week of rehearsals Judi's tone of voice and manner suggested that people might not take her seriously or do what she said, a nervousness that was quite unnecessary, as the whole Company was more in awe of her than she was of us. Although Judi had made very sensible cuts in the play, she was terrified of giving them to the actors, who she plainly thought might mutiny. But laughter began to break down the barriers, and amid general hilarity the cuts were noted, moaned about noisily, and the read-through proceeded with first-day nerves starting to disappear.

Relieved and slightly hysterical actors broke for lunch and I went to a meeting with a film lawyer. Stephen had decided to go ahead with *Henry V* and had crazily agreed to the timetable which I had put forward. With the airy certainty of the blissfully ignorant, I had told him that the film would cost £2½ million. I don't know where I produced this figure from, but I reckoned that at least it would frighten him. He had managed miraculously to produce £250,000 for the Shakespeare season, and I was hoping he might respond to the challenge. He'd insisted nevertheless that I produce a screenplay on which a full budget might be based. I had no choice – if I really did believe in a film version of *Henry V*, then I had to do something about it. All through January I slaved over a hot typewriter to produce a text and detailed stage directions which would allow my conception of the piece to be visualised by others, and to be broken down into budgetable scenes.

I delivered the script, and with it the virtual ultimatum that I would not do it unless filming began at the end of October, immediately after the Shakespeare season finished. God knows where this chutzpah came from, but I had very strong instincts about the whole project. The pace of events at Renaissance had developed so rapidly that I think my mind and ambition were racing ahead. Anything seemed possible: the Shakespeare season, which had once seemed impossible, was shaping itself into a nationwide tour with a London season; we were moving from a 150-seat Studio auditorium into large theatres up and down the country, and would be playing (we hoped) to up to 2,000 people each evening. I had a blind and ridiculous faith in the venture. We were still in control, and my instincts told me that, if Judi's first comments were anything to go by, then *Much Ado* had the potential to be very special, and I was sure that the other two productions would at least be exciting. We were on the verge of finalising a West End season that took us to the end of October, and, again, I had a hunch that the possibly triumphant arrival of Renaissance in London for a three-month season could be the showcase which might produce the final bits of finance for the movie. Money men, distributors, anyone could come and see us in the flesh providing the 'popular' Shakespeare which the company and all three directors would be trying to create.

At this point film plans were highly fanciful, and yet Stephen and I both knew that if they had any chance of being realised then, all through the nine months of the Renaissance tour, we would have to be arranging meetings, fixing studios, sorting out designs and organising everything as if shooting really was set to start on 31 October 1988.

In early February we had a screenplay, an actor/director, and the goodwill of Judi and Derek, who had already agreed to be in the imaginary movie as Mistress Quickly and Chorus respectively, making an impressive start for the cast. We'd *have* to make it. The film lawyer did not agree, and asked many of the questions which would plague us over the coming months – it's been done before, why do it again? How do you know Shakespeare will work on film in the eighties? How do you know you can direct? In short, he produced a number of very sensible responses to what seemed like a pie-in-the-sky project. I reported back to Stephen and then lost myself in *Much Ado*, where I was simply an actor doing a job, and not a film mogul.

Judi felt her way carefully through the first week. She didn't enjoy the initial 'blocking', but far preferred the work on character that she was starting with each of us, and on the speaking of the text, which she was determined should obey strict rhythmic rules. By the second week she was firmly into her stride and the laughter in rehearsal was almost as great as the discipline with which she conducted each session. She was particularly savage with my Benedick. She had not wanted to cast me in the role originally but as several actors turned it down and as I made a good pair with her preferred Beatrice, Samantha Bond, I got the part. I found it extremely difficult to get to grips with the role and, though striving for the opposite effect, I was making him very broadly comic. Judi jumped on this immediately. A great comic actress, she was not going to have Branagh's vaudeville act disturb the balance of her production, and she led me very much in the direction of the heartfelt warmth and naturalism of Samantha's Beatrice.

Watching Judi at rehearsals was marvellous. She was like a clear glass through which one could see the mood of the piece ebb and flow. Her instinct was infallible: like an orchestral conductor she knew exactly where to place each pause, each rest, and each acceleration. As the weeks went by her directorial gifts blossomed, and she always resisted the urge to act the scene out for you, searching instead for the words and the imaginative suggestions which would release the actor further into the part.

Judi's ideas for the design of the set and costumes developed and in look and tone she was catching a delightful Mediterranean quality which could convey the light and shade in the play. Confidence was growing all the time, right through the Company – Judi could really direct and the Company responded vigorously. We were already discovering a gold mine in Pat Doyle, who had provided a marvellous score for *Twelfth Night* and was now producing some beautiful tunes for *Much Ado*. The music would be performed entirely by the actors, which was another element that bonded the Company together and reinforced our sense of commitment. We really were all in it together, and there was a sense of something very special in the air. As the month's rehearsal in London drew to a close we looked forward to the opening in Birmingham with real anticipation.

It was impossible not to be excited. Judi had informed me before rehearsals started that she'd just got 'a marvellous job for the panto season', which was a delightful way of announcing herself as a Dame of the British Empire. The newspapers were full of Judi, and I was doing endless publicity myself. There was no choice. Birmingham Rep wanted to celebrate our arrival and we were concerned about the box-office: even with a sold-out run at the Studio, Renaissance would be left with a deficit of £80,000. This was serious money, and I was aware of the danger involved. We were in a financial corner, and forced to draw as much attention as possible to a project that we had hoped to initiate quietly in order to protect the delicate conditions of this new actor/director experiment.

We arrived in Birmingham to receive the joyful news that we had indeed sold out, and were now faced with a flood of letters of complaint from people who couldn't get in. *Hamlet* had sold out its fifteen Birmingham performances on the morning that booking opened. Although we were worried about its effect on the quality of the shows, I was relieved to think that by taking the shows to larger theatres on tour, more people would be able to see the plays than at Birmingham. I hoped that one day we might find the right balance – studio Shakespeare is great, but only for the 150 people who manage to get in. How is intimate acting in Shakespeare shared by lots of people? By making a film of *Henry V*. But more of that later.

We began the technical rehearsals for *Much Ado*, the most unfamiliar area for our novice directors. The studio setting helped, as the smaller stage seemed fairly manageable and Jenny Tiramani's set of an elegant Sicilian Villa could be lit relatively easily by Judi, who was working with her long-time colleague and lighting designer, 'Basher' Harris. Judi remained a stickler for detail in this technical area. She hated sloppiness in production or acting, and the actors and stage managers rallied, with everyone in the eighteen-strong team making themselves available for scene changes. There was a tremendous sense of togetherness – everyone knew the precarious-ness of our financial position and everyone had access to Company accounts. This openness produced the sense of goodwill that creates that hard-to-define quality of a marvellous 'Company feeling'.

It doesn't always follow that this produces a marvellous perform-ance. Although friends who were in loved it, the first preview of *Much Ado* was a tense affair. The first performance of a comedy is always difficult: people never laugh when you expect them to, and it is very difficult to find a playing rhythm. For our first-time director it was a harrowing experience. The actors are occupied with the play and at this stage are simply concerned with their own performance, but Judi was discovering the unfamiliar feelings of directorial helpless-ness and a tense concern which embraces every aspect of the production. She walked slowly into the large communal dressing-room after the show, looking white and shell-shocked. I had seen her in the tiny auditorium where everyone was frighteningly visible, hunched over her director's notebook and suffering with every stumbling attempt by her inexperienced cast to get it right first time. Now it was all over and her voice was hoarse with anxiety. 'It was like watching a pile-up on the M1.'

There was laughter all round but it was clear that she was quite shaken. As everyone disappeared to a local Indian restaurant to mull over the lost laughs, Judi stayed behind and took me by the arm. 'Oh, Kenny – it was like giving birth to a baby that isn't breathing properly. You watch it trying to walk and then it falls over and can't get up, and you can't *do* anything. It's agony.'

Judi went back to her hotel and came in the next day with new resolve and an armful of notes. The next performance picked up enormously, as we relaxed and allowed the audience to relax as well which – surprise, surprise – allowed them to laugh. On the Sunday I spent my day off in Manchester, where I danced on a giant record player as my last contribution to Emma Thompson's new show. The change was as good as a rest and Emma, who had seen the first preview, was very encouraging.

I left for Birmingham on the Monday morning which was the

Company morning off. This allowed them a slightly longer weekend away from an increasingly frenetic work schedule. The local press night for *Much Ado* was Tuesday, but before that on Monday afternoon we had our first rehearsal for *As You Like It*. There really was no stopping: note sessions with Judi had to be fitted in after *As You Like It* rehearsals, or grabbed over beans on toast in the Rep canteen. Financial dictates had forced us to contract the rehearsal periods like this, and I was already wondering whether I would be able to stand the pace.

With a shaky Benedick in performance and a Touchstone about to start rehearsal, I still had far too many other things to think about. Stephen Evans had secured Elstree Studios for our hypothetical production of *Henry V* and I was needed in London for meetings with a producer who seemed to be the next step towards realising the project. Bruce Sharman was an experienced film man with an impressive list of credits, and over another precious free Sunday we talked about the production, its difficulties and the budget. With an accountant he had produced an accurate figure to confound my fly-by-night fancies: we would need £4.5 million, and more if we went on location. I had talked idly about putting the battle scenes on Dartmoor, but this was out of the question – it would add weeks to the schedule, go across Christmas and add millions to the budget. No. Turn again Whittington. I returned to Birmingham and put my feet on another step of what was at least an exciting treadmill.

The Tuesday press night for *Much Ado* went well, and afterwards Judi, who was now much more relaxed, was already reluctant to say goodbye to the Company of which she was becoming very fond. She had come through with flying colours and the local press concurred by saying all the right things, bar one critic who made the cardinal error of saying I was rotund. I am still looking for her.

The weeks were flying by but the rhythm changed dramatically with Geraldine McEwan whose much slower, more methodical approach to *As You Like It* was in sharp contrast to the swift and breezy atmosphere which Judi created for *Much Ado*. Both had judged the moods of the plays perfectly and rehearsed them in just the right way. The seeming fragility and breathtaking honesty of Geraldine's personality defined the delicacy of this play – a beautiful discourse on love. She was extremely patient with a young cast and produced marvellous things from Tam Hoskyns and James Larkin as Rosalind and Orlando. The Company were all helping each other, and on this production in particular there was a good level of mutual help and support. Company feeling had not diminished – we were united in exhaustion, if nothing else.

With confidence growing in my Benedick, I was encouraged by Geraldine to take great risks with Touchstone. She had chosen an Edwardian setting for her *As You Like It* and this allowed the Fool to emerge from the music hall. I didn't have to be asked twice, and armed with a marvellous arrangement of 'It was a lover and his lass' from Pat Doyle I set to work on developing a Touchstone that borrowed from Max Miller, Archie Rice and about every professional comedian I'd ever seen. It was a loud performance, but was just about legitimate, and it was borne with great patience by my fellow actors who had every sympathy with a comedian who has to make the following joke on his first entrance:

ROSALIND	Where learned you that oath, fool?
TOUCHSTONE	Of a certain knight that swore by his honour they were good pancakes, and swore by his honour the mustard was naught. Now I'll stand to it, the pancakes were naught and the mustard was good, and yet was not the knight forsworn.

Boo-boom. You try making that funny. Shakespeare might have been amused by it for a week in 1599, but in Birmingham in 1988 it provides certain difficulties. Archie Rice it was. Forgive me, father.

The candle continued to be burned at both ends. Monday mornings meant film meetings in London where the salesman in me would try to persuade the latest contact of Stephen's to part with a million pounds. This time it was the Completion Guarantors, who were, in effect, the film's insurers, and without whose approval the film could not be financed. Their main concern was my directing as well as acting. Thinking on my feet, I produced Hugh Cruttwell out of the air. He was already advising in Birmingham, and without permission I instantly unveiled him as artistic advisor on the movie and in so doing proved to them that I had a sufficiently strong insurance policy. They were satisfied. Yes, they would guarantee the film. *And* I could direct.

Phew!

If we found the 4½ million.

Ah. Back to Touchstone.

Bold though my performance was, I was not rising sufficiently to he challenge of Touchstone. As Hugh pointed out at a preview I imply wasn't on top of the text. Of my three roles in the season, I ound Touchstone the most difficult to learn with the famously complex and unfunny 'lie' speech being a particular pill. It was the first sign of the work-load taking its toll. I bought some vitamins and went back to the text. Since *Romeo and Juliet*, it had been eighteen months of solid hard work, and I really was going to have to be careful. *Hamlet* hadn't even started.

As You Like It opened to enthusiastic local press and audiences. Like *Much Ado*, the plaudits were for its freshness and wit and lack of pretension. Both shows were elegant and simple, allowing the plays to breathe through, and placed great emphasis on the acting itself which was developing in confidence all the time. As well as the two principals here, there was a fine Jacques from Richard Easton and a lovely Celia from Sophie Thompson. We were developing new talents, which fulfilled an essential aim of the Company. The only drawback was the pressure on everyone who, by the time *Hamlet* opened, would have been rehearsing and playing solidly for three months.

My own pressure was, of course, self-imposed. As Derek arrived from a triumphant Broadway season, we began *Hamlet* rehearsals, were playing *As You Like It* and *Much Ado*, and Tim Harvey, the designer for *Henry V*, came to stay with me in Birmingham to work on plans for the film. By this stage so much time, effort and now money had gone into *Henry V* that we didn't dare let it drop. In that first crazy week with the moody Dane, I was rehearsing from 10 am, breaking at 5.30 pm, playing one of the comedies, then having design meetings over a late supper for a movie that might or might not happen. Was I doing too much? Yes. Was it any good for Hamlet? God knows.

Derek started rehearsals at high speed. He wanted a dramatic and highly theatrical production that acknowledged the rich store of theatrical imagery in *Hamlet*. He worked amazingly fast and knew every single word of the text, so that when anyone dried he was ahead of the stage management in prompting them. At first I resisted his suggestions, and I was determined not to be hurried or over-awed. There were a couple of days' wariness, and then we both began to trust each other and went to it with a vengeance. The play was blocked in a week. He had marvellous ideas for the women: there were extra entrances and even re-allocated lines to help produce a truly heart-rending Ophelia from Sophie Thompson and a very strong Gertrude from Dearbhla Molloy.

Derek directed my Hamlet with amazing sensitivity – I had my own instincts and he shaped them. There wasn't an acting problem in the part that he hadn't already faced and analysed himself, and the alternatives that he offered me were fascinating. He was also of tremendous help in colouring speeches and knowing when to rest on the lines, which was particularly useful for the closet scene, which seems to me the Becher's Brook for Hamlets. At Drama School I had fallen into the trap of ranting through it and running out of steam early on, but Derek showed me how to pace myself and find enough breath and energy to get through *and* to make sense of the lines. He seemed to take to directing like a duck to water.

Derek and I developed a form of telepathic shorthand where short phrases and words would take the place of long explanations. Hugh balanced this by watching run-throughs and following up with typed notes which charted my development in the role. Everything Hugh said was aimed at deepening my performance, for my propensity for superficial energy was at points betraying the intellectual content that Derek sought to illuminate. But between Hugh and Derek I made great strides.

The first performance was electric. There was a packed house and a large returns queue, and I had the strange sensation of being followed right up to my very first entrance by an American TV documentary crew who had been filming throughout rehearsals. During the performance the time passed in a whirl of worrying about getting on and off, but there was undoubtedly something in the air. At the end of the play we had taken several curtain calls and were back downstairs in the dressing-room shrieking with relief when people started commenting on the ferocious banging noise which came from above us. The audience was stamping its feet and still cheering. The cry went round, 'We've got to go back. We've got to go back.'

Exit fifteen hysterical actors who stumbled and fell across the tiny Studio stage where they were greeted by a magnificent standing ovation. People occasionally rose to their feet at RSC shows I'd been in, but it was the first time I'd experienced the full-blown version. We dragged Derek down onto the stage and eventually made our tearful exit, looking forward to a long and strong drink.

Over the following weeks I learned about the uncomfortable phenomenon of playing Hamlet twice on Saturdays. The stomach-wrenching sick feeling that overtakes one as the first soliloquy begins is truly terrifying and it's impossible not to be aware of quite how far you have to go in this Everest of a role. But at that point we'd stopped rehearsing full time and whatever the controversial response might be to Derek's production, it was a very honourable addition to a trio of excellent shows. A local press night was followed swiftly by a national press night. The major critics had already visited the comedies and been warmly enthusiastic. With the usual cavils, we seemed to get away with Hamlet, too. There were raves, and, as always, there were those for whom I could never be Hamlet in a million years and who found the production an offence to their sensibilities. The daily tide of congratulatory mail confirmed that the general public response as well as that of the critics had been very positive.

There was certainly no opportunity to rest on any laurels. As soon as *Hamlet* had opened, David and I were forced to ask the Company to agree to understudy each other, as a cover system was necessary for the big theatres that we would play in. At Birmingham we had simply taken a risk on everyone staying in good health. If an actor had been off, then the performance would probably have been cancelled and 150 people would have been disappointed. Touring to large houses, a guarantee of performance was required in order to fulfil insurance obligations. The result was a very complicated cover system where people in smaller roles could cover the larger ones and still manage to play their own part if an emergency arose. The logistics of this meant that almost everyone had extra parts to squeeze into their already heavily taxed Shakespearian memory banks. It was not an ideal situation, but the Company responded magnificently with people actually volunteering for particular roles that interested them. It meant extra work all round for stage management and an impingement on the actor's precious free time while on tour. I felt extremely guilty, as I had watched the pressure on the understudy system at the RSC and had always wanted to improve such a difficult area. We had clearly not thought this one through sufficiently. Things would be different next time.

Towards the end of our stay in Birmingham, Prince Charles asked if Renaissance could provide a Shakespearian entertainment for a private party at Windsor. Judi Dench, Derek Jacobi, Emma Thompson were all available to perform in this 'Miscellany', and we rehearsed some of the Bard's greatest scenes in the Patron's Bar at the Birmingham Rep. I directed the show, which was excellent practice for *Henry V*. It was terrifying to be directing great actors, but I was relieved and delighted to find that they were prepared to listen to me. They all headed south with their fifty-minute programme, while the rest of us set off across the water.

On with the shocks. The Opera House, Belfast, and we went from 150 people to 1000 people. There was a full house. I'd spent all day doing 'local boy makes good' publicity, and in the late afternoon, when I saw our Studio set seemingly adrift in the expanse of the great stage, my heart sank. I was learning quickly that being a small-time impresario and playing Hamlet four times a week was an uneasy mixture. For various reasons, Derek had not been available to see his show transfer to a big house, and by the time I arrived, David and the stage management and design teams had been working for hours to do an instant conversion. The cast turned up, and although we had attempted rough re-blockings in the last week at Birmingham, we were faced with immediate adjustments which dealt with sight-line problems that had been impossible to predict in advance. We did what we could on the spot and at seven o'clock I retired to the dressing-room/office I was sharing with David. Peace seemed very

hard to find and this seemed the very best or the very worst preparation for an evening as the moody Dane.

The warm reception from our Belfast audience resolved most of the problems of tiredness and adjustment. They were just plain delighted to see us. After the performance we attended the first of the many parties that would be a feature of the tour, and which were often provided by one of the local sponsors that Stephen had encouraged to support our week in a particular town. The reaction of our Belfast hosts was ecstatic, and there, in full glorious loyalty, were my parents, who had flown over especially to see the great home-coming. They were in danger of expiring with pride.

The bookings for the week ahead were near capacity, there was a great deal of publicity. Walking into town from Uncle Jim and Aunt Kathleen's house, where I was staying during the Belfast run, I was often recognised and stopped. Local people were no longer sus-picious about Billy's English accent – they'd read the papers, they'd seen *Fortunes of War*, and they now seemed to accept that I was an Ulster one-off. There was a funny sort of inverted snobbery and pride about my involvement with Shakespeare. They liked the idea of one of their lads showing the English how to do it and they were delighted that Belfast was first stop on the tour. The recurring uneasiness that I felt about my Irishness was beginning to disappear. Suddenly I was being accepted for what I was and not what people thought I should be. I left Belfast with more peace of mind than I was used to experiencing in my home town, and it was a feeling that would thankfully remain with me.

The towns rolled by, and I felt as if I was in a montage sequence from one of those American movies where the train steams across the plain and those whirling place names rush up into the frame. Only this time it wasn't the Cohan family from Yankee Doodle Dandy steaming through Ohio and Nebraska. It was Dublin and Bath and Brighton. Up and down reviews, up and down sponsors and, thank God, packed houses – it looked as though we might recover the £80,000. David Parfitt's anxious gaze at the weekly figures became slightly less manic. In between advance publicity for the towns ahead and the dreaded understudy rehearsals, Stephen would grab me for work on the film, and likely punters would be brought along to see the show when we were within shouting distance of London. During the week in Brighton, I commuted and found time to deal with the latest film crisis.

After detailed planning with Tim Harvey about how to produce Agincourt in a car park, Elstree Studios was sold overnight in a mysterious deal which left us without a place to shoot. It seemed like the death of the project. Pinewood and Shepperton both had problems with our dates, but we almost managed to complete a deal with Pinewood who then had to pull out and go ahead with a more definite offer from another movie. It seemed unlikely that Shepperton would be available. We were forced to wait for a cancellation and to carry on raising money, although no studio had been booked.

Manchester, Newcastle and Richmond. It was all travel, and Sundays passed in a haze. Although I tried to keep one day free every week, Renaissance activities continued to impinge. Most extreme was a trip to Denmark. After months of detailed negotiation, we had produced a wonderful bonus trip in the shape of a visit to Krönberg Castle, Elsinore, to perform *Hamlet* in its actual home for a two-week season. The green spires of this Renaissance palace were an impressive sight. The place had extraordinary majesty, and once across the moat and inside the inner castle with its sea-facing battlements, we all felt an undeniable frisson – one could imagine sea battles and ghosts of all kinds. Several months in advance of our August trip

David, Derek, Sophie and I gave up yet another Sunday to drum up publicity for the Danish run. They knew and loved Derek who had already played there, but they didn't know me from a bar of soap.

Tiring though it was, the trip did confirm the marvellous atmosphere that could breathe out of this strange Renaissance castle, where a troop of Shakespeare's actors were reported to have played in the 1590s. It was impossible not to be affected by their ghosts or those illustrious actors who had played the Prince at Elsinore in the current century – Gielgud, Olivier, Burton. Heady stuff.

Theatrical romance does not a movie make. Bruce Sharman needed a second draft of the script. On the Monday of our appearance in Newcastle I found myself in Teddington practically manacled to his desk and doing the re-writes which were necessary for rebudgeting. Bruce dropped me at Heathrow airport so that I could catch the 4.30 plane, and on checking in I found that there was an unspecified delay. It was our opening night of *Hamlet* in Newcastle, and I was stuck in the Departure lounge at Heathrow. At 5.45 we took off, David met me at Newcastle airport, and I arrived in the theatre at five past seven. I must never play Hamlet under these conditions again.

It was difficult to resist the intoxicating momentum of the movie. It still seemed like a crazy notion but we now had a detailed budget, designs, a pencil booking at Shepperton (it looked like there would be a cancellation), a business expansion scheme which looked as if producing £1½ million, and now there was interest from the BBC who were prepared to consider an investment in this unmade film in return for the television rights.

In the latter stages of the tour I found myself on planes and trains commuting from the North in order to attend the latest vital meeting. We were just about to start official pre-production, that is, have offices, a skeleton staff, and begin the long-term preparation that was necessary if the movie were to start shooting on 31 October. With the last-minute preparations for Elsinore taking up more and more time and the tour fatigue at its most extreme, Stephen Evans called a two man council-of-war in Manchester after the midweek *Much Ado*. He had grafted relentlessly on the project and had maintained enthusiasm and belief at a time when many others were expressing doubts. How could I possibly prepare for the first movie I had ever directed if I was playing eight shows a week in the West End?

The objection was fair, but I reckoned it could be done, and something told me that if we didn't strike while this particular iron was hot the movie would never be made. The spectacular and surprising success of the Renaissance tour seemed to make anything possible, or at least, that's what I thought.

On a bleak rainy night in Manchester, Stephen did his utmost to persuade me otherwise. He could have pulled out there and then, and without him the project had no chance. I could persuade as many people as possible over lunches and dinners but he was the one with the contacts, the introductions and the financial know-how to make it work. Instead of threatening me, he tried to make me see sense. It was surely wiser to start in the New Year, to have a rest after the Renaissance season and then have a completely clear period in which to prepare the film. It all made total sense, but I was also sure that in the weird world of movies, it would ensure that once people had enough time to think about its drawbacks, the film would never be made. I said as much and left it to him to make up his mind. I took a cab back through a miserable Manchester night to the digs I was sharing with David and his wife, Sue, and wondered what would happen.

And then there was David Puttnam. A rescue plan seemed ready to dispel Stephen's doubts and renew my belief in the whole thing. Through Brian Wenham, whom Stephen had inveigled onto the Board of the newly formed Renaissance Films PLC, and through the recommendation of Prince Charles, David rang our office. He spoke to our brilliant new miracle-working administrator, Iona Price, and arranged a meeting. At his mews office in Kensington he and his partner, Colin Vaines, quizzed me in great detail about the usual things: directing/acting, what crew I wanted, the tight schedule, my physical condition. I'd faced this kind of questioning before and was ready for anything. David was cautious about the project, but was interested in helping us. He had a deal with Warner Brothers who had distributed all of his Enigma movies, and we now had £2½ million. He suggested that he go to Warner Brothers to see whether on his recommendation they might be prepared to put some money up front in order to buy the American distribution rights and allow us to make the movie. It was an exciting move. Quite what David's involvement would be wasn't clear, but we would work that out if and when Warner Brothers showed an interest.

This was giddy news to take into the last week of the tour in Leeds, and it coincided with confirmation that the BBC would make an investment in the film. The week ended in a flurry of phone calls as I pursued the busy David Puttnam for news of the Warner Brothers' response. The silence was deafening, and it reinforced another harsh lesson of the movie world – if you're supposed to hear on Tuesday, you'll hear on Friday; if something is definitely going to happen on Monday week, then it happens on Wednesday fortnight.

Stephen and I were finding ourselves in this uncomfortable position halfway through the Elsinore stay and with pre-production dates winging towards us. Action was necessary. On my one day off from twelve consecutive Danish *Hamlets*, I flew to London for a meeting between David, Stephen and me. It was at least a respite from the relentless Danish glamour that had already produced two Royal visits in our first week at Krönberg, including one from our own Patron, Prince Charles, and one from the Queen of Denmark.

As David appreciated, time was not on our side. Warner Brothers were hedging over the project, and Stephen suggested that we forget their involvement. He was confident of raising the rest of the money in this country, but we needed to know if David would definitely become involved. David confirmed that he would take on the position of Executive Producer, providing this was acceptable to Bruce Sharman and as long as Stephen could convince him of the strength of the money. Stephen was sure he could and was even more convinced that with David's name and the BBC's attached to this quintessentially English project, that the other £2 million could be found easily. Proof of David's direct style and commitment had been given by his instant decision to fly to Elsinore the following Saturday to see *Hamlet* and to discuss some of the details of the film production.

The international airline timetables had been kind to me once more, and I arrived back at the Castle with an hour to spare. All of the male members of the Company had been assigned roles in the movie and they were relieved that my mission appeared to have been so successful. The proof of the pudding was David's appearance the following Saturday. If I had any doubts about his interest they were swept aside by the candour with which he answered all of my post-show questions about crew, schedules and his involvement. With his extremely able assistant, Lindsay Posner, he seemed ready and willing to make the whole thing work. On his return to England he met up with Bruce Sharman and the two of them planned a way forward for the movie on the existing schedule and at Shepperton.

At last it seemed I could relax about the financing of the movie and take a breather before the full horror of working out how to direct it. This was accompanied by a delicious week's break in which I experienced all too rare moments of utter happiness in the front room at Camberwell, with the summer sun pouring in through the window and all seeming well with the world. Then the phone would ring – it was definitely Shepperton, so could I go and see the studio and plan Agincourt for the third time? It really did seem to be coming together. Not only was there Tim Harvey as designer, but we now had a production supervisor, Vincent Winter, and a director of photography, Ken MacMillan, who had shot *A Month in the Country*. It was late August and we traipsed round the Thames Water Authority's field opposite Shepperton Studios, still a million pounds short, but with David Puttnam on board and the world's longest tracking shot developing in the mind of Camberwell's Orson Welles. The next three weeks would be nerve-racking. If we pulled the plug on the project at the end of this period, then Stephen would lose £80,000, and for every week after that the total would rise. Turning back would be an expensive process.

The West End openings of our Shakespeare season were set for late August and early September 1988, and the plays were launched over consecutive weeks with relative ease. Not only had the performances grown enormously through theatres large and small, indoors and out, but the directors themselves had visited the plays regularly to service the productions and to curb my worst excesses in the comic roles. By this stage we were ready for anything. Our experience in Denmark of playing sometimes obscure Shakespearian comedy to a largely foreign audience had stiffened the sinews. West End first nights lost a little of their oppressive tension when one remembered a rain-soaked Danish matinée of *Much Ado* where Benedick's first soliloquy was accompanied by an air-sea rescue taking place at the back of the sea-front auditorium. When the Danish Queen saw the production, the rain was so insistent that Gertrude played the closet scene in an oil-skin in order to protect her nightgown. There really were worse things than opening nights, and since the season began we had had our fair share of them.

With the plays open to yet more good press, with the usual reservations about my Hamlet, and with queues round the block at the Phoenix, attention turned full time on the film. We had no choice but to start intensive pre-production. Actors were ringing me daily asking whether it was on or off, and technicians and specialist crew were being lined up by Vincent and Bruce. We all sat like greyhounds in the slips hoping that the combination of Stephen's financial acumen and David Puttnam's film experience would secure the last million pounds. There had been an ominous silence from David's office since the Elsinore visit, and I was uneasy when summoned to a special meeting with him which turned out to be on the afternoon of the press night for *Hamlet*. I seemed destined never to let this performance have the benefit of a clear day's rest.

David's news was bleak. 'I'm sorry to have to say this, Ken, but it is my absolute belief that this film will not be made.' Oh fuck. 'I've been in this situation before. Every warning signal is flashing. I believe totally in you, and I believe totally in Stephen. What I don't believe is that you have enough time. With the best will in the world, and with the best skills in the world, it just will not be possible to do the paperwork in order to get this money into place.'

'But . . .' He was unshiftable. He would continue to act as advisor and could not actually stop us from going ahead, but his feeling was absolute. The potential damage to my career was enormous and unnecessary.

'I am convinced that this film will collapse either two weeks before or two weeks after shooting begins.'

That was that. Exit David Puttnam from Renaissance film world and enter Kenneth Branagh as the gloomiest gloomy Dane the West End had ever seen. I found myself between scenes and during the interval sharing my misery and fear with Stephen and with Emma and managing to stop ringing people like Judi and Geraldine and everyone else to whom I felt morally obligated. Stephen refused to be down-hearted, and still felt the film was possible. He believed Puttnam was referring to finance that came from more usual sources. The great strength of Stephen's contacts was their relative lack of cynicism, and their basic unfamiliarity with the film business. Like me, he was also alarmed but encouraged that down at Shepperton necessary work was already proceeding on some of the larger sets, which had to happen if we were to start on time. The enormous wall that I had asked Tim to design for the 'Once more unto the breach' section was already being constructed and there was also a fiercely impressive plaster model. This was exactly Puttnam's point. We must not be wooed by the excitements of these apparent signs of the film being a reality. Everybody was subject to two weeks' notice. If we stopped the next day, it would cost us *three* weeks' money for everyone, apart from the materials and other costs. Bruce was keeping a beady eye on all of this but it was clearly not good for film morale that the increasing numbers of staff should be living under the threat of collapse.

Now it was Stephen's turn to convince me to carry on. There were still key areas of casting to finalise. We talked about mortgaging our various properties to keep it alive for another few weeks while he and his associate, John Wilson, had a chance to do the paper work on the last million. It never came to that but it was with trembling heart that I sat opposite the tea table with Paul Scofield and Ian Holm in an attempt to persuade them to join up. Both were kind, courteous, asked sensible questions and believed totally in my ability to make the film happen. The fear which attended the whole venture had focused the mind wonderfully and if I didn't have a movie confirmed, then I did have a dazzling clarity about the movie that I would one day make. Ideas for colours, costumes and storyboards spilled out. The nearer it got, the surer I was about the gritty realistic approach that was necessary to make it the truly popular film I had in mind.

My enthusiasm was fitful, and alternated with bouts of extreme fatigue and utter depression and doubt about the whole project. Each day meant that we were further committed. Pat Doyle, who I knew instinctively would be the right composer for the piece, had been engaged to produce a demo tape. More money. I was at Shepperton every day, meeting with actors, casting directors, construction managers. The sets were growing at an alarming rate. There were three weeks to go and we still didn't know whether we had all the money in place. As I continued to grab between-show meetings with Stephen, and David held the theatre company together my mind was full of every cinema hardluck story from Zanuck, Welles and onwards. The final stumbling block was a bank guarantee for half the money. I still don't quite know what that involves but we couldn't proceed without it, and nor could we keep the actors hanging on indefinitely. All the deals had been done, but we had asked everyone to wait patiently for 'confirmation'.

After yet another late-night sponsors' event where I had said a million thank-you's and drunk too much cheap white wine, I found myself at midnight in Joe Allen's with Stephen over a dinner where I gave way to my overpowering depression about the film's fate.

'We've done it, mate. I'm relaxed on that.'

'Relaxed?' I said wanly, my face hardly emerging from the black bean soup. 'Then can I confirm with all the actors?'

'Give it another forty-eight hours.'

'Oh Christ, Stephen.' The face went back into the soup. The end. I could take no more. I had no more enthusiasm with which to stall the increasing number of apprehensive actors who were desperately seeking reassurance. Nor could I continue to run from the equally understandable curiosity of the numerous backstage visitors that came to see the Phoenix shows.

'But I'm telling you we've done it.'

It was useless. I'd now got to the stage where I would believe we'd done it when I was watching it in a cinema in 1989. And I was forced to realise that there would be no perfect, golden moment when an individual or a company would say wholeheartedly, 'Yes, it will all work out, the film will be made.' The film industry doesn't operate in that way.

Stephen was right. Although I went through the following days like an automaton, it was clear that we were going to make it. I was summoned to the latest high powered meeting of Renaissance Films PLC where I signed anything that was put in front of me. The consequent paper work made up a volume the size of a telephone directory which catalogued the deal by which the £4½ million would be produced and released in time for us to start shooting on 31 October. My scepticism remained. If it did fall through at this late stage I wanted to be able to get up in the morning. Things went on happening – the actors were confirmed, and a full construction crew was engaged. I had to have conversations about camera equipment with Ken MacMillan and, with ten days to go, we had a full read-through of the piece with the entire cast.

Of all the dreams that this scheme had included, this had seemed the most unlikely. There, under one roof, in a film to be directed by me, were gathered the entire Renaissance Theatre Company, actors from *Public Enemy* and *Twelfth Night*, as well as Paul Scofield, Ian Holm, Derek Jacobi, Geraldine McEwan, Alec McCowen, Brian Blessed, Judi Dench, Richard Briers, and Emma Thompson, in short, one of the greatest casts which could be assembled for such a venture. A mixture of young and old, and all hugely talented. If I discovered that I couldn't direct on film I would still have to go a long way to obscure the talents of this remarkable group. I took a deep breath as I looked around the great table at which we were all nervously sitting. Debilitating nerves were one thing I could no longer afford. I plunged into my directorial address. This was the one time they would all be together, and I wanted this to be a 'Company' picture. Here was the one opportunity to establish the tone and taste of the movie so that we all understood. Everyone listened. I played Pat's marvellous demo and the atmosphere was thick with a sense of rare occasion. A disaster it might be, but a singular one. Everyone was glad to be there. We few, we happy few.

And few were the days of movie rehearsal that followed. Actor availability and my commitments to both film and theatre meant that there was one chance to go through each scene before the actors disappeared. Paul Scofield would rehearse all his French Court scenes in one day before returning some six weeks later to film them, by which time we would hopefully have completed three quarters of the movie. In these brief walk-throughs of the scenes I found myself being dangerously dogmatic. I simply trusted that the people involved would challenge me on my worst excesses. There was no time to do anything else. Again not an ideal situation but the only one in which to get this particular thing done. I had to believe I was right.

The Friday afternoon before shooting. I'm sitting on a strange piece of camera equipment actually practising for the opening shot on Charles Kay. Trying to get used to people calling me 'Governor'. Back to the theatre for the weekend marathon. Two final Hamlets. All the thank-yous and well dones were over. We'd had our end-of-season parties and tearful last performances. I felt very proud of what the whole season had achieved and although there was effort of a different kind ahead, my chief feeling as I vacated my dressing-room was one of relief that the undeniable slog of eight shows a week in demanding roles was over. There was a lot of Hamlet in Henry V but I would only have to produce it in short bursts and not in front of a thousand people between 7.30 and 11 pm. One of the things I looked forward to most was having the evenings to myself.

I had a quiet restful Sunday, part of a delightful and important habit that I was developing. At this stage dread seemed pointless. I'd done everything I could to prepare. I owed it to myself to enjoy the following seven weeks as best I could. Otherwise what was the point? The chief joy of that day was the continued sense of being unshackled from the gloomy Dane and the relentless pressure of the theatre. *Henry V* seemed a much lighter affair by comparison. I said a short prayer, took a rare sleeping pill and continued to hope for the best.

Good night, sweet Prince.

222

TEN

In the maelstrom of thoughts and activities that made up the filming of *Henry V* it was very hard to keep a grip on reality. Very soon days began to blur into one another, and the only way to assess how one was feeling and how it was going, was to try and record things as they happened. The following is a rough diary account of this highly charged period, on which I have imposed some kind of retrospective order.

Monday 31 October
Day One. The first scene of the piece, and a scene which is vitally important for establishing through the clerics – Ely and Canterbury – the tone of the whole first section of the film. A conspiratorial political mood; an unfriendly palace and a dark world beyond. Ken MacMillan responded to my request for some very atmospheric lighting. At the same time I wanted not to be aware of it, and wanted this scene to feel like a documentary. For all sorts of reasons I'd made the shooting of it extremely simple. It made the business of the first morning easier and somehow I quelled the paranoia that this hugely experienced crew would suspect me of filming the entire film in the same way. Other elements helped to make life easier. When I rolled up on set to munch on the obligatory bacon roll I was mightily relieved to see the reassuring and smiling faces of Charles Kay and Alec McCowen, who were playing the clerics.

My chief concern with the first shot was not to repeat the experience of a short test that we had made on St Crispin's Day, 25 October. The purpose of this had been to experiment with hair, make-up and costume, and allowed me the first chance to direct Colin Hurley, a young actor who had learned the part and who would stand in for me as Henry V. Despite the propitiousness of that date, I had still been certain that the fates were against me. I could remember clearly David Tringham, the first assistant, shouting for quiet, calling for the camera to turn over. Nothing was happening. It

223

wasn't until I received a friendly dig in the ribs that I barked, 'Action'. I was determined that this should not happen on my first official day. Indeed, the reverse happened, and I found myself mumbling 'Action' before we'd even rehearsed. Calm down, Branagh. Charlie and Alec were brilliant, absolute pros who knew their lines backwards and were giving me the benefit of every doubt. The set began to give out the necessary atmosphere of trust that I needed in order to work.

By midday the seven set-ups were complete and the scene was finished. I couldn't believe it. A morning gone and we were on schedule.

The afternoon was tougher. Because of the speed, what I had dreaded had come to pass – I would be required to act on my first day. It was a baptism of fire. The entire English Court was required to be present for my opening speech, which meant twelve actors and behind them, in this vast medieval hall set, literally dozens and dozens of crew all thinking (as I imagined) 'Come on then, let's see what you can do'.

I did get on with it, even though my voice went up an octave. Despite Hugh's already excellent help I sensed I'd be doing this one again. Six o'clock arrived, and with it a huge sigh of relief.

Tuesday 1 November
Still in the English Court, and most of the pressure off me as actor, thank God. Instead the pleasure of watching Charles Kay make brilliant sense of the difficult Salic Law speech, Brian Blessed acting superbly, and providing a wild anarchic presence to relieve any potential tension.

'You can't direct for toffee, you big pouf.' He yelled this at the top of his voice, and the whole studio was in uproar. I laughed loudest and decided I loved the man to death.

Once a large number of important characters are gathered together and facing each other on a set, technical problems begin. I wanted to capture the paranoid atmosphere among these politicians, and this meant a great deal of coverage. I needed many different set-ups to record the reactions of all these important characters who figure throughout the film, and wanted the audience to be very familiar with them from the start. Unless one is extremely careful it's very easy to lose track of who's looking at who, and when. If you don't get it right, then it can make editing impossible. This whole concept of what is known as 'crossing the line', of actors appearing to look one way and sometimes looking quite the other, was an unfathomable mystery to me. I understood the principle of it but no element of its practice. I was saved, as I would be continually, by Annie Wotton, the script supervisor, who not only kept me right on this, but with David Tringham, suggested valuable shots and adjustments that I hadn't even thought of. Though it was early days, a sense of team work was developing. I was being supported.

And we were still on schedule.

Wednesday 2 November
A slight sweat on today. Alec McCowen had to be released by lunchtime in order to get to Chipping Campden for an evening performance of his latest one-man show. Deadlines like this seem to guarantee delays, but we got away with it, if only by the skin of our teeth.

Lighting this picture would be difficult. I wanted a smoky, fire-lit, medieval darkness in which we could still see people's faces and which was not too dour. Possible, but very time-consuming. Already I was unreasonably impatient about delays, and I reckoned that I had about a week in which to prove myself as a director. I had an unwritten agreement with Stephen that if things started to go wrong early on, he would take me off the picture. There was far too much at stake. I resolved not to get behind schedule through any fault of my own but I finished Wednesday by re-shooting my opening speech which was considerably butcher after the disappearance of my first day nerves.

Thursday 3 November
A new set for the conspirators' scene. It was very cramped and exactly what I wanted for the Hitchcockian underbelly of this sequence but, try as I had, homework had not yielded up the right way to shoot it. There was a dangerous rehearsal in which I was sure people would rumble my indecision. But as I was to learn on a daily basis it is not possible, or even healthy, to plan every move and set-up in complete detail. Things can occur on the day which change any preparation you might have made and, with helpful advice coming from actors and crew, there are often improvements. So it proved with this scene, which I wished to make fast-moving, tense and violent. Once the set was properly lit, we were able to shoot the scene

quite fast and bring something of that quality to our actual working methods. Once again the professionalism and discipline of the actors was a fundamental element in keeping us on course. No one dried. No one misbehaved, and Blessed's encouragement continued unabashed.

'Your direction's crap, Ken. Do you understand? *Crap.*'

I really couldn't take myself seriously.

Friday 4 November

By lunchtime it was clear that we were going to finish this scene by the end of the day, which put us a whole day ahead. Bruce and Vincent called me off the set to discuss this unexpected contingency. I had naively thought that we would have the day off. Not a chance. Another set was ready – the English Camp at night, but I hadn't done my full homework on that one. It was an exterior sequence, shot inside and I hadn't a clue what to do, or how to use the large number of actors who would be appearing for the first time and out of sequence.

'Well, we could always do your long speech, Ken.'

I understood the practical elements of Vincent's suggestion but 'Upon the King'? I wasn't ready to do that. My whole system was geared to the schedule. I didn't believe I could cope with this kind of change. Perhaps I could make up some new shots for the conspirators' scene?

Saturday 5 November

'Upon the King' it was, and all in one glorious set-up. Whether it turned out to be any good or not remained to be seen. At least there had been a psychological advantage in gaining a day, and I think the crew seemed genuinely impressed that their baby director could remember all of this four-minute speech in one go. Unusual in films. We celebrated by finishing early. I went home relieved but now newly apprehensive for the week ahead of night shooting on the 'Once more unto the breach' sequence.

Sunday 6 November

A recce for an opening sequence shot on the south coast which would later be cut. With divine wisdom we had chosen the day of the London to Brighton car rally and spent the hour-long journey either way in three-hour traffic jams. It did offer a lot of time to think, and I was able to mull over the rushes that I had seen that week. They were screened during lunch and provided me with the extremely difficult task of monitoring performances and trying to find my chicken salad in the dark. Mike Bradsell, the editor, had already produced a rough assembly of the first sequence. It was impressive enough to be shown to Stephen and some of the money folk who were beginning to make their appearances on set. The week ahead would draw them even more strongly. The Harfleur set was a magnificent epic structure – dark and brooding. And bloody difficult to shoot.

Monday 7 November
Arrived at 4 pm to examine the chaos, which looked as though it would never be converted into a highly disciplined and dramatic battle sequence. Everyone was called at around 5, but I knew that we'd be lucky to have anything on film by 9 pm. I had a quick canter on my horse. Vic Armstrong, the brilliant stunt director, had patiently encouraged me with lesson after lesson during the pre-production weeks to revive the Roy Rogers of old. He'd provided a magnificent white horse that felt as easy and safe to drive as a tricycle, but looked much more butch.

The weather was on our side, although it was amusing to see the high fashion eccentricities of a film crew preparing for the cold. David Tringham was moon-booted up to his armpits. David Crozier, the sound mixer, was in a jump suit, redolent of Pussy Galore, and Annie Wotton was encased in what seemed like a blue eiderdown warehouse. I worried about how we were going to talk to all these people. They had so many clothes on I was convinced they wouldn't hear me.

I spent the first two hours saying, 'What's happening, David?' to the crazed first assistant who, with his two deputies, was trying to marshal our 100-strong English siege force into the positions that I wanted. The complicated tracking shots that I required were not only difficult to light on the back lot at Shepperton, but they also required complicated camera equipment and cranes.

We had a go at last, and the atmosphere of friendly chaos seemed to work for the mood of the scene and the famous speech. Henry's words became passionate, almost desperate pleas of persuasion to a confused army who had been driven out of Harfleur for the umpteenth time. Things were going slowly but it was undeniably exciting to see Ian Wingrove's special effects lighting the Shepperton sky and giving the convincing effect of Harfleur in flames. The only problem was it all took so bloody long. Maintaining energy and concentration as the night wore on was difficult. Even the midnight supper break for stodge intake could not prevent the onset of fatigue.

Tuesday 8 November
Home at 7 am. Up at 3 pm, and on the set at 5 pm. More of the same, and more difficult with each passing night to rally all our troops and persuade them that spending another cold night in an increasingly muddy field would be exciting and fun. As the nights wore on there were less people available, and the shooting schedule had to be planned so that we covered as much large-scale action as possible early in the week, before it really was a case of we few, we very, very few. Keeping track of what we'd shot was difficult. Annie was a genius, and David Tringham also helped in my instant education about film grammar. The weather gods continued to smile on us and no time was lost through rain or snow, an extraordinary achievement in the middle of an English November.

Wednesday 9 November
The English army principals had behaved remarkably all week. They were all there in the cold, John Sessions, Ian Holm, Richard Briers, and Robert Stephens. No complaints and all the hallmarks of really fine performers: total concentration on a scene when they were off camera, and everyone helping each other out. The unit was beginning to take on the aspect of an army under pressure, led by an inexperienced director who nevertheless wasn't losing his bottle. The camaraderie helped us deal with our first stroke of bad luck. Malcolm Vinson, the camera operator, with whom I had already formed an excellent working relationship, was injured when a piece of camera equipment sheared and the crane he was sitting on threw him to the ground, fracturing his pelvis. Rapid diagnosis confirmed that he was fine and would recover comfortably but would not be able to complete the picture. We stopped shooting early and went home to think.

Thursday 10 November
One of the more bizarre things to deal with that week was having a second camera unit. I hardly knew what to say to the first one. When

Trevor Coop, the main operator, would ask the familiar question about a set-up, 'What would you like here, guv'nor?' I found myself answering, more often than not, 'Anything you like, love. As long as it's exciting.'

My incompetence had endeared me to Trevor who saw us through this last night of the Harfleur sequence while the second camera unit doubled for him. With a television documentary crew also following us around the set, I wasn't sure at times what camera I was supposed to look at.

Friday 11 November
The rushes for Harfleur looked great. Much to my surprise, there was sufficient scale and drama, and in the scene between the four national captains, a marvellous sense of impending danger in the British ranks. As I had hoped the whole sequence at times resembled other kinds of conflict, most notably the First World War and its trenches. I was convinced the material could combine to make a truly exciting sequence, but I was relieved that I didn't have the nightmare job of Mike Bradsell, the editor. Harfleur would be a challenge, to say the least.

The English night-time sequence would be a great challenge for me, and the change of rhythm a great shock after the chaos of Harfleur. It felt as though one was hardly doing anything and that this was the point where the audience would leave the cinema. But my instinct had told me that this sequence was the very heart of the play – the reflective, melancholic, sombre pause before the battle seemed to fascinate Shakespeare. My hopes for the sequence were confirmed on shooting Robert Stephens' definitive performance as Pistol, which managed to retain the feeling of despair that we had caught in the rehearsals for the Boar's Head scenes. Really fine acting.

Saturday & Sunday 12–13 November
At last a weekend off to sleep and recover from having actually filmed one of the great set pieces that people would be inspecting with such scrutiny.

En avant.

229

Monday 14 November
We do the Outside English Camp at Night, inside during the day. My senses were becoming very confused. Mike Bradsell had worked slavishly to produce a rough assembly of what we'd shot to date, and it included my version of 'Upon the King'. I could see it wasn't right and, with the omnipotence of a director who's a day ahead, I decided to do it again. David Tringham had made valuable suggestions as to how it might be shot and I knew that Ken MacMillan was delighted to have another crack at lighting this very difficult set. I revelled in this unexpected luxury and planned it for the next day, and settled back to enjoy a superb performance from Michael Williams, who brought great compassion and intelligence to his Shakespearian namesake.

Tuesday 15 November
With a peculiar irony I embarked on the second shot of 'Upon the King' as Prince Charles came onto the set as part of a visit to Shepperton. He'd been shown round the design department and some of the other sets, had seen some footage and was now faced with Henry's very personal soliloquy on kingship. With his customary patience and tact he waited until I had, in my view, got it right and then chatted to me about his continuing support and interest in the project. He certainly was a Patron, and a great supporter. He'd even turned up in Bath, informally, to see our *As You Like It*, and his reaction to my Touchstone had been identical to my grandmother's in Belfast: both of them did an instant dressing-room impression. It is delightfully disconcerting to see either your aged grandmother or the heir to the throne flicking their cuffs, bending their knees and mimicking my classical Tommy Cooper.

He left me to get on with it, and told me that he really would be looking forward to this film premiere. There was one convert. Another 4½ million, and we'd get Stephen's money back.

Wednesday 16 November
The system has finally adjusted to being back on days. The English Camp sequence is finished. Stephen and Bruce are still pleased with the rushes. Something must be wrong. Disaster is obviously round the corner.

Thursday 17 November

Back outside and time to hang Richard Briers. Shakespeare kills Bardolph off-stage, but I wanted to show the effect on Henry and on the army. And of course I wanted it to rain. During the Agincourt campaign it had rained for eleven days and nights on the long march from Harfleur. It had been disastrous for the English army, and the man-made precipitation that we arranged was far from welcome with our film crew. Everyone gets wet, of course. Permanently. Equipment has to be covered, the sound is difficult to record, and the special effects people need time to control the flow of water through their numerous hoses. It was time-consuming and difficult. But rain it was.

Friday 18 November

A certain campaign weariness began to show itself. Teddy Jewesbury, our Old Sir Thomas Erpingham, had suspected shingles, and I feared that he would take me to court for having brought them on. And, despite the brilliance of Peter Frampton's prosthetic nose for Richard Briers, the artificial appendage had a limited life-span under the effects of continual rain. In addition, the weather was mucking us about. Sun, would you believe – sun in mid-November. We had to crack on with this scene before the clouds parted completely, Richard's nose fell off, and we suddenly found ourselves shooting *Carry On Agincourt*. The absurdities of the situation, and the fact that the light went at 4 pm, put a spring in our step. To my utter amazement, we'd gained another day. This was a tremendous boon, as I had felt more and more strongly that the film itself, and the Boar's Head sequences in particular, needed the help of a more direct reference to the character of Falstaff. Not only would Judi Dench describe the man's death in heart-rending detail, but I wanted the audience to be aware of his tremendous influence on the young Hal. I assumed no previous knowledge of the other plays on the part of the wide audience I wished to reach and had resolved to insert a flashback scene which would give the film more emotional weight. I scoured the *Henry IV* plays and constructed a scene that described Falstaff's relationship with Hal and with all the low-lifers. What I needed urgently was a fine actor to play this flamboyant, life-loving character. It required instant, full-blooded acting that could be sad and funny in the space of one short scene.

The gods decreed that Robbie Coltrane was available to take his first swipe at a part which must be his birthright. A brief telephone conversation to this extraordinary Scotsman confirmed for us both that he could and should do it.

Saturday 19 November
First day on the splendidly filthy, spew-ridden Boar's Head set. Judi Dench's first appearance. She was nervous and vulnerable but, as always, ready to plunge in and trust her director and fellow actors. There were problems in trying to judge the exact mood and tone for the first appearance of each character, but the main problem was in controlling the giggling that went on, chiefly occasioned by Richard Briers' transformation into a lewd, gross Bardolph. With the Neanderthal Nym of Geoff Hutchings, the spit-spurting Pistol of Robert Stephens and Judi's own filthy Mistress Quickly, the incongruity was powerful and often comically infectious. The scenes needed to be funny, but we tried to keep the sense of underlying danger.

Sunday 20 November
Rest. Sunday had now become an oasis of calm and peace that was supremely important to me, the only day in which I seemed to live in the present. On the film, and throughout my work with Renaissance, I seemed to be preoccupied with the past or, more often, with the future, and consumed by an obsessive anxiety that allowed me very little real or lasting satisfaction as I went along. This sense of achievement was something I almost consciously denied myself, a complex debt being paid for feelings of guilt about my success. It is not a condition designed to produce happiness, or which allows you to consider alternative ways of life.

Monday 21 November
Proof, if it were needed, that Robbie Coltrane had the potential to be the definitive Falstaff. He was funny, melancholy, alive and deeply moving. I was delighted.

Tuesday 22 November
Rushes confirmed my on-set opinion. The flashback sequence seemed to work marvellously. And as we moved into the scene which recounts the death of Falstaff, it was clear that Judi, having played the scenes with Robbie, could infuse her lament for the dead knight with even greater feeling. The play is so infinitely varied that these

232

scenes felt as though they belonged to a quite different movie, so marked was the change in tone. It augured well for the finished piece.

In the meantime, I was revelling in not acting through the tavern sequences, and the mounting irritability that I was expressing about delays, the amount of smoke, and anything else that seemed to be in my way, was accepted with good humour by the cast and crew who, I suspect, put it down to fatigue.

Wednesday 23 November

Back outside for some mopping up on the Bardolph sequence, and the first appearance of Derek Jacobi. Securing Derek's availability for the film had involved Houdini-like escapes from previous commitments on his part. As it was, we could only call on him for brief periods, as he was about to open in London as Richard II and had already started rehearsing *Richard III*. If scrambled Shakespeare was whirring through his brain, he gave no indication with his first speech as Chorus, the difficult 'Now entertain conjecture'. The lunchtime rushes were a blow, as they presented numerous technical imperfections on what had been a glorious take of Judi with the death of Falstaff speech. We had no choice but to do it again.

Thursday 24 November

More smoke, more delays, more irritation. But against all the odds, an even better performance from the ever-patient Dame. It was 7.30 in the evening before we had cracked it. I'd insisted on the whole thing being done in one, a five-minute take where many things could go wrong. The tension on set as we attempted the umpteenth take was almost unbearable. Only Judi's example prevented me from flying into an impotent rage against someone or something. Not worth it, love.

Friday 25 November

Patience had proved to be the right course. The rushes were superb. Just as well, as we were now back outside with a vengeance: the English Camp before the battle, and, for me, the hurdle of the St Crispin's Day speech. This needed a tremendous epic setting and we were back on the famous Thames Water Field. Behind us were pylons, to one side was a modern housing estate and on the other side was a reservoir. This called for great ingenuity on my part, and as many trees as we could use to disguise the modern world. As if this wasn't enough, the religious calm of the speech was regularly punctuated by the sonic horrors of the Heathrow flight path.

Saturday 26 November
More air traffic, but miraculously the weather remained constant. There were no breaks for rain or sun, just pauses while we waited for the noise to die down. It was well worth it. Attempting to re-record this kind of dialogue in a studio was very difficult, and from my own point of view as an actor, almost always less successful. We had to have as much live sound as possible. We stayed on schedule and headed off for the weekend with our toughest week ahead of us.

Sunday 27 November
Panic.

Monday 28 November
We were off. 8 am on a frighteningly empty field in Shepperton. Annie Wotton and David Tringham looked at me with nervous anticipation: how do you start filming the battle of Agincourt? They weren't the only ones who wanted to know. We had 150 extras, thirty horses, numerous carts, actors and stuntmen. Fuck it. Bring 'em all on.

The numbers might be small, although they seemed pretty bloody enormous to me, but I knew that somehow we could achieve the effect I wanted – the brutal, savage scrum of Agincourt. It was important to fill the frame with as much activity as possible. There was a basic story-line which involved most of the principals, but with so many people and animals milling around in apparent pandemonium, and two camera crews, it was very hard to keep control of the narrative. It would have been very easy to get carried away and forget the basic colour coding that we'd employed and actually let the French win.

Tuesday 29 November
Having spent most of Monday in the saddle, I was megaphoning my way around the field as a bow-legged arthritic wreck. Reports of rushes were good. A relief.

Wednesday 30 November
We started on the slow motion stuff, which would be used to cover

234

the middle and end sections of the battle. With seventy-two frames per second whizzing through the camera, it meant that rushes' sessions stretched to over an hour at the end of a battle-weary day. The mud was getting deeper and each day was merging in with the rest. We needed a computer to work out who'd fought who.

Thursday 1 December
Not content with the time-consuming demands of slow motion, I now wanted rain again. Brian Blessed and the rest of the English army were getting used to this sadistic approach from their director. At this end of the week, they really did feel as though they'd been in a battle.

Friday 2 December
With the second unit starting to look after the residual stunts of horses falling, people being shot by arrows and everything else that was nasty, we moved back into the English Camp to film the aftermath of the battle. This scene which involves the death of the boys and the listing of the dead, is extremely affecting and was beautifully played by Ian Holm, who caught Fluellen's Welsh sentimentality exactly. Acting with him was like playing a racket game with someone very much more skilled. One was never sure how the ball would come back, but it would always be exciting and unexpected. He is a master of film technique. I'd heard the Ian Holm School of Acting described as follows: 'Anything you can do, I can do less of.'

Saturday 3 December
It was a funny sensation to read the list of the French dead while Europe's holidaymakers were whizzing overhead. I felt so much heavier and older after the experience of directing the battle, and of fighting in a great deal of it, that it was not hard to convey the immense relief at seeing light at the end of our particular tunnel.

Sunday 4 December
Rest. Calm and contentment.

Monday 5 December
The greatest tracking shot in the world. That was my theory, anyway. It was certainly bloody long. After the close-up carnage of

our Agincourt, I wanted to reveal as much of the devastation as possible. On our limited location we had not only built a 500 foot tracking platform, but Tim Harvey and his team had constructed a terrifying battlefield, where our 300 extras would mingle, wounded and dead, with horses and large numbers of dummy horses and people. To the accompaniment of a single voice starting the *Non Nobis* hymn, the exhausted monarch and his men would march the entire length of the battlefield to clear the place of the dead. As they marched, the music (provided on playback by Pat Doyle) swelled to produce a tremendous climax. There would be no question about the statement this movie was making about war.

David Tringham made this chaos work, and with our massive crowd and our remote control camera on its strange electronic arm, we began by 12.30 on that long day to start on the amazing shot. It was the last instance of my taking an inexperienced risk. Everyone had been suspicious that the shot would not work. We needed more coverage. Well, we did at least put another camera on the same track to gather close-up material, but I was convinced that the whole thing needed the sweep that the main tracking shot could give it. After each take, during which I carried Christian Bale the length of the field, we would watch nervously the video playback facility which we had specially employed for the day. The quality was poor and we had no alternative but to keep going. The visibility on Trevor Coop's monitor set was so poor that it was impossible to know what the remote control camera was picking up. Live, the action looked marvellous. As for the finished product, we would have to sweat.

I arrived home exhausted and somehow defeated and, for no good reason, burst into tears.

I felt as if I had come back from the war.

Tuesday 6 December
No acting. Hurrah! There were the French scenes to do now, and first on the list was the 'Comanchees coming over the hill' shot which I envisaged for the French generals pre-battle. I was delighted that our French seemed properly civilised and elegant, quite distinct from the rough English, but just as military. In the Olivier film they had been dangerously effete, which for me undermined the whole story. You had to believe before the battle that the English had no chance. With Richard Easton as the Constable and Michael Maloney a wonderfully fiery Dauphin, the French were a formidable force.

Wednesday 7 December
Back in the warm at last. I was glad not to have the wind whistling round my cod-piece any more. After the gory detail of the battle, it was a relief to direct the tense but still comic scene in the Constable's tent on the night before the battle. Derek came into this scene briefly and it was a comfort not to have the life-or-death dash to the theatre that had accompanied his filming during the battle period. We needed him for night shots and so had to wait until the light had dropped at 4.30 pm. We then had to take the scenes very quickly in order to rush him into a car and back to the Phoenix Theatre in time for *Richard II*. I would look at his haunted face, remember myself in that position and think, never again.

Thursday 8 December
Calm arrived with the appearance of Emma Thompson and Geraldine McEwan, both brilliant comediennes who transformed the French lesson scene into a beautiful, tenderly comic affair which manages in brief to show the woman's role in this depressingly male piece. She and Geraldine – fresh from her success in *Lettice and Lovage* – worked a treat together.

Friday 9 December
Enter Paul Scofield. If ever anyone was born to play kings, then it was this Titan, with his regal frame and haunted majestic face. I was more in awe of him than of any of the other legends working on the film, and yet he was the shyest of them all. He had no choice. Brian Blessed broke up any potential for undue reverence with his midday yell across the floor after I had given him some notes as Exeter. 'You never give Paul Scofield any fucking notes. You're just a bloody arse-licker. You've destroyed my performance.'

Scofield helpless under his crown.

Saturday and Sunday 10–11 December
Twenty-eight today. Bloody hell. The props boys made a surprise attack on me at the surprise birthday party while I was cutting the surprise cake which was in the surprising shape of the Harfleur wall. Wes and Gary's surprise involved two plates of shaving foam and much loss of dignity on my part. I licked my wounds on the Saturday night at the nicest birthday dinner I've ever had. Quiet, among

friends, and the whole delicious rare feeling lasting through Sunday.

Monday 12 December
Once more unto the breach, and it was the last week of filming. Signing the treaty. Scofield, me, Blessed, everyone. Hysteria. When the greatest seriousness was required, the greatest giggles started. I saw Scofield with the tears pouring down his face, pointing to Blessed and grabbing hold of Emma to say, 'Keep me away from that man.'

A VIP arrived on the set in the shape of the great director, Fred Zimmerman, who had directed Scofield in *A Man for all Seasons*, a marvellous film in which Scofield had given one of the all-time great screen performances. During breaks I listened in on their friendly gossip. About how Orson Welles had turned up on the set of that movie to play Wolsey and didn't know a line. Blimey.

Tuesday 13 December
The nobles disappear and leave Emma, Geraldine and me to get on with the wooing scene. It's a strange episode to place at the end of such a play and needs playing of the utmost delicacy if it is to tell us any more about this troubled monarch, and this strangely sensitive princess. The scene is both funny and tremendously sad. The princess has no choice, but she is spirited and intelligent, and subtly challenges Henry, who is unusually vulnerable in the scene. At the read-through, Judi had told me how much she had enjoyed playing this small role on three separate occasions in her early career. It is brief but beautifully written, even in broken French.

Wednesday 14 December
Hugh continued to be an enormous help. My insides were screaming out, 'only a few days to go', but I also felt a growing sadness that this marvellous family atmosphere on the set was about to be broken up.

Thursday 15 December
The very last lines of the play and most of the English and French armies were on set, with Derek, who was taking yet another break from *Richard III* to deliver the final Chorus speech. From Derek and

Paul the wonderful gravitas of the last movement of the piece is beautifully clear. All the lines seemed to be about resolution, with peace and hope emerging through the terrible experience of the play. As we waited for the last take to be checked, the atmosphere in the studio was thick with emotion. A brief moment of hysteria while the unit photograph was taken gave way to a moving scene where we said goodbye to all the actors. Only Derek had scenes left to do. For everyone else, it was the end. From Paul, Brian, Emma, Michael and everyone who had been part of this remarkable seven-week period, there was a tearful pride in the parting. It had been a glorious job and these last days had been among the happiest I had ever known, either personally or professionally. I shook as many hands as I could without giving in to sobs and reserved my warmest hugs for Brian, and for Emma.

The rest of the day was spent catching up on what are laughingly called 'inserts'. Shots of maps, feet passing, anything that we needed to help Mike edit. The mood on set was melancholy. I became irritable and found myself arguing with Annie Wotton for the first time in seven weeks about the way a map should be folded. What had happened to me?

Friday 16 December
A fresh breeze blew away the nostalgia of the previous day with our one location trip to Beachy Head where the Shakespeare-stuffed Derek would be required to deliver a Chorus speech while looking out at the French coastline. I arrived at the spot ridiculously early and found the place eerily quiet. We were on a deserted National Trust clifftop where the birds had decided to shut up temporarily to allow some Hamletian reflection on what had passed in the previous two months. Derek came and went, performing the speech beautifully. We tried unsuccessfully to get another shot which I had felt at one stage could open the movie – a pan across the French coastline eventually taking in the White Cliffs of England and ending on the contemplative face of yours truly. The whole thing was accompanied by the hollow crown soliloquy from *Richard II*, which seemed to express something of the message of our *Henry V*. The shot did not work and I decided to drop the Richard anyway. It simply didn't belong.

Saturday 17 December
A gesture towards Christmas shopping.

Sunday 18 December
The last day. In true cinema tradition, the last shot we filmed was the first shot of the movie. Derek was exhausted, but recovered after lunch, which is about as long as it takes us to get the tracking shot right. Stephen arrived for the last take and when the gate was checked we realised that we had actually finished filming a new version of *Henry V* in 1988, in seven weeks, one day ahead of schedule and amazingly under budget. I poured champagne into my dazed frame. We had done it.

Monday 19 December
Tidying up. Rushes good. Mike Bradsell confident that we can see a rough cut of the whole movie on Friday. Strewth. Meanwhile the wrap party. I went through in a state of high intoxication and endless thank-yous. I must have thanked everyone twice and when I started on the third circuit it was time to go home.

Friday 23 December
The week had passed in a blur of Renaissance meetings. Now it was time to look at the topic of our meetings. This first rough cut ran for two hours and forty minutes. Far too long. I knew that I would take at least twenty-five minutes out. That was OK. It was a little bare without the music but the potential for sound and orchestra was enormous. We'd invited heads of departments from the movie team to see it, as well as a selected group of close friends. They were all astonished at what we'd achieved so quickly. The possibilities for the film seemed limitless. As we sat over a late breakfast (the showing had been at 7.30 am) there were about thirty people in the room.

Several bacon rolls later I returned, exhausted, to my office and mulled over the enormous task ahead. There was a quote from *A Midsummer Night's Dream* which someone had scribbled on the noticeboard. It seemed an appropriate line for the months of post-production which loomed before us: 'Take pains, be perfect'. Fair enough. Here we go.

POSTSCRIPT

'Sit down and rest'
THE TEMPEST

And what then? Well, there's been lots of 'then'.

A brief holiday and then a whirlwind introduction to the world of film post-production, where the director seems to have a frightening power. Supported by a brilliant editing team, headed by Mike Bradsell, and with a consultative rather than interventionist policy from Bruce Sharman and Stephen Evans, I have enjoyed this very demanding job. And thanks to the miracles of cinema technology, I have been able to produce exactly the film I wanted. It will not be to everyone's taste, but for me it succeeds in realising what we set out to do. The ensemble acting is superb, the work of each department is excellent, and an indefinable element of commitment and heart shines through the picture. It *is* a popular, accessible and yet serious view of an underrated play.

At least, that's what *I* think. For the moment. In whatever way time, distance, objectivity and the judgements of others affect my view of the film in the future, it seems essential to be able to enjoy the results of all that work in the here-and-now. It is not something I have always been capable of doing, but it's an attitude towards my work that I shall try to maintain.

What effect will this have on Renaissance? I hope that it means we lose some of the frenetic energy which seemed necessary in the early days – the nightmare timetables, the constant fatigue, and the incessant drive towards the future, while the very reasons for the formation of Renaissance were neglected. With inevitable compromises over working conditions, occasional thoughtlessness about Company welfare, an unsatisfactory understudy system, and other teething troubles, we have fallen at times into every trap that I had set out to avoid.

Having had time to reflect, it is clear now that an enormous amount has been learned. Slowly but surely the moves to create and protect our chosen conditions of work are becoming more effective. The manic autumn of '88 showed us the dangers of stretching ourselves beyond reasonable limits. At the same time the success of Renaissance has allowed us to carve a theatrical future that is no less exciting, but less unrelenting in its demands on the Company.

A world tour is now being planned where, nevertheless, continued financial pressure will make rehearsal time relatively tight, and will force us to make a number of compromises. But even then, the administrative structure, understudy system and workload will have improved as a result of the lessons learned over the first two years of the Company's life. Of course there will continue to be tensions for the young theatrical puritans, but they will resolve themselves. In time.

Time. One thing that I can at last enjoy – it has been mercilessly overstretched during the last two years, and it has been my greatest personal loss. Things are changing. David and Stephen are developing their own strong ideas for the Company, both on paper and in practice, and I am very happy to share responsibility, and to allow the Company to develop a character which is distinct from me as an individual, and which can stand on its own as a positive force in the theatre. This is happening in many ways: the success of the London season has allowed Renaissance to buy back the offices which the book originally helped to pay for, and its financial independence is complete.

Now that this book is finished, there is time for me to have a break. A great deal of *Beginning* was written at the same time as editing *Henry V*, and the self-imposed restrictions of time created enormous pressure. Now, at least, that way of working can change, both through desire and circumstance. The final cathartic thrust of finishing the movie has quenched the roaring ambition of a young man in a hurry, although it has not stopped me from wanting to realise particular projects in the future. I feel as passionate about certain plays and parts as I have ever done, but it is clear to me in retrospect that my success has not been accompanied by any real sense of sustained enjoyment or achievement. I have never given myself the chance to make any serious assessment of my work, and I have thus denied myself many chances to improve as an actor, which now stands as my primary concern. I shall continue to write and direct, and I shall also revel in the chance to see other work of all kinds. Yet another casualty of the last two years has been the lack of opportunity to see other actors' work in current theatre and films – a very dangerous situation.

It seems to me that a profound change has occurred, a shift of perspective which I welcome. At last I can see that a balance between professional and personal life can be achieved, and I hope that I continue to keep it in view.

Here's to it.

The readiness is all.

London, May 1989.

244

Praise for *Broken River*

"Compelling from the first page, and then smart, sophisticated, suspenseful and satisfying throughout—*Broken River* is a first-class ride" Lee Child

"Hypnotic and unsettling, *Broken River* weaves a dark, compelling spell" Mick Herron

"*Broken River* is a novel with multiple identities: it's a ghost story, a crime story, a coming-of-age story, a story about love and a family and fiction itself. What is astonishing is how well all these elements work together, how they intertwine as seamlessly as the fates of Lennon's characters. As good as fiction gets" Ben Winters

"An intimate portrait of the violence we do to each other, about family and art and the scars of unspeakable acts. *Broken River* blisters and rips and ultimately soars. I loved it" Lauren Beukes

Praise for *Familiar*

"J. Robert Lennon's beautifully written new novel bristles with menace and suspense—a terrific and disturbing read" *Daily Mail*

"This highly convincing nightmare reads like a thriller; Lennon is painfully truthful about grief and parenthood" Kate Saunders, *The Times*

"Tight in focus as well as in construction ... an otherworldly narrative" Leo Robson, *Evening Standard*

"Dazzling" Justine Jordan, *Guardian*

"A writer with enough electricity to light up the country" Ann Patchett

"A literary puzzle, a marvelous trick of the mind ... as tightly wound as a great Alfred Hitchcock movie" *LA Times*

"So breakneck and harrowing, so grab-you-by-the-lapels astonishing, that you may not notice until nearly the end how many questions about your own life it makes you ask" Elizabeth McCracken

"A novel that imposes itself on the imagination from the opening sentences ... Lennon's brisk prose is both vivid and precise; the dialogue is clear and authentic, often funny. In fact, considering that this is a deadly serious, often bewildering and affecting novel, *Familiar* is witty and satiric. It is obvious that its genius lies in Lennon's feel for metaphysical contradictions that consistently undercut the realism ... *Familiar* is fresh and original; it is also disturbing in its strangeness, because that strangeness is eerily real" Eileen Battersby, *Irish Times*

"The direct present-tense narration and instantly engaging plight prove an irresistible combination ... One of the clever things about the set-up here is how neatly it invigorates some of drearier procedures of conventional fiction ... a meditation on family and identity likely to stir brain and heart alike" Anthony Cummins, *Observer*

"Lennon is an American writer whose novels delicately probe the psychology of their protagonists ... In *Familiar* Lennon uses his sci-fi vehicle to create eerie fiction. The notion of parallel universes becomes a metaphor for life choices and their results ... immersion in her alternate realities prompts reflection upon the aleatory nature of our own life, in all its uncanniness" Peter Carty, *Independent on Sunday*

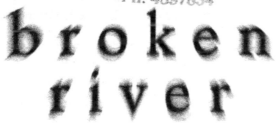

broken river

J. Robert LENNON

First published in Great Britain in 2017 by Serpent's Tail,
an imprint of Profile Books Ltd
3 Holford Yard
Bevin Way
London
WC1X 9HD
www.serpentstail.com

First published in the USA in 2016 by Graywolf Press, Minneapolis, Minnesota

1 3 5 7 9 10 8 6 4 2

Printed and bound in Great Britain by Clays, St Ives plc

A CIP record for this book can
be obtained from the British Library

Hardback ISBN 978 1 78125 797 5
eISBN 978 1 78283 335 2
Trade pbk ISBN 978 1 78125 800 2

broken river

Part One

1

It is a few minutes past one in the morning when the front door slams shut. Anyone remaining in the house—but there is no one—would be able to hear, through the closed door, the footsteps of three people hurrying across the porch and down the stairs. There are voices, too—a man's and a woman's, and a child's. The adults are quiet, or they are trying to be quiet, but their voices betray strong emotion: fear, in the case of the woman; and in the case of the man, impatience and frustration, which could easily be interpreted as a response to his own fear. The child's voice is plaintive and confused, as though she (a girl, most likely, of around five) has been awoken from sleep and hurried out of the house without explanation.

The state of the now-empty house would suggest that this is precisely what has happened. Many of the lights have been left on. In the kitchen, dinner dishes are still soaking under sudsy water in the sink, and a drawer and a cabinet have been left open and disordered, as though objects have been removed from them in haste. Three of the four mismatched wooden chairs that surround a small table—its laminated plastic surface scratched and gouged and peeling up at one corner—are pushed neatly underneath it; the fourth is lying on its side upon a linoleum floor that is equally scratched and gouged. A few coins lie on the tabletop, along with a half-empty pack of cigarettes, one of which burns in a white plastic ashtray.

Anyone standing in the kitchen right now would hear, through the screened, half-open window over the sink, footsteps on gravel outside. The three people—the man, woman, and child—have evidently reached a driveway or parking area adjacent to the porch. The man and woman are arguing, and it is possible to determine from their tone that they are trying to decide upon something quickly and don't agree about the proper course of action. An especially perceptive listener might describe the woman's voice as accusatory and the man's as defensive, and might be willing to imagine a scenario in which the man is to blame for this crisis, and in which the woman is registering her displeasure about the circumstances that led to it. The child, meanwhile, has begun to cry and is demanding something that has been left behind.

If an observer in the house were to climb the stairs that lead up from the kitchen, he or she would reach a narrow hallway interrupted by three doorways. Two of them are open right now, and light spills through them onto the frayed hall carpet. The first of the doors is on the left, and behind it lies a small bedroom: clearly the child's. The bed is unmade; open drawers interrupt the face of a painted bureau. Some clothes appear to have been hastily grabbed from these drawers; a few articles have fallen on the floor. One drawer has tumbled out of the bureau entirely and lies facedown on the pink-painted wide-plank floor, on a pile of small socks and underpants. Also visible on the floor, between the upturned drawer and the bed, is a stuffed toy frog. Perhaps this is the item that the crying child is demanding.

If so, the child's parents do not sound enthusiastic about the possibility of going back to retrieve it. Instead, their footsteps in the gravel outside have stopped, and the jingle of keys can be heard in the still night air. It is even possible to see them now, from the child's room: if an observer here were to turn off the overhead light and move to the open window, he or she could make out the family standing around a station wagon parked at an awkward angle on a weedy gravel drive. The car is a Volvo, from the mid-eighties, perhaps, with rust eating away at the edges of the doors and in the wheel wells. It is hard to tell the color by starlight (tonight is a clear night), but gray or light blue would be a good bet. The man has gotten the driver's-side door open and has dived into the car, and the woman is shouting at him to unlock the other doors. The man curses, and there is a moment of relative quiet wherein an attentive observer could discern the sound of the other locks popping open. The child is wailing now—she is clearly terrified by this strange nocturnal excursion and by the unprecedented desperation of her parents. The woman flings the rear passenger-side door open and pushes the child inside. She is in there for several long seconds, attempting to reassure the child that all will be well, in a tone of voice that indicates the precise opposite. Perhaps she is attempting to fasten the child's seat belt. The man is shouting at her to just get in, fucking get in with her and close the door. In the end the woman obeys, and before the door is even shut, the engine has been started and the car begins to execute a sloppy three-point turn. At last the car is pointed away from the house; it is thrown into gear, and the tires spin, sending a shower of gravel out behind it.

If the observer in the house were to leave the child's room and continue down the hallway to the next open door, the one on the right, he or she would find a larger, similarly disrupted bedroom. It would seem to belong to the man and the woman. The bed is mussed, with the sheets pushed down to its foot, but only one side appears to have been slept in. A collection of items on the small table at this bedside—a paperback romance, a snarled elastic band with several long hairs tangled in it, and a single earring (its twin is lying on the floor, in the shadow of the bed)—make it appear likely that it is the woman who lay here alone tonight. Perhaps, then, it was the man who stayed up smoking at the kitchen table.

The third room will have to remain unexamined for now, because a new sound is demanding our observer's attention. It is emanating from the now-darkened child's bedroom: or, rather, from its open window. The sound is that of a car—the mid-eighties Volvo station wagon, it would seem—scraping through brush and crashing against the trunk of a tree. There is a shout—the woman's. Something, some obstruction or unexpected event, has caused the man to steer the car off the drive and into the woods. As the observer turns and approaches the room for a second time, light sweeps through it, and out the door and into the hall: headlights: not of the now-disabled Volvo but of a new vehicle that has come up the drive toward the house. Car doors open with a rusted groan: the Volvo's. Another car's doors can be heard to shut, cleanly, quietly: this car is newer, denser, larger.

Heavy footsteps break twigs and crush leaves. There are shouts—men issuing commands, to one another, to the fleeing family. Someone, doubtless the woman from the house, is screaming—at first in surprise, then in alarm, and then in outright terror. Then, for a few moments, the woods are quiet. The chaotic action that immediately followed the accident has ceased. The woman, for now, is no longer screaming. Only the man can be heard; he pants and grunts; he weakly protests. Now the woman begins to cry. Deep male voices ask sharp questions, issue threats. The man and woman attempt to respond, to comply, but their efforts are evidently ineffective. Flesh can be heard to come into violent contact with flesh. The man groans. The woman yelps, begs.

It is unlikely that any genuinely feeling person could bear to hear the sounds that come next, not for more than a few seconds. And so let us assume that our observer is not a real person but merely the idea of an observer: an invisible presence without corporeal substance, incapable of engaging emotionally with the sounds that reach the house. These sounds are to last for nearly fifteen minutes. They are the sounds of suffering: the man and woman are enduring physical and emotional agony. It is unclear whether information is being extracted from them; or if they are being punished for something they have done, or are supposed to have done; or if these acts are merely sadistic. In any event, they are acts of physically violent, sexual, and psychological torture, and the man and woman react the way any human animal does when the last of its defenses have been stripped away and it is facing the inevitability of its own death. It is not necessary to describe those reactions here, only that they come to an end following two short, sharp noises: gunshots.

There is silence once again. Then the male voices return, quieter now, more efficient. Three of them: it is not necessary to discern the differences between them. The three men are working together. They

effect movement in the brush; they grunt, as though lifting something heavy. A quiet metallic snick implies the opening of a car trunk
or rear door, and a thump indicates that a heavy object has been
placed roughly inside. This sound is accompanied by the clanking
of wood and metal, as though some tools have been displaced by the
heavy object: shovels, perhaps. This process—the lifting, conveyance,
and depositing of something heavy—is repeated, and followed a moment later by the opening and closing of the newer car's doors. The
glare from its headlights, which during the chaos of the past half hour
has remained fixed upon the walls of the child's bedroom and of the
hall outside it, once again begins to move, and the sound of the car's
engine recedes into the distance. And then one of the Volvo's doors
opens and closes, and its engine starts up. It seems that, with some effort, its new driver has managed to extract the station wagon from the
brush and navigate it back onto the gravel drive. Soon it, too, is gone,
in the same direction as the new car, albeit with an altered set of wheel
and engine noises: scrapings and knockings and a rhythmic clanking, as of a fan blade bent off true. The Volvo is not right. Surely it is
barely roadworthy. Our observer might conclude that the car, like its
former occupants just minutes before, was nearing the end of its func-
tional life. In fact, it is likely that it will never be seen or heard again.

For some time, the only sounds audible from the house are of the
wind in the trees—it seems as though a storm may be coming—and
the creaking of the front door on its hinges. The door was left open by
the fleeing man and woman. The wind has come into the house, and it
has begun to move other things—some papers left out on the kitchen
counter, a bit of onion skin on the linoleum behind the pantry door.
The lit cigarette in the ashtray burns faster, and the wind pushes its
smoke away, at an acute angle, toward the farther recesses of the house.
The cigarette is propped in one of the three heat-discolored notches cut
equidistantly along the ashtray's edge; in twenty minutes the line di-
viding the intact cigarette and the ash has reached the notch, and the
remaining unconsumed cigarette tips back and tumbles silently onto
the table's surface.

Now, in a gust, doors slam shut throughout the house. The front door is the last, and loudest. Rain—big drops of rain—begin to fall outside, intermittently at first, then in a steady if irregular rhythm, and then in a torrent. After three minutes of this, rapid footsteps sound on the porch, and the front door opens only wide enough to admit a lone person before it closes again behind her.

It is the child. She's crying—sobbing wildly, choking on her sobs— and mucus drips from her nose and over her lips. She locks the door behind her and calls out to her parents. Of course there is no answer. The child does not appear surprised. She knows that something unprecedented, terrible, and irreversible has happened and that her parents are not likely to answer. At the same time, she believes the opposite: that her parents are nearby and will soon come to her aid. This is, after all, the only arrangement she knows. For a few minutes more the child stands in the vestibule, continuing to cry, her arms hanging at her sides, her eyes darting wildly, surveying the interior of the house, which our observer might guess she suddenly sees as alien, subtly and permanently changed, as though in a dream. At last the crying stops, and the child stands panting and rubbing her face. She takes a few steps into the kitchen. It appears to frighten her. She takes note of the fallen chair and the few scraps of blown paper lying beside it. After a time, she moves a few feet to her left, slowly, her back sliding along the kitchen wall. Then she lowers herself to the floor and sits there, her legs splayed out like a doll's.

The child is wearing a thick cotton nightgown printed with pictures of suns, rain clouds, birds, and umbrellas. She moves a hand up to the neckline and begins to twist the fabric around her pointer finger. She then puts this knot of cloth into her mouth and chews on it, champing with her bicuspids like a dog with a bone. Her eyes stare straight ahead, unseeing, and the fabric is soon dark with saliva. She falls asleep, and the nightgown-wrapped finger drops from her open mouth. But the finger remains tangled in the wet fabric, and her arm hangs there, stretching out the nightgown at the neck. The child snores. The rain continues to fall.

....

As dawn breaks, the child wakes on the kitchen floor, briefly appears frightened and confused, then gets up and hurries to the stairs. From down in the kitchen, our observer hears the sounds of a toilet being used. Footsteps can be heard, first across tile, then carpet, then wood. Bedsprings creak. The child can be heard to speak a single word, "Froggy," uttered in evident relief.

The child appears at the top of the stairs. Her nightgown is dry now but wrinkled and distended around the neck, and she is clutching the stuffed frog. She gazes down into the kitchen, her eyes passing over and through our observer, and she calls out to each of her parents. There is no answer.

After a minute, the child comes down the stairs, slowly and warily. But when she reaches the kitchen she appears to gain confidence— she walks quickly now to the pantry and emerges with a box of cereal. She places it on the table, then heads to the refrigerator for milk, and to a drawer for a spoon. Once these items have joined the cereal box, the child rights the fallen chair and drags it over to the cabinets. She climbs onto it and retrieves a china bowl from a shelf. These actions are deft; the child is clearly accustomed to them. The bowl secured, the child now moves to the table, prepares her meal, and eats it.

Once the child has put away the breakfast ingredients and carefully balanced the bowl and spoon in the sink, on top of the previous night's dishes, she walks briskly out of the room. For a few minutes she is audible moving through the recesses of the first floor. Not long after, her footsteps sound in the upstairs hall—there must be another staircase at the rear of the house—and roam through each room. The third door, the one closed the night before, under which no light shone, now opens, then quickly closes. The child calls out to both parents again, this time in evident, if theatrical, frustration and impatience, as though the previous night's fear has been transformed into irritation at their inconvenient absence.

The child's footsteps can now be heard entering her own bedroom again. Drawers are opened and closed. Muttered words are spoken: she is talking to herself, or perhaps to her frog. When our observer sees her again, she has come down the stairs and is passing through the kitchen on the way to the front door. She is dressed in a pair of bell-bottom jeans and a white tee shirt covered with small pink hearts, and her face wears an expression of determination and mild but growing anger. What else can we learn from her short trip across the floor? The child's eyes are large and deep, and the pale and faintly translucent skin beneath them is purpled by crying and by the disruption of her sleep. In the set of her shoulders, the tightness at the corners of her mouth, and the complex expressiveness of her brow— she is scowling in apparent concentration—we may detect evidence of a troubled and agile mind, one that, at this moment, is attempting to contextualize, explain, and reshape the events of the night before: to give them a form that she will be prepared, if not to grapple with, then at least to tidy up and get out of the way.

But we are out of time. The child has opened the door and is marching through it, into the bright and muggy morning. She throws it closed behind her, but with insufficient force, so that it fails to latch and falls partway open again. This enables us to hear the child calling out for her parents, in a tone both plaintive and scolding, the way she might address her stuffed frog when she has invented a wrong for it to have done. For several minutes the child's footsteps sound through the rain-drenched woods, and her chastening voice grows more distant. And then the house is silent again.

It remains that way for fourteen hours, during which time our observer can hear, through the open front door, the sound of water dripping from the leaves of trees and onto other leaves and the ground. This sound slowly gives way, as the water evaporates, to the busy noises of insects and rodents in the woods. For a brief time around 8 a.m., and again around 5 p.m., the distant hiss and rumble of traffic can be discerned, barely. Then, when darkness has fallen, footsteps approach from the rear of the house and make their way around it toward the front door. The footsteps are stealthy, but once they reach the porch, it's easy to tell that they belong to two men. The taller and more muscular of the men shoulders open the half-closed front door, and, though it is dark here, our observer can see that he is holding a pistol at his side. His partner, who is shorter, thinner, and somewhat stooped, carries something long and heavy: a crowbar, or perhaps two of them, one in each hand. The two men explore the first floor of the house, then head upstairs, where for half an hour or so we hear them taking apart the third room, at the end of the hall. Evidently un-satisfied with their findings, they proceed to do the same to the two bedrooms. Then they come downstairs again and proceed methodi-cally through all the remaining rooms. They make a lot of noise: fur-niture barks against wood floors, doors are ripped open, objects are cast about. Sometimes a crowbar is used to pry back pieces of floor or wall material, and we hear the groan of old nails being wrenched from wood, and the snap of wood breaking. Light bulbs pop and shat-ter; one or both of the men swear. Every now and then, a particularly noisy vehicle is audible on the road below, and the two men stop and listen and, eventually, return to work.

By the time they reach the kitchen, the two men are clearly frus-trated. They expend particular effort here, pulling cabinet doors off their hinges, smashing jars of molasses and dried beans and lentils, and ripping open bags of powdered sugar. Drawers are emptied onto the floor, and at one point the smaller man throws a blender across the room, inadvertently striking the larger man in the ankle. There is a shout, an oath, an argument. The larger man, our observer now sees through the evening's gloom, is more than large; he is enormous, and densely constructed, a hulking yet agile ogre of a man. The smaller man, we can now conclude, is of average height; he is small only in comparison with his counterpart.

After two more hours of effort, the men leave with the tools they brought and nothing else. The house is in disarray.

The next morning police arrive: first a couple of plainclothes offi-cers, who take one look in the door and then back away, talking into their radios. A pair of detectives shows up next, a man and a woman, both wearing suits. They slip on latex gloves and Tyvek shoe covers and pad through the house, taking notes, one in a little notebook, with a pencil, the other out loud, into a tape recorder. Technicians ar-rive, a photographer, and a number of other functionaries whose im-mediate purpose is not clear. The detectives leave after a couple of hours with a few objects sealed in plastic bags, but for the most part they appear dejected and bored. Eventually the police clear out. By late afternoon, everyone but the plainclothes officers is gone. Through the windows (for the door has at last been shut) our observer can see the uniformed police stringing yellow plastic tape around the place. They stretch it from tree to tree, doing a little maypole dance around each one. They appear to be having a pretty good time. Eventually a man arrives in a marked van—a locksmith, its panel would suggest— and he removes the locks from the front door and replaces them with new ones. Our observer then hears him doing the same in a distant part of the house: a back door, no doubt. Then car doors slam shut and engines start and the house is left in peace.

············

It is a matter of weeks before anyone enters the house again. During this time, the food left in the refrigerator browns and shrinks, and mice and insects discover the boxes of cereal and packaged snacks and sacks of grain. Ants march across counters and floors, and moths flutter through the kitchen. Squirrels, who have always lived in the largely unmonitored attic, sense the absence of human beings and take up their daily activities with less furtiveness. Still, the house seems more or less as it was left, to the untrained eye. The female police officer who enters the place twenty-five days after the initial incident curls her nose as she lets herself in, and gazes with apparent surprise at the destruction the two unidentified men wrought here. She wends her way through the kitchen holding a cloth shopping bag and a piece of paper. Let our observer look over her shoulder for a moment, at the paper. Words have been printed there: *red trousers, yellow dress, ukulele, Lego, tennis shoes, flip-flops, books.* The police officer makes her way up the stairs, speaking into her radio as she goes: *Nobody here*, she says, and a distorted echo of the words sounds from the front porch, where a partner doubtless stands guard. We hear the officer in the child's room, bustling around for ten minutes or so; when we see her again, her bag is bulging and she is walking quickly, as though mildly frightened. She slows her stride as she reaches the front door, as if to conceal her nerves from her partner. She pulls the door shut behind her and we hear the deadbolt lock. Low words and footsteps follow, then silence again.

Months pass. For a time, mice populate the house in great numbers. But pretty soon the food is gone, and the mice retreat. The house smells bad at first—feral and rotten—but after a while it just smells moldy and stale. It's autumn, and then winter. The first snow of the year falls and heaps itself onto the trees, and then a wave of unseasonable warmth turns the falling snow to rain, and branches, heavy with saturated snow, begin to break. The sound, recorded and speeded up by a factor of ten or twenty (and let us imagine that this is how our patient observer might perceive the passage of time), would sound like muted applause through the house's sealed windows and doors—that is, until a massive sugar maple standing outside the kitchen sheds a snow-burdened bough, which falls twenty feet, slides down a lower bough, and shatters the window over the sink. Now the applause is deafening. It peters out by midafternoon: show's over.

But a new one is beginning. New squirrels enter through the broken window and build nests in the house, and then, one afternoon in midwinter, a couple of teenagers arrive. A boy first: long haired, pale skinned, he appears unthreatening but unhappy. He picks the remaining bits of broken glass out of the window frame, then wriggles through, landing headfirst in the dish-filled sink and tumbling noisily to the floor. A voice outside asks him if he's all right, and he says he's fine. He goes to the front door and unlocks it to let his girlfriend in.

She's slight in build, but her face is wide and her color high. If our observer were inclined to form an opinion about these two, it might be that the girl has some potential for a long and happy life; the boy, not so much. In any event, they are together now. They explore the house, talking to each other in low tones. While they are upstairs, we smell marijuana smoke, then hear the sound of gentle laughter, and then the noises of sex. When the sun is about to set, they leave.

The boy and girl come back several times over the next several months, and then, on the first warm day in April, the boy returns alone. He's got a canvas army-surplus satchel with him; it dangles at his side limply, as though it contains nothing. In fact, it contains letters, a surprisingly neat, thick sheaf of them, in business-size envelopes. Our observer might deduce that they are from the girl and that, given the expression of grief and rage on the boy's face, the two have split. He sits down at the kitchen table, pushes aside the coins and the ashtray and the stub of cigarette lying there, and heaps the letters in the center. After a moment, the boy picks up the letters again, crumples each in his hand, and puts them back. Now the pile is larger— satisfyingly so. He pulls out a lighter and sets the pile on fire. He's crying. He mutters an oath. Then, apparently on impulse, he quickly pulls an envelope out of the burning pile, shakes the flames off it, and removes the letter inside. He doesn't read it. Instead he pulls a plastic pouch from his satchel, pinches an amount of weed from it, and rolls an awkward joint using the half-burned letter. He smokes it as he continues to cry. Meanwhile the pile burns down to ash, save for a few miraculous scraps, which he leisurely touches with the flame from his lighter until they become ash, too.

When the boy leaves, it is for good.

The coming year finds the house occupied by all manner of vagrants. Drug addicts, vandals, genuine hoboes. Graffiti covers the once-clean white plaster walls. Looting takes place, of course; clothes, furniture, and appliances disappear, while other items are destroyed by rough use or by the unfocused rage of the house's temporary inhabitants. Gradually the interior of the house comes to resemble what it is: an informal shelter for the marginalized, angry, disenfranchised, and mentally ill.

A few years down the line, after a particularly raucous gathering— a loud and violent party that can be heard even at a great distance— one man, no doubt a neighbor, attempts to take matters into his own hands. He's hale, big in the shoulders, determined, around sixty or perhaps sixty-five. He enters through the front door and deadbolts it behind him. Then, grunting, he wriggles out the broken kitchen window. Soon his face reappears, a cluster of heavy nails clutched between the lips. Our observer (still here!) watches as he hoists a piece of plywood into place over the kitchen window, and five noisy minutes later the house is again sealed off from the elements.

Not long after this, though, the plywood is torn off, and the house returns to its state as a hangout for teenagers and down-and-out adults.

....

Six years after the events that left the house empty, a car comes up the drive. The door opens, and three people appear on the threshold: a woman in a neat business suit, holding a clipboard; a casually dressed man of evident means (our observer notes his evenly tanned skin, long, tapered shoes, and designer jeans); and a weathered-looking man wearing a tool belt. The last of these three lets out breath: we can only imagine that he is about to be tasked with cleaning up the mess. The trio takes a tour of the place. At times, the woman points at something—an architectural feature, a spot of damage—and the men nod. The man with the tool belt takes notes in a small spiral notebook. The man of means nods at things the woman and the other man say. Soon they're gone.

The following week, the front door opens and the house fills with people. It's a work crew. Over the next few weeks they tear up the water-damaged and moldy carpets, rip out the waterlogged plaster, and peel up the worn-down, torn, and filthy linoleum. An electrician replaces faulty and hazardous wiring and installs three-pronged outlets in every room and ground-interrupt outlets in the bathroom and kitchen. A plumber repairs a number of radiators and replaces the upstairs bathtub and kitchen sink. Meanwhile the kitchen cabinets have been restored and a new range and microwave oven installed. The walls are sheetrocked and painted, and the broken window is repaired at last. Men can be heard scaling the outside walls, scuttling across the roof. When the work is complete, the woman with the clipboard and the man of means return to examine it. Satisfied, they leave. Our observer, whom none of the recent visitors has noticed, hears the clank of metal striking metal coming, faintly, from the end of the driveway. It's a real estate sign, no doubt, being driven into the ground. Our observer might also, however, have noticed a headline on the newspaper a workman left in the wastebasket underneath the new sink: KABOOM!, it reads, UPSTATE HOUSING BUBBLE BURSTS.

This headline might offer an explanation for the events of the year that follows: the woman with the clipboard leads potential buyer after potential buyer through the empty house, gesturing enthusiastically at the various amenities that seem less valuable, less appealing, with every passing day: the synthetic marble countertops; the laminate flooring, printed with a wood pattern; the bathroom fixtures that already show signs of rust, though they have never been used. Meanwhile the number at the bottom of the page on the woman's clipboard gets lower and lower.

The second year that the house is on the market, the buyer visits peter out and eventually stop. One day the man of means appears with a second man of means—this one younger, more ill at ease. They tour the place, then shake hands. A new woman soon appears, with a new clipboard and a new series of visitors, but once again the visits dwindle. The house is beginning to look abandoned again. Our observer doesn't venture outside, but it's safe to assume that the weather has taken a toll both on the recent renovations and what's left of the original eighty-year-old construction. Over the next year, rodents begin to move in again. Vandals come back—our observer can hear their spray cans being shaken, the hiss of their tags being laid on the siding. A vagrant breaks a new window, and once again people begin spending the night here, doing drugs, having sex.

Then, a year and a half after the last appearance of the second clipboard woman, she returns. She is followed by a man. He's tall, bespectacled, heavy in the middle, thickly bearded. He's wearing jeans and a leather coat and expensive shoes and is about thirty-five years old. The clipboard woman appears bored. She isn't trying very hard to make the sale; she's been in this position many times before. The man follows her around, gazing with apparent equanimity at the drug debris, dirty rags, and muddy footprints the visitors of the past year have left. The two climb the back stairs, move from bedroom to bedroom, and come down the front stairs. Words are exchanged in the kitchen, right beside our observer, who notes a certain dawning understanding in the clipboard woman's face. My god, she seems to be thinking, he's going to buy it. Numbers are proffered, adjusted, returned. The man nods. The woman nods. They shake hands. Clearly the woman cannot believe her luck. Her expression suggests an impending day of unexpected celebration—a boozy lunch, a night on the town.

Now it's late February, and the ground outside is covered in snow. Big machines come up the drive and clear a path to the backyard: a dump truck, an earth mover, a cement mixer. As the weeks pass it becomes clear that an outbuilding is being constructed. Low, blocky, with an angled roof and a continuous row of small square windows, it speaks of careful and understated design and appears built for some inscrutable aim. If our observer were, at this stage of its existence, capable of curiosity, this structure would no doubt pique it; the building's minimalist style, coupled with the bearded man's scruffy urbanity, implies some kind of creative or otherwise artisanal activity.

Now, for the second time in five years, the interior of the house is being torn apart. The sheetrock is replaced with plasterboard, the laminate flooring with wood, the cheap plumbing fixtures with bespoke ones of obvious durability. The imitation marble countertop is demolished and a three-inch-thick butcher's block laid in its place. The plastic and aluminum replacement windows, results of some long-ago renovation, are soon gone, and custom-made wooden sash windows are hung.

From time to time over the next few months, the bearded man returns, sometimes with another man—doubtless a building contractor, judging from his tape measure, dusty blue jeans, and military-grade cell phone shell—and sometimes alone. One time he arrives with a woman. Slender, small breasted, black haired, she peers around the place with evident astonishment. She coos with approval as she walks from room to room. The bearded man appears pleased as well. It is Sunday, and the two are the only people present in the house. In an act of evident ecstatic abandon, the woman turns a slow circle in the living room, then strips off her clothes. Does the man appear reluctant at first? Alarmed, even? Never mind. He is soon naked as well, and they make love pressed against one of the freshly painted plaster walls. With this act, their faces and bodies seem to assert, we hereby claim this house as ours.

Another four weeks pass, during which time the workmen attend to the final details of the renovation—painted trim, splashguard tile, a wood-burning stove. And then a moving van pulls up outside, and men carry boxes into the house, each marked with the name of a room. The men consult a hand-drawn diagram and haul the boxes to their proper places. Plastic-wrapped furniture follows, then tightly rolled oriental rugs, wooden crates full of paintings and photographs. Two objects of indeterminate identity are left in the living room; they stand at five and seven feet high respectively, upon their heavy hardwood bases, and reach up to two feet wide at their widest points. From beneath the translucent plastic sheeting and packing quilts that cover them, an occasional heavy appendage or extension pokes. The mysterious objects appear to be made of steel and glass.

Three days pass. These days are hot and sunny, and the interior of the house has grown muggy. Late in the evening of the third day, the driveway gravel is audibly disturbed by an arriving car. Its doors open and close. Light, fast footsteps cross the porch, and the knob jiggles. "Hold on, hold on!" comes a voice, one that our observer might recognize as that of the black-haired woman whom the bearded man brought here more than a month ago. Heavier footsteps land on the porch now, and keys jingle. In a moment, one of them crunches into the door lock, and the front door falls open. The woman and man are back, but bounding ahead of them comes a girl: their daughter. She is tall like her father, fine featured and dark like her mother, and she says, "Oh, *man*!" She runs from room to room in an obvious state of excitement, then races up the stairs, presumably to find her own room.

"Welcome home," the man says, to no one in particular. To his family. To the house. To the Observer, who floats silently, substancelessly, in the kitchen, looking on without judgment.

2

Irina is sitting on her bed with a spiral notebook open on her lap, a pencil poised above it. It's a special pencil, one from a box that her mother bought her—a long-defunct brand that has been brought back to life by the kind of people who miss old pencils. They are silvery gray, with soft, dark leads; the eraser is flat and rounded and encased in a rectangle of squashed gold metal. These pencils cost twenty dollars for a box of twelve; Irina looked them up online. Her mother would disapprove—a gift is a gift, however much it costs—but in this case, the price has made her like the pencils more. They are precious. They can't be used for stupid things. Which is why she is using them to write her novel.

She likes it here. She liked it the moment Mother described it to her: "A small house, in the woods, far from anything fun." In the months leading up to their move, when they were still living in Brooklyn and Mother was angry at Father, she would ask Father what was being done to the house today to make it ready for their arrival, and he always had an answer. "They're replacing the kitchen counters today," he would say. "They're sanding the old floors." "They're painting the walls." Perhaps he was making this stuff up—how could he know what was being done at any particular moment, in a distant place he'd visited only a couple of times? But Irina enjoyed the notion of the house being transformed for her benefit. She imagined her room, with its window onto the trees. In her conception of the future, she could sit cross-legged on her bed and gaze out at a heavy tree branch that squirrels and crows would perch on, and she could talk to them and possibly, eventually, feed them from her hand. In the meantime she would work on her novel. She started it in Brooklyn; it's about a boy who gets on the wrong subway train and ends up in a previously unknown sixth borough of New York City where women wear gigantic dresses with bustles that prevent them from ever getting closer than six feet from one another, and men who are brothers or close friends or who started businesses together would allow their long mustaches to intertwine, making them physically inseparable. When one of them kisses his wife (the wives have to lean far forward, due to the bustles), the other feels, through his very sensitive mustache, his brother or friend or business partner's lips moving, and this makes him jealous, and he desires to kiss the wife himself. Also, in this borough the most distinguished job you can have is street magician, electric power comes from monkeys riding stationary bicycles, and the borough president is twins. The borough is called Quayside because it is an island cut through with man-made channels, and people live on boats as well as in apartment buildings, and most of the cabs are boats, too, yellow boats painted with checkerboard patterns, and when you step onto one a recorded message in the voice of a famous Quayside actor or comedian reminds you to put on your life vest.

So far, a week after arriving here, life has gone pretty much according to her desires, if not better. Her room is awesome. The window really does look out onto the trees, and she sees squirrels and crows all day long. She hasn't befriended any, but that was just idle fantasy. She has written 14,734 words of her novel (she counts each day's output in the evening, before going to sleep, and pencils the total at the bottom of the day's last page) and has persuaded her parents to let her be homeschooled, just for the fall, before they enroll her in the public school in Broken River, which she is not so secretly hoping never gets around to happening. Broken River seems to her a meager, sad little place, with its empty storefronts and depressed-looking old people heaving themselves up and down the sidewalk, but it has its charms—an old-fashioned (though abandoned) movie theater with a marquee bearing the now-fragmentary names of movies from three years ago, an old-fashioned (not abandoned!) drugstore counter that serves ice-cream sodas ("Not old-fashioned, either," her father corrects her, in her head: "Retro"), a busy and not-at-all-old-fashioned coffee shop, complete with the horrible sucking sound that results every time somebody orders an expensive drink. Actually it reminds her a little bit of Quayside—certain neighborhoods in Quayside, anyway, where it's all white people. Broken River is all white people, and every other place they've had to drive thirty or forty minutes to get to this week—WalMart, Home Depot, and the like—has been all white people. That's fine, their family is also white people, but Irina cannot help but think that these people are hiding from everyone else, either out of fear or because (she hopes) there is some secret appeal to this part of the world that they don't want other kinds of people to find out about. For what it's worth, she hasn't figured it out yet herself.

She has spent a lot of time out in Father's studio, helping him, or perhaps mostly watching him, get it set up. He is clearly excited about the space, which is a twenty-foot square with cement floor, sloped metal ceiling, and clean, white walls. He has been lecturing her on the operation of the forge—it is new, stainless steel, "heats up fast, Irina, really fucking fast"—and on the positioning of his anvil and his wheeled rack of blacksmithing tools. He is quite geeked about the wall-length rack he made, out of plywood and two-by-fours, that holds his supply of thick slab glass—some clear, some milky, some smooth and shiny, some sandpaper-rough—and iron and steel, sheets and bars of the stuff. As he talks, which he has been doing pretty much incessantly since their arrival, she walks up and down the wall of glass and metal, running her fingers along the edges of the slabs and sheets and bars, gripping them with her fingers, trying to budge them. If her mother were out here, she would shoo Irina away from the wall of heavy materials, any one of which could fall on her and injure her, or shatter and cut her; her father does not. Her explorations have given him pause—many times he has stood, interrupted in midsentence, staring at her dazedly, his forehead creased as though with concern—

but she isn't sure if this is because he's worried about her safety or just surprised and alarmed to realize that she is there, that she exists, that he has a daughter, that the daughter is her, that they have moved hundreds of miles from home to this strange, isolated place, and that this is their life now.

If it's the latter, Irina understands. She feels that way, too: alarmed, amazed, uneasy. It should not be a secret to her father that she is a little bit afraid of him, a little bit in awe of him, a little bit skeptical of his status as an adult responsible for her upbringing. She's had friends, though not great ones, and she has met their dads. Her dad is not like their dads, not even back home in Brooklyn, where everyone's parents are weird or creative. Her friends' dads smiled when they saw their daughters, kissed them hello and goodbye, explained things to them (often things that didn't really need explaining, to be honest) in a bright and really kind of corny tone of voice. These dads kept their beards trim, their jeans cuffed, their glasses polished, their balding heads buzzed. Her dad, on the other hand, talked to her friends as though they were adult women (or maybe he talked to women as though they were children? She is very proud of this insight and jots it in the margin of her notebook for possible eventual insertion into the novel), asking them if they wanted a cup of coffee or what they were working on or what they thought of various books there was no chance any of them had read. Her dad didn't comb his hair and beard, he grew them as long as her mother could stand (she was the one who periodically hauled him into the bathroom and sheared them off with clippers), let his glasses grow hazy with sweat and dust. Her dad was as much ape as dad. He was an ape dad! It was an ape dad who loped around the studio, fondling the tools, rearranging and reorganizing the work table, the hooks on the pegboard, the standing fans. It was an ape dad who made these big weird scary awesome things that he sold, apparently, to people in New York.

"You are not to return for one year," Irina heard Mother tell Father one night a few months back, while they lay in bed after sex (and yes, she knows what sex is and what, unfortunately, it sounds like), meaning that he is not supposed to set foot in New York City, not even to sell his sculptures. "The service can deliver them. You don't need to be there. Gert will take care of everything." Gert is the woman who runs Father's gallery, or rather it is her gallery in which his sculptures are sometimes shown.

"I know," Father said, groaning, "I know."

They didn't know how loud they were. Or maybe they did but figured Irina tuned out any kind of information that wasn't obviously relevant to her. Irina, in fact, didn't tune out any information that reached her from the adult world. She was very eager to reach adulthood and wanted to be able to step into the role with the ease of a seasoned professional. She asked one friend, Sylvie, if her father had ever had an affair, and Sylvie, even though she was *thirteen*, didn't even know what that was. "It is where he meets another woman who isn't your mom and he falls madly in love with her." Sylvie said, "That's stupid," and Irina said, "But has he?" and Sylvie said, "No!" and pretty soon Sylvie's mother was calling Irina's mother to tell her to come get her. (There was a long pause, and then Sylvie's mother said, "I'm sorry, Eleanor, I cannot put a twelve-year-old girl alone onto the subway," and Irina saw which way the wind was blowing, excused herself, and slipped out of the building to sneak off to the F train. Very probably she will never see Sylvie or her mother again.)

Personally, Irina herself doesn't see how it's possible to be with one person your whole life, or even overnight—"You would have more friends," Mother once said to her, "if you would agree to more sleepovers," to which Irina replied, "Exactly"—and if a day arrives when the idea of removing all your clothes in someone else's presence does not horrify her, she thinks that she will not feel compelled to limit herself to one lover. She intends to be a novelist, a famous one, like her mother but more so, and also much more frightening and intimidating than her mother, who even on television appears like a fairly normal person—somebody's mother, in fact.

Their house is small. This part, she didn't expect. The front door opens onto the kitchen, and between it and the stairs lies a living room where her parents have put books, a sofa, and Father's two giant, frightening sculptures. The kitchen is disproportionately large and has big windows on two sides and so is Irina's favorite room besides her bedroom. It's everyone's favorite, actually. Upstairs there's a narrow hallway from which Irina's room, her parents' room, and her mother's study may be entered; all three are basically twelve-foot boxes. There is also a spiral kitchen staircase with tiny steps you can't even fit your entire foot onto, and Irina habitually uses it instead of the main one because it is weird. On the outside of the house, which is brownly shingled and frankly kind of ugly, the spiral staircase is contained in what looks like half of a cardboard toilet-paper tube somebody glued onto the exterior wall. There's a little turret on top, for no evident reason.

Perhaps the most interesting thing about the house is that something bad happened to the people who used to live here. They are dead, anyway. This is apparently one of the reasons the house was empty for such a long time and thus needed to be renovated before Irina and her parents moved into it. Irina is aware of this fact only because she overheard two workmen talking as they were installing a new refrigerator: one of them said, "You know this is where those people got killed," and the other one said, "Yeah, except it wasn't in the house," and the first one said, "But still," and the second one said, "Hey," and then kind of tilted his head at Irina, who was sitting at the kitchen table wearing headphones, but, cleverly, the headphones were not plugged into anything. This is a trick Irina would have played around her parents as well if her parents made any effort whatsoever to conceal what they said to each other.

In any case, the identity of, fate of, and story behind the previous inhabitants of the house is something Irina intends to research while she is here. If the results are interesting, maybe she can incorporate them, somehow, into her novel. Because at the moment, the novel has no real plot—it's just descriptions of things. That's what Irina is good at. She believes that she inherited this deficiency from her father, who is a visual artist and does not require narrative to make something of value. But if that's her cross to bear, she will do it stoically.

It's 11 a.m. Not yet time for lunch. Mother and Father are working. The novel isn't going anywhere, not today. But it's a sunny summer day and the woods outside are beckoning. She closes her notebook and shoves it under the mattress, then goes out to the studio.

Irina's father is wearing goggles and thick gloves and is bending a glowing iron bar around the edge of an anvil. It is somewhat disappointing to her that her father doesn't do more pounding with a hammer. This is what you're supposed to do with an anvil, isn't it? Instead Father mostly bends. She is not sure if the lack of pounding is the cause of his underdeveloped upper arms or the result of them. She says, "Father, I'm going to the woods. Can I borrow your phone?"

He doesn't look up. Instead he plunges his iron bar into a metal bucket of water on the floor, and the water roils and bubbles and hisses, and steam surrounds his face. Then he straightens, holds the bar up to the skylight, turns it in his hand, squints critically at it. Frowns. "Sure, it's on the bench."

"Thank you." She goes to the workbench, picks up the phone, and puts it into her pocket. Father is moving to the forge to heat his bar again. He says, "Don't answer it if it rings. I'll call them back."

"Okay."

"Don't fall off a cliff or into a river."

"I won't."

"Don't fall in a lake, either." He's looking at her now. She stands in the open doorway, her hand on the knob. "Or a hole, don't fall in a hole. Don't threaten a bear, especially a bear cub, especially if the mother is around. Don't get eaten by wolves or carried away by pterodactyls. Don't get alien abducted. Don't spontaneously combust or become a drug addict or a prostitute. Don't marry an asshole."

"Stop bossing me around," says Irina. "I'll marry whoever I want!"

"That guy's no good for you. Don't let his fancy car fool you."

"You don't understand me, or Chad! You'll never understand our love!"

"Fine!"

"Fine!!!"

Outside, she wakes up the phone, finds the maps app, opens it. There is central New York, and there is Irina, a blue dot. She was delighted to discover, a few days after moving in, that the woods surrounding the house are adjacent to a state-owned nature preserve that is crisscrossed with walking paths. These paths are actually documented in the maps app on the phone, and Irina has figured out how to drop a pin representing their house on the map, so that she can always be directed back to it as long as there's a cell phone signal, which there does in fact seem to be everywhere near the house. She walks north, through her parents' land, to the sign that reads THREE VALLEYS WILDLIFE MANAGEMENT AREA STATE OF NEW YORK DEPARTMENT OF ENVIRONMENTAL CONSERVATION. Catchy name, New York! Now the path becomes wider and better groomed. She walks for five minutes or so to where there actually is a cliff she could fall off of, if she isn't careful. The path goes left and right and is marked by yellow paint marks on trees; she has previously taken the path to the east, so now she goes west. The path is crooked, following the line of the cliff, which she peers over from time to time, not without some anxiety. Father was not kidding: the dropoff is steep, and though she might survive the fall she would most likely end up drowned in the river two hundred yards below, and her body would be carried away. She wonders where the people got killed—the previous owners of the house. Were they thrown off the cliff? Why did it happen? Did they mess with the wrong people? Were they innocents who happened across the commission of a heinous crime, and knew too much? Were they bad guys themselves? It's hard to imagine criminals living in their house, which is so awkward and charming and peculiar. The house is a nerd. They're living in a nerd!

After a while the path slopes down and the cliff face becomes less sheer, and pretty soon she is walking along a ridge that leads her to the river itself. It's just barely a river—she would call it a creek, really. But the maps say it's a river, the Onondakai. She finds a sunny grassy patch by the water and sits cross-legged on it: "Indian-style," a teacher of hers once said, and was corrected by an aide who told her that was racist. The aide did not last long! She googles the river and finds out that it got its name from a Seneca chief. The name means "destroy town." She imagines the river rising, inundating a village, sweeping the houses and people away. On the other hand, the town it runs toward is called Broken River: are the two at war? She wishes she had brought a notebook so that she could write all this down for her novel—maybe that could be the plot, the waters of Quayside are rising and only her protagonist can fight them back.

The phone rings in her hand. No face appears on the screen, no name, just a number.

Father has asked her not to answer, and she doesn't intend to answer, but who can resist answering a ringing phone in their own hand? Also, the ringtone is shrill and unsettling—a nondescript beeping that sounds like a digital alarm clock. It is out of place here in the woods, by the river, and it needs to be stopped. She swipes the screen and raises the phone to her face.

"Hi, this is Irina."

"Oh! Hello," says a woman. She stutters for a moment, then says, "I'm trying to reach—is this Karl's number?"

"He's—I borrowed his phone."

"Hello."

"Hello."

"If you call again in half an hour, he'll answer."

"I'll do that, then."

Irina ought to just hang up now, but instead she says, with a precipitous kind of feeling, as though she is falling off a different kind of cliff, into a different kind of river, "I won't mention that I talked to you. I wasn't supposed to answer."

"All right . . ."

"So maybe you won't mention it, either?"

"No, I won't."

"So we're cool then."

The woman does not sound entirely comfortable as she says, "We're cool."

Irina hangs up. She feels bad. She wants to be on her father's team, but only in the most abstract way. Because she believes she takes after him and wants to protect him from a world that doesn't appreciate him enough. On the other hand, she senses that she has just involved herself in a part of her father's life of which her mother might not approve.

The phone is still glowing in her hand. For reasons not entirely clear to her, she is suddenly mildly angry with her father, and she pokes the phone icon, imagining that it is his shoulder: Hey! Hey, you! His call history pops into view. Father doesn't make a lot of phone calls, but there is one number, with a 212 area code, that he has called about five times in the week they've been here, and it's the one attached to the lady she just spoke with. The conversations are long—like, forty minutes to an hour—and occur at the times (lunch until dinner) when he's typically in the studio.

Hm.

She decides to forget about this. It is none of her business.

She gets up, climbs back up the hill along the cliff, turns south, passes the back of the nature preserve sign (onto which a yellow POSTED PRIVATE PROPERTY sign has been stapled), and hurries down the path to the studio to give the phone back to Father. He is hard at work bending hot metal again, so she slips the phone onto the workbench and edges toward the door.

"That's you? Not a ghost? You didn't fall off the cliff?"

"Nope."

"Which way did you go?" He takes off the protective goggles and wipes sweat from underneath his fogged-over specs. He is wearing baggy jeans with suspenders and a tee shirt bearing the name of a summer camp. He looks cool. He always does. She feels her irritation draining away.

"I went west. It goes down a hill. It looks like there's a bridge over the river at some point, I want to find that."

"Yeah, you should."

It occurs to her, not for the first time, that her father never addresses her by name. A nickname, sometimes. She was named after a photographer her father knew—a haughty gray-haired woman who wore long flowy things. Irina met her at a gallery show in New York, to which, thinking of it now, she had probably been brought solely in order to meet her namesake. Suddenly she doesn't understand the role of women in her father's life. Suddenly she is not sure how she is supposed to feel about him.

They look at each other for a couple of seconds, and then his phone rings. They both glance over at the workbench.

"Better get that," Irina says. Her father's antennae go up. She slips out the door and closes it behind her.

....

The physical and emotional rigors of the afternoon have left Irina almost too tired to eat dinner. After her walk, she returned to her room and tried to add a couple of pages to her novel. Then she tried to take a nap, but every time sleep endeavored to drag her down, some noise from outside the window—a bird or falling branch—would distort and magnify itself in her nascent dream and jerk her back to wakefulness, where the things she didn't want to think about awaited her. Now Irina is grumpy and displeased, even with the food her mother has made, even though it is spinach lasagna, ostensibly one of her favorites. The spinach is stringy and it's sticking in her teeth and the sauce is bland. She entertains a moment of guilty nostalgia for the days, years ago, when her mother was sick and they got takeout all the time. At some point during the silent meal she drops her fork on the plate, falls back in her chair with a sigh, and crosses her arms over her chest.

"Yes?" her mother inquires.

"That's not a question," Irina points out after a few seconds.

Her mother contemplatively dabs the corners of her mouth with a cloth napkin. The napkin is printed with a cartoon of the New York skyline. They got it at Fishs Eddy in Manhattan. They can't go there anymore! They don't live in New York! Mother says, "What is the source of your dissatisfaction, Daughter?"

"Nothing."

"So you are not, in fact, dissatisfied."

"I *am* dissatisfied," Irina says, "but I am telling you that my dissatis*faction* has no *source*."

"It's parthenogenetic," Father offers. "It's ambient." He has a nervous look on his face.

Irritated, Irina says, "I don't know the meaning of the first word."

"Virgin birth. Asexual reproduction."

"That's not the same as having no source." As she says this, she thinks of the river, *her* river, the Onondakai, running in a circle, like one of those tail-chomping snakes whose name also, she's pretty sure, starts with an O. It comes from nowhere, and it never reaches the ocean. It can't rest! It just goes and goes, in an endless loop, destroying every town it touches.

Her father shrugs, pooches out his substantial lips. "I guess you're right."

The conversation has had the effect of spreading the bad mood around. It really is ambient now. Father keeps glancing over at her, significantly, and she doesn't know why. Mother keeps glancing at Father and then back at Irina.

This is stupid! "I'm going to take a bath," she says.

"You don't want dessert?" her mother wants to know.

"No."

Irina gets up, scrapes her lasagna into the trash, slots the fork and plate into the dishwasher, and climbs the stairs. In the bath, she hums quietly to herself while trying not to have thoughts; afterward she dries off and puts on her summer pajamas, which consist of pink, lacy shorts and a tee shirt with an owl on it. She goes to bed and tries to read. But it's still light out. It's weird to be in bed. After a while her mother comes into the room and lies on the bed with her. Yes, Mother, that's just what I need, for my hidey-hole to be invaded by grownups. Irina pretends to read for a while. Then her mother says, "It's strange to be in a new place."

"That's not why I'm dissatisfied."

"So why, then?" says Mother.

Instead of answering the question, Irina says, "What happened to the people who used to live here?"

After a long pause, Mother says, "I didn't know you knew about that."

Irina narrows her eyes and says, "You don't know a lot of things."

Mother has been facing Irina, who has been lying on her back, but now she lies on her back, too, and puts her hands behind her head.

She says, "They died? It was a long time ago—they think it had to do with drugs or something else illegal. We're not in any danger."

For no particular reason, Irina replies, "That's what *you* think."

"Irina," says Mother, after what sounds to Irina like a strategic pause, "did something happen today? On your walk? Or with your father?"

Oh, no, you don't, thinks Irina. She digs in: "*How* did they die?"

Mother narrows her eyes, and for a moment Irina is frightened: she has seen her look at Father this way, when she thinks he is lying about something. Is this what it feels like to lose Mother's trust? It isn't a good feeling.

"They were murdered, Irina," Mother says, her voice steady. "By two or more assailants. Their bodies were never found, but the physical . . . evidence suggests they were . . . that they died. In the woods."

"Hm," Irina says.

"And that's all I know about it," Mother concludes, and now she's the one who's lying. Her mouth twitches and she glances away.

And without thinking (though of course she has been working up to this, and it is not unrelated to the subject at hand), Irina says, "I think I am more than old enough to have my own computer, don't you?"

The hesitation that follows is brief, and then her mother answers, "Sure, okay. What are you planning to do with it?"

"I'm going to edit my writing. And do research."

Her mother appears impressed. Irina allows herself the small luxury of believing she is not faking this time.

"Also," Irina adds, "I will stop borrowing yours! Won't that be a relief?"

"Well," her mother says, "it's maybe good for me to not have access to a computer now and then. But all right. We'll order one tomorrow."

Well! That was easy. "Can I borrow yours now?"

Her mother turns her head and Irina looks right into her eyes. "Yes, sure," Mother says. "You want me to get it for you?"

"Yes."

A nod, and then she hoists herself up off the bed with a groan and disappears down the stairs. There has been more groaning than there used to be; her parents' middle-aged bodies no longer recover so quickly from the lifting and transferring of heavy boxes. A few minutes later she has her mother's laptop on her lap and is opening the browser. Her mother looks on.

"I know how to use it. I don't need help."

"Just—"

"I'm not going to snoop in your personal things."

Mother's eyebrows go up. "That's not what I was going to say. But all right."

"Thank you."

"You're welcome." There's an awkward moment when she seems to want to say something but can't. In the end, she just says "Good night" and disappears into the hall.

This feels like some kind of victory to Irina, for a short while. But after staring into the empty browser search bar for several minutes and listening to her mother move around listlessly in her computerless office, she begins to feel sad. She looks up at her closed bedroom door, opens her mouth to summon Mother back.

But what would she say? That she was suddenly sad and didn't know why? No. That would be stupid. Instead, she shuts her dumb mouth, lays her hands on the keyboard, and types the familiar words *Broken River NY unsolved murders.*

....

Because Irina was lying, too: she has had no trouble, over the past few weeks, finding information about the murders and probably knows as much about them as anybody but the killers. Those workmen were right that it didn't happen inside the house; it actually happened close by: right next to the driveway. What was known was that the people, a man and a woman, attempted to flee the premises in their car but ended up driving it off the driveway and into the trees. There they were "taken from their vehicle" and shot. Police found bullets and shell casings at the scene of the crime; DNA evidence established that the blood "and tissues" of both victims were present "in amounts that strongly suggested that the victims did not survive the shootings."

Neighbors claimed to have heard none of the commotion; anyway, gunshots were not unusual in this area and tended to be ignored and quickly forgotten. Police weren't alerted to the crime until the following day, when a child appeared on a neighbor's doorstep and announced that her parents were missing. Police found the house ransacked, the door left open, and tire tracks leading off the drive and into the woods; a tree had been crashed into, and the evident murders had happened not far away. The child was able to provide some additional detail, including the probability that there were multiple perpetrators and that they drove to the scene of the crime.

But beyond that, there was nothing. The child had evidently run into the woods and hid with her hands over her ears. She had not seen the killers. She took refuge in the house for the night and left in the morning, to search for her parents. Instead, the neighbor heard her calling for them, took her in, and phoned the police.

Those, as far as Irina has been able to learn, are the actual known facts. But they don't tell her anything about what she really wants to know: what happened to the girl. It appears that her name was Samantha Geary and she was put into foster care, but beyond that, there is nothing. The girl disappeared from the public eye. Luckily, this is precisely the kind of mystery that the internet likes to speculate about, and Irina has found a great deal of said speculation on an internet messageboard called CyberSleuths dot net (no doubt named when "cyber" seemed like a forward-thinking prefix that everybody would be using in the future, while wearing eyeglasses with screens on them, LED wigs, and e-scarves crawling with stock tips). CyberSleuths is the meeting place of bored and morbidly curious people like Irina who think they are clever enough to solve crimes the police have given up on. And they are right! There is a HALL OF FAME thread where the messageboard's successes are archived: and there are many! The information is out there, and the CyberSleuths are on the job, combing through old news reports, Facebook-stalking murderous creeps, connecting unidentified bodies with missing persons, and generally being completely brilliant and heroic from the comfort of their own homes. Irina has registered under the name UncleJ. This is a reference to a character from her novel. Additionally, it pleases her to think she might be mistaken for an old guy. She is discovering that, with a man's name, she does not get talked to like the twelve-year-old girl she actually is. She just gets talked to.

Not that she posts much. She's merely dipping a toe, so far, into the thread unmemorably called *Geary murders, 2005, 2 vics, no bodies*. So many people saying so many things about events Irina now feels, thanks to her move upstate, somehow in the center of: it is immensely exciting, and she feels as though she needs to exercise patience, not let it all take her in too quickly. She both fears and savors the experience.

Irina logs in (she doesn't let the browser save her username and password, as she wishes to spare Mother from the knowledge that her imagination has grown so dark) and scans the thread for new stuff. There isn't much, just some idle speculation. She studies, for the umpteenth time, the iconic photo of Samantha Geary—someone named smoking_jacket found it in a school yearbook—as a kindergartener, wan and stringy haired, her face long, her eyes large. Irina googles the girl—she would be seventeen now—and finds plenty of people by that name on Facebook and Twitter. Some of them are probably seventeen. But it's not an unusual name. And if Samantha got new parents, they probably changed it. That's how things like this work, the child gets a new name and psychologists use hypnosis to make her forget what happened. Probably they replaced her memories with puppies and ice cream cones. Anyway, these Samanthas don't look like her Samantha. They look like regular girls, uncorrupted by proximity to murder. Irina thinks she would know her Samantha anywhere. They are housemates, soul sisters, cruelly separated by time and circumstance. When she sees the girl's eyes, she will know it.

She spends ten minutes rereading old posts on the Geary thread, then another twenty clicking idly around other threads: murders, rapes, disappearances, all of them attended by people even more obsessed than Irina, all of them unsolved, abandoned by the police. An increasingly familiar sense of futility and dissatisfaction settles over her, and she throws her head back onto her pillow pile and stares at the cobwebs swaying nauseatingly on her bedroom ceiling. Here it comes again: her dissatisfaction deepening, mutating into something harder. She is beginning to feel resentful. It's nothing in particular that is making her angry, just the vague and growing sense that she is little more than a pawn in her parents' lives. A powerless thing to be pushed roughly ahead, and sacrificed if necessary, as Samantha Geary nearly was in the woods that night. Of course just this morning she was feeling deeply enchanted with her new home, the wooded path, both of her parents, her novel-in-progress. Now that's all gone. Why? Is this irrational? Is she just being moody? From inside the emotion, it's impossible to tell. She's as angry with herself as she is with anyone else. She imagines, briefly, that *she* is Samantha Geary, never mind that the years don't add up right. Maybe she's actually seventeen and her physical development has been arrested by the violent trauma of her childhood. She has been dropped into this life by a team of social workers, and her memories have been replaced. It makes a certain kind of crazy sense.

Impulsively she navigates to the forum entry where Samantha's childhood photo has been posted. Irina doesn't look like that and never has: apple-cheeked, pigtailed. Bah! She opens the image file in a new tab and hits PRINT. She tosses the laptop aside and runs down the hall to her mother's office, where the printer is. It's dark now, and the printer is wheezing, and spitting the paper out underneath a blinking red LED. Irina snatches it up and returns to her room. Samantha is grainy and small, up in one corner of the page. At her desk, Irina cuts out the photo and tapes it into the back of her notebook. Then she opens up the browser history (*muscle fatigue remedy, back pain remedy, achy bones remedy, massage therapy*, read Mother's recent queries), erases her tracks, closes the laptop, and climbs down the stairs. Her parents are sitting on the sofa, drinking whiskey and looking mildly depressed. She sets the laptop down on the coffee table, says thank you, and runs away before anyone can say good night to her.

Only when she gets back in bed does she realize she never kissed them. Oh well. There's a first for everything. She doesn't need the habits of youth. She's a new girl now.

3

Summer is nearly at an end. The air is heavy and wet and the sun appears larger in the sky, diffused and magnified by the haze. Clouds are massed at the edges of this valley but seem to lack the motivation to climb the ridges and pour in. If there were a large town here, its inhabitants might crowd into the Onondakai to cool down. In the wide, shallow stretch where it bends toward the wildlife preserve, and where large, flat stones offer paths to the far bank or islands to spread towels and lie in the sun, the Observer might find people relaxing, talking, playing with their children, unwrapping wilted sandwiches and unscrewing thermoses containing diluted iced tea and a few foamy slivers of what used to be ice cubes. If there were a town here, one of the natural pools that has formed at the base of a small waterfall, accessible by two miles of rough footpath, might be informally designated a spot for skinny-dipping. Young people in love with each other and with their youth might strip off their clothes here and swing into the water on a rope slung over a branch; old hippies might join them, and a pervert or two might lurk in the woods with binoculars. But there is no town, and the Observer finds no one.

Instead the Observer moves southeast along County Route 94. It has discovered that it can leave the house: can go anywhere, really. Faster now, faster than a car, the Observer flies along the river, in between hills, briefly above a defunct railroad, sometimes past a half-empty village or struggling farm. Once the Observer arrives at flatter land, there are more paved roads, more farms, low houses. Soon there are car dealerships, fast food restaurants, big-box retailers surrounded by half-empty parking lots. It's Broken River. There is the Broken River State Prison, and there are several prison-themed bars and a prison museum. There is even a street called Hoosegow Lane—doubtless part of a doomed effort, at some time in the recent past, to draw visitors based upon the only claim Broken River has to fame.

The Observer is not interested, however, in the center of town (the defunct movie theater, the walk-in medical clinic, the senior center, the strip club, the local bank that closes half an hour before everyone else gets out of work), choosing instead (because with freedom of motion has come the need to make choices) to continue down Onteo Street, through three traffic lights; to make a right at the hospital and parking garage; to follow an Afro'ed, baggy-panted kid on his bicycle toward the long, low glass-fronted building where an unwashed, multiply dented Greyhound bus is idling. It doesn't matter where the bus has arrived from. The Observer elects not to care. Passengers file off: a pale kid with sunken cheeks and a trucker cap that bears the Playboy logo, who hitches his backpack higher on his shoulder and fist-bumps the kid on the bike; a very old woman whom no one is helping down the steps, and who meets no one on the pavement; a thick-necked middle-aged man in a Buffalo Bills tee shirt and gigantic basketball shoes who can't seem to stop coughing; and a teenaged girl.

To see this girl at rest, and from a distance, might be to regard her as waifish—she appears, at first, to be very thin, malnourished, even, and she seems to have mastered the art of stillness, as though in an effort to conserve energy. Her straight hair covers much of her face, but large eyes peer out from beneath it—are they frightened? wounded?

But to see her in motion would bring doubt to one's initial assessment of the girl, for she moves purposefully and with preternatural poise, as though holding back some hidden strength. And if you approached her, as our Observer now does, her thinness would reveal itself as, rather, a leanness. She's tall—five feet nine or even ten inches—and she carries her army-surplus duffel bag as easily as though it were stuffed with balled-up newspapers. It is not. It's heavy. Our Observer can tell by the thump it makes as it hits the ground at her feet. She has dropped it there, not ten yards from the bus she has just exited, in order to consult a paper map, printed from the internet. She studies the map, squints at her surroundings (the Wilson Farms convenience store, the electric power substation, the empty stucco box that once contained the local chapter of the SPCA), examines the map again. Whether what she sees is a disappointment to her is unclear. Her face is impassive.

Clearly no one has arrived to meet her. But perhaps she didn't expect anyone. There is resignation in her eyes and in her posture: the slight stoop a tall girl learns to assume, an inward curl of the shoulders. She folds the map, jams it into her back pocket, hoists the duffel onto her shoulder. She's wearing a gray V-necked tee shirt that conceals small breasts and, on her left arm, the lower half of a crude tattoo of uncertain design. Her well-worn jeans hug narrow hips, and her shoes are garish running sneakers bearing the logo of a popular brand. She walks briskly but without particular haste. She heads up to the light, followed by our Observer, turns left at the hospital, then beelines through the center of town, rarely turning her head to peer into a shop window or acknowledge the appraising look of a passerby. She does not invite, with her posture or facial expression, the male gaze. But certain boys and girls she passes—kids hanging around on stoops and in the doorways of abandoned storefronts—are interested in her.

The girl ignores them. She passes the strip club and medical clinic and movie theater, crosses the town's main intersection, then heads down an incline past one, and then the other, prison-themed bar. Of course: she's going to the prison. This is not an uncommon walk for an out-of-towner to take—the bus station to the prison, eight shameful blocks enduring the curious stares of the locals. But the girl isn't ashamed. She isn't anything. She's walking to the prison, that's all: past the museum, with its electric-chair logo, past the hot dog stand, over the train tracks, and in the main entrance.

Our Observer doesn't follow her inside. An hour passes, then another. After a third hour has passed and the sun is low in the sky, she emerges. Now her body betrays some weariness: she carries her duffel as though aware of its weight, and her color is off—she looks a little peaked. She looks hungry.

And as though to confirm this impression (for the Observer hasn't moved in the three hours the girl was inside), she heads toward the hot dog stand. There's a small line there, as visiting hours at the prison have just ended, and a collection of tired- and sad-looking people is queued up at its small yellow-lit window. But the girl doesn't get in line. She arcs around and past it, then stops in front of a pay phone bolted to a telephone pole, not fifteen feet away. It's standing in darkness, for the insect-encrusted streetlight above it has burned out. Surely it doesn't work, this phone? But no matter: the girl pulls an outdated folding cell phone—its fake chrome plating pitted and worn down to a patina of streaked black plastic—out of her pocket, and leans against the defunct pay phone kiosk to make a call. (The Observer can see that the cultural memory of a space apart, dedicated to communication at a distance, remains strong, despite the obsolescence of the technology that made it necessary. Where else should one go for a private conversation? Or, more to the point, what else is there to be done with such a space?) She pulls a map from her bag; this she unfolds, turns over, and holds up before her eyes, evidently trying to make out, in the light from the hot dog stand, something written there. She punches a series of numbers onto her phone's keypad, waits a few moments. She says, "It's me," then has a brief conversation. Her body language changes as she speaks; it's clear she does not savor this conversation, in which she is doubtless at some kind of disadvantage. She is, perhaps, asking for a favor.

After a minute, the girl hangs up the phone. She gazes at the hot dog line as though contemplating the possibility of eating a hot dog. Her hand burrows in her pocket as if palpating the coins there. But in the end, she walks another half block from the prison, just to the other side of the tracks, and settles onto the guardrail underneath the closest functioning streetlight.

She sits there for twenty minutes. If she wore a watch—she does not—she might periodically gaze at its face. She closes her eyes, then opens them quickly, as though wary of the consequences of falling asleep.

At last a car pulls up. It's a four-door Ford Taurus from the nineties; rusted in places, primed and sanded in others, it sits low on its tires and emits a scraping sound as it idles. It is too dark to see the driver, but a hairy arm tells us that it is a man. The girl leans in the passenger-side window for a brief chat. Then she lifts her duffel, opens the back door, and tosses it in. Hastily, as though she's afraid the driver might take off without her, she opens the passenger door and folds herself into the car. The Taurus continues past the hot dog stand, takes a turn around the prison visitors' lot, then bumps over the tracks and heads toward the center of town. Before it gets there, though, it makes a right, disappears briefly behind some houses, then reappears long enough for our Observer to see it vanishing around a hillside.

The Observer could follow but chooses instead to remain. It is interested, it realizes, in the negative spaces the people leave behind, spaces they fail to occupy in the first place. Objects and events not missed but gone unnoticed, unanticipated, unconceived of. The Observer will catch up to the human beings later. They're slow, moored to their physical forms, to each other.

In the next half hour, the hot dog crowd dwindles. Cars leave. Visitors walk toward the bus station in silence. For another hour or so, the hot dog vendor reads a magazine. Then the guard shifts change—men and women in uniform arrive in their cars; others leave through the front gate. Most of them buy a hot dog. When this rush is over, the hot dog vendor switches off his yellow light, padlocks a hinged piece of plywood over his window, and leaves on a moped that was parked, out of sight, behind the stand.

4

Several weeks later, Eleanor is doing what she has done every Tuesday and Friday afternoon since they moved here, which is to take Irina to the Broken River Public Library and sit with her in downtown's only coffee shop with their piles of cigarette-reeking, broken-spine hard-covers. It's unusually hot for September, and the coffee shop—it is called Frog and Toad's and is located in a kind of difficult-to-find mini-mall behind an abandoned bank—has the air-conditioning going full blast. As a result it's quite crowded. Eleanor is self-conscious about occupying a table in a crowded coffee shop; she can sense other people waiting, studying her for evidence of impending departure. When potential customers walk in, see the crowd, frown, and march back out, Eleanor feels responsible. She wants to leave now in order to accommodate what she perceives as other people's more pressing needs. But she has identified this quality in herself as a personality flaw, and she doesn't wish to pass it on to her daughter. So she pretends she belongs here and deserves this table.

Irina's drinking coffee too. She asked for a cup, just now, in line at the counter. Their conversation went like this: Irina ordered coffee, Eleanor laughed, Irina said, "What's so funny?"

"You're serious? You want to try coffee?"

"I don't want to *try* it, Mother, I want to *drink* it."

"So you've had it before?"

She recognized Irina's scowl from her father's face: that broad fore-head so effective at advertising hurt. "I have it *all the time*."

"Where?" Eleanor asked, though she knew.

"Father's studio."

"He has a coffeemaker out there?"

The barista, through a tiny, tight mouth, said, "Two coffees, then?"

"Yes, please!" Irina chirped. "Milk in mine, please. No sugar," she added, proudly. Eleanor immediately recognized this pride not as a manifestation of her own emerging faith in herself but rather of Karl's natural, effortless, self-satisfied bluster. She checked herself: now stop that.

The girl poked the cash register iPad with one hand while point-ing at the condiment station with the other. Irina blushed, obviously embarrassed at having blown the protocol. You'll learn, young one, Eleanor silently reassured, and a gray funk settled over the two of them.

Now they're sitting together at a tiny table by the window, pre-tending to read their books. People in business casual drag themselves damply down the street, casting the occasional envious glance into the coffee shop. Whenever one meets Eleanor's gaze, she offers up a small, embarrassed smile. She is thinking about the coffee in Karl's studio. What else has he got out there? Packages come for him regularly; she has seen the cardboard boxes, neatly broken down and stuffed under-neath the advertising circulars and egg cartons in the recycling bin. These expenses do not show up on her credit card statement, and so he must be paying for them himself, with his own money.

She doesn't go out to the studio very often, and when she does—to bring Karl mail or ask him if he wants lunch—she rarely steps over the threshold. He invites her in now and then to look at what he's working on, but it seems perfunctory, an effort to demonstrate that he has nothing to hide. In New York his rented studio was where he had his girls, and, though there are no girls now, she still feels as though it's his private space, which she shouldn't invade.

She does not know why she is affording him this courtesy.

For her own part, she is blocked. Early on in this project, before they moved, she had been sending chapters to her agent, and her agent claimed excitement. He wanted to sell early, get her an advance. But instead of moving forward with her outline, she has decided to go back and tweak things a little. Nudge them a bit. "I'm making some changes to those chapters," she told the agent, and he said, "No need to do that. Just move forward. Move forward, and we'll work on it together." Craig Springhill is his name, a smooth-faced, honey-voiced white man with prematurely silver hair and a charmingly patronizing manner that she used to find reassuring. He came from the dying world of old-school New York publishing and treats her as though she's the only lady novelist in his stable, a titillating unicorn. When she comes to town he buys her twenty-four-dollar cocktails at the Algonquin Hotel and laughs hysterically at everything she says.

They had a relationship. Well—a thing, anyway. It was a long time ago, before he represented her, when she worked as his assistant. She was twenty-three; he was nearly twice her age. He's the one who first called her Nell, the name all intimates now use to address her. They were in her apartment, his fingers were fondling the top button of her blouse, and a query appeared in his eyes: "May I undress you?" was the question she expected, but the actual question, which he posed while undressing her without requesting permission, was, "May I call you Nell?" Yes. Yes, you may call me Nell.

He was married then and slept with most of his assistants. Divorce was inevitable, but what came next was a surprise, at least to Eleanor: he found someone, a woman three years his elder, and entered into an evidently stable relationship with her that brought the assistant fuckings to a close. Eleanor has met this woman, a foxy, silver-haired, rather intimidating television critic named Shannon something-or-other.

Eleanor was glad when Craig settled down, or she told herself as much at the time. In truth, however, she had chosen to see Craig's serial infidelity as a manifestation of the general incorrigibility of men, something she needed to believe was real if she was to tolerate Karl's sexual exploits. Craig's rehabilitation, then, could be taken to mean that she was, in fact, married to a jerk. And there was no avoiding the other plausible lesson here: that, unlike Shannon the TV critic,

Eleanor was not the kind of woman who inspired men to abandon their promiscuity.

In any event, she did not take his advice. She changed the chapters, rewrote every sentence. And when she sent them to Craig, he said, "Very compelling, keep at it," and when she sent him yet another draft of the same pages, he said, "Brilliant, genius, love them."

"Good."

"Of course I adored the original version, before you changed it. And the second version. But these are also fantastic."

"The other drafts are gone now, Craig," she told him. "They're deleted. The new versions are the real ones."

"Yes, got it," he said, and then, after an awkward pause (awkward, in particular, for Craig, who is so very skilled at filling empty spaces with words): "Nell, dear, you do realize that these are all roughly the same."

"They are not remotely the same," she replied, attempting to suppress the stirrings, in her breast, of panic.

"The words are different—"

"Yes."

"—but what they say is not. They are variations on the same thing. It's the same novel."

"I wouldn't say that," Eleanor told him, weakly.

"I think," Craig Springhill told her, with gentle condescension, "that it is time to move forward on this book. To write new pages."

"These *are* new pages."

"To write the pages that come after these pages, Eleanor. To write," he said, with uncharacteristic irritation, "the rest of your novel. To begin to finish it. Don't you agree?"

"There's only one acceptable answer to that question, when a man asks it."

"Eleanor," he said, and at this point his voice had adopted the tone of exasperated finality that she had previously heard only while sitting in his office, waiting for him to get off the phone with someone else, "writing your damn book is a gender-agnostic good. Just do it, please." And he hung up.

Eleanor's books are about, and ostensibly for, women. Both the women she writes about and the women who read what she writes are young, smart, reasonably affluent, white, and firmly middle- to upper-middle-class. Her protagonists have been called "sassy" by leading entertainment magazines. The pastel-colored covers of Eleanor's books are the kind that display shoe-clad disembodied white women's legs or a fancy warm-weather hat or a signifier of free time such as a beach umbrella or shopping bag. (Eleanor was disdainful of these design clichés in the years before her name was embossed over them: reassuring expressions of conventional femininity, promising womanly universality through the promise of capitalism. She has since learned to do her sneering exclusively in private.)

The common parlance for the kind of book Eleanor writes is "chick lit." If asked, Eleanor will say that she writes "literary chick lit," an awkward and redundant term that nevertheless gets across the intended message: that she recognizes the essential frivolity of her work but insists upon approaching it with intelligence and a dedication to craft. She has learned, in the ten years her career has spanned, that certain other writers, ones with more intellectual cred than she possesses, read her, and regard her as a guilty pleasure. "Smart-lady trash" is what Craig calls her work. "As reliable a racket as this business has seen since the celebrity tell-all." Each of her books has sold better than the one before, and she is on the cusp of achieving genuine entrenched semistardom. "This," he told her, speaking of the new book, "will be your first number one bestseller." He didn't mean that the new book was better than the others—he meant that because it was functionally identical to them, it would not impede her career's natural rise. The book, in Craig's conception, should be cart, runners, and grease, all at once.

She has admitted to herself that he is right, at least in that it truly is time to move forward. But she is hopelessly blocked.

············

Irina lets out a noisy sigh and theatrically slams her book shut. She says, "I don't think I'm good at reading."

"That's silly," Eleanor replies, with a reflexive strenuousness that unpleasantly reminds her, every time, of her own mother. "You're a great reader."

"I start reading a paragraph and then something reminds me of something and by the time I get to the end I realize that I've been thinking of the thing *in my head* and not the thing I just read, and I have to start over!"

"Oh, that," Eleanor says.

"I've read this paragraph five times! And I don't know what it's about!"

"Maybe it isn't very good."

Irina says, "What's with all this reading, anyway? Like, how long have humans been doing it? Compared to all of history, I mean. A zillionth of a percent of time, I bet. It's unnatural!"

"But on the way here you said it was your favorite thing to do."

"That's the *point*!" Irina cries. "It *is* my favorite thing, but it's never *good enough*!"

She picks up her spoon and idly stirs her milky coffee while Eleanor tries to think of something to say. Irina, always precocious, never satisfied by the simple pleasures of childhood, has lately been witness to an abundance of adult troubles; and instead of shunning them, of regressing into prepubescence, she seems perversely eager to shoulder them herself. The bitterness of coffee is one thing, but Eleanor had hoped to shelter her from the bitterness of everything else, at least for a few more years.

Her instinct is to reassure, but the truth is that she agrees with Irina, she feels the same way about books: about everything, really. Your favorite things are never good enough. They're idealized by nature; their favoriteness is derived from Platonic forms, perfect realizations that existed only once, usually the first time, if at all. No book, no meal, no sunny day ever equals the one in your head. She should tell her agent this. She should tell her husband this. She *did* tell her husband this when Rachel, the Last Straw, cast her lumpen shadow over their already-compromised union. Go to her, Eleanor told him, and find out. Find out just how happy she makes you. Instead, he agreed to an arrangement that Eleanor presented as months in the making rather than the drunken whim that it actually was: a year upstate, and then we'll see.

When Eleanor met him, Karl was a graduate student in sculpture at the School of Visual Arts in Manhattan and lived in a fairly spacious fourth-floor walkup in Bushwick, on the same block as a barber who used only clippers and an illegal Jamaican speakeasy and gambling den. He was thin then, with broad shoulders and narrow hips; his arms and chest were naturally well developed from his handling of the heavy materials—concrete, iron, glass—that his sculptures were made from. He was very handsome. His heterosexuality was so pronounced as to seem, in the heavily diverse, non-gender-normative environment of early-2000s art school, almost radical. He came off as arrogant. He was arrogant. He loved, or professed to love, the stridently masculine painters of the American midcentury: essentially, anything Clement Greenberg liked in 1963, Karl liked in 2005, and for this his fellow students hated him. He identified more powerfully with painters than with sculptors—"I'm painting in three dimensions," he used to tell Eleanor—for which his fellow students and most of the sculpture faculty hated him.

But women loved him, even the ones who hated him. Within his grad school cohort (some of whom Eleanor eventually got to know), fucking and then hating and then grudgingly admitting you really still kind of liked Karl was practically a rite of passage. She met him at a party. He had arrived with one woman, an experimental portrait painter, and left with Eleanor.

Months later, when she realized she was pregnant, she mounted a campaign of emails and phone calls, none of which he answered. So she went to Manhattan, found Karl in his studio at school (where he was scraping German curves into a chunk of veiny sandblasted glass with a hand chisel while singing along to whatever noise was pumping out of his giant insectile headphones), and in front of two other sculptors working in separate corners of the room shouted, "Hey!"

He didn't look up.

"Hey, man!"

Now he saw her. His face registered nothing. He raised a finger:
Hold on a minute.

"How come you're ignoring me!"

"Jussec, jussec . . ." *Scrape, scrape*, went the chisel. *Tockatocka-tockatocka* went the headphones. For fuck's actual sake.

"Dude!" Eleanor shouted. "You knocked me up! What are you going
to do about it!"

"Oh shiiiit!" came a voice from behind a precarious-looking sculp-
tural pile of corrugated cardboard. From the other side of the room, a
snicker sounded. Karl appeared to sense the shift in vibe. He removed
his headphones.

"Hey," he said placidly. "What?"

She told him. He didn't appear surprised or alarmed. He swore
he hadn't been ignoring her—or, rather, he'd been ignoring everybody, working on this project. "Look," she said. "Do you want to
pay for the abortion? Do you want to come to the clinic with me? Or
would you just like to be a garden-variety dick?" Something in Karl
inspired this gleeful vulgarity, which was otherwise out of character
for Eleanor. Later she would understand that bluster was necessary,
when addressing this man, to conceal and undermine strong emotion. You didn't want to cry in front of him. You didn't want to be
weak. You wanted to win.

He said, "Oh, no, don't do that. Have it. Have the baby."

Her only response was a snort.

"No, I mean it." He jabbed with a dusty finger at the portable CD
player attached to his belt, and the pulsing hiss emanating from the
neck-slung headphones stopped. The room dropped into a kind of
hush. Karl spoke quietly. "I'm sorry. Have the baby. We can't kill it.
Let's move in together."

"That's insane. I have a life." Though this wasn't true. She had half
a shitty novel draft and worked for her ex-boyfriend.

He shrugged.

"We don't know each other," she said. Save me, she didn't say.

"Sure we do. Also, I have money. Family money. This is great, actually.
We'll be a couple. Didn't you tell me you were a writer? That's perfect."

He took two steps and gathered her into his arms. The feeling was extraordinary: like being picked up by a warm gust and deposited on some sunny, grassy hilltop. "It's perfect," he said. "We will be amazing. The baby will be amazing. He'll be an opera singer, or a tattoo artist or something. All three of us will be fucking famous."

"Let's get coffee and talk this over."

"Yeah. No. Coffee's no good for the baby. Remind me of your name again."

Someone else in the room said, "Awwww, so sweet."

"Eleanor."

"Yeah. Right. Eleanor."

"But you can call me Nell."

"Okay, Nell. Let's go get some herbal tea or something."

They went out for tea, and Eleanor got coffee and felt bad about it.

············

She supposed she knew he was going to sleep with other women. Or, rather, she told herself he was without really believing it and found herself surprised to have been right. It was hurtful and cruel and she didn't like it, but it also felt very grown-up to let him do it; it felt like a clever heterodoxy, an artsy relationship hack of which she elected to be proud. She was allowed to do it, too, of course—sleep around. Once she had had the baby, nursed it to toddler strength, regained her former slim figure, found a babysitter, and managed to attract a guy who was interested in extramarital sex with some kid's mom, she would really go crazy with it.

Uh huh.

Anyway, they stuck it out, and they got better at what they did, and they lived the lives they thought they wanted. And then, somewhere in there, she got sick. That's the way she thinks of it now—the illness as one event among many: or, in the terms of her trade, a subplot. Cancer as a minor character, who appears in chapter 8 and fades away, like an old boyfriend or nosy neighbor, into the fog of memory. Like her mother and her aunt before her, Eleanor survived it, she *beat* it, leaving her corporeal and emotional selves intact. She kept her breasts, her husband, and her life, and she did so without joining a support group, without registering for an internet forum, without wearing a pink ribbon. She quietly triumphed. There are still friends who don't know she had it.

Of course, the illness scraped their bank accounts down to the metal and then some: her insurance policy, even after a deductible you could buy a used Mercedes with, left her footing 20 percent of every bill. After years of strongly worded letters and daily phone calls from collection agencies, the sales of the Brooklyn apartment and her un-written fourth novel finally erased the rest of the medical debt, with enough left over for a down payment on the place upstate, while Karl's family income (which had not proven as substantial as he made it sound) would pay the mortgage.

The irony that Karl's infidelity helped to finally balance the books is not lost on her. But no matter. She is healthy now, and she is writing.

Well, in theory, she is healthy. In truth, she needs to make an appointment at Sloan Kettering. She hasn't been in for a checkup in almost two years. The last one she scheduled, she didn't keep: just walked up to the automatic doors, watched them part before her, then turned around and left. She figured one of these days the scans wouldn't be clean anymore. And she did not want that day to come. So she faked it. Went through the motions. Took the train to Manhattan and walked aimlessly around the Upper East Side. Soon after they moved here, she did it again: four and a half hours in the car, five hours of solitary wandering, a night in Craig's girl-friend's apartment, and home. "All clean," she told Karl, making sure Irina was in earshot.

And she is writing, too, only in theory. Actually, she hasn't writ-ten a word since they moved. She has decided to see this fact as a mere technicality. The novel manuscript is open on her laptop screen every single day: that counts. That's writing!

Her daughter, of course, really is writing, for hours at a time, with the kind of feverish intensity Eleanor can only enjoy in distant mem-ory. (Or maybe that's yet another idealized experience she has invented to torture herself with.) She is proud of Irina, and proud that her pride is not merely a euphemism for jealousy, at least not yet.

Irina is turned around in her seat, staring out the window. Her forehead is pressed against the glass, and her body is tense. Tall and narrow, jointed like a crane, she has a kind of accidental grace: she ought to be bumbling, with her big head, nascent hips, and prominent knees; instead she navigates her environment with spidery lightness, leaving behind little evidence of her passage. It's not that Irina has mastered her body, not yet; it's as though her body has mastered the world. Like her father, she is going to get away with almost everything she tries.

Only in her eyes and mouth does she resemble her mother, and that's too bad, because Eleanor has made a life project of being hard to read. Irina's features are placid but composed: something is unfolding itself in her head.

"Hey. Irina."

She starts, spins around. "Can I get an ice cream?"

Through the window, Eleanor can see, a half block down Onteo Street, some kids lined up in front of a Dairy Queen. She says, "Well . . . we could leave here now and get some on the way home."

"No, I want to stay! Just let me go and come back."

Irina is avid. She is gripping the table with both hands and blinking a little too fast. The latter is familiar to Eleanor: she has seen herself do it on television, while dissembling about her work.

"Um, sure. Yes. Sure."

"Thank you!" Irina shoots a quick final look out the window, as though to make certain the ice cream stand is still there. Most of her coffee is still in the cup; pale continents of milk fat drift on its surface.

Eleanor feels a moment of relief: the girl is still a child, after all. She hands over some cash, and Irina extracts herself from her chair and tugs down the hem of her tee shirt. She moves through the tables to the door and in moments is outside and is briskly walking, almost skipping, down the street.

It is in a similar spirit of optimism and youthful energy that Eleanor is now able to push aside the piles of library books and lift her small laptop up onto the table. Ahhh, the freedom to write. Except that, of course, the moment the screen flickers on, she minimizes her un-touched word processor, with its bloated cargo of doubts and second-guesses, revealing a web browser open to her current obsession, the CyberSleuths forum, specifically the *Geary murders* subforum, which she has rescued from obscurity under the screen name smoking_jacket.

She doesn't want to admit to Karl how excellent his choice of house was; she'd held its shortcomings, not entirely consciously, in reserve as something to resent him for later. But in fact she likes the place very much—its musty, woody odor that even the professional cleaning couldn't suppress; its dark and twisty corners and cramped spaces; its dirty windows, busy with densely packed trees, that only the most oblique rays of sun occasionally touch.

And the murders—how they excite and obsess her. How much more interesting they are than the petty dalliances of her novel-theoretically-in-progress. She feigned indifference to Karl on the subject and didn't mention them to Irina at all—fat lot of good that did—but of course they intoxicated her. She'd begun her internet re-search before they even left the city; Karl had told her about the kill-ings only in order to explain the great deal they got, but she dug in like a starving dog. Since arriving here she has made secret forays into the library's paper and microfiche archives. There, she found a par-allel, digitally unsearchable narrative of the crime, as reported by a short-lived competitor to the then-already-terrible *Broken River Daily Reporter* (now chain owned and called, depressingly, *Broken River Week*) known as the *Onondakai County Shout*. Its editor and primary writer, a man named Zane Ellsburgh, was prone to wild speculation and overheated prose, excellent qualities in a writer if what you want is to blather recklessly on about his subject on an internet forum. The paper died with him, and his life's work was now archived, to no great evident interest and in thrillingly perishable form, at the Broken River Public Library alone.

Eleanor is now giddy with power, if only in the small virtual world of CyberSleuths. She has single-handedly transformed the *Geary mur-ders* subforum into a minor sensation with her previously unavailable newspaper clippings, police quotations, crime scene photos, and evidentiary culs-de-sac. She, or rather smoking_jacket, has taken to referencing Ellsburgh by his first name, as though she and he were close. Eleanor thinks of smoking_jacket as a brassy gal of around forty-five, maybe a career diner waitress with an unfinished college degree in semantics, or philosophy, or some other impractical and ultimately unsuitable area of study: she moved back to Broken River at age twenty to take care of her invalid mother, got a night shift at the Chomp Stop or Lyle's Sandwich Parlor, and never left. When her mother died, s_j renovated the house and took an older lover: yes, the shambling and jowly (but smart and charming) Zane Ellsburgh, whose motor mouth and sweaty brow served as titillating correctives to the trials of life with Mother. It was tragic, his coronary (he was in his prime, the *Daily Reporter* eulogized out here in real life, in what seemed to Eleanor a tone of barely suppressed gleeful relief); smoking_jacket inherited little, save for the violent mystery that distracted Broken River, more than a decade ago, from the long, boring project of its own decline and death. She reads the archives, calls up a few retired cops. Posts her results online.

That is, Eleanor does so, in the voice of her character, whom she has inhabited with greater enthusiasm than perhaps anyone she has yet invented. Maybe it's the refreshing lack of mediation that makes this project so much fun—no agent, no editor, no publisher, no bookstores. Or maybe she wishes that her life were a little more like smoking_jacket's: solitary, obsessive, and straightforward.

Eleanor doesn't have anything new today, so she answers a few questions other forum members have asked. From ladygumshoe2: *Any idea what agency, state or local, administered Samantha Geary's care and eventual adoption? No,* she replies, as smoking_jacket; *if you've read the thread, you already know that I think we ought to leave Samantha Geary alone.* From DotOnTheTrail: *Is there any new information about the identity of Mr. Chet, the drug kingpin the crimes have been linked to?* Eleanor: *If Mr. Chet is alive or active, he is probably using a new name, because I haven't been able to turn up any information about him that originates after 2005.*

And then, this, from UncleJ: *Has anyone gone back to the house to see if they can uncover new clues? Is it true that there are new owners?*

It gives her a chill, this post. There is nothing, of course, overtly threatening about it, but it represents the first time her own corporeal existence has been referenced, however obliquely, on the forum. She is suddenly aware of the smallness of the world, this town, this coffee shop.

Eleanor looks up from the laptop and out the window. Irina is in line now, behind a small, dark-skinned child and a big man with flowing blond hair. She is fidgeting, as she often does, hopping from one foot to the other as she reads, presumably, the menu.

Whoever wrote that post knows about her family, is implying that maybe they ought to be visited, interrogated, their home searched. In the politest possible way, of course. Time for smoking_jacket to nip this one in the bud. Eleanor writes, *Dear UncleJ, haven't met the new people yet, but I'll stop by and say hello. If they've found anything, I'll let you know. But don't hold your breath. The place has been gutted and rebuilt more than once.*

In other words, back off, dude.

Satisfied that the threat has been neutralized, Eleanor looks up to reassure herself, once again, of her daughter's safety. But her view has been blocked, by a man wearing a zipped-up windbreaker. He is standing here in Frog and Toad's, right in front of her, holding a coffee mug and a plate bearing what looks like a blueberry muffin. He's a big man, not quite monstrously so, with a jumbled pale face punctuated by a crooked nose and enormous ears, one higher than the other; his hair is mussed and graying, both on his head and on the backs of his rough and meaty hands. The coffee and muffin clank down onto the table's surface, and the hands push aside Irina's pile of library books. He sinks onto Irina's chair with a groan and the chair groans back. He looks like a fat vulture occupying a fence post.

"That's my daughter's chair," Eleanor says.

For a moment the man continues to look out the window, and then, seconds later, turns slowly to face her. His eyes are gray and expressionless. They are like glass eyes. She endures a moment of terror as they lock onto hers; then she shakes it off.

"My daughter," Eleanor says again. "That's her seat."

The man blinks, takes up the coffee mug, silently half-drains it of coffee. Then he puts it back down on the table and turns back to the window.

The gesture is peculiar enough to shake Eleanor's social confidence. How do you react to being utterly ignored? She tamps down a sudden spike in anxiety and leans around the man to find Irina.

Her heart clenches: Irina's gone.

No. Wait. There she is; she's off to one side, sitting on a wooden barrier, made out of railroad ties, that separates a parking lot from the sidewalk. She's licking a giant vanilla soft-serve cone beside a tall girl who seems to be in the latter stages of the same activity. The two are talking.

Whatever the big man is looking at, it isn't her daughter. He seems to be staring directly across the street, at a row of empty storefronts. Occasionally somebody passes by on the sidewalk, but the man's eyes don't follow them, not even for a second. He is just staring. For a moment Eleanor wonders if the man is homeless or has escaped from something. His jacket is clean, as are his unfashionable tan pants, and from him issue the faintest scents of soap and aftershave—yet there's something overly mannered and contoured about his grooming, as though he learned to do it from an old book or a social worker. He seems designed to deceive.

Meanwhile the tall girl has gotten up, and Irina has, too. Irina is turned three-quarters away from Eleanor and is gesturing excitedly with both hands; the ice cream cone, still largely uneaten, wobbles alarmingly. The tall girl is bending over slightly, scowling in apparent concentration. She speaks a few words, then is silent for a time as Irina talks and gesticulates. At one point she looks up at Frog and Toad's. Eleanor feels as though their eyes have met. The girl looks back at Irina, speaks, and then lowers herself back onto the guardrail. Irina sits beside her, and the two are again engaged in conversation.

Eleanor's not sure why this situation unnerves her. It's typical be-havior for her daughter: an introvert by nature, Irina is nevertheless prone to periodic bursts of intense social engagement, and it has been months since she has had the opportunity to be around people. So of course the girl wants friends.

But why this girl? She looks like a teenager, or older. The two are sit-ting close, and the tall girl is listening, nodding. It's almost as though Irina chose her, targeted her for friendship from afar.

Now Eleanor is distracted by a movement in the foreground; the man in the windbreaker has turned from the window. He is gazing at his blueberry muffin with the same mooselike affect he previously employed to examine Eleanor herself. He picks up the muffin, hefts it, turns it over in his hands, like it's some unfamiliar piece of tech-nology. His meaty fingers pick at the pleated paper baking cup, seek-ing purchase; little grunts escape the man's throat as he concentrates. Finally, his thumb and forefinger get a grip, and the paper is torn away like a cocktail dress. The muffin disappears into the man's mouth in two casual bites.

The entire operation has made Eleanor extremely anxious. She gathers up the library books and computer and dumps them into her cloth tote from the Strand (18 MILES OF BOOKS! promises the logo, and it sounds to Eleanor like a death march); she slings the bag over her arm and collects the dishes she and Irina have dirtied. The table trembles a little as she does it, and the man's coffee sloshes around in his mug; as though its motion reminds him of its existence, he seizes the mug and pours the liquid down his throat. He's like a robot that's been programmed to eat and drink, to appear more human. She says, "All yours," but by now the man has turned again to the window and appears to have forgotten she was there.

It's hotter outside than when she entered Frog and Toad's. It has to be ninety. That's just not right. It's September! Upstate! She has exited on the far side of the building and has to loop around to Onteo Street, and by the time she's halfway to the Dairy Queen, Irina is walking to-ward her down the sidewalk, daubing at her hands with an enormous wad of paper napkins. Behind her the guardrail is empty of sitters. "Oh my god, it's so sticky," Irina says. "Hi, did you get my books?"

"I have everything. Some weird guy stole your seat and I figured it was time to go. Who was that?"

"Who was who?" Perfectly innocent. Eleanor has turned around, and now they're both walking toward the car, which is parked in one of the diagonal spaces in front of the empty strip mall.

"The girl you were talking to."

"Oh! That's Sam."

"You seemed to know her."

"No, we just started talking."

"Why did you suddenly just start talking to a girl twice your age?"

"She's not *that* old, she's seventeen." A pause. "Well, I think she's around seventeen. She had a Brooklyn shirt on, and I was like, hey, I'm from there!"

Eleanor doesn't remember seeing a Brooklyn shirt, but she didn't see the girl for long, and she was far away.

"She's never been there, actually," says Irina. "She's from Buffalo, supposedly. She's in town visiting her brother and living with her uncle."

"She's visiting the brother, but she's staying with the uncle? Not the brother?"

"Umm," Irina says, "yeah, I don't really get that, I guess the uncle's got the extra room. Anyway, she seems cool. I gave her my email."

They've reached the car, and Eleanor unlocks it with the button on her fob. She wishes she could have started the engine from two blocks away and turned on the AC so that it would be ice-cold by the time they got in. Then she chastises herself for such a miserably bourgeois desire. She says, "I don't know how I feel about that. You shouldn't just befriend an older kid on the street. If she's seventeen, shouldn't she be in school? I mean, she's staying with her uncle and going to school?"

"I guess, Mother. I only talked to her for five minutes."

"Well, I'm not going to let you just go into town and be friends with an older girl I've never met."

"Okay, okay." They are in the car now, and Irina is not looking at her. She doesn't appear angry, just off in her own world.

They drive in silence down County Route 94. The library books lie in a heap at Irina's feet, spilling out of the tote bag, and she is rhythmically pressing her thumb to her middle and ring fingers, then pulling them apart, over and over again. Feeling, no doubt, the stickiness of the melted ice cream that the napkins couldn't clean off.

The gesture unexpectedly fills Eleanor with sadness. She suddenly believes that her marriage is going to fail. Indeed, it was never going to work, was it. They married for Irina, and she tolerated Karl's philandering for Irina, too. But there's more to it than that: the philandering was useful to her. It gave her a moral advantage, a reason to serve as the default parent, a license to make Irina into the ideal friend and roommate that her own prickly nature never allowed her to find outside her family.

She loves Karl, but her love never wrung her heart out or made her feel like she would die if it weren't reciprocated. Of course, that kind of love doesn't last—just read one of her dumb books—but maybe this kind doesn't, either. She's annoyed when Karl enters a room she is in, as often as not is repelled by his touch, cringes at the sound of his voice. Prevented from fucking for forty-eight hours, he paces like a caged animal until she relinquishes herself to him. He actually said to her last week, rolling off her, "How was that?" and she replied, truthfully, "Kind of rapey." He didn't seem to be offended—he nodded and reached for his phone, and soon tiny video game sounds filled the bedroom.

She is aware that all of the things about him that presently vex her—his intensity, amorousness, and imperturbability—are the very things that attracted her to him in the first place. But now he has hurt her too much. Right?

They get home and she feels as though she has wasted the journey: oughtn't they have talked? Irina jumps out of the car and sprints for the front door while Eleanor heaves herself oldly out of the Volvo, grunting: her back is still killing her, weeks after the move. How did she end up hauling so many boxes when Karl was supposed to be the family muscle? In retrospect, he seemed mostly to have scratched his beard over how things should be arranged in the truck. Her anxiety has seized upon her muscle aches, found them to its liking, declared them permanent.

She hobbles around to the passenger side and gathers up the library books from the floor. She would like to spend the evening on the sofa, reading these while Karl's hands massage her legs and feet. He is good at that, and when he does it she is willing to forgive him almost anything. Suddenly she does want to forgive—she wants to be put into a state where she can do so. She gazes up at their house. It's beautiful, really, in a rough-hewn, workaday sort of way; she understands why Karl found it so appealing. He might have built it. Its low shoulders and slightly awkward angles resemble his art, which in turn resembles automobiles that have been crushed into uneven cubes.

She's shouldering through the front door now—Irina has already disappeared up the stairs—and hoisting the bag of books onto the table, and she spies his two favorite sculptures through the archway to the living room, standing there on their steel tripods like a couple of obsolete machines that have been powered down for good. It's getting late and she ought to start cooking dinner—though who wants to do anything hot in this weather—but she walks into the living room and stands before them, telling herself that they deserve to be appreciated, they deserve to be understood. It seems wrong that they receive less of her daily attention than the television set that now stands beside them, a concession, on Karl's part, to conventional matrimonial togetherness.

They are called *Flow (frozen) #4* and *Flow (frozen) #11*, but Karl refers to them as Huck and Jim. He has proudly claimed that they are the two ugliest things he has made. Each consists of a massive glass block, cracked, drilled, and broken in several places, with inch-thick steel beams tunneling and bending around and through them. Huck stands about five feet tall and two and a half feet wide; Jim reaches seven feet but is nowhere wider than eighteen inches. They remind her of trees that have grown through fences—or of a trick her father showed her once. Take a block of ice—in Dad's case, the size and shape of a two-gallon bucket he had commandeered in order to illustrate this phenomenon—and place it on a grate over a tub. (He used a baking rack from the oven and their actual bathtub, doubly irritating her mother.) Gravity will pull the ice block through the grate; enthalpy will fuse it back together. In the case of the oven rack and the ice bucket, the healing was nearly seamless. Dad lifted the ice-gripped grate with his skinny arms and held it over his head, laughing. Then Mom made him run hot water over it into the sink so that she could have her oven back.

Her father probably intended this experiment to illustrate some philosophical principle, or maybe some commonplace of human behavior. Our tendency to return to our original state after a tragic event? The persistence of our preconceptions in the face of contradictory evidence? She can't remember. Today, though, it tells her that there is a force that keeps intact things intact. An object wants to stay whole. One may expend great energy attempting to break it apart, but it may gather itself back together regardless. She doesn't even know how Karl does it—how he gets the steel in there, how he cracks the glass and fuses it back together. Some rough magic, the same stuff he has used to keep her.

There's enough space in the corner for Eleanor to walk behind the two sculptures. She hasn't seen them from this angle since they moved—actually, it's probably been years, because they stood in the same configuration in Brooklyn as they do here. Why on earth did they waste so much precious apartment space on them? Even here, they dominate the room. It's strangely intimate, back here in the corner, behind the sculptures; she reaches out and touches them both, runs her hands up and down them. They're cool to the touch, despite the heat, and the air around them is cool. There's less light here, almost as though it's a separate time zone or dimension. Above her the ceiling is filthily stained where it meets the wall, and is dotted with mold: the third contractor mistake they've found so far. She's sick of calling them, demanding that they come back, giving them more money.

She wants to see her husband. She wants to make up for her traitorous thoughts in the car. Does he feel this way about her? Does he stand out there in his studio, cleaving glass and bending metal into shapes and regretting falling in love with somebody else? Imagining it seems to make it so. She calls up to Irina that she's going out back, walks out the door and around the house, knocks on the studio door and enters.

He's standing with his back against the west wall, his pants unbuttoned and his hand in his boxer shorts. His other hand has pushed up his tee shirt and is stroking his belly hair in a gentle circular motion. In front of him, on the work table, his laptop computer is open, and a woman's tinny moans emanate from it. He looks up, startled, slaps the computer shut. "Um," he says.

She can't help laughing. She forgives him for everything, the idiot. She goes to him. "You're not done yet, are you?"

He appears absolutely horrified. He jerks his hand out of his pants. "Um, no?"

Eleanor mashes herself up against him. He's still hard: good. She pushes his jeans and shorts down and takes over for him. He has already created a sticky preemptive mess. She remembers, against her will, Irina's ice cream cone and her sticky hands. She says, "Can I fuck you, or do you want it like this?"

"Fuck," he manages, so she hikes up her dress and puts his hand on her, and when she's ready, they do it. He is good at it, and when he is doing it, he puts everything he has into it, and into her pleasure. He makes her aches disappear. Her cries sound to her like sudden epiphanies, as she discovers forgotten pockets of love.

Afterward he's dressed again and is holding her and stroking her hair. They are panting, leaning against the wall. He says, "Uh, sorry about the . . ."

"I get it," she says. "I wasn't home. You're a horny guy."

"I guess . . . yeah, I suppose."

She wants to look at his face and he doesn't seem to want to let her. Finally she disentangles herself. He is staring over her shoulder at the door, though when she turns to see who is there, it is closed. "Hey— are you all right?"

"I'm great. That was—thanks. Sorry."

"I don't care, Karl."

"Yeah, no—that's—I appreciate that."

She pulls back a little farther from him, leans back against the workbench. "Did you not want that? Would you rather have done it alone?"

"No!" He's looking at his feet. "I mean, that was great. I was just . . . I thought I locked the door. It could have been Irina walking in."

"So remember to lock it."

"I will."

She stares at him until he looks at her. He seems to wince. Then he gathers himself and gazes into her eyes. "I love you," he says.

"I love you, too."

Twenty minutes later, while she is cooking dinner, it occurs to her that maybe she ought to have opened up the laptop to see what was on the screen.

5

After the woman with the books exits the coffee shop, the man in the windbreaker sits in silence for fifteen minutes, blinking, exuding heat. At last he stands up from the tiny table, jostling the patron sitting behind him: a pale, strawberry-bearded man in conversation with a willowy, sleepy-looking young woman. The bearded man's mouth opens, as though to issue a complaint, but then he swivels around, allowing himself a view of his tormentor. His mouth abruptly shuts. This small series of events appears to catch the young woman's attention. It rouses her from her torpor. Her gaze follows the man in the windbreaker as he makes his calmly bullying way through the crowd, and when she returns it to the bearded man, it is as though she is seeing him in a new light. Subtly, but not so subtly that the bearded man fails to notice, she wakes her phone—until now lying dormant beside her coffee cup—with a poke of her middle finger. She appears to take note of the time and quickly puts the device back to sleep. The bearded man seems to realize that some spell has been broken. The young woman is no longer interested in him. He looks down at the notebook open before him. It is covered with hand-copied quotations from Kierkegaard and Wittgenstein. A sour expression seizes his face and he closes the notebook with a sigh.

The Observer is interested in these wordless events that span mere seconds. Serendipitous encounters, subtle reactions, inscrutable social cues that alter the course of events, nudging the plot—one plot out of an infinitude—this way or that. But the Observer understands this plot to be a distraction. The important thing now is to follow the man in the windbreaker as he pushes through the heavy glass door as if it were no more substantial than a bead curtain. To follow him down the street, to the twin painted lines between which a car, presumably his, is precisely parked.

It isn't like the other cars around it. Lower, longer, less sleek. Its sharp corners are accentuated by its unusual color, the blue of a robin's egg, with interior accents of a warm off-white, the color of pages in an old book. Though this car appears better cared for than the ones around it, the Observer deduces that it is, in fact, older than they. It is, among the humans, an ostentation, an eccentricity. The man in the windbreaker climbs into the car. Moments later its engine turns over and the car backs into the street and joins the flow of traffic.

The car's route through the town of Broken River seems, to the Observer, uncoupled from any kind of predetermination. It circles, doubles back. At times it pulls up to a curb, or into a graveled verge, and pauses there for five minutes, ten minutes. Now the man in the windbreaker pulls up beside a bleak and unshaded playground strangely empty of children. He sits there for half an hour, staring out through the windshield. It is clear that he has been drawn to this place, is driven to occupy and survey it—or perhaps he is merely acting instinctually, like the bird of prey the Observer spotted in the unpopulated hills outside this town, diving out of the sky in pursuit of a tiny flash of gray flickering between leaves of grass in the field below. His patterns of behavior resemble the bird's more than they do most humans', whose primary purpose seems to be to engage with—or, alternately, to avoid engagement with—the others. It's as though the man in the windbreaker is also an Observer, if one without any particular observational objective.

(But then, what is the Observer itself? What is its objective? The patience of the man in the windbreaker has caused it, for the first time, to reflect upon its own purpose. Already its years inside the abandoned house seem inconceivably dull: how could it have remained there, in a state of mute forbearance, when it might instead have moved, followed, investigated? Suddenly the Observer is aware, as it never was before, of the existence, the scope, of time and space; it sees itself as an entity within a frame of reference. It is a thing that exists: and if one thing can exist, then other things, perhaps, cannot. Did the Observer ever not exist? Did it *begin* to exist, or has it *always* existed? Is it more like the man in the windbreaker, or is it more like the other humans? Is it the diving bird, or is it the flash of gray?)

The day has grown warmer, but the man in the pale-blue car has not removed his windbreaker, nor opened the car windows. He betrays no evidence of discomfort, however; his pink skin remains dry and gives the impression of softness, like a child's, despite its pits and scars. Indeed, the man might be described as a big baby, with his large head and socially unsophisticated affect; he seems to apprehend the world as a child might, unconcerned with the context of people and objects, alternately fascinated and distracted. He appears, overall, disconnected from the larger world, driven by forces invisible perhaps even to him.

Now the sun is falling in the sky. The temperature is starting to fall, as well. The man in the windbreaker drives to a gas station and waits. Inside the small attached convenience store, the sole employee watches a sporting event on his phone. Neither man moves for nearly two minutes. Then the man in the windbreaker begins to honk the car's horn, first in a staccato pattern, scattershot, like the first drops of a rainstorm, then more deliberately, the notes longer, more insistent. Finally the man in the windbreaker presses the heel of his palm into the horn and leaves it there.

The clerk emerges from the convenience store and approaches the car. The man in the windbreaker releases the horn. The clerk says, "What's up, man."

"Fill 'er up."

"Self-serve, man."

"Fill 'er up."

The clerk looks over his shoulder, back at the store, then squints, in the honeyed light of the setting sun, back at the man in the windbreaker.

"You do it yourself, man. That's how it works."

The windbreaker man's response is to resume honking. The horn is quite loud: it fills up the world of this gas station like a thick fog, like a darkness. "Okay, okay," the clerk says, and the honking lets up only when the nozzle has been inserted into the car and the gas begins to flow.

A few minutes later, the pale-blue car is moving, this time more deliberately, the Observer senses, down one of the roads leading away from Broken River. The Observer recognizes it as the road leading to the house in the woods, the one that the man and the woman from the house drive along most days to get to town. If the Observer were to be seated beside the man in the car, it might be possible to discern a change in his demeanor: in fact, yes, the Observer is doing this now. The flesh at the corner of the man's mouth is twitching, very slightly; his eyes are blinking at a faster rate than before. Is the man in the windbreaker aware that his body is betraying some inner turmoil? Probably not. He is acting on instinct. He is the bird.

The car arrives at the bottom of the long gravel drive that leads to the house. Instead of turning right and navigating the car up the hill, the man in the windbreaker pulls over and pauses on the side of the road. He switches off the ignition.

For ten minutes, the man in the windbreaker sits very still. His hands remain on the steering wheel, clenching periodically; the knuckles whiten, then go pink, with each clench. Now the man has begun to sweat, even though the sun is all but gone from the horizon and the sky has turned purple-black. (It is as though this man exists in his own private world, with its own unfathomable climate.) His chin quivers and his right eyelid has begun to spasm.

If the Observer were capable of registering surprise, what happens next would likely qualify as a triggering event. The man in the windbreaker turns, then peers past the Observer and out the passenger-side window, as though in an effort to see, through the trees, the house where the man and woman and girl reside. This is not possible, but the man does it nonetheless. And then the man's gaze is drawn to where the Observer's eyes would be, were the Observer corporeal. The man in the windbreaker is staring at the Observer, acknowledging its presence. The man is aware that he is an object of observation; perhaps he has been all day long. A smile cracks the man's face. The smile is for the Observer.

"My name is Joe," says the man in the windbreaker.

The Observer has no power to respond, no mechanism for doing so.

The man in the windbreaker says, "My name is *Joe.*"

The man in the windbreaker says, "Watch." Then he starts the car, puts it into gear, and pulls out into the southbound lane of the county highway. The Observer remains behind, watching. The car recedes into the distance and disappears behind the curve of a hill. It is only now that the Observer rouses itself to follow, and it does so at some remove. The man in the windbreaker instills in the Observer a sense of disquiet: a disturbance, a warp in the mesh of cause and effect.

He is the bird. Who is the flash of gray?

6

A man named Louis is sitting on his front porch in Argos, New York, at noon, smoking a Camel and eating a baloney-and-cheese sandwich with yellow mustard, on wheat bread. Inside his house, behind him, his kids are eating the same sandwiches, all of them made by his wife, Pam, who is eating nothing, because she's "way too fat." This actually isn't the problem with Pam, the real problem is she's way too thin. She is wasting-away-type thin. For a while Louis tried to get her to put the pounds back on, but now he's given up. It's some kind of psychological thing. It's fucked up. It worries him. The other thing that worries him is that he's got another half dozen years of parenting ahead of him, at minimum, and he's too sick of his kids to eat lunch with them. The little one, Fred, doesn't bug him so much, though he never stops talking except to stuff food in his mouth. It's the older one, Janine, who is fifteen, who is really getting to him—she complains about everything, won't get up off her ass to do shit, slathers her face with makeup and goes around trying to look like a slut. He doesn't know how it happened. That is, she's a teenager, he understands that much, but the rest, what the fuck? It's all invisible to Pam, she can't see the kid turning into a skank, she bought the girl fucking thongs, none of it makes any sense. His wife and daughter are going nuts together. And he bets Janine won't eat half her sandwich, which will please her mother. And Louis also predicts that he himself will eat the other half of the sandwich once they've all left the room, and will find a way to wash it down with a couple of beers. And then the rest of the day will be hazy, and he'll fall asleep, and blammo he'll have wasted the only day of the week when he doesn't have to go into the carpet warehouse. It all feels inevitable. It's only noon, and the day is over.

It is into this moment of reverie that a powder-blue Cadillac pulls up in front of the house. The house is in a crummy cul-de-sac and is a crummy seventies ranch with a roofless cement porch, aluminum siding, and nonfunctional aluminum shutters bolted next to aluminum-frame windows. Metal! They were into it, back in the seventies. Louis can remember when his father ripped the clapboards off their old house and replaced them with aluminum. "Never have to paint again!" It looked like shit, of course, but Louis didn't know that at the time, he was fucking six. This car, the Cadillac, is out of place here. It's the kind of car his father used to issue a low whistle over every time they drove past one on the highway. "Someday, baby," his father used to say, as if he was some kind of up-and-comer, an ambitious kid with a twinkle in his eye and a spring in his step, who was going to hustle his way to the top of the heap and make a killing. When in fact he was a fucking dipshit who lost his actual car—the family station wagon—in a poker game, and his right eye in a knife fight the following day, trying and failing to get it back.

But if Louis is irritated to have been reminded, by the sight of the Caddy, of his father, he is bewildered when he realizes whose car it actually is. He can see the man's silhouette in there, humped behind the wheel like a small mountain: it's Joe. That's Joe's car.

Louis feels a burning sensation on his upper lip and realizes that it's being caused by actual burning: his cigarette, forgotten in his mouth. He spits it out, and it falls onto the baloney sandwich fragment he has apparently been trying to crush to death in his hand. He says fuck and from inside he hears Janine's voice also saying fuck and Pam's voice yelling at her not to fucking say fuck, and Freddy's voice laughing and laughing and Pam's and Janine's voices telling him to shut the fuck up.

He doesn't want Joe at his house, or in contact with his family, who suddenly seem like the best thing that has ever existed in the world. He wants to put them on a plane to Florida right now, and himself on it with them. He lets the sandwich fall onto the ground, along with the still-burning cigarette, and he stands up and closes the front door behind him.

The inside voices are cut off. Birds are singing and a dog barks a couple of blocks away. At the far end of the street, cars whiz by on Route 81. It's a sound Louis used to hate and then gradually came to love, as it promised a quick escape from his bullshit life, if it ever came to that; and now he's back to hating it, because it is the sound that brought Joe to his doorstep. How did he even know where Louis lived, for shit's sake? He's moved since his time with Joe, and his number and address are unlisted. Because of Joe. And why in the hell is Joe still sitting there, in the car? What is he doing?

As if in answer, the Cadillac shudders and then springs up as it relieves itself of Joe's weight, and then the man himself is standing on the sidewalk, looking up at Louis standing there looking at him.

Like an idiot, Louis waves. Joe does not wave. But he is smiling. His face doesn't appear accustomed to it, but that's a smile all right. He comes halfway up the sidewalk, stops with a grunt, and says, "C'mon. Let's take a ride."

"How ya been, Joe?" Louis says, because he doesn't want to say no, not directly. But there is no way he's going anywhere with Joe.

Joe says, "C'mon."

He doesn't look older. He doesn't look different in any way from the way he looked twelve years ago. He's even wearing the same windbreaker and tan pants, though they're unlikely to be the *very* same clothes, given the level of untidiness they were reduced to that night. For his part, Louis soaked his in gasoline and burned them to cinders in a trash can.

"I got my family in here, Joe," Louis says with a thumb over his shoulder, regretting it immediately.

Joe, still smiling, nods. He looks to be chuckling a little, even, though he makes no sound. Then he takes a step forward, and another one, and before Louis can stop him (and who is he kidding, he couldn't stop Joe from doing anything), Joe has climbed onto the stoop, brushed Louis aside, and walked in the front door.

Louis follows him. "Hey, man, hey. Get outta here. Seriously. Joe. Come on."

"Are these them?" the big man says. They're in the kitchen. Pam and Fred are sitting at the table, both of them with a hand in the same big bag of potato chips. Janine is sitting on the counter in her tight jeans and tee shirt, drinking a Coke. They're all frozen, staring at Joe.

"Yeah. Joe, you gotta go."

"You're the wife," he says to Pam. It's not a question: Joe is showing off his deductive powers. Pam looks at Louis, not angrily, not yet, anyway, just asking, with her eyes, for a little guidance.

"Come on, man, let's go. It's cool, I'll come with you. Let's go."

"And these are the little kiddies. What are you called," he says, looking at Fred.

Fred just stares. But Janine says, "I'm Janine."

Joe's smile broadens. His chuckle is audible now. The kitchen is extremely cramped with Joe in it.

Louis says, "Hey, look, Pam, I gotta help this, ah, customer out with something, I'll be back in a jiff." To Joe he says, "All right, man? Let's go."

"Janine," says Joe. "You're a little woman, aren't you."

The girl wants to say something witty, something to prove how cool and grown-up she is, but she fails. She doesn't look like a wiseass now, she looks frightened.

"Hey, man, leave her be, she's just a kid. Let's go."

"This is the one that saw the thing, huh," Joe says. And now Louis realizes that this is his fault, that he has made a terrible mistake.

"No, man, that's . . . let's go, Joe, let's talk about it in the car."

Now that Louis has agreed to the ride, Joe is all smiles. "Good to meet you," he says to no one in particular. He sounds like he's speaking a foreign language. Pam and Fred still have their hands in the chip bag—they haven't moved. Joe turns and walks out, and Louis goes after him, with a parting glance over his shoulder.

"Sorry," he whispers. "I'll be back."

The fuck? Pam silently mouths, and all Louis can do is shrug. He follows Joe to the car and climbs in.

....

The reason Joe has come for him is that Louis called him. He had to go through his old, defunct address book to find the number— *J* is how it was listed, except under the *Q* section, which is how the Louis of a decade and a half ago figured he would deceive any cop into whose hands the thing might inadvertently fall. Because he was a fucking idiot.

Anyway, Pam is into those true crime paperbacks, the kind you can get at the supermarket, on a rickety wire rack that might also display marked-down store-brand beef jerky and hamburger seasoning. Years ago, a few years after the thing in Broken River, somebody wrote one of these books about it, a lady named Lisa Halverson. She kicked out a new one every four to six months, crappy little riffs on unsolved killings or mysterious disappearances, usually based on whatever newspaper reports had come out at the time, plus a few new phone interviews and a lot of ominous-sounding made-up bullshit. The publisher padded these things out with pages and pages of grainy photos with captions like *The scene of the crime* and *In happier times*, knocked out a bunch of copies on cheap puffy paper, shipped them to grocery store chains. Louis knows all about it, he looked into it at the time. Everything about the book was pretty much wrong; the lady figured it was a mob hit and went off on these crazy tangents about New York City and the Jersey Shore and, implausibly, Juárez. Pam had bought the book, and Louis read the whole thing. He didn't bother telling Joe, back then—for all Louis knows, Joe can't even read. And there was nothing in it to make them worry. If anything, the book was doing them a favor.

But last month it surfaced again in the house from whatever closet shelf or rotting cellar box it had been banished to, this time into the hands of Janine, who had picked up her mother's habit. The two of them had really bonded over these books—and not just Halverson's, either. There's a whole raft of these lady writers, all them mad as hell that there are murderous, unprosecuted man-monsters roaming the earth, and Pam and Janine get equally mad as hell at the kitchen table together, snorting and tsking and quoting passages to each other. And Janine read the Broken River book, and she said to her mother, "Hey, this happened right near here, a couple hours from here," and Pam said, "Yeah, I wonder what happened with that, if they got the guys, wasn't it supposed to be Mexicans or something?" and Janine said, "I dunno, but I'm gonna look it up." And then she got on the internet.

Yeah, so, the internet. Louis has to admit that he's never had great facility with computers. (Not that he's much of a hands-on guy, really; his efforts to build a doghouse a few years back eventually led to their returning the dog to the shelter. Honestly, he's not much of an animal guy, either. The different kinds of guy he is not are too many to count.) So he didn't realize that unsolved crimes had become kind of an internet phenomenon and that pathetic unemployed shut-ins all over America had taken to cracking cold cases using only Google and their mountains of free time.

"This lady says it's not Mexicans," Janine told her mother over the dinner that Pam had spent an hour cooking, filling the house with greasy smoke and wilted-vegetable stank, and now was eating barely any of. "She thinks it was local guys. She knew this reporter. He had all kinds of inside dope."

"The Mexicans thing was an excuse," Pam said. "So they could give up on it. Cops are lazy."

"The guy was probably a drug dealer. It was small-time. There was weed in the house. Residue and stuff."

"I bet it was the cops that killed them," Pam said.

"Fucking pigs," said Janine.

"Watch your mouth," Louis and Pam told her at once, then glared at each other, as if, what, each of them valued the privilege of scolding her alone? What is wrong with my fucking marriage? Louis wondered.

Fred just snickered until Pam and Janine yelled at him to stop.

That night, after everybody had gone to bed, Louis got a little drunk and got on the computer and found the site that Janine had been talking about. It didn't take long: the Broken River case was right on top. And what Janine had said was true. Some lady who went by the name smoking_jacket had found a bunch of old newspapers and notebooks and put together a much more plausible—correct in almost every particular, in fact—scenario. The number of perpetrators, the order of events, the kind of car they were driving: it was all more or less right. And the house, which had stood empty for a decade, was occupied by new owners. And some other guy was planning to get in touch with these people. And maybe search the place.

Surely, Louis thought, there was nothing here to worry about. They spent only an hour in the house after what happened. The work was awkward and hot. Maybe one of them dropped something? *Maybe*, if this something existed, it could have survived the police investigation, the years the house stood empty, the renovation, the new people? It seemed unlikely.

But here was the thing. Like three weeks before, a guy showed up at the warehouse—big guy, big beard, big glasses, weird, womanish walk—and started pawing at the samples. He refused assistance at first, instead just walked around, putting his hand on swatches of thick pile, closing his eyes, tipping his head back and kinda mumbling to himself. If Louis was the kind of guy to ever want to look at a cop again in his life, he might have called them.

Eventually the guy picked out some ecru Infinity PermaSoft and said, "Hey, can you put this in my living room?"

"Right, sure, that's from our American Heritage line, nice selection, but lemme ask you, what kind of usage situation are you—"

"Don't do that, man," the guy said. "This stuff. Can you come put some in my house?"

"Yeah, you bet. Just, these are only a few of the varieties—"

"Hey, yeah, listen, knock it off. This is the stuff I want, okay?" The guy's voice was calm but Louis could tell he was pissed. Okay, fine. He'd dealt with guys like this before. They wanted to make their decision without your help and then they called you a week after installation asking why the chocolate milk stain wouldn't come out. But Louis knew when to cut his losses.

"You got it," he said.

"Come install it in my living room, okay?"

"You bet. How about I come make some measurements?"

"That's more like it," the guy said, and gave Louis an address outside Broken River. Which, sure, it gave him a chill. But he was a professional, he made an appointment, and a couple of days later he drove out there as promised.

He wasn't really paying attention. His mind wandered, and he just let his phone tell him where to go. But the closer he got, the more uneasy he felt, and by the time he was rolling up the driveway in the company van he was sweating like a fucking horse, his heart clenching, his stomach spasming. He pulled up between the dude's Volvo and some builder's truck, gulping air, listening to the sound of hammering and boombox contractor-grade hit radio emanating from the house, and thought, Holy fucking shit, this is it. This is the place. Fuck. Fuck.

Louis didn't hesitate. He just threw the van in reverse, made a three-point turn, and sprayed gravel the hell out of there. The guy called him twenty minutes later. "Hey. You coming, man?"

"Sorry, can't make it."

"You were just in my driveway."

"Yeah, no, yeah," Louis said, and hung up. When the phone rang again a couple of minutes later, he pulled over, rejected the call, and blocked the number. Nope. Not doing that. Nope.

So yeah, that night, drunkenly reading the CyberSleuths website, Louis got paranoid. He opened up his address book to *Q*, and he called the number next to the letter *J*. And left a voicemail after the beep. And regretted it immediately. He had a full day to think that maybe Joe was dead or at least didn't have that number anymore, or got the message and didn't care. A full day and a morning. And then Joe showed up. And now Louis is sitting in his Cadillac, wishing he'd kept his fucking mouth shut.

They drive in silence for ten minutes through increasingly marginal neighborhoods until they arrive at a former drive-up bank that has been half-assedly converted into some kind of dwelling. They park under the collapsing awning and Joe gets out. "Stay here," he says.

"Right," Louis replies, though the door has already slammed shut.

A brown drape repaired with duct tape has been drawn across the drive-up window, and a stripe of interior is visible through the crack between the curtains. The mechanical teller drawers have clearly been deemed a security threat and are welded awkwardly shut, with big, ridged beads of metal resembling lava flows that have almost but not quite devoured a highway. If this guy is involved with drugs, as Louis figures he must be, this seems like a waste. The teller drawers would be perfect.

A bit of motion is visible between the curtains. Bodies moving around. Louis hears perhaps one small yelp through the glass, high pitched and choked off. Then the motion stops and Joe reappears at the corner of the building. He hitches up his pants a little, as if whatever he did in there required a bit of stretching. He re-enters the car with a grunt.

"Everything go okay?" Louis asks, like an idiot.

Joe says nothing. He drives Louis home. At the curb, Louis reaches for the door handle, and Joe says, "Nah."

"Okay," Louis says, and waits, staring straight out the window at his neighbor, who is berating a chained-up dog.

"Don't leave messages," Joe says.

"Okay."

"What's the thing called."

"What thing?"

"Computer thing."

"A website?"

Insofar as it is possible to assign feelings to anything Joe says, Louis detects annoyance in the words "No fucking shit. What's it called."

"It's called CyberSleuths. It's these people, they research old—"

"Yeah. Get out."

Louis gets out of the car. It's barely past two. Clouds have rolled in and a very light rain is falling. He feels a lightness, like the one he used to feel upon leaving church with his mother, the feeling of stepping out from under the judging gaze of an angry god. He wants to embrace his asshole neighbor and the dog both.

Joe says, "I'll check it out."

"Okay."

"Don't go anywhere."

Louis doesn't know what this means, exactly, but he doesn't like the implication. He says, "Okay."

"Close the door," says Joe.

"You got it," Louis mutters under his breath, and the car barks away from the curb the second metal hits metal.

A minute later he enters, with relief, his house. He breathes in the greasy air, holding back tears. Pam finds him moments later, still standing in the middle of the living room with his hands in his pockets.

"The fuck was that, Louis?" she would like to know.

"Ah, it was nothing," he says.

"That guy. I don't want that guy in my house ever again."

"Haha, yeah. Yeah, right?"

She comes right up to him, stands ribs to tits, and uncharacteristically kisses him. "Seriously, Louis. Keep him out of here."

"I will."

"Hm," she says, and heads to the kitchen to resume the cigarette and paperback she has taken up for the afternoon. Louis thinks, Well, hell, I should be doing that, too. He goes to the kitchen and sits down and lights up and grabs a book from the pile. It's about a cold-case double murder—go figure!—this time one that he has nothing to do with. He and Pam stay there until dinner, then send out for pizza, earning the temporary love and respect of their children. Later that night they have sex for the first time in a while, and they sleep with Pam's skinny body curled up into his, just like the old days.

It's only in the middle of the night that he wakes and begins to shake and shake and cannot stop.

7

Of all the stupid things Karl has done over the past few months, the stupidest has got to be leaving an entire fucking ounce of weed on the G train, in a mason jar sharing space inside a paper grocery sack with a pile of celebrity gossip magazines, three twelve-packs of haw flakes, a wholesale box of green-tea Kit Kats, a couple bags of Boy Bawang garlic bites, and a lemonade-iced-tea Snapple. He realized his mistake the second the doors slid closed behind him: screamed an oath, spun around, literally clawed the windows of the moving subway car. Some kid with headphones the size of Cinnabons had just sat down next to the bag and was starting to unroll the top to see what was inside, and it was probably Karl's frantic screaming face that tipped him off to the fact that it was something really good. As the train gathered speed, Karl contemplated sprinting the four or five blocks to Bedford–Nostrand: maybe that was where the kid was getting off, who knew. He even ran up the stairs, yelling at people to move aside, but by the time he reached the street, he was too winded, too overheated and dejected, to go on. He leaned against the brick wall of the Indian drugstore, an air conditioner dripped on his head, and he fucking cried. He actually cried for the first time since this whole mess began. Five hundred bucks' worth of weed! And where the hell was he going to find Asian munchies in fucking Broken River, New York? He walked across the street to the playground, tears and sweat sluicing down his face, and sat on a park bench. He fell asleep and woke up only when his phone rang in his pocket, startling the couple of kids who were looming over him, probably about to steal it. A small blessing, he had supposed, on that shitty-ass, roasting-hot final full day in Brooklyn. He was hoping maybe it was Rachel, but it was Nell, obviously, wondering where the Chinese takeout was (she was careful to identify the food's absence, not his, as her primary concern); she and Irina were starving, and there was still packing to do before the movers showed up the next morning. He guessed it was sort of almost nighttime? The light was impossible: heavy and golden, as though ladled out of a smelter. He promised to be home soon (home: ha!), flipped off the already-retreating delinquents, and dragged himself back across the street to buy some fucking dumplings. Fuck moving. Fuck upstate. Fuck everything.

That was months ago, though, and he has discovered that it's no big deal to buy whatever obscure foreign eats he likes online and have them delivered to his studio door. He also thinks he's found a weed connection, just in time for the consummation of his trifecta of vice: he's going to bone Rachel.

She's here. In Broken River. She's staying at the Upstate, an old hotel in the middle of town, and in about half an hour Karl is going to get into the elevator (if the place even has one) and ride it up to her room, and they are going to get stoned and screw. He kind of can't believe his audacity, his blatant flouting of the very simple rules set forth in the plan to rehabilitate his marriage, his logistical acumen in the pursuit of the things he needs to feel alive. He is a masterful deceiver, a scoundrel, and he is so, so excited right now.

"Father?"

"Huh?" he says to Irina, whom he forgot was in the car with him. He forgot, in fact, that he was in a car at all.

"Do you have a stomachache or something?"

"What? No. What?"

"You're moaning."

"I am?"

"Well, now you've stopped. But yeah."

He wipes his palms on his knees, and the denim darkens with sweat. "Oh, yeah, that. Yeah, actually, I kind of do have a stomachache."

Irina says, "So you do have one, then?"

"It's probably something I ate."

"Probably," she says, gazing out the windshield.

Karl looks at her. She doesn't look back. Is she being sarcastic? Does she know? He says, "Haha, it usually is."

"What?" His daughter looks startled. Her electric guitar is pinned between her knees, and her hands clutch its neck through the gig bag.

"When people have a stomachache. It's usually because of something they ate. Right? I mean, why else?"

"I guess you're right."

"So I have one, then," he says. "And that's probably why."

She nods slowly, gazing at him in apparent confusion, then turns again to the window.

Karl has got her signed up for an art class and a guitar lesson, both on Saturday afternoons, and offered to bring her to Broken River every weekend to attend them. He has managed to contextualize this effort as a form of filial magnanimousness rather than the act of total selfishness that it actually is: while Irina is getting her double dose of culture, he'll be up in Rachel's room. He made these arrangements using the secret email address he has created for the affair, the password to which he has not written down anywhere and which he has instructed his browser never to memorize.

The problem is that painting is from 1 p.m. until 2 p.m., and the half-hour guitar lesson doesn't start until 2:20 because the guitar teacher, a dreamy, long-haired man of about sixty named Jasn (not Jason) Hubble, takes a smoke break at 2:00. "That's my smoke break," he told Karl last week, as if the idea of teaching guitar at two was absurd, as though Karl should have known. The yellowness of the man's handlebar mustache, drooping over the edges of a puzzled frown, lent credence to the seriousness of this caesura in his daily routine.

Of course, Karl indeed should have known. He *did* know. That was how he met Jasn Hubble, after all. Stalking through downtown Broken River one early autumn afternoon, he spied the denimed old bastard leaning against the wall in the alley next to the guitar shop, and he thought, There's my guy. He marched right up, said, "Hey, man, how's it going," and Jasn Hubble said, "Right this second it's going pretty damned good, friend, what can I do for you," and Karl said, "Where in the hell does a person score some weed in this town?" and Jasn Hubble responded with a big, yellow grin. They passed Hubble's cig back and forth for a while and pretty soon he'd gotten Irina signed up for guitar lessons and the whole plan came into focus.

The guitar shop is several blocks away from the Community Arts Center, so last week, when Karl took Irina into town to buy a guitar, they walked back and forth several times between the two buildings. "Okay, see this? You're going to go past the laundromat, the abandoned pet store, the abandoned deli, the adult bookstore, and the bank. Then you're going to go left on Shearn Avenue, and you can see it from here. See?"

"I get it, Father."

"And on the way back, it's the same thing in reverse. Shearn to Erie to Onteo, and you're at the arts center. But you don't have to do that. I'll meet you at the guitar shop."

"I *know*." They were standing in the street on the corner of Erie and Shearn. Irina squinted in the bright sunlight, wearing her pink jean jacket that Karl kind of envies. She appeared annoyed with him.

"So what's the matter? You can do this."

"I *can* do it."

"So what, then?"

"*Father*." She looked up and down the street, and he followed her gaze.

And then, of course, he saw. The dumpster in the parking lot beside the pizza joint, behind which a couple of teenaged junkies were sleeping off a high. The wino on the stoop of the former pet shop muttering angrily to himself about all the people he was gonna kill. The piss-stained, rusted mailbox. The skeletonized Chevy Impala. The tattooed guy chain-smoking and walking in a circle. The heavy metal shaking the apartment window. The three blocks between the arts center and guitar shop were fucking terrifying.

"Yeah, right. Sorry, dude."

"Thank you, Father."

"This stuff's invisible to me. From growing up and all." Which was bullshit, of course—Irina herself grew up in rougher neighborhoods than Karl had. But—"Yeah"—she accepted this, and they trudged back to the guitar shop. Jasn offered them a 5 percent student discount, and in the end he bought Irina a cheap starter electric and a small amplifier. ("I'll have that special order of yours next week," he told Karl with a wink.) She chose not the Hello Kitty–branded pink guitar Karl himself would have chosen were he to inaugurate a rock-and-roll subcareer, but a thoroughly black, rather masculine-looking piece with three pickups and a whammy bar. Since then, he has been listening to her picking out chords and warbling in a not-bad-at-all rock-and-roll kid voice up in her room all week and has several times wondered why she needs a lesson at all, if she can do so well on her own.

Now, in the car, he is trying to conceal his excitement, which is to say his boner, with a right arm casually flung across his lap. He'll have an hour, basically. Less, because it will take a couple of minutes to walk each way from the arts center and to ride the elevator or climb the stairs to and from Rachel's room, and of course he doesn't want to show up late to pick up Irina after art because the teacher is this witchy sixtiesish lady who can see right through him, and when it comes time for Nell to take Irina to her lessons for one reason or other, Karl does not want this lady to casually mention that last week her husband showed up ten minutes late, reeking of poontang and hotel soap.

He has a life that can be ruined and a daughter whose respect for him may be hanging by a thread, even without the taint of marital infidelity, and he is totally getting off on it. And isn't this the age when, if a kid gets exposed to her parents' sexuality, it fucks her up? It probably fucked him up, honestly. He saw his naked father pull his mother's braids until she screamed, one time near the end, when they were evidently trying to fuck themselves back into love with each other. What does Irina always say? "Epic failure"? Anyway, that. He doesn't want her to be shit-talking him in some college dorm six years from now, but he also doesn't want her to have to tell her hot college pals that her father, the sculptor, was boring. Best to err on the side of feeling good. In fact, that's his life philosophy in a nutshell: he doesn't want to do anything to anybody except make them feel good, and he doesn't want anything done to himself except that which makes him feel good. That's an achievable goal, right? It ought to be, anyway.

They arrive in Broken River early, for lunch. As they pass the Upstate, he looks up at the windows, trying to catch a glimpse, but the uncharacteristic sunshine obscures them with glare. Is she there yet? Anyway, she wouldn't be looking out the window. She would be reading or something. He and Irina go to the crap diner with no name next to the empty theater, and as they eat, Karl wonders what Rachel's rental car looks like. Is it out there, on the street? Has she checked in? Surely she has by now. What is she wearing?

"Father. Stop looking out the window when I'm trying to talk to you."

Irina is gazing at him, deadpan, a single french fry held before her like a scare quote. He's startled: she looks like Nell. The outline of her face has always been Karl's, but the features are his wife's, and they are trained upon him, pinning him, with Nell's casual intensity. She doesn't even realize she has this power—her genes speak directly to her face, without the intervention of the adolescent ego, its vestigial narcissism.

"Sorry, dude."

"No worries, Ape Dad. I was telling you about what I'm going to do in art class."

"Sorry. What?"

"I'm going to make maps and draw clothes for the people in my novel."

"Novel?"

Irina shakes her head. "For real, Father?"

"Wait. Yeah. You told me. The, like, it's Brooklyn under water or something?"

"No. Well—close enough."

"I dunno if you'll get to just do what you want," Karl says now, finding a thread he can tug. He picks up his largely uneaten burger. "Art teachers are stuck up. They want everybody to do the same thing. The same snowcapped mountain reflected in the same fucking lake. Or decoupage or whatever. I flunked art in junior high."

"I know."

"Then I got suspended in high school for drawing my girlfriend's—"

"Ugh, Father, I *know*."

The two of them sit in silence, eating. Karl checks his phone for texts. He has missed one. *I'm here room 405.* He suddenly wishes he hadn't had a cheeseburger; he feels greasy and bloated. Usually he absorbs and assimilates food with preternatural speed; today he feels like any other warm-blooded organism laboriously breaking down chemical bonds.

As though reading his mind, Irina says, "This can't be any good for your stomachache."

She appears genuinely concerned. How fucking gross does he look?

"Oh yeah, that's gone. I guess I was hungry," he says.

"Okay." Quiet now, as though chastened, though he has not chastened her. Has he ever? He forgets that he's authorized to do that. But why would he? Irina is such a good kid. This realization hits him hard. Irina is a *good kid*. He doesn't worry about her at all. She's not going to do stupid things and be self-destructive and make bad choices. She knows how to live in the world. And she's nice! She's a nice girl. Hey, he thinks: why don't I tell her that?

"You're a good kid, Irina."

He doesn't know what he expected, but bemused surprise wasn't it. "Thanks!"

She doesn't say that he's a good dad, though. He says, "Let's go."

"It's early."

"Yeah, no, I know."

"I don't want to be the first one there."

"You won't be."

She is, of course. He doesn't want to talk to the art teacher, so they wait in the hallway outside the classroom on a wooden bench beside a Pepsi machine, and he texts with Rachel.

be right there
good I'm getting ready
show me

A point-of-view selfie arrives, Rachel's skirt pulled up, her hand in her underwear. Karl draws the phone closer to his face so that Irina can't see.

save some for me
it's all for you

"I'm bored," Irina says. "I'm going in."

Karl has another erection, so he tugs his hoodie pocket down over it. "Yeah, cool. Okay, so, I'll see you in an hour?"

"Okay! Good luck!" Irina chirps, jumping to her feet, and she walks through the classroom door and shuts it behind her.

Good luck?

....

In the elevator (the hotel does indeed have one), Karl stares at his shlumpy, furry, blurry reflection in the polished metal doors and wipes his sopping palms on his sweat-stained jeans. He is shaking a little bit. It has been a month and a half since he has felt sexually satisfied. Not that he hasn't been fucking Nell, but she feels insubstantial to him now, like a wastrel, and has ever since the cancer. Rachel's zaftigness, her full round thighs and breasts, her gnarled mess of hair, the folds of belly fat he snuffles and snorts in like a rooting hog: these things have come to define sex for him in a way that Nell's body—no woman's body—ever has. And, though there is no question of Nell's attractiveness, it's like the beauty of a statue next to the beauty of a living being. Rachel is the fulfillment of a fantasy he didn't even know he harbored: a woman his age (older!) he can't get enough of.

Fantasies, for Karl, have always been a cinch to realize—you could call them "plans," really. Even the upstate house search, ostensibly designed as a punishment for him (or maybe, ultimately, to get him the hell out of the apartment for a few days, he thinks now for the first time), ended up turning fun; he came across the house, the one they bought, in the binder of inkjet-printed, plastic-sleeved info sheets the real estate agent provided, and was immediately attracted. He likes a found thing. He likes restoring life to a thing that has been abandoned. To the agent, a square-jawed, heavily made up young woman whom he considered trying to fuck, he said, "Why's it so cheap?"

"The previous owners were murdered."

That made him sit up straight. "Seriously? Why tell me?"

"Seriously. It's the law. I have to tell you."

"When? How? Why?"

She leaned forward a little. Her eyelids drooped, barely perceptibly. "Ten years ago. A dozen years? Anyway, guns? Drugs? I don't really know."

"They didn't catch the guys that did it," Karl said.

"No, I don't think so."

"Nobody wants to live where there are killers on the loose."

Her chin was puckered and her mouth was a hard, straight line. "Guess not."

"Let's go check it out."

The house was set back a couple hundred yards from a county two-lane, at the end of a shitty gravel drive. It stood on twenty-three acres of new-growth pine forest. Propane heat, well water, fourteen hundred square feet, two bedrooms and a study. Or three bedrooms. It would be a teardown if it were anywhere anybody wanted to live. The place was awkward to look at—a combination of incompatible styles. An arts-and-crafts-bungalow-cum-alpine-chalet with cedar shakes and a chimney and fireplace made of river stones. He liked it. The agent told him it was designed and hand built, presumably with somebody or other's assistance, by its original owner in 1922. Inside, it looked like ass, with evidence of recent and thoroughly tasteless landlord-caliber renovations that were already starting to seem old and ruined. "This'll all have to go," he told the woman, and she said, "Uh huh."

He was already designing the studio in his head. It would be huge. He'd have his own forge. Fuck yeah. He would make knives—that was going to be his new thing. The money they were saving on the house, he could pour into the studio, and he would spend all his time out there, being angry at Nell and at himself, jerking off, and making knives. Glass-bladed art knives. He would teach Irina to use them, and the two of them would stalk around in the woods wearing loincloths and stabbing shit.

Once the agent overcame her shock at his evident interest in buying the place, she pulled out her clipboard. "I need the name of a contractor," he told her. "Somebody who can rip out all that cheap-ass shit and also who can make me a blacksmithing shop. Can you find somebody like that for me?"

She was scribbling wildly. "Blacksmithing shop. Right," she said, her voice struggling to maintain its warily sardonic tone. It was no use. Karl had heard it before. His enthusiasm was infectious. Virulent.

"And the town," he said. "Where do people go? For stuff, I mean. Groceries. Movies. Fun."

"I will print you a map. I will mark some things for you."

"Right on. Awesome. Get back to me on that offer, okay?"

"Oh, I will. I will."

It all went so smoothly, his crazy plan. The contractors weren't dicks and showed up and did shit on time (if not at precisely the rates they had promised, but whatever). At one point Karl heard an ad on the contractors' boombox for a carpet warehouse down the road in Argos, and on a whim he went out there and found the exact carpet from the living room of his childhood home, the carpet he used to lie on watching TV on summer afternoons when he ought to have been outside, years before his parents got divorced. But the bastard who was going to install it bailed and then didn't call Karl back, so he never did get around to carpeting the living room. Other than that, though, everything's been golden. When Nell and Irina arrived and saw what he had done, they loved it. They fucking loved it! His studio is awesome. The forge is badass.

Two small problems.

One of them is that his agent, Gert, has sort of dumped him. Via email, no less. She gave him three months to either pay to have his remaining unsold sculptures shipped to him or to come down and get them. *I'm sorry, Karl,* she wrote, *but I can't sell this work, and it is taking up space. You will be better off with representation that better suits your needs.* Which is to say, somebody who still likes his shit. Of course she waited until Karl had left New York to tell him, the coward—and now, unless he wants to explain the whole thing to Eleanor and beg for an exception to the no-New-York policy, he can't go down there to find another agent, or to find somebody to unload his stuff onto until he figures out what to do.

The other problem is the matter of his family money—the income he's been getting for his entire adult life, which originated from the Canadian gold mine his grandfather owned. At some point, he'd reasoned, the old man would kick off and leave him a nice nest egg (Karl has been sending "I love you Pop-Pop" postcards every few months for fucking ever). But last week, a terse email from his father arrived, informing him that the family business was ruined and had been for some time. His grandfather had been revealed as corrupt and might even, at the age of eighty-three, go to prison. The remains of the company were being sold and its assets used to pay its debts. *Just to be clear,* his father added, in a postscript, *don't expect anything from your stepmother and me, either. We're as fucked as you are.* Karl's mother had long ago donated everything she owned to the new age cult that was now her entire life, so he was, at last, on his own. With a failing marriage, an upstate mortgage, and a fifty-thousand-dollar outbuilding dedicated to the creation of experimental cutlery.

You might have some luck with these on eBay, Gert told him in her breakup email, which he now understands to have been precipitated by the box of prototype knives he sent. (Those, anyway, she had the common decency to send back.) So okay, fine: he started an account, started figuring out how to auction the shit off. He had a blast concocting the marketing narrative—some bullshit about his having been inspired by fucking ancient Japan or the Norse sagas or something, a riff about his secret processes and rituals. He laid out the auction template using plenty of corny clip art, set all the display text in Papyrus. But so far nothing has sold. He's not sure what he's doing wrong. Meanwhile he's put on weight, despite his brisk walks through the creepy woods, and he seems to be getting sweatier, especially when he's turned on. Indeed, the elevator ride isn't even over, and his palms are drenched again.

The doors open and he steps into a musty-smelling brown-carpeted corridor lined with corroded brass sconces, half of them bearing burned-out bulbs. Everything's brown: the doors, the wallpaper, the stained stucco ceiling. The dirty window at the end of the hall. He finds 405. The door is off the latch; a thread of variegated light lines the jamb. He knocks and enters.

The room, to his surprise, is welcoming: creamy sunlight through gauzy curtains, clanking radiator, two roses in a vase, doubled by an oval vanity mirror, and behind the flowers' reflection, a mussed king-size bed bearing the seated form of Rachel, draped in a black night-gown he's never seen before (or maybe he has, the lady owns a lot of black nightgowns), her hands folded together in her lap. She is wearing an expression that strikes him, initially, as expressing more pity than desire. He turns, now, to face the actual Rachel, and in the time it has taken him to look away from the mirror, the pity has vanished, and her gaze appears smoky, hungry. Or maybe the pity was never there; maybe it was the mirror, half-desilvered with age, that lent her a bygone gravity, like a figure in a daguerreotype.

He goes to her, falls upon her, and they gobble each other up. Her mouth on his is frantic, hot with need, yet the pity from her reflection has lodged in his mind, he can taste it on her, he can feel it in her touch. There is something of the nurse in the way she pulls him back, settles him onto the pillows, interrogates his body with her hands. It's as though she's giving him more to conceal the fact that she has less, like a poor mother who has saved up all year for a plentiful Christmas.

Stop thinking, he tells himself. He mostly succeeds. They do all the stuff they do, and it's finished after twenty minutes. Now, to his surprise, there is time to kill. Now they have to lie here talking.

She fills him in on the neighborhood characters, the same way she used to back in New York. "Nancy finally let the police arrest her gentleman friend," she says. "Her regret was immediate. She cried out his name for the better part of an hour in my apartment, until Mrs. Chang brought her something to eat. Let's see . . . Carlos's little dog bit a passing child, or its mother claimed it did, though Carlos insists he could see no bite marks and Nugget would never do such a thing . . . she has threatened legal action, but we'll see what comes of that. The leaves outside my window are turning, soon I'll be able to watch those Honeymooners across the courtyard fry things and read newspapers and argue."

She's got her glasses on but is otherwise naked. Her voice is so composed—where's the conspiratorial whispering, the tears, the desperate texts? He would like to be able to get it up again, but it's too soon. She wants to know how his work is going.

"What?"

"Your work. In your fabulous zillion-square-foot studio?"

"Pretty good," he says. "New project cooking. Crazy stuff." For some reason he doesn't want to talk about it. He knows she wouldn't care. The women in his life don't, generally. That's fine by him.

He says, "What's up with your thing. The . . . magazine."

"Magazine?"

"The poetry thing. That you put, you know. That Eleanor was in."

She smooths the bedsheets over her thighs. Her fingernails are chipped and bitten, painted red. "Ah, yes. Haven't published that in years. As I believe you know. Believed."

There's a long pause. The small of Karl's back suddenly itches like a mofo, and he grunts as he snakes his arm back to scratch it.

"I don't think we're really connecting," she says.

"Now you know what it's like to be in a committed relationship with me."

"Ha," Rachel intones flatly. "Ha."

Get it up, he tells himself. *Come on, man.* He reaches down and fondles his wiener, glances over at Rachel. He glances down at her crotch, back at her face. She rolls her eyes, spreads her legs a little, touches herself.

When Nell was declared cancer-free, she presented herself to him, sexually, morally, as a survivor. *I kept these for you*, she seemed to be saying every time she unbuttoned her blouse and let her bra slip down off her shoulders. *Respect this body.* Truly, he doesn't understand why he can't. He didn't used to like sloppy, curvy women like Rachel. He's supposed to be the sloppy one—his women are supposed to be tidy and sleek. But Nell's poise, her grace, now feels effortful to him, her bulwark against the cancer—she is taking care not to wake it up. Her body is an advertisement for its own weakness.

And an advertisement for his, he supposes. Because, ultimately, he didn't do shit when Nell was sick aside from drive her to and from the hospital and hang out with Irina during the treatments. He'd expected, when the diagnosis came—and they were both expecting it, anticipating it—to feel more . . . heroic, maybe. Or at least sort of useful. They sat in dirtily upholstered plastic office chairs, facing the doctor's freakishly tidy desk, and he put his arm around her, squeezing her tighter when the bad news arrived. He was almost excited on the way to the parking lot. "We're gonna beat this thing," he told her. "Fuck it! Fuck cancer!"

But she didn't seem to appreciate the rhetoric and gently chastised him one night, while he was administering some pep. "You don't have to say that," she said quietly, touching his knee.

"I know, baby, but I'm doing it. I'm on your team."

She almost seemed to say something then but held her tongue. Afterward, she became more private about her treatment, about the progress of the illness. She scheduled meetings with the oncologist at awkward times, encouraged Karl not to come. She didn't complain of aches or nausea or exhaustion, just quietly endured. The quiet endurance became a thing. He could tell she was proud, and she was not interested in his sensitivity or praise. "Dude, you're amazing," he tried to tell her. "You're a fighter." But she wasn't having it. Her answering smile, her pats on the shoulder, were dismissive. It was her body. Her fight.

Karl does not think of himself as a jealous man. If Nell was fucking somebody else, he'd be down with it. Surely she already has? Is doing so now? After the cancer was over, after she beat it, she would take the train to Manhattan routinely, for checkup appointments at Sloan Kettering. And she has gone there once since they moved here, too. But last week, he got a feeling, or maybe it was a hope, and called them, ostensibly on her behalf, to double-check on the time. They didn't have her down for an appointment at all.

"When was the last time she came in?"

That clammed the lady right up. "I have already said too much" was the reply, and she hung up on him.

So yeah, what can that be but an affair? Right? It was almost a relief. The less Nell thinks about cancer, the more she thinks about sex, the better. Even if he isn't the one she's thinking about. Breast cancer is the thing he was jealous of. Her relationship with it was more serious than her relationship with him. Her commitment to it was deeper.

Not that Karl's commitment to their marriage is anything to crow about. And yet they are still married, aren't they? And he's a good father to Rinny, he's pretty sure. Or at least a good something to her—Karl isn't sure what a father is supposed to be like and is deeply skeptical of any model of parenthood imposed from without. Whatever he is, he digs hanging around with the kid, really respects her, thinks she's hilarious. He teaches her stuff, helps her to be chill. She's changed, Irina has; she used to be uptight, worried about everything. Karl has helped her learn to occupy her own self, he thinks. To be confident. Like him.

He isn't feeling terribly confident right now, playing with himself, watching his girlfriend play with herself, while up the street Irina daubs tempera paint on a fucking sheet of newsprint. He says, "Hey, so, does your building have, like, a storeroom or something?"

Rachel raises her eyebrows; they arch over they tops of her glasses: now she looks like a hot librarian. But at this point his anxieties have returned and are crowding out all desire. His palms are dry now. His dick's limp.

She says, "There's one in the cellar?"

"How much space do you have?" he asks her.

"This is a strange line of questioning, Karl." She lifts her fingers off her junk and wipes them, discreetly, on the bedsheets.

"I'm in kind of a situation."

"Okay . . ."

"I gotta get my pieces out of Gert's place or she'll junk 'em. I can't afford to ship them up here."

She pulls the covers up over her lap. "I see."

"I don't want to ask you to move them for me . . ."

This gets a laugh out of her. "Sure, sure," she says. She reaches for the nightstand, checks the screen of her phone.

And then he remembers. "Oh shit!"

"What?"

He jumps out of bed, finds his sweatshirt. He shoves his hand into one pocket, then the other. "You want to smoke? I bought some weed!"

"Don't you have to meet your daughter in a few minutes?"

"There's time!" He fumbles with the baggie, digs out the little pack of papers Jasn Hubble had been kind enough to include.

Rachel looks at him with a kind of amused affection. She climbs off the bed, says, "I'll open the window," and on the way back finds her underwear in the mass of black cloth on the floor. (Add a pointy hat, it could be the spot where the Wicked Witch melted.) She steps into her panties, says, "I'm not going to smoke with my pubes exposed."

"Why not?"

She gives it a moment's thought, shrugs. "I don't know, actually." Back in bed, she accepts the joint he has lit, takes a hit, hands it back. "Karl," she croaks. "Is this really what you want?"

He hates being asked questions like this, especially by women. "Is what what I want?"

"This," she says, exhaling. "Long-distance infidelity. Stolen hours. Minutes, really."

Karl is concentrating on the joint now. It is with a kind of rote anxiety that he says, "It sounds like it's not what you want."

"Of course it isn't what I want," Rachel says. "I came up here because I'm in love with you. But eventually, you know. Things will have to change."

"Change how?"

"You decide to leave Nell and come back to New York. Or not. In which case we'll split."

Some distant part of him begins to panic, but the weed is pushing it back. He closes his eyes, tips his head back, smokes, hands over the joint.

"I can't deal with this right now," he says. "Please tell me you'll come back. That we can do this again."

After a silence, she sighs, or maybe she's just letting the smoke out. "I'll come back."

"Thank you."

"This supposed future time, when you'll be able to deal with things," Rachel says, not without humor. "It exists, I trust?"

"Sure," he says, drifting. "Sure it exists."

8

By the time Irina has walked into the guitar shop with her gig bag strapped on her back, she has already mastered the chords D, G, C, and E minor; has tried, with some success, to teach herself tablature; has haltingly strummed her way through some Beatles songs using transcriptions she has found online; and has tried her hand at songwriting. She is feeling quite pleased with herself and is looking forward to the moment when Jasn says to her, "Okay, kid, let's learn some chords," and Irina says, "Chords, you say?" and bangs out her own personally written song, complete with lyrics. Bam!

Instead what happens is Jasn wants to teach her scales.

"I thought we were going to do chords?" Irina says.

"Aw, you can learn that stuff off the internet," her teacher says with a dismissive and oddly dramatic wave of the hand, like he's trying to dispel a cloud of smoke from a joint. Irina suspects Jasn smokes a great many joints because he smells quite powerfully of them and because he treats her like she's about forty and they are in a band together. "If you wanna learn some really tasty licks, you need to know scales."

"I don't think I need to do that. I'll just play chords, like Bob Dylan."

Jasn appears appalled. "Who the hell told you to say it that way? It ain't *dialin'*, like you're makin' a phone call! It's *dillin'*, like you're, I dunno—"

"Eating a dill pickle?"

"Ha! Exactly!" He holds up his hand as though for a high five, so she gives him one. "Anyway, even a rhythm guitarist needs to know scales, kid. There's notes in between the chords, and the notes come from the scales. Trust Daddy J. Okay!"

He takes his own guitar in hand—they are plugged into the same very large, very smooth-sounding amplifier—and begins to instruct her in the G-major scale, since that was the key whose chords she admitted she had already learned. Sometimes her fingers don't seem to reach, and Jasn removes one from the fretboard with his own long, yellow fingers and places it in the correct spot. She is surprised that she doesn't mind being touched by him. He is the least threatening and intimidating adult she has ever encountered. By the end of the lesson she can limp through the G scale with a reasonable degree of confidence and is already thinking about which of the notes she has learned will go in between which chords of her new song.

The lesson's almost over. Her father will be back shortly. She says, "Hey, I wrote a song, you wanna hear it?"

"Why in the hell not?" Jasn replies.

"Excellent," Irina says, then fishes from her jeans pocket the paper she has written the words on. They are an expression, of course, of her obsession with the Geary murders, which have dominated her thoughts for weeks; she could easily write a hundred more songs on the subject, based on a hundred little details mined from the CyberSleuths forums. But she doesn't yet know enough chords to keep from writing the same song over and over. She unfolds the paper, looks around for a place to put it, sees none. "Hold this, okay?" she says.

"Right on."

Jasn holds up the paper in the air between them, and Irina draws a breath and sings:

> *Ohhh, poor little Samantha Gee*
> *You poor little orphan of Route Forty-Three*
> *Ohhh, Samantha Gee, where did you go?*
> *Samantha Gee, I think that I knooooowwww*
> *Samantha Gee, I think that I knooooowww*

You came back to fiiiind
Oh, you came back to find something you left behind
Walkin' around, down that lonely street
I'm the one you were destined to meet
You'll be glad you met me, Samantha Geeeee

"The route number is fictional," Irina says quickly, to head off criticism. "It's sort of a blues song."

"I noticed!"

"You don't think it's very good."

"I think it's real good! Play it again, kid."

She plays it again, and this time Jasn plays along, adding a kind of bassy part under her singing and inserting these little melodies—these must be the tasty licks!—at the end of each line. It's so good! It sounds like a totally professional song. She only wishes she could sing better. But Jasn says, "You keep singing, kid, you've got a good natural voice for blues."

"Don't patronize me," she says without thinking. It's what her mother tells friends who claim to like her books.

This makes Jasn laugh like a hyena. "I wouldn't dare, kid! It's the truth! I mean, you sound like you're ten or whatever—"

"Twelve."

"—but you've got the makings of a real good singer-songwriter."

"I'll practice my scales, I swear. Those little noodles you were making are cool."

"That's what a lifetime of noodling gets you, kid!"

She likes this guy. She likes his droopy mustache and goofy enthusiasm. She likes that he calls her "kid," even though it's probably because, like many adults, he isn't able to retain her slightly unusual name. She has been called Helena, Irene, Ileanna, Irma, Ellen, and India. One teacher at her old school always called her Caroline, but that's because a girl with that name used to sit in her seat. Anyway, it's time to go. She and Jasn emerge from the practice room, and the mean girl behind the counter, who has dyed hair and about thirty tattoos and does not ever seem to smile, is nevertheless smiling at Irina's father.

"Hey, little buddy!" says the mean girl, about half an octave above her regular voice. "You sounded awesome in there!"

"Um, thanks?"

"Are you in a band?"

"I'm twelve," Irina says for the second time in five minutes. There's no worse age, when you get down to it; you're not, in any sense, a teenager, and so are not given allowances for such traits as sullenness and not wanting to get out of bed. You're supposed to still be energetic and cheerful, even if you are, at heart, a grumpy and basically lazy person. And meanwhile you have to endure the trials of puberty, one of which is repeatedly hearing adults utter the word *puberty*, the most horrible word in the English language. It contains all the awful words: *pubes, beauty, boobs, pretty. Über.* Über pretty booby pubes! "Are you noticing any changes in your body, Irma?" the dumb doctor wanted to know at this year's checkup. Yeah, I'm noticing it wants to run screaming out of this office.

"She could start a band," Jasn says, clapping her on the shoulder. "A few more scales and she could play lead guitar in Hubble Bubble!"

"I'm guessing that's your band," Irina's father deadpans.

"Classic rock covers," the clerk says, recovering her former bitchiness. It is embarrassingly obvious that she's trying to impress Irina's father, who, to his credit, seems less than receptive to it, even though the girl is kind of sexy. Indeed, Irina's father is now actually, literally licking his lips. Maybe they are just dry. He also smells weird and has ever since he met her at art class to walk her over here.

"Yeah, rock and roll, man!" he says, idiotically, handing Jasn twenty bucks.

"Catch you next time, Karl," the clerk says, with a wink in her voice. "See ya later, Rinny!"

Rinny! Her father must have referred to her this way in the girl's presence. But that doesn't mean the girl can. Is nothing sacred? Suddenly Irina feels as though everything is going to pieces. Too much that used to be certain is suddenly confusing and new and not necessarily very good.

Jasn is speaking to her now: "Okay, kid, bring me your best stuff next week, got it?" But Irina has already hitched the guitar up onto her shoulder and is pushing her way out the door and into the overcast and mildly stinky fall day. She feels bad for letting the real world seize and dispirit her so quickly—at the very least she should have been happy to see her dad. But when he emerges, slowly, from the guitar store, drawing a pack of cigarettes out of his jacket pocket and a cigarette out of the pack, and says, "Hey, man, lemme smoke this, okay?" she pretends not to know him and instead leans up against the brick wall of the abandoned storefront next door and pulls out her iPod. She can get a weak Wi-Fi signal from the guitar shop (*$uper$hredders* is the password) and uses it to Instagram a fortune-cookie fortune she has found adhering wetly to the sidewalk: TODAY MIGHT BE THE BEST DAY OF YOUR LIFE. Thanks, cookie. Her father smokes placidly six feet away, thumbing at his phone; he takes a handkerchief out of his pocket and mops his face with it. To distract herself from her profound disgust with the handkerchief and the concept of the handkerchief, she opens her email app and reads, once again, the email correspondence she has been engaging in with her new friend—or acquaintance, really but they are going to be close, Irina just knows it—Sam.

From: irinaofthedeep@gmail.com
To: lee.samuel.fike@yahoo.com

Remember me??

From: lee.samuel.fike@yahoo.com
To: irinaofthedeep@gmail.com

Dear Irina
Hi, yes, I remember you. It was nice meeting you at the Dairy Queen. You said something about knowing something about me, but like I said I don't think we have met

before? I am curious though, so here is an email like you asked for.
Your friend Sam

From: irinaofthedeep@gmail.com
To: lee.samuel.fike@yahoo.com

Hi Sam I am glad you wrote to me! Yes its true I have SUSPICIONS about you. I believe you have an identity be-sides the one you think, maybe you don't even realize you're somebody else, but I think you have been in Broken River before and you're back to try and learn something about your past and I think I can help you. To fill you in about who I am my father is a sculptor and my mother is a writer, and we live by the state forest in a house that I think if you saw it would bring back memories of your past. I'm from Brooklyn which is part of New York City but I don't miss it. I'm home schooled which mostly means reading whatever I want and sometimes taking a test altho I have not had any of the tests yet. Write back if you know what I mean or want to know more

Sincerely Irina

From: lee.samuel.fike@yahoo.com
To: irinaofthedeep@gmail.com

Dear Irina
Well I definitely don't want to disappoint you but like I said I'm from Buffalo and I'm here because of my brother. To be completely honest he is in the jail. He'll be out before long, so I'm just helping out my uncle and working at Denny's, and then I guess I'll see what happens when my brother gets

out. My life is pretty boring and I don't get what you mean by me being somebody else. Though like I said I'm kind of curious.
Sam

From: irinaofthedeep@gmail.com
To: lee.samuel.fike@yahoo.com

I'll be frank, I think you are a girl called Samantha Geary who's parents were MURDERED in 2005 in my house and who disappeared. Samantha/you was 5 then and now would be 17 which I think is about your age. If you want to know more lets meet.

I.

From: lee.samuel.fike@yahoo.com
To: irinaofthedeep@gmail.com

Irina,
I'm 19 and my parents are alive as far as I know. My mom definitely is, anyway. My Sam is from Samuel, not Samantha, because of a dead uncle. For some reason I have boys names haha. You're an interesting girl though. Maybe I will see you around.
Sam

Irina knows a brush-off when she hears it, but there's that last sentence, *Maybe I will see you around.* It could be politeness, or it could be an invitation. It could be an *unconscious* invitation. Irina is going to take her up on it, one way or another. She pokes Sam's email address to add it to her contacts and then adds a photo: the one she surreptitiously took

while standing in line at the Dairy Queen. It's grainy and smeary, because she had to zoom in, and Sam's face is half-obscured because she
was bending down to her ice cream cone. She looks at the new contact
card she has made with a certain amount of pride—A friend! I made a
friend!—and then, after a moment's thought, replaces the photo with
her internet-swiped Samantha Geary yearbook shot. They look similar, there's no question. Maybe Samantha was actually seven when the
murders happened. Her parents were probably druggies or something,
maybe they probably couldn't keep track! Or maybe Sam is lying a
little bit, to appear more grown-up?

Irina got a feeling when she saw her sitting there on the guardrail
next to the Dairy Queen, working her way down her vanilla cone. She
had a feeling Sam was not an ordinary girl, so she lifted up her iPod
and pretended to check her own hair in the selfie cam while in fact taking the photo. The line was long and the weather was hot and she became increasingly concerned that Mysterious Vanilla Cone Girl would
finish and leave before she, Irina, even had her own ice cream in hand.
But in the end, there was time not only to sidle on over with her own
vanilla cone (for solidarity) but to say hi, compare personal facts (both
new in town, both enjoy ice cream, etc.), and *exchange names.*

When Sam said her name was Sam, Irina's body turned into pure
electricity, and she said, "Samantha Geary!?" and Sam said, "No,
sorry, Fike," and Irina said, "Samantha Fike?" and Sam said, "No,
just Sam," and then they stared awkwardly at each other for a couple
of seconds, Sam appearing amused and alarmed, Irina squealing inwardly, her toes madly tapping the sidewalk. "But you're from here
originally," Irina said, and Sam said "No, sorry," and Irina said "But
you're here now," and Sam laughed and said "Sure, you could say that,
I guess." Irina gave Sam her email address, which Sam did not write
down but did repeat out loud, and Sam gave Irina *her* email address,
which Irina typed immediately into her iPod. "I will email you!" Irina
said, and Sam laughed again and said okay, and Irina liked her so
much, she likes her *so much.* And now, a bunch of emails later, she
likes her even more.

She's Samantha Geary. She has to be. If she isn't . . . If it's not her . . .

"Father," Irina says now, loudly, to try to keep the quiver out of her voice. "Are we going?"

"Yeah," he says, still thumbing away. At least the hankie has been stashed.

"Like, now?"

"Lemme finish this, Rins."

The two of them stand there, eight feet apart, leaning against the crappy-ass guitar shop wall. Irina stares up at the crumbling hotel facade across the street and tries to think of something, anything, that will keep her from crying. So she thinks about the comic-book shop near their apartment in Brooklyn, the one run by the angry little man with the big white dog. She never liked it, though she pretended to Father that she did because he liked taking her there. She isn't into comics, she didn't like the angry man, she doesn't like dogs. And the kids—and adults, for that matter—who were always hanging around in there frightened her.

Yet, in spite of what she told Sam, suddenly she misses it. The emotion she was trying to suppress is attaching itself to it. It is a real place, it's a place she used to go into because it was there, and it has carried on without her! Irina's plan has backfired. She is going to cry! She is looking forward to this aspect of childhood being over—this thing where you can't control your emotions and they aren't even about the things you really care about.

"Father, please."

"In a minute."

She can't help it—she lets out a single strangled squawk, and then she is crying and crying.

A moment later she feels her father's arm around her shoulder and he's saying, "Jesus, kid, what the hell."

"I just want to *go home*."

"I know I'm a shitty father."

"This isn't about *you!*" she says.

The arm disappears. She can hear his back cracking as he stands up straight. "Okay, yeah," he says. "Sorry, let's go."

Her chest is still hitching as they walk back past the arts center—it seems like years since the painting class she was just at—and to the car. They get in it and pull out of the space and some guy honks and her father hits the brakes hard and swears. Their heads bobble back and forth. "Sorry, Rinny."

"Stop apologizing!"

She realizes that she's mad at him. Maybe it's the nickname. He's overusing it today, probably because the guitar store clerk liked it. Her mother doesn't, and Irina doesn't particularly, either. But she likes that he devised it for her, and she has imagined that it's the kind of thing her future husband might call her, if she ever gets married.

But no, it's not the nickname, or even that he told it to that stupid girl. It's the *smell*. He smells like an ashtray in a gym in a department store. She looks over at him, and he's sweating and clenching his teeth as he flips off the guy who honked at him and then jerks the car out into traffic. "Goddammit," he says, and then he wipes his forehead with his hideous snotcloth.

She can't hold back. "Do you blow your *nose* into that thing? You blow your *nose* and then you wipe it all over your *face*?"

He hazards a glance at it as he shoves it into his jacket. "Ahhh, yeah, but . . . it's in a different part of . . . yeah. I guess that's kinda disgusting."

"It's completely unacceptable."

Unexpectedly, he gets mad. "Hey, man, you don't get to tell me what's acceptable and what's not," he says.

"No, *nobody* tells *you* what to do."

That shuts him up.

They drive home in almost total silence. At some point he says, "What'd you practice," and she says, "Wouldn't you like to know," and immediately feels bad, almost worse than before. She manages not to cry again. When they get home she runs to the stairs, passing, along the way, a duo of worker dudes who are dismantling a corner of the living room that has succumbed to blossoms of blue-black mold. The men smell like cigarettes, gross ones, grosser than Father's weed. In her room, she takes clean clothes out of her dresser and heads for the shower. She can hear the clickety-clack of her mother's laptop down the hall: doubtless she has her earbuds in and can't hear, otherwise she would come out and ask how the classes went. Irina doesn't want to talk about how the classes went. Adults buy you something, anything, they think they deserve detailed reviews and progress reports. Just pony up and leave us alone! She slips through the bathroom door, locks herself in. Then she runs the water and gets undressed while it heats up. She wants to wash Broken River off herself, the tears, the car ride, her father's weird smell. She is naked when a knock comes on the door. It's Father, loudly whispering. "Hey, what are you doing in there, man?"

"I'm taking a shower," she loud-whispers back, because that's what you do.

"*I* need to take a shower!"

"So do I! Which is *why* I'm *doing* it!" That was less a whisper than a quiet shout.

His answering whisper isn't even loud. "No, like, *now.*"

"Too freaking bad!" Irina actually shouts, full throated and genuinely angry, and she gets under the water and flings the curtain shut. Through the wall behind the faucet handles she feels, rather than hears, the sound of her mother's wheeled office chair being pushed back, then feels a door opening and closing, and then a knock.

"Irina?"

"I! Am taking! A shower! Leave me alone!"

"Are you all right?" her mother says.

"I am fine! Go away!"

"Where's your father?"

"Mother, I don't know!" Irina screams. "Go away!"

She goes away, and Irina cries for a little while longer under the hot water. She is aware that it will soon stop being hot. She washes quickly, then continues to stand there, making sure she uses up every drop so that her father will have to wait. When the hot water is gone, she gets out, dries off, and puts on her clean clothes. She enters her bedroom and closes and locks the door. The smell here is a comfort—familiar, a little rank due to feet and unwashed laundry, a little piney because of the open window and the close-hanging boughs, and a little musty, on account of the mold blossoms that have appeared behind the headboard, which she has not had the heart to tell her parents about. Also, she kind of likes the mold blossoms. They make the wall soft—they feel alive to the touch, yielding and slightly clammy. She climbs onto her bed, shoving aside the laptop her mother, as promised, has bought for her, and reaches behind the headboard to stroke the dark patches. Her fingers are dusted with spores, and she gives them a disconsolate sniff.

She opens up the laptop and dies a little bit inside. It's been a few weeks since she has added anything to her novel. When she got the computer, she decided she ought to be writing on it, so she typed everything she had so far into a word processor file, changing things a little as she went. Then she tried writing new bits. But it wasn't the same. She missed her notebook. So she got out the notebook and tried writing in that, but it didn't feel like the novel was *in* the notebook anymore, it was in the laptop now, and so she couldn't write in the notebook, either. After that, she just didn't feel like writing anything, and she put the whole Quayside project on hiatus.

Now, though, she opens up the Quayside file and starts typing. She has her boy protagonist, Aiden (a name she picked at random; she doesn't like it; she's going to change it) meet a girl called Kimmifer (they all have weird names in Quayside) who has amnesia and is trying to discover her past. She's older than him, seventeen, so she has just started wearing the bustle—until then, she just wore regular pants. She is very frustrated, she can't do the things she likes to do, and her mother tells her she'll get used to it, all women do, and she's a woman now. But she hates it. It is impeding her range of motion. She keeps having to ask men for help with stuff—getting into water taxis or reaching for a birdcage in a birdcage store, which is another thing grown women in Quayside are supposed to be into. (Privately, Kimmifer really does like birdcages.) Aiden (ugh, that really has to go) suggests they take a water taxi down to the Quayside Department of

Records, which he knows about from his research into trying to get back to Brooklyn. She agrees, and of course he has to help her into the cab, and he gets very excited touching her hand, although it feels sort of wrong somehow to feel that way. (Irina's thinking is that she is actually his long-lost sister? which will have to be written into the opening chapters somehow. But in a subtle way, so that it isn't obvious the moment Kimmifer arrives on the scene that she is the sister. Irina is aware that she is ripping this off from *Star Wars*, but *Star Wars* probably ripped it off from something else, so no big deal.)

There: she did it. She worked on her novel. The words are on the page now, they're real. So why do they feel fake? Why does she feel like a fraud? Would anybody else notice the difference between the fraudulent words and the real words? Would the Irina of three years ago, or of three years from now? Is this what a real writer feels like all the time—unsure if she is real? She hears voices—Mother speaking to the repair guys. The phrases "temporary fix," "probably come back," "could be everywhere," float up the stairs. She could ask her mother this question, but even the question itself feels fake. She closes the word processor with a couple of angry keystrokes, and the word *bad* escapes her lips. She opens her browser up to the Geary thread.

Not much new stuff, although smoking_jacket is at it, again promising to contact the new owners of the house about having a look around. Irina has been waiting for this to happen. Maybe it already has and Mother or Father has declined to let smoking_jacket come. Or maybe they have said yes and they are just waiting for the right moment—that is, when she, Irina, is not at home. At some point she should come clean to them about knowing everything about the murders. She can handle it, after all—she has not only been handling it, she has been enjoying it! But something is holding her back. Maybe even her parents don't know. Maybe *they* couldn't handle it, given the problems that they have been going through. Let the murders, and CyberSleuths, be hers alone.

Now she does something impulsive. She opens up a new-post window and types, *I think that I have found Samantha Geary. I know her name. She moved far away after the killings but now is back in the area. I*

entend to protect her identity and privcy but here is a photo of her. I asked
her if she was her and she did not say no. The dates match up. I think she
is hopeing to solve the mystery of her parent's deaths.

Irina uploads the Dairy Queen photo, making sure there are no details in it that would identify Sam or where she is standing. Then she
spell-checks the text and corrects *intend, privacy,* and *hoping.* Then
she hits POST.

If she expected an adrenaline rush, and she admits to herself that
she did, it doesn't arrive. There's just a silence as the post appears on
her screen. She refreshes the page a couple of times over several minutes, and nobody has responded. Well—maybe nobody will believe
her. She can live with that; she knows the truth! It will out, eventually. Is that how you say that: the truth will out? It doesn't sound right.

Irina sits in silence for a few minutes, refreshing the browser page,
hoping for a response. From down the hall comes the quiet clackety-
clack of Mother working on her novel. It makes Irina feel guilty about
not working on hers. Then the clacketying stops, Mother's office chair
creaks, and a response appears on the screen, from smoking_jacket:
Interesting, if true.

Footsteps. A knock on the door. For crap's sake.

"I'm busy."

The door opens. Mother walks in.

Irina is too shocked to react at first. Walking in is *not done.* Mother
comes across the room and flops down with a groan on the bed beside
Irina, stretches out her legs and crosses one over the other, squeezes
her hands in between her knees. "What are you working on?"

Irina glances down at her laptop. The blurry photo of Sam is right
there on the screen, beside the name *Samantha Geary.* She snaps the
laptop shut. Guiltily!

"Novel."

Her mother pauses, staring at the space where the browser page
was. That didn't look like your novel, Irina expects her to say, but instead, after a little grunt of acknowledgment, she says, "You said you'd
been having trouble after switching to the computer."

"Yeah . . . I think I've got it now."

"Good. You need to have problems and then solve them, if you're going to be a novelist."

"What do you want," Irina says, perhaps a bit too nastily, perhaps annoyed with herself for wanting to lean against Mother, whose bony shoulder is *right there*.

There's a pause. Mother cracks her toes. "Your father is . . . did something happen? In Broken River?"

"No."

"I heard him raising his voice. Did you have a fight?"

"No."

Another long pause, during which Irina considers slipping out from under the covers and escaping to the kitchen. But Mother says, "Sorry, baby. I don't think it has anything to do with you," and her tired voice induces in Irina another wave of longing. "I mean, I'm sure it doesn't."

"I miss New York," Irina says, and feels her small advantage slipping away.

"Me too, sometimes. Though there are fewer distractions out here."

"*I* wasn't distracted there. *You're* the one who was distracted."

Mother opens her mouth, then closes it again without speaking. It gives Irina a chill. It's like something a ghost would do.

"It's not like I want to move *back*," Irina goes on, lying. "I just want to visit. And go to our places. I miss the Sandwich Dungeon. I miss Grawlixes Comics, even the jerky guy and the dog, even though I don't like it. And WORD Brooklyn. There's no bookstore in Broken River."

"Maybe we just haven't found it yet?"

"I looked it up. It was called the Book Nook. It's out of business. You can still see the shelves and whatnot through the window."

"Oh."

"It was probably no good anyway because it had a stupid name and it's full of those wire spinning display things that always have romances or Jesusy things on them."

Irina's trying to sound hard, but her mother laughs. "You're probably right. Okay, sure. We should go back. Maybe I'll have a draft of this book soon and will have to meet with my agent—maybe you could come with me. We can see a show. We'll take pictures of Times Square, like tourists."

And like that, Irina forgives her for . . . whatever it was she was mad about. "Yes! That would be excellent. Is Father invited?"

She has said it without thinking. Of course Father is not supposed to go to New York. And Irina is not supposed to know that. And she has accidentally behaved as though she doesn't, even though she does. The layers of regret are piling up. Her mother seems to consider for a moment, then quietly says, "If you want."

"Maybe just you and me would be good," Irina says, and Mother's body relaxes.

"Deal."

"Deal."

Mother kisses the top of her head and gets up from the bed. Or tries to. She kind of convulses instead, and a small sound escapes her, a little squeak. Then she draws a deep breath and slowly peels herself off the mattress. This series of motions gives Irina a chill, though she doesn't understand why.

"Are you all right?" Irina asks her.

"I have a backache. I hurt myself moving our stuff."

"Maybe it's stress."

This gets her mother's attention. She's standing beside the bed, pressing a hand to her spine, curving herself backward like a blade of grass in a wind.

Irina says, "When I was fighting with Sylvie, I got pains in my jaw and shoulders, like, all the time."

"You never told us you were fighting with Sylvie," her mother says.

"It wasn't a big deal."

For a second she looks like she's going to respond, but in the end she just nods. She goes to the doorway, steps into the hall. Looks back.

"But seriously," she says. "What's that you were looking at, on your laptop?"

They stare at each other.

"Research?" Mother prompts.

"Yes."

Another few seconds of staring, and then the door latches quietly shut.

Irina is left with a complicated series of feelings: mild sadness that Mother has left the room; relief that their conversation is over; irritation that it was Mother, not she, who broke contact; annoyance at the complexities of adult existence in general and her parents' in particular; puzzlement at the parental intent in this whole encounter; and a niggling feeling of dissatisfaction, as if they were supposed to have accomplished something, or reached some agreement, or solved some problem, when in fact they have not. Was it her fault? Is there work she's supposed to be doing, as Child in Chief, that she has neglected? She squeezes her eyes shut and tips her head back and takes deep, deep breaths through her nose, and hums something in a minor key. And then she's through it.

Irina considers returning to CyberSleuths to see if anyone else has responded, but no: once she makes a habit of that kind of behavior, there will be no end to it. Instead she picks up her guitar to practice her scales.

She likes unamplified electric guitar: it's private, as much feel as sound. She plays all the chords she knows, in a random order. Each one vibrates differently against her body. Each one seems to touch some different interior part of her. She starts making up chords now, just random fingerings, to see how they make her feel.

And then one of them makes her feel something very specific and strange. It is the feeling of being watched. And not watched as in monitored, like there's a hidden camera and somebody somewhere is observing her on a screen. The watcher is here in the room with her. A presence. A thing without form or motivation but with a consciousness. It isn't evil, but it is scary. Something is watching her.

She is startled—so much so that her body jerks and she drops the guitar. The headstock dips and bumps into her laptop, and she cries out and snatches the instrument back up and examines the computer. There's a scratch on the case, a little scuff, but it isn't cracked or anything.

Irina looks around the room. It's just her room, that's all. The sun's low in the sky and very bright, and the shadows of branches are moving against the far wall. Soon she will be called downstairs for dinner. She hears voices, Mother's and Father's, and soon Father's footsteps sound on the stairs and the bathroom door opens and closes. Water runs. Irina's sense of this presence is draining away. It was here, she's sure of it. The chord, it was the chord that did it, and she tries to work out what the notes were—where she'd placed her fingers. She tries several combinations, but they're all wrong. It's hopeless. She isn't going to get it.

The experience has left Irina with a sense, strangely enough, of calm. She lays the guitar down where her mother was sitting. She shuts her eyes and listens to the vigorous splashing and thumping of her father's shower. She listens to the breeze moving the branches outside. She's going to sleep now—she'll sleep until dinner. She sends her thoughts out to the thing: Watch over me. It isn't here anymore, but perhaps it can hear her. Father's shower has combined with the wind, and now there is a sizzling from below, from the kitchen, where her mother is cooking, and the distant sound of traffic from the road and the creek as it runs over and around rocks. It's the sound of the world, and the thing watching her is part of it, and this feels like the solution to a problem: that's why the chord revealed the thing, it's because it's made of sound! It's this feeling, the feeling of the problem presenting itself and being solved, that tips her over into dreamless sleep.

Part Two

9

But earlier that day, in Broken River, the dark-haired woman lay on the hotel bed she had paid for, her hands laced behind her head, scowling at the stuccoed ceiling shot through with cracks and wreathed in cobwebs that trembled in the steady wave of warm air rising from a large, white-painted radiator. The Observer might have expected the woman to smile, or perhaps to drift off to sleep, but instead she seemed agitated, uncomfortable in her skin.

The woman stood, smoothing her nightgown down over her belly and thighs, though there was no one else in the room to notice the wrinkles it had developed in her overnight bag and in the struggle to remove it an hour ago. The Observer followed her across the room and to the window, and her gaze to the street, where the man, her lover, leaned, smoking, against an exposed-brick wall a short distance from his daughter, the girl.

The dark-haired woman, having taken notice of these two, now pulled back from the window, perhaps in fear of being seen. Across the room, her phone buzzed, and she hurried to find it in her handbag. A small smile appeared on her face as she took in what the screen displayed; soon her thumbs were in rapid motion, tapping out messages, presumably to the man on the street.

The Observer didn't presume to understand the lines of affection and repulsion, hope and disappointment among these three: the man, the girl, and the woman. It was not clear why this mode of communication—the encoding of short bursts of information into digital signals that were then transmitted into the upper atmosphere and back to earth—was preferable, in this instance, to simply shouting out the window. The girl's face was gripped by intense animation, at times evincing consternation (when she happened to glance over at her father) and confusion, at other times excitement (seemingly in reaction to the messages on her own device). The girl's hold on her childhood was slipping; before long the word "girl" would no longer apply.

The dark-haired woman issued quiet breaths, small grunts, as she gazed, alternately, out the window from a safe distance and at the text-filled bubbles scrolling down her screen. Eventually, the girl, having pocketed her device and failed in her struggle to maintain an adult demeanor, began to cry. The man looked up in surprise and went to her: there, on the sidewalk, he threw his arm around her, engaged her in a brief but intense conversation, and led her away. Seemingly in response, the woman fell silent, her face still. She gazed out for several minutes, as though deep in thought, at the place the man and child had occupied.

Now, hours later, all is quiet and calm. The dark-haired woman is leaving Broken River, having quickly changed her clothes, gathered her things, and departed the hotel. "Checking out? Already?" asked the desk clerk, and the woman replied, with audible disdain, "Family emergency." She sits, motionless relative to her speeding car, not singing along to the pop radio station that can't seem to maintain a clear signal here among the mountains.

The Observer lets her go. It is time to turn its attention to the family many miles to the north, though the Observer is increasingly aware that it needn't choose one time, one place, one group of human beings to attend to. Indeed, it is quite capable of observing anything, all things. But it has begun to recognize that its purpose, as opposed to its ability, is limited: or, more precisely, its purpose *is* to *be* limited. It is unconcerned with, bored in fact by, the immensity of its power. It is interested only in the strategic—the aesthetic—winnowing of that power.

It has been brought into existence in order to amuse itself.

What has caused it to come into being is not clear, and the Observer is not sure that it is interested in knowing. It is new in this world, yet it feels that it has always existed: or, rather, it has existed as long as the humans have. Its identity is connected to the self-awareness of the humans, and to their awareness of the world around them. The humans are already limited in what they can notice, compared with the Observer, yet they elect to be even more selective in their perception, filtering out those obvious truths that might nudge them away from their established trajectory. They refuse to seize available opportunities that might expand their experience even slightly; they maintain obsolete habits rather than adjust promptly to new circumstances. They seem almost to prefer ruin to voluntary change.

Yet the humans seem to think that anything is possible, that life is limitless, which is entirely and obviously wrong.

Of course the humans die. Quite possibly all of them. Perhaps the Observer will die as well; it doesn't know, and it can't imagine what it would do differently if eventual death were a certainty. But the humans, it suspects, know. This is likely why, years ago, at the beginning of the Observer's existence, the murdered man and woman screamed, even before any damage was inflicted upon their bodies: they were justifiably fearful that their lives were about to end. If the humans know that death is coming (and, by the Observer's standards, it would seem that it tends to come very soon), their words and actions must all be profoundly influenced by that fact. They fear making wrong choices, so they avoid making any at all. They keep very still, hoping that death might fail to take notice of them.

The man and girl have now returned to their house, and the girl is in bed, asleep. The breaths she draws are even and silent. She is curled on her side, this child who is already half an inch taller than she was when the man and woman made love in the unfinished house. The man and woman don't appear to have noticed this yet about their daughter. But it is clear, or it should be, that the girl has grown out of her fall clothes and that they ought to buy her some new ones. Perhaps they have other things on their minds.

Indeed, the girl herself seems to have failed to notice the space between the bottoms of her jeans and the tops of her shoes, and the fact
that she can now see half of her wristwatch (she found it sitting on
a bench in the subway—it's a cheap ladies' Timex with a rectangu-
lar golden face and little hash marks instead of numbers to mark the
time, and her parents have not asked her where it came from) poking
out from her shirt cuff. Her sneakers still fit; she isn't in school, and
so there's nobody to mock her, no one whose gaze she could feel self-
conscious in. Perhaps, the Observer thinks, the girl, the whole family,
could go wild out here, forget about the existence of other people and
their judgment. Their hair could grow long and tangled; they could
kill their dinner with their bare hands.

But no: the man and woman have not forgotten themselves. There
are clues. In the bathroom, the shower has stopped, and the man
is standing, naked and dripping, in the steaming stall. He's staring
straight ahead, at nothing in particular, and scowling. His left hand
is idly stroking his belly, which has increased in girth in proportion to
the girl's increase in height; his right hand cups his flaccid penis in its
nest of dark hair. After a moment he shifts his left hand to his creased
forehead, where it digs and massages. Perhaps the man has a headache. He really ought to turn the shower back on and let its powerful
spray soothe his face. But the girl used all the hot water, and the heater
in the basement has not had time to fully replenish it. He's going to
have to just get out, which he does, violently flinging aside the curtain
and stepping, still dripping, onto the rug. He buries his face in a towel
and leaves it there longer than our Observer is interested in watching.

Downstairs, the woman is standing at the stove. A blue-and-white
pinstriped apron covers her usual uniform of black jeans and sweater.
In her left hand is a wooden spatula; her right hand grips the handle
of a stainless-steel wok. The wok is filled with vegetables, and they are
steaming and sizzling. On the burner behind the wok sits a pot full of
rice. Behind the woman, the table is set for three.

The vegetables are cooked. They were cooked some time ago. In a
few moments, they will be overcooked. The woman is standing quite
still. The expression on her face is one of thoughtfulness tinged with

concern and perhaps, at the corners of her eyes and mouth, the slightest hint of terror. Has she realized that her husband's erratic behavior this afternoon is consistent with continued infidelity? All the necessary information is there for the woman to make this determination. But she seems unable, or unwilling, to do so.

The woman's hand reaches around behind her. Her brow knits in concentration, and then she winces and her body jerks. Her reverie broken by the evident pain, she looks down at the wok, emits a small gasp, quickly removes it from the heat. The words "Oh, shit" escape her lips. A few flicks of the spatula confirm that half the vegetables are blackened and shriveled. The woman sighs, slumps against the counter. For a moment, the Observer wonders if she is about to collapse onto the floor.

But then the woman opens the cabinet beneath the sink, scrapes the burned food into the trash bin. She sets the wok back on the burner, turns off the gas, and sets to work chopping vegetables again.

This delay in the completion of the family dinner gives the man's natural energy and grumpy good cheer enough time to reassert themselves. The girl's nap markedly improves her mood. The three appear to enjoy their meal and, afterward, a filmed entertainment in the living room. Their laughter will indicate that the movie is a comedy, but the Observer can find no appreciable difference between the onscreen human folly that evokes merriment and that which induces sympathetic misery.

It's time for the Observer to move on: again above Route 94, along the river, past the hills and railroad, past the farms and villages. Back to Broken River. It could go there instantaneously, of course, but at this moment it prefers to take its time. Without impending death to hurry it along, why not? The temperature has dropped—it's been dropping all day, down to levels at which the humans begin to complain—and now it's snowing, even though there are still a few days left in October. The Observer reaches the flat land where Broken River begins, and moves through town, past the abandoned theater, which an angry teenaged boy is attempting to break into through an alley door (he will succeed); past the apartment building where Jasn Hubble is watching a YouTube video of the Average White Band's cocaine-fueled performance on *Soul Train* that originally aired November 22, 1975, and where his eyes follow, with longing, the movement of a Lake Placid Blue Metallic Fender Mustang bass with matching headstock; past the empty animal shelter that now once again shelters animals, a family of stray cats here of their own volition who got in through a rat-chewed hole in the rotted plywood back door and who are being fed daily by the old man who lives on the other side of the disused, weed-choked parking lot; and finally over the cluster of jail-themed bars and the prison itself, a mile beyond which a trailer park lies. It's large and fairly tidy; compared with most of Broken River, it is thriving. Many of the streets that run through it are paved, and the pavement is in decent shape; the rest are graveled and reasonably free of ruts. At the end of one of these streets stands a neat beige doublewide around which a small deck has been built. Light shines from the trailer's windows, yellow from the lamps inside and blue from the television, which is showing a baseball game to a compact, overweight, alert-looking man in his fifties. Our Observer, however, remains out on the deck, where the girl called Sam is standing, clutching herself against the cold, which her thin cardigan sweater and baseball cap do little to protect her against. One hand holds a cigarette, the other a phone.

She says, "He didn't say anything about coming home."

She says, "He didn't say anything about your letters, Mom."

She says:

"I don't think it's about you, Mom. He's just got other things on his mind."

"No, I don't think he's coming back to Buffalo."

"No, but I'm going to stay here for a while, okay? Uncle Bobby's fine with it."

"I said he was fine with it. I think he's lonely."

"I haven't met any girlfriend."

"Well, I didn't meet any boyfriend, either, so I don't know."

"I don't know, Mom."

"I have to go. I love you, too. I have to go. Goodbye."

10

Sam is standing on the deck, gripping her phone, snow falling all around her. It's cold out and she is shivering, but she isn't eager to head back into the trailer and pass through the room containing her uncle on the way to another lonely night in her bedroom. Not that she doesn't love her uncle or appreciate the room: she's kind of surprised to realize she's okay with both, for now. She had been led, before coming here, to believe that her uncle was little more than an embittered, self-satisfied loser whose dominant conversational mode was that of explaining why all his problems were the result of other people's failings. And it's true, there's more than a little of that in him. He seems surprised that the world hasn't given him more, hasn't brought him the riches he thinks he deserves. But, as far as Sam is concerned, he doesn't have it so bad. He's got a job, anyway, as the site manager and retail clerk at a stone quarry, which is why this doublewide is surrounded by rock gardens, low stone walls, and frankly weird and incongruous intentional piles of what he calls "irregular flag." He always seems to have some rocks in the trunk of the car, and she suspects he steals them from work: his miniature rebellion, a thumb on the scales of justice.

Anyway, even if her uncle was little more than an insecure prick with some very slightly suppressed creep impulses, Sam would be all right with it. She adores the old man. When he still lived in Buffalo he was her favorite surrogate father; they used to play cards together, and he took her to the track with him most weekends. But then his wife left him, his sister's crazy got unbearable (Sam's father and poorly considered namesake, Lee Samuel Fike, was already gone before she was born, and Uncle Bobby liked to mutter under his breath that he didn't blame the guy), and he packed up and moved here. Sam hadn't seen Uncle Bobby for years, and it was only when Daniel got three to five for growing weed under lights that she ever considered even visiting. By this time she was already planning to move away—she hated school, despite her excellent grades, and had GED'd her way out at sixteen, plus living with her mother was a nightmare—and she figured she could come out here with the stated intention of getting Daniel back on his feet. She would crash with Uncle Bobby for a few weeks, then help Daniel find a place, live with him for a little while, and decide what to do once she had the lay of the land.

Instead, she has mainly bonded with Bobby and at the moment has no plans to move out. She admitted to him, a few days before Daniel's release, that she felt guilty about abandoning their mother. "Look, she's suffering, no doubt about it," Bobby replied from the other side of the sofa, gesturing at the glowing, silenced television with his burning cigarette. This was how he talked: at the TV, regardless of where in the room you actually were, or if it was on. "But just 'cause you're suffering don't mean you got the right to make everybody else suffer with you. The crazy bitch sent your brother up the river. I'm not saying he wasn't breaking the law, I'm saying your fucking mother ratted him out. She pretended not to know what she was doing, but she did.

"That's what she's like," he went on, cracking open a beer and changing the channel. Sam couldn't discern any logic in the channel changes, neither in their timing nor ultimate destination. Now, many weeks later, she has decided that the TV is like an animated painting for Uncle Bobby, a series of abstract patterns and colors; he's not actually interested in human narratives, finds them tiring, despite his fairly acute sensitivity to human personality. "She's sneaky. She's a manipulator. She was a manipulator when she was three fuckin' years old. She learned to get me blamed for all the shit she did: stealing from the neighbors, leaving a turd in the bathtub, setting the fuckin' cat on fire.

"I'm pretty sure your granddad was making her suck him off, though. I mean, I think that's what that's all about. Or maybe she's just a psycho. Anyway, go ahead, feel bad for your mother, but don't let her make you feel like anything's your fault. She's forty-eight. She's got her health and she's no idiot. If she can't make her way in the world without you, fuck her.

"Am I right?" he asked the TV. "Am I right? Fuck her!"

"Yeah, okay," Sam said with a laugh. "Sure."

So no, none of the three of them has any reason to be here, really, except that they all want to be far away from Mom and Broken River is a town few people think about or want to go to. For Sam, the place is probably a stepping stone, though to what, she has no idea. Like her brother, she is smart and decent-looking and built to endure. Daniel, too, is unlikely to stay here long—he tends to develop ambitions, and even if the ambitions center mostly on growing pot, he will likely achieve them and will either grow out of Broken River or end up back in prison.

Daniel was good at prison. He kept himself up-to-date on changes in the world of weed: new varieties, new methods, looser laws. "If I'd been caught only a year later," he told Sam once, over the glass partition, "I woulda got off with six months in county." He probably wouldn't have been caught at all, of course, if it weren't for their mother; it was her basement he'd been growing in. She was lucky not to lose her house, actually, a fact that Daniel still refuses to acknowledge. He had enough plants down there for twenty years in federal— his light sentence was the result of a liberal judge who'd been apprised of the family situation and who made frequent eye contact with their mother during the trial.

She was late to pick him up on his release day. It was literally the only reason she came to this town, and she was late. Uncle Bobby's Taurus wouldn't start—he'd left the passenger door open overnight after bring- ing the groceries inside, and the dome light ran down the battery. They had to get a jump from a neighbor two trailers down—a broad-hipped, ex-beauty-queen-looking lady of around sixty, perpetually bathrobed, eyeglasses on a chain—who clearly disliked Uncle Bobby but appeared accustomed to the ritual of helping him start his car. Sam expected to find Daniel pacing up and down the street or doing jumping jacks or pushups or something, looking thin in his years-old clothes, but when she arrived, there was nobody in sight except the hot dog man, a couple of kids using dirt bikes to prop up their lanky, loose bodies, and an idling brown Oldsmobile with poor suspension.

Sam parked, turned the engine off, then winced: had she driven long enough to charge the battery? Well, she'd soon find out. She thumbed through a wrinkled and muddy issue of *Motor Trend* she found in the passenger side footwell while she waited, wondering if she'd gotten the time wrong, or the date, or if something had happened inside the prison to detain him, like becoming friends with the warden. After fifteen minutes she got out of the car and started walking around—like brother like sister—and eventually she made her way past the idling Olds. There was nobody behind the wheel, but in the passenger seat lay a little pile of hot-dog-stand debris; the window was open a crack, and into the crisp autumnal air drifted the scents of sausage and chili and tomato ketchup. While contemplating getting a hot dog of her own, Sam noticed that the back seat was occupied by two people: one a curvy girl with straight black hair, like a late-night television diva. She was wearing a lot of makeup and a lot of black. The other person was a man, thick, curly light-brown hair, broad shoulders, little girlish ears. He had his face buried in the woman's neck, and his hand was squeezing her tit. Sam couldn't see the man's face, but it bore good-humored, thickly lashed brown eyes, plump lips, a sharply cleft chin, and a scattering of freckles. She knew this because the man was Daniel.

The girl saw her first and flipped her off. In response, Sam knocked on the window. The girl said, "Fuck off, perv!" and at that point Daniel turned, and his sleepy face woke up, and he said, "Sam!"

The car door flew open and Daniel flew out. "Sis! I'm free! Fuckin' hi!"

"Hey, Danny," she said as he embraced her; she angled her hips away from him so as to avoid contact with his hard-on. He smelled of old sweat and hot dogs and somebody's perfume, presumably the girl's. "You made a friend."

"Oh yeah. Yeah, this is Yetta. Yetta, this is my sister Sam."

The girl still appeared hurt to have been interrupted but made an impressive attempt at friendliness, leaning across the width of the backseat and peering up at Sam. "Hey, sorry."

"It's okay."

"She was coming to visit somebody, and we got to talking!" Daniel said, combing his hair back with his fingers.

"That's great."

"My boyfriend's in for assault," Yetta told her, with an eyeroll. "Not on me. He was a teddy bear with me."

"He's supposed to be in for a while," Daniel explained, by way of reassurance. "I know him, actually!"

"Oh, he's a fucking tool," Yetta said with a wave of the hand.

Daniel shrugged.

"The hot dogs were for him," Yetta went on, "but . . ."

"Haha, right!" Daniel said. "Yetta and I met in the hot dog line."

"That makes sense," Sam said.

"Yetta was ready for a change!"

"Goddamn right I was."

"Sure," Sam said.

In the end all three of them went to Yetta's and had some beers. (Sam was right to worry: the battery in the Taurus had indeed failed to charge, and Yetta had to give the car its second jump of the day.) When it came time to take Daniel back to Uncle Bobby's, he told her, apparently in response to some wordless invitation of Yetta's, that he was going to stick around here for a while. Yetta nodded. Sam said fine, went out to the Taurus, which she had left idling, and went home to Uncle Bobby, who seemed relieved.

That was a month and a half ago. Since then, Daniel has taken over Yetta's ex's semidormant weed operation, expanded and refined it, and gone to market with the product. With what money, she has no idea. Money has never been a problem for Daniel. People do things for him, invest themselves. Women, mostly, but also a certain kind of boy as well, the impressionable loner with no social skills and limited charisma, who looks up to him and aspires to his particular kind of cool. When Daniel is seen at all, he is usually seen with one or more factotum or fuck buddy trailing along behind him, laughing at his jokes and looking around to see who is noticing that they are with Daniel. Sam looked up to him too, when they were growing up; in his presence she felt an uneasy mixture of pathetic inferiority and secondhand chic.

It embarrasses her to find that, even now, even here, Daniel still makes her feel this way: invisible except in the light of his glory. It doesn't matter that he's a stoner ex-con in a shitty town. He's Daniel, and she's Daniel's little sister, and ever it shall be.

That is, if she can't find something to do with her time besides read library books, hang out with her uncle, and go over to Yetta's house to hang. Another job would be good. She could save some money and move someplace more interesting—a city, maybe. Although, again, what she would do there, and what stimulation she thinks her mind requires that this place could satisfy, remains unclear. Maybe all three of them will just live here until they die.

The snow is picking up. It's adhering to her clothes now, faster than her meager body heat can melt it. She finishes her cigarette, stubs it out in the now-snow-covered china plate that lives on the porch railing, and goes inside, shaking herself off. Bobby raises a hairy arm to her as she heads to the kitchen, and she raises a pale one back. She prepares a grilled cheese sandwich and eats it standing up while staring at her own reflection in the kitchen window. Even after the sandwich is gone, she remains standing there, waiting for the next thing to happen.

That thing is that her phone rings in her pocket. She answers, and Daniel says, "Come on over, we're having a party."

"I was thinking of going to bed."

"It's nine thirty!"

"Okay. Hey, I just talked to Mom."

"Sam-Sam, come on, I just told you it's a party. No Mom talk."

"You should call her."

"Okay, okay," her brother says. "You coming?"

"I don't want to walk in the snow."

"I'll pick you up, yo."

"I don't know."

"I'll pick you up, yo."

Ten minutes later they are fishtailing down unplowed Onteo Street, nearly missing several parked cars. Daniel reeks of weed. He's talking nonstop about having met a guy who knows a guy. He says the words "untapped potential" and "power vacuum." The radio is on, but only static is coming out of it. Sam is listening to the static, out of which little bits of words keep emerging—vowels, consonants. She isn't even high yet, but this is what Daniel does, he transforms his milieu into a zone of mild intensity and confusion. He induces susceptibility to his frame of reference.

The party is hot and close and loud beneath the low ceilings of Yetta's late mother's house. She's been dead for a few years. Her things are still here—her knitting, her bedroom slippers, her cardigan sweaters—scattered throughout the place. "I keep thinking she's coming back. I keep thinking she's here," Yetta told Sam a few weeks ago, over mugs of the sickly sweet instant coffee that her mother favored and that is still stockpiled in the cabinets as though against some future societal collapse. They're friends now. Sam kind of knew they would be, even when Yetta was giving her the finger over her brother's shoulder in the car. Yetta is impressive. She's bitchily confident and has a loud laugh, and she managed to keep her ex's pot situation going in his absence. (He was in for assault, not drugs, though it's inconceivable that the cops don't know about what's going on downstairs. Sam has decided to try not to worry about this.) It's no wonder she and Daniel found each other. She has invited Sam to deal for them.

"I don't know anyone. I'm an introvert."

"You could deliver out to the boonies. Where the weirdos like you all live."

"Hey," Sam protested, though to be noticed in this way, by Yetta,

sent a little shiver of pleasure through her. She has indeed driven
Yetta's car out to where a few amiable hermits live, and been treated to
a lot of rambling anecdotes and political rants that Yetta was probably
tired of listening to. It's fine. She does like it. She likes Yetta. And she
is surprised to find that she likes this party.

Sam was unaware that parties of this intensity and magnitude even
existed in Broken River. There is a lot of beer and a lot of box wine
and everyone is eating brownies and passing joints around. People
are gathered in tight clusters everywhere and the clusters are gathered into larger clusters. Wild-card guests form little pockets of pecu-
liarity here and there: a totally ripped guy in a sweater vest is lying on
the floor in the hallway, talking to a girl who looks like a hairdresser
and who is rubbing his temples. There's a miniature boombox in the
bathroom with Christmas carols coming out of it and a yellow sticky
note on it that reads LISTEN CAREFU because the author ran out of
space. Some unbelievably tall guy in the kitchen is telling a story about
Antarctica, and a girl who looks like a very sexy horse is giggling uncontrollably. A long-haired dude in his fifties or sixties is talking about
opening for KISS in 1979, and he's making air-guitar gestures. Sam
consumes chemical refreshments for hours and everyone is so friendly
to her, asking her name and saying it's so cool she's here. A black guy
wearing glasses picks her up bodily for no clear reason and carries her
on a tour of the house while shouting out the names of the rooms:
living room! bathroom! hallway! bedroom! She thinks: Are we going to
stop in the bedroom? For a moment she is very nervous and begins
to tremble; she's about to tell the guy to put her down. But then the
guy puts her down and picks up somebody else, and she misses him
a little. She overhears her brother telling some kids, "Yeah, I fucked
some dudes! Everybody fucks dudes there!" At some point some girl
standing behind her kisses the back of her neck and squeezes her
breasts and whispers "I like you" and disappears before Sam can get a
glimpse of her, and at another point she is challenged to put her finger
into a sleeping man's nose. She does it, and people cheer.

She's not the only one to spend the night. She wakes up on the coat
pile. Some of the coats are on top of her. She's holding someone's hand,

someone also buried under coats. It's a nice hand, long and white, probably a girl's. Sam endures a moment of desire: for what, she's not sure. The hand is warm and slightly moist and there's a scar on the back of the thumb. The fingernails are unpainted and bitten short. The wrist the hand is attached to is slender and translucent and a vein pulses pinkly under the skin. She touches the wrist with her lips and feels panic begin to rise.

And then the hand is withdrawn, abruptly, into the coat pile and a little moan sounds, and Sam needs to get out of there. She sloughs off the coats, leaves the room, and moves down the hallway, blinking. A small group of mostly young people is arrayed around the kitchen, drinking coffee and eating eggs that Daniel has made. He's wearing the apron, anyway. The heat's turned up high, and Yetta's in her panties and a sweatshirt. Sam can see her pubes sticking out.

"Mornin', Sam-Sam," says her brother.

"Hey. Hey, everybody."

Conversation is quiet and unanxious. Everyone seems happy. Sam eats the eggs; they're just scrambled, but there's something extra in them, something delicious. She has another helping and drinks a lot of coffee.

When everyone but her has left and Yetta has gone to take a shower, Daniel says, "Come check it out." She follows him through a door that she thought was a wall—given that it is covered with shelves, and the shelves with jars of dried beans and grains and cans of vegetables— and down a narrow set of stairs to the weed operation, which consists of a giant clear-plastic tent, or series of tents, with thick hoses running in and out of them. The tents fill the basement, leaving room for only a washer and dryer in one corner, and a series of bookcases filled with mason jars of harvested buds. They enter the tent complex by pulling aside the plastic and step into a warm, bright, reeking spring. The plants are growing in soil underneath racks of makeshift lamps; Daniel has created track lighting using what look like discarded garment racks, plastic shower-curtain rings, and cheap hardware-store workshop task lights. There is a low hum from the fans that ventilate the tents.

"Wow" is all she can say.

"It needed an upgrade. Barney was small-time." Barney is Yetta's violent ex.

He points out various features of the operation, the way the air flows through the tents, the carbon filters, the ozone generator that eliminates the smell of the plants when the air vents outside. "Didn't smell it when you got here, did you?"

"No," she says, but she isn't really listening. She's thinking that Daniel will probably end up in jail again before too long. Not, she hopes, in the same cell block as Barney. Watching her brother talk, watching him point at his creation and talk about his future plans, she is moved, embarrassingly so, and lets out a little gasp of emotion. He stops talking and looks into her eyes with that disarming alertness his girlfriends both love and can't stand too much of, and he takes her into his arms. "I love you, little sis. I missed you when I was in jail. I can't believe you're a grownup now."

"Don't get caught, Daniel."

"Aw, I won't. Unless Mom finds out."

Upstairs, he offers to drive her home. She declines, and walks. It's sunny out, though still cold. With every step away from Yetta's house, she feels lonelier. When she gets to her uncle's, it's past noon. He's reading magazines and coughing and doesn't say hello. She goes to her room, opens up her laptop. It's old, the fan runs all the time and makes an incessant clicking noise. There's another email from the girl who is obsessed with her and thinks she survived a murder in 2005. The email consists of more plot summaries of a story the girl is writing, along with complaints about her parents.

She sighs. She's due at Denny's in an hour and a half. She writes to her mother and her only remaining friend from high school, who she doesn't even really like. Then she writes back to Irina and asks, *Not that you're a baby, but*, do her parents need a babysitter? Because she is cheap and available and needs the work.

11

A week later, Louis and Joe are driving from Argos to Broken River. It's an unseasonably cold day and the heat barely works, and that bothers Louis. But he knows better than to complain to Joe, whose car they're riding in. The car is in perfect condition—Louis has identified it as a 1973 Eldorado—with immaculate paint and impeccably gleaming chrome trim, but the interior looks and smells like a dumpster. He's sure it says something about Joe that he only cares about the outside of this car, but isn't sure what. He asked him once: "How come your car's such a mess inside?"

"Who cares?"

"I'm just saying. On the outside it's perfect, on the inside it's a pigsty."

"So take the fucking bus."

"I'm not complaining, I'm just asking."

A moment of silence before, once again, "So take the fucking bus."

Joe is kind of like those frogs they cut up in high school. They attached electrodes to the leg and made it twitch. Joe reacts to things. He doesn't think about them. He looks kind of like a frog, too, with no neck and big hands and a big mouth and bulging eyes. A couple of hours ago he called Louis up and said, "Gotta go north."

"Can't."

"Mr. Chet says."

Louis didn't want to do anything having to do with Mr. Chet ever again. He said, "I can't go now, I got a delivery coming in tomorrow and that kid Duane doesn't know how to do shit, and so I have to be there when the truck comes in."

Silence on the line. A childish disappointment combined with brooding anger.

Louis said, "And also Pam and the kids—"

"I'm comin' to pick you up," Joe said.

"Nope, can't, sorry." Though he knew it was pointless.

"Comin' over." And the line went dead.

So here they are, driving three miles an hour under the speed limit in Joe's Cadillac with the windows cracked open, because the car is a dumpster and the smell is unbearable without fresh air. Ineffectual late autumn sun is beating down on a boarded-up farm stand, a Jehovah's Witnesses' Kingdom Hall, a motocross track, another Jehovah's Witnesses' Kingdom Hall. The road is lined with the dead stalks of those tall weeds that turn out yellow flowers in the summer.

Louis says, "Hey, you want me to find something on the radio?" and Joe says no and Louis says "Is that no as in you don't have a preference or no as in you don't want me to do it?" and Joe says, "Don't fuckin' do it."

He sort of regrets coming, despite the implied threat in everything Joe says and does. But it's true that the kids are driving him bananas, and Pam is going through one of those phases where nothing he does is right, and his job is boring, and the new kid Duane is girl crazy and won't stop talking about "chicks" he wants to "bang," apparently figuring that's the only possible topic of conversation when you're alone in a carpet showroom with another man, even one twice your age.

The other night Janine and Pam were sitting on the sofa with their heads mashed together, staring at the laptop, and when Louis asked what they were looking at—because he wanted to know what could possibly cause them to non-accidentally touch each other—Pam said it was the Broken River case, the missing girl. Somebody had found her, somebody posting on CyberSleuths. She was back in the area, this person said. "I know her name," said the person. There was a picture.

"Lemme see that," Louis said, and they scootched over and he added his head to the cluster, pressing it against Janine's. He suddenly remembered when she was, like, two, before Fred, before Broken River, how they'd sit this way, in the old place, on that shitty sofa they used to have, the one that would swallow you up when you sat on it and that smelled like cat piss. Him and Pam, with the kid nestled between them, looking at a book or watching TV. His arm around Pam's shoulders. He did this now, snaked his arm behind the two of them. They let him.

He didn't get any chill, any shock of recognition. It was just a girl, kind of blurry, on a sunny street. Could have been anyone, could have been anywhere. Maybe she looked kind of like those people, but Louis had only ever seen them at night, in motion, illuminated by headlights.

Louis didn't ask Joe if this trip was about the girl in the picture. He didn't ask because he didn't want to know. Now, though, he has got plenty of time to think about it. Plenty of time to sit in silence without the radio to distract him, and contemplate what possible other reason there could be for Mr. Chet to suddenly be back in their lives, telling them to go north.

Louis first met Joe at the carpet warehouse, more than fifteen years ago. Joe was working part-time for the franchise, making a delivery of boxcutters, tacks, carpet pads. They got to talking, sort of. Joe was in contact with other drivers, people who knew just how shoddy their bosses' record keeping was. They hauled appliances, electronics, basketball sneakers: stuff you could sell. Louis had a big old warehouse here, with plenty of unused space. After twenty minutes they shook hands, and soon afterward Louis's take-home pay began to rise. That was the longest conversation he ever had with Joe. They did all manner of jobs together, usually secured through Joe's contacts, shadowy people known only by their first names or by no names at all.

One of them was a guy Joe called Mr. Chet. Everybody else they worked for or with seemed to Louis to be small potatoes, but Mr. Chet was somebody. If they had a big job that needed doing, Mr. Chet was typically behind it. You'd only ever hear him on the other end of a pay phone. His voice was calm and quiet, but high, nasal—it begged to be imitated, though you didn't dare. He never involved himself directly. He didn't show himself.

Until the thing with the guy and the lady in Broken River a dozen years ago. That was the first and last time Louis saw Mr. Chet. Everybody disappeared afterward, went quiet, and Louis put that part of his life behind him. When he knocked Pam up again, they decided they'd better get married, and after a while Louis got used to being out of the game, managing the carpet store, bringing up the kids, being more or less fucking stuck here in his shit house, with his crazy wife, never making quite enough money. Sometimes—more so back when the kids were little and he was still unaccustomed to lying to Pam—he lay awake at night panicking that Joe or Mr. Chet might throw him under the bus. Pin Broken River on him somehow. Sometimes he would dream about Broken River and wake up screaming and sweating, and Pam would bolt awake next to him saying "Jesus Christ, Louis, what is your fucking problem?" Nowadays she's taken to wearing earplugs to bed. She can't hear if one of the kids gets sick, or if the phone rings, or probably even if the fucking fire alarm goes off. It's all his responsibility.

But whatever. It's fine. He doesn't wake up screaming anymore. Some days he barely even thinks about it. Today started out as one of those days.

....

An hour later they reach the outskirts of town. It's nothing much to look at. Shitty houses, a car dealership, a Chinese buffet. Once they're in town proper, it's no better, with everything as broken-down and depressing as he remembers. Maybe it's a good thing, being here, Louis thinks; it makes Argos seem cosmopolitan by comparison. He is recalling their meeting with Mr. Chet a dozen years ago and tenses up as they approach the turn that led to the empty, chained-off parking lot where they rendezvoused. But Joe drives past it without a glance. Louis says, "Is he here? Are we meeting him?"

"No."

Well, that much is a relief. "So what are we doing?"

"Talking to a guy."

"What guy?"

No reply. Joe turns onto Erie and then onto Shearn and pulls up in front of an abandoned storefront, yellowed newspaper falling away from one corner of a window that is already more than adequately obscured by dust. Joe turns off the engine and says, "Come on."

Louis doesn't move. Something has just occurred to him. Maybe Mr. Chet is just trying to tie up loose ends. Maybe this is all a ruse to get Louis far away from home without telling anybody where he's going. Joe probably told Mr. Chet about the girl showing up on the website, and Mr. Chet probably told Joe to take Louis somewhere and kill him. So now Joe's going to kill him. Louis is the weak link, the amateur. He always was. Joe's got a little pistol with a suppressor on it tucked into his big canvas coat, and he's going to push Louis into this abandoned store and pop him in the back of the head and leave him there. It'll be weeks before his body is discovered, if not longer: weeks before Pam and the kids even realize he didn't run off with another woman.

Joe has gotten out of the car and shut the door. Now he's opened it again and poked his big, ugly head in. "Come on," he says, in precisely the same tone of voice he said it in the first time. This only reinforces Louis's fear. His blood has turned to sludge. He unbuckles his seat belt and sort of leans against the door, then unlatches it and lets his weight push it open. Ahh, fuck. His feet hit the ground and he is able to stand on them. They propel him slowly around the front of the car and onto the sidewalk, where Joe meets him and leads him not into the abandoned store but into the guitar shop next door.

Oh god. Thank you, god. Guitars are hanging on the walls, amplifiers are stacked on the floor, and there's a tattoed girl with punk rock hair working behind a glass counter full of electronic-looking shit. She glances up without saying hello.

"Where is he," Joe says.

"Teaching a lesson."

"Tell him Joe's here."

"He's teaching a lesson," the girl says, dropping a shoulder and cocking a hip. She doesn't drop her gaze.

Joe turns to Louis, stares blankly at him a moment, then jerks his head toward the hallway in back, from which the sound of halting electric-guitar scales can be heard. After a moment, Joe manages a frown.

"What?" Louis says.

"Get him."

"Oh."

"Hey, he's in a lesson. You gotta wait," the girl is saying, but Louis is happy to disobey, happy to have an errand, happy to be alive. He follows the sound of the guitar to an unmarked white door, knocks and enters.

There's a guy here, older than Louis, long gray hair, smoker's mustache. He's sitting in a plastic folding chair, and across from him's a girl a little younger than Louis's daughter. They're both holding guitars. The guy says, "Hey, sorry, man, Cherise can help you out front," and Louis says "Joe's here," and the guy says "What?" and Louis says "Joe." In response to the guy's puzzled frown, Louis pantomimes Joe's considerable height, large girth, and bald head with a series of creative hand motions.

"Oh," says the guy. He turns to the kid. "Smoke break, Shooter. Keep noodlin'."

....

Out in the alley behind the guitar shop, the guy looks pale and nervous and confused. Also cold. He's a skinny bastard; in his puffy purple ski jacket, which must be something one of his students left behind, he looks like a length of insulated PVC pipe. He smokes his cigarette in little sips and jogs in place every few seconds.

"Yeah, I remember you, man," he says to Joe, offering Louis a half glance as though to acknowledge, or invent, the possibility that he remembers Louis, too. Which he doesn't because Louis has never met him. "What's up?"

"Who's the new Barney," Joe says.

"I dunno who that is, man."

"There's a new Barney. And a girl making deliveries."

"Don't know any girl, Joe." The guy's in kind of a permanent shrug. Born shruggin'. He looks tiny in his big coat.

Joe turns to Louis. "Stand at the end of the alley."

"What?" Louis says. Then he looks at the guy, who now appears terrified, and realizes why, and says, "Oh, okay," and goes to the end of the alley and looks up and down the mostly deserted street for, what, he doesn't know, a cop? A rival thug? There don't seem to be many of either in this town. From behind him comes a squeal and a moan and then a lot of low, fast talking on the part of the guitar guy. When he turns around a few seconds later, the guy is scuttling back in through the alley door and Joe is lumbering toward Louis with his fingers twitching and an expression of mild distaste on his face.

"C'mon," he says, and Louis follows him to the Cadillac.

They drive back through town the way they came. "Where're we going?"

"House," says Joe.

But they don't go to a house, not right away. Instead they go to a diner. Louis is grateful for this; lunchtime was an hour ago, and he's hungry and mildly nauseated from the hunger and from the smell of Joe's car. The diner is mostly empty save for a farmer-looking guy falling asleep at the counter and, over in the corner, a Hispanic lady with makeup tattooed on her face who at first seems to be talking into a Bluetooth but actually just turns out to be nuts. The waitress takes their order. She's a tall dyed-redhead of around forty. She and Joe know each other. Pretty well, by the look of it. Louis is jealous, the waitress is his type. Pam's not. Louis isn't sure why he is attracted to his own wife. It doesn't make sense. Anyway, he's never been unfaithful to her. He supposes he just still likes her in spite of everything.

The waitress—her name is Shelly—brings their food, and they eat it. It's club sandwiches. Louis now understands why the diner is empty: the lettuce is wilted, the bacon is clammy, the turkey doesn't have any flavor. Joe takes huge bites of his sandwich, champing and

smacking like a dog with its face in a bowl, and licks his fingers—
every one of them—when he's finished. He gets up, carries his plate to
the kitchen, and emerges with Shelly. Louis is only halfway through
his first sandwich half.

Joe says, "I'll be back." Shelly is taking her apron off and hanging
it over the back of Joe's chair.

"Seriously?"

The two of them head for the door, Shelly leading the way, and as
they pass into the street, Joe smacks her behind. They climb into his
car and drive away.

Louis sits there, bewildered by this unexpected development. The
mentally ill lady has stopped talking and is now moving her hands
as though saying the rosary, but her hands are empty. The farmer is
gone; a young guy is standing with his arms crossed behind the counter, scowling at the front door. The cook, Louis supposes, and then, in
a burst of insight, realizes that he's Shelly's son. He can't be more than
twenty. How does he feel about his mother taking a nooner with some
tough from out of town? Louis again remembers when Janine was
still a little girl, when her room was pink, and lousy with bears and
lacy garbage and posters of horses and princess shit, and how much
he hated all of it, and how much he misses it now that the horses
have been replaced by rappers and the tiaras by heels, and he wonders
if someday—who knows, during her heroin-addiction-and-hooking
phase, maybe—he will feel nostalgia for what he hates today. He is
trying to get this bite of turkey club successfully chewed and out of his
life. It's taking forever. And then he finally stops trying and just swal-
lows the damned thing, and nearly chokes, and he coughs, and tears
up from the coughing, and then he has to calm himself down to keep
from straight-up crying.

He didn't mean to kill anyone. Jesus Christ, he never dreamed
that was what they were doing. They didn't even need a third man,
that's the crazy thing—Joe and Mr. Chet could have handled it all
by themselves. They pulled into the driveway and met the Volvo coming out, and the Volvo swerved into the woods and hit that tree. Joe
and Mr. Chet were out the doors in an instant, and Mr. Chet tackled

the guy and Joe the lady, and they got the two of them up against a couple of trees in the headlights with guns up under their chins, and Mr. Chet started muttering to the guy, asking him unintelligible questions punctuated by insults: You little fucking twerp, you limp-dicked little hippie.

All they'd told Louis was they had to go pick something up. And they needed him to drive, and maybe to serve as backup in case things went a little screwy. And he would get a nice little payout if it all went well: a thousand bucks. No promises, but how's that sound to ya, Louie? Eh? Pretty good, Mr. Chet, pretty good. Mr. Chet didn't seem so intimidating at first—he was smaller than Louis had expected, though big-shouldered and amiable. More talkative than Joe, which wasn't saying much, but he didn't seem to mind Joe's silences on the long drive to Broken River. "Whaddya say, Louie," Mr. Chet said every fifteen minutes or so, and Louis said Sure, right, definitely, Mr. Chet. What did Louis know? He was twenty-eight. He worked at his uncle's carpet store. He could use a thousand bucks.

And then, when the guy up against the tree was saying they didn't have it, they didn't have it, that Mr. Chet's people had robbed them, they fucking robbed them, why don't you ask them yourself? the lady started screaming. She just screamed and screamed until Joe's hand clapped itself over her mouth, and she must have bit the hand because it reared back and smacked her. And then . . . Jesus. Louis couldn't believe what he was seeing. Joe was raping her, that's what he was doing—he had apparently got it into his head that this would make the guy talk, or maybe he just felt like raping somebody. Anyway, what the guy did instead was make a break for it, to try to save the lady, or maybe he was just a coward and was leaving her to die. And Louis heard Mr. Chet say "For fuck's fucking sake" and somebody shot the guy, and after a while, after way too long, somebody shot the lady, it was dark and hard to tell who did what, and the guy and the lady ended up bleeding to death on the ground while Joe hiked up his pants and tucked his shirt back in.

Louis had been half-watching all this from the gravel drive, where he was standing with one hand resting on the driver's-side door of

Mr. Chet's Expedition and the other on the butt of the gun they'd given him and which was half-buried in his jeans pocket. Now he just said *oh Jesus oh Jesus* under his breath over and over while the smell of discharged firearms dissipated in the air.

"The fuck," Mr. Chet said.

"Sorry," said Joe.

"The *fuck?*"

"Yeah. Sorry."

"This is a real fucking mess, Joe," Mr. Chet said.

"Sorry, Mr. Chet."

"You're sorry. You're sorry. Louis!"

oh Jesus oh Jesus oh Jesus

"*Louis!*"

"Yessir?"

"Open the back. There's tarps. Get out the tarps and clear the rest of the shit out of the way. Then bring 'em over here and let's fix this shit. Hurry it up."

He did as he was told.

Joe and Shelly return to the diner sooner than Louis worried they might, though Shelly's facial expression (bleary, small private smile) and body language (slow, sashaying walk with lots of hip action) indicate satisfaction, and Joe clearly feels confident enough in a job well done to smack her on the ass again as she heads for the kitchen. Is she aware that she just had sex with a rapist and murderer? Maybe she is. Maybe it's a selling point. Louis has paid—the kid accepted the money—and left a significant tip, despite his waitress having abandoned the restaurant for forty-five minutes. Joe does not comment on the cost of lunch or on what has transpired. If there is evidence on Louis's face of his recent bout of reminiscence, Joe betrays no awareness of it. He just says, "C'mon."

In the car, Louis asks where they're going and Joe again says "House." Louis asks if he can be a little more specific than that, and

Joe says nothing. Okay, fine. Joe's got his phone out and the lady in it is telling him how far to go down what streets. They're there in five minutes—it's a little warren of fifties bungalows, most of them in disrepair or in need of paint. Old cars are parked in cracked and weedy driveways—not interesting old cars, old cars from when cars started looking the way they now look and will probably look forever. It occurs to Louis that Joe's car is spectacularly inappropriate for criminal activity. Maybe what's happened so far today, or is about to happen, doesn't fall into the category of criminal activity. Mr. Chet's car back in 2004 was stolen, it turns out. A throwaway car. When, someday, Joe arrives at Louis's house in a ten-year-old Toyota Camry, Louis will know that he's about to once again be put into service as an assistant murderer.

No car sits in front of 1313 Gauss Lane, though. The name on the mailbox is JANDEK. Louis follows Joe up the front walk and watches him bang on the screen door, five times, with deafening force. No one answers, and no one flees out the back. It's snowing again, harder now, so maybe the owners will not notice the footprints Louis and Joe leave as they case the joint. Joe looks at the first-floor windows, presumably to see how secure they are; he crouches and peers down into the basement window wells. Either these are blacked out or it's really dark down there, but nothing is visible through the dirty glass. Joe sniffs the air, squints up at the chimney. He grunts.

"Well?" Louis says.

A shrug. "We'll come back."

"Look, man, I don't have time to come back."

"Gotta. Nobody here."

"I don't get it."

Joe turns to face him, gazes uncharacteristically into his eyes. "Our money, idiot. New people took over. They got our money."

"How do you know, man?"

"I found out."

"How?"

Joe says, leaning alarmingly in, "It's that piece on the internet, idiot. In the picture. Her and a guy. She's makin' deliveries."

Louis says, "Internet?"

"That thing you told me about."

"Yeah, but—"

"It's the kid that got away that night. She's back. She got our money."

The two stare at each other. Louis says, "How can she . . . ," and Joe smacks him on the face. Not too hard, just hard enough to indicate how much it would hurt if hurting was what Joe wanted to do.

"Shut up, buddy," Joe says.

Joe turns around, returns to the front door. He takes a folding knife out of his pocket and cuts a large gash into the screen with one deft stroke that creates a very satisfying *zwoop* sound in the muffled, snowy air. Joe turns back to Louis, smiling. The knife blade has scarred the wooden front door as well, lending the action a more definite intentionality.

"Leavin' a note," says Joe, turning and heading for the car.

"What's it say?" Louis asks, trying to keep the fear out of his voice.

"We'll be back."

They climb into the Cadillac. The across-the-street neighbor, Louis notices, is watching them through a window. He is old and frowning and appears installed there, like a subject in a portrait. As Louis watches, the man's frown deepens and his face fades into darkness. Joe has either failed to notice him or doesn't care.

As they leave town, exhaustion overcomes Louis, and he realizes he's going to fall asleep. Part of him believes that he should remain vigilant in the presence of Joe, but really, what is vigilance going to get him? If Joe is going to get him killed, or even, eventually, kill him, attentiveness isn't going to change anything. It will only make the experience more miserable. The ancient windshield wipers creak and moan as they clear the snow; Joe's headlights penetrate weakly into the blizzardy late afternoon. Louis closes his eyes.

Louis says, "I don't understand why I had to come along on this thing."

Joe doesn't say anything.

He helped them. Helped them move the bodies. Helped transport them deep into the state forest, far off any path, and bury them. He drove the dead couple's Volvo: followed Mr. Chet and Joe to the chop shop, crying all the way. And later he and Joe turned the house over, looking for money, Louis supposed, and for anything that connected the dead people to Mr. Chet. But there was nothing. Louis thought for sure the bodies would be found, but they never were. The missing people were named in the papers, some family members made a fuss, but eventually the whole event faded away as more people did stupid things and died.

It was while they were tossing the house, the next day, that Louis realized: there was a kid's room. There was a kid. On the way home, he asked Joe, Did you see a kid? What happened to the kid?

Wasn't no fuckin' kid, Joe told him.

But the bedroom—

No fuckin' kid.

Joe was wrong, of course. The kid turned up. The kid told the cops what she heard. In the end, though, it wasn't enough. The cops gave up. The kid disappeared. Louis has thought about her every fucking night since. What happened to her, where she's been. Most nights, when he can't get to sleep, because he can never seem to get to sleep, he imagines a scenario in which the girl's existence is known and he has been ordered to find her in the woods and kill her. Sometimes, if he falls asleep while enduring this fantasy, it turns into a nightmare. Sometimes he finds the girl and the girl is a monster and he kills her. Sometimes he shoots the girl and she dies but is still conscious somehow, and lies on the forest floor, in a pool of blood, telling him that it's all right, that he is forgiven. Sometimes he finds the girl and it's his daughter and he needs to explain to her why she has to die now. Awake, during the day, he has tried to imagine lives for her, far away, teaching a kindergarten class or working in an office or being a singer or something. He is obsessed by the possibility that she might re-surface, that she might remember something, that she could lead the detectives to reopen the case and catch them at last. If that happened, Louis thought, he would surrender. He would tell them everything and beg for mercy.

He never imagined that this would happen, though. The girl as a drug dealer? Maybe she's hard—maybe she'll end up a killer, too. He pictures her, tattooed and dead eyed, loitering outside Janine's high school, selling her weed. Or meth! Janine gets addicted—she can't pay. The girl threatens her, beats her. And what if it comes out that Louis killed her parents? The girl would show no mercy. She'd exact revenge on Janine. And Pam. And on Fred! Even Fred, Jesus Christ.

"Joe," Louis says now, because he really, really does want to know. He wants there to be, to have been, a point to any of this. "Why am I here? Why did I have to come along."

Joe makes a sound deep in his chest like a purr. "Because I like you, buddy," he says, and laughs, very quietly, for a long time.

12

The Observer has been taking liberties.

For a dozen years it was not self-aware. If it could be said to have possessed any consciousness at all, any perception of its existence outside the things it observed, it might have imagined that its work had some purpose, that it had been tasked by some entity, or for some ultimate goal, to record the goings-on around it, without prejudice, without the burden of interpretation. But for whom, or what, it monitored the house, it could not have guessed, nor would it have bothered to try.

Nor did it notice the passage of time. In the great immeasurable before, all events were equal, regardless of their duration; some events contained others, some bore no relation to others. But the Observer did not acknowledge—indeed, had not considered the potential for—cause and effect. One event, one object, was as good as another. The destruction of a human life carried no more weight in the Observer's understanding of reality than the paralysis and imprisonment of a housefly in a spider's web.

But that has changed. The Observer has begun to make judgments. It has become . . . interested in the doings of the human beings. It cannot be said to have acquired emotions, or morals, but it is increasingly compelled by the intricacy of human interaction. The humans are logical but unpredictable. They set things in motion. Their lives intersect in unexpected ways. The Observer has increasingly elected to follow them, to watch them more closely, at the expense of other phenomena it once regarded as equally significant—the volume of rainwater draining from the roof, dots of mold developing under the eaves, the deterioration of roads and stones and paint, patterns of light projected upon the wind-bowed trees. And with this new dedication to mobility, to *pursuing an avenue of investigation*, the Observer has developed a distaste for immobility. In fact, it has begun to experience a feeling akin to regret, a sense that it has "wasted" a portion of its "life." But these concepts, pressing as they might seem, point to broader questions that the Observer is not prepared to ask itself, questions about its origins, its *duration*. Because no entity can embrace the notions of time, of cause and effect, without the concept of mortality intruding upon its thoughts.

The Observer senses that its powers are greater than it has thus far appreciated. Or, rather, its power is enormous, perhaps infinite, within its narrow range of ability. The humans, it understands now, are weak and limited as observers of themselves and others, of the intersecting events and phenomena that make up their universe. But, unlike the Observer, they possess agency. Their corporeality enables them to effect change in their immediate environment, sometimes more broadly even than that. The Observer is aware that there are humans it could study—powerful leaders, great thinkers—whose words and actions have real consequences for the community of men and women. But, like the physical reality they inhabit, the humans embrace the same patterns of cause and effect regardless of their importance. Much can be learned about the humans, the Observer suspects, by studying any insignificant collection of them, in much the same way that patterns of ice growing overnight on a cold windowpane resemble, in a vastly different scale of time and space, the patterns ocean water etches into a rocky coastline.

The Observer senses that its existence will extend far beyond its meager entanglement with these people; yet it suspects that it will see these patterns repeated over and over again as long as human beings remain its subject.

For now, however, the Observer can feel the gears of cause and effect locking together, increasing in rotational velocity. Previously hidden truths will soon become known to its subjects. Events long gestating in the womb of possibility will soon be dramatically born.

The woman, Eleanor, can feel it. Changes in her relationship to her husband, her daughter, are imminent. She fears and craves those changes, is aware of the fear but not of the craving. Her body tries to inform her of both. It is the middle of the night, and she is awake, writing.

13

She is awake in the middle of the night, writing.

No. *In* the middle of the night, *she is awake, writing.*

Eleanor stares at the laptop screen, her fingers lying inert on the keys. Minutes pass. Her office window is cracked open, because she needs fresh air to work, but it is almost winter and it's snowing, so the space heater, that reliable gray cube, is gently rumbling at her feet. Every couple of minutes it switches itself off, having heated the underside of the desk to its evident satisfaction, and then Eleanor can hear the very quiet sound of heavy snowflakes thudding gently onto the windowsill and the pine boughs outside. Cold air flows in and settles on the floor, and the space heater kicks back into life with a wheeze.

Several cycles of heating and cooling later, she deletes the line and types *She is awake writing in the middle of the night.* Then she deletes that and types *It is the middle of the night. She is awake, writing.*

There.

It is the middle of the night. She is awake, writing. What she is writing is the scene, at the end of her novel, in which one of her two protagonists, the woman dying of cancer, is awake in the middle of the night, writing a suicide note. She has decided to spare her family the agony of a protracted decline and is about to ingest the bottle of painkillers that her friend, a nurse, has gotten for her, at great risk to herself. The bottle stands at the corner of her protagonist's desk, where in the equivalent spot on Eleanor's own desk stands a coffee mug, empty of coffee.

Eleanor's novel is almost finished. It has been a constant companion to her anger and anxiety for weeks now; it has obsessed her like nothing else she's written. The first thing she did when she discovered the renewal of Karl's infidelity was to open up the file and start deleting sentences. This led to deleting paragraphs, and then chapters. Once the book had been reduced to an invalid, she began to build it back up, into something new. A monster, nourished on internet cancer research, CyberSleuths, and mistress stalking. The book is about her marriage now, about the ways adults hurt children by being the assholes who love them. It's about the way things you thought you put behind you can come back to kill you.

She has started taking naps during the day so that she can stay up late working. As a result, she and Karl have been sleeping, on average, two or three hours a day in the same bed together, tops. If she continues to work on the book (and she feels as though she could do this forever, repeatedly scrapping, abandoning, rebuilding, relocating, in the manner of robins or wasps), their sleep schedules will come to be entirely out of phase, and they will be effectively transformed into roommates, and not even friendly ones, at that.

But she is not going to continue working on the book. She is going to finish it. Tonight. She stands up, stretches. Her back screams. She wants more ibuprofen, but it's too soon; she took three of them two hours ago. Already they are making her feel nauseated, or maybe it's the back pain itself, or whatever is causing the back pain. But no, we're not going to think about this now, we are going to sit down and write until we are finished.

She sits down and writes.

At some point Karl comes stumbling into the office, rubbing his big red face, and says, "Hey, man. That shit's loud."

"What is," she says, typing.

"Typing."

"Welp," she says, typing, "I am typing the food onto your table, so I will stop when I feel like it and not a minute sooner."

He pauses at the threshold, his head resting against the door-jamb. She has not yet confronted him about what she now knows he is doing. First things fucking first.

"All right," he says. "As long as you're awake, do you wanna screw?"

"What do you think, Karl." Don't stop typing.

"Yes?"

"No."

"Okay, well . . . all right," he says. "I'll see ya later."

"See ya."

An hour later, she's done. It used to feel like something, finishing a book. She would time it, announce its proximity to completion, create an opportunity for celebration. Champagne would be chilling in the refrigerator, or reservations made for someplace nice to eat. Nowadays, even under the best of circumstances (and these are not the best), declaring a thing finished is a convenient lie. There is no finishing. Many drafts, dozens, are to follow. Even with the book in stores, the writing continues in her head. Only another book can stop it. It's like a nuclear meltdown, a destructive reaction that feeds on itself and renders everything around it toxic. At best, finishing a draft these days feels like inadvertently knocking something off a table—a bowl of soup, say—and gazing at it there, slowly spreading at your feet, and thinking, I guess I'm not going to eat that anymore.

It's 4 a.m. Eleanor goes to the bedroom. She finds Karl balled fetally in a snarl of blankets, a pair of headphones askew and tangled up in his hair. The sound of rain—a white noise app, running on his phone, on the bedside table—issues quietly from the vicinity of his head. The sight of him, vexingly, moves her. There is something about Karl's sleeping body—its essential childishness, she supposes—that induces affection and pity, emotions she does not wish to experience right now. So she jerks the blankets out of his grasp, collapses beside him, and, without touching him, tries to drive herself, like a railroad spike into a tree trunk, to sleep.

But she's kidding herself. Her back is on fire. The pain is reaching up into her neck and shoulders and down to her calves, as if to snap her in two. She knows what the problem is: her cancer is back, and she is going to die, die, die.

....

Nevertheless, at some point, she wakes up. Which means she has been asleep. Her back feels better, though it also feels stiff and bulky, as though there's a pine plank gaffer-taped to it. No pain, though it's right there, around the corner, waiting for her. She gets up, levering herself off the bed, and stands in the bedroom, listening to the house. A shower is going. It's probably Irina. She should do something with her daughter—invite her to go downtown, maybe—but she doesn't want to. She wants to escape. She's still wearing the clothes she had on last night. After a moment's thought she gathers up her computer and charger and totters downstairs and out the door.

Smoke is pouring from the studio chimney. He is out there doing one of the stupid things he does. Making knives, he has told her, which was too stupid for her even to believe, at the time. She should leave him, she tells herself as she gets into her car and navigates down the snowy driveway to Route 94. She should have left him when she discovered that his usual monthly income from his family "investments," the money from which their mortgage was being drawn, hadn't been deposited into their account on the customary day and she extracted from him a confession that said money was, in fact, gone for good. But she did not. And then she *really* should have left him when she realized he was still in touch with, still fucking, Rachel Rosen; and again, she did not. She hasn't even confronted him. She is too tired.

Rachel Rosen! Editor of *Vera*, the shitty poetry magazine that Eleanor had given a couple of poems to years ago, before she discovered her evident calling, writing schlock people actually want to read. Rachel Rosen, blowsy fatty, she of the coarse black tresses and excessive eye makeup. Rachel Rosen, moneyed poseur. A year ago, when this idiotic drama began, she thought, No, that can't be right. He can't be sleeping with Rachel; she is an actual grown woman. But then

Eleanor started sleuthing. She found Rachel's blog, a dreadfully writ-ten exercise in formalized middle-aged narcissism packed with vague references to romantic passion with an earthy man-child called K and a lot of post-feminist bullshit about the pleasures and humiliations of submitting to the capriciousness of male desire. Then came the con-frontation, the shouting, the tears, the apologies. The nights apart. The reconciliation. The deal: say goodbye to it all and move upstate. As if that was ever going to work.

She should have known it wasn't. It was easy to figure out, once she had decided it was time to know again: she waited until he was in the shower and looked at his phone, just like she had a year ago. There she was, her name expunged but the number in black-and-white, just like before, over and over in the call log. And then the series of local numbers that did not correspond to the pizza place, the guitar shop, or the art school and that she discovered belonged to hotels and mo-tels, which Rachel was presumably staying in. She checked the Skype contacts on his laptop while he was taking a dump and found her there (complete with, for fuck's sake, a fucking come-hither *profes-sional portrait* of the woman, as though she was ever going to publish an *actual book* that would necessitate such a thing); she remembered interrupting his self-abuse in the studio and his bizarre eagerness to shower when he got home from Irina's lessons. He had been having sex during Irina's lessons! He had driven their daughter home with Rachel Rosen on his dick! He had carried the woman's spoor into their home!

Yes, she has known, really known, for weeks. But how long she has *sort of* known is something she doesn't wish to contemplate. Because the answer, probably, is: for a long time. The whole time, maybe. And what does that say about her?

It says that she was distracted. It says that she is afraid.

The colder it gets—and it is indeed getting colder—the earlier Eleanor has to arrive at Frog and Toad's to get a seat. It is the only coffee shop in town besides Dunkin' Donuts and the only one with Wi-Fi, and all the people who in warmer weather took their coffee break in the park or leaning against an outside wall of their place of employment are taking it in here now, and they are not getting up once their cups are empty.

Nevertheless, she manages to find a seat, at a table with a frantically texting older woman who has left her scone untouched. Eleanor doesn't blame her. They drizzle everything with icing up here: the scones, the cinnamon rolls, the cookies. Nothing is sweet enough for these people. She gulps three ibuprofen and washes them down with coffee, then, over the course of an hour, rockets through her completed manuscript, correcting spelling mistakes, making meaningless small changes to make herself feel like she's improving it. Finally: Save. Quit. She attaches the file to an email and sends it to Craig. Then she looks up over the lip of the laptop as if watching the thing fly through the coffee shop and into the router on its way to New York.

She reaches into her bag and pulls out her phone. In a minute she is speaking to Craig Springhill. She says, "I just sent it to you." The blond man, ghostly pale, who replaced the old woman half an hour ago looks up, startled; he is annoyed that Eleanor is talking.

"I have it here," Craig tells her. "This was fast."

"I was on a roll."

"Very, very good."

She says, "How soon can you read it?"

"End of next week?"

"How about the end of this week? I'd like to come down."

There's a pause on his end, the click of computer keys. "I can move a few things."

"Thank you."

"You don't sound quite like yourself, Nell."

This annoys her, though she knows it's just a friendly expression of concern, of sympathy. It annoys her because who in the hell is he to say who she's supposed to be, who it is she ostensibly sounds different from? It annoys her because it's in his best interest for her to be the woman who wrote the books that other women wanted to buy, so of course he's concerned that she sounds like someone else. It annoys her because she wants and needs this kind of attention, because she is not getting it from Karl. It annoys her that the question makes her want to cry.

She says, "Well, lots of changes these days, you know."

"Anything I should know about? New, that is?"

"No." Although she is tempted to just tell him everything. He is a man of keen empathy; he will deliver the succor she craves. But, no.

"Well, all right," he says, and she is mildly disappointed that he gave up so easily. "Friday lunch?"

"I'll be there."

"I cannot wait. And I will have read your next great novel."

She packs up her things, returning the blond man's dirty look, and is she right that he looks surprised, hurt? As though he didn't realize he had been giving her the stink eye? As though he might, in fact, not have been? On the snowy sidewalk to her car, she shakes out her arms and legs, restoring lost feeling, waiting for the pain to return. (Where is it? Suddenly its absence is as alarming as its presence was last night.) She starts up the engine and turns up the heat full blast, though it is not yet warm. In the idling car, she watches people enter and exit Onondakai County Credit Union and reflects upon all the ways in which her very existence has revolved around the accommodation of male need. She cooks when Karl is hungry (though he could do the cooking, he knows how, he is competent at it, but when it is his responsibility, it tends to get done when it gets done and not when she and Irina are hungry; and sometimes it doesn't get done at all, and she and Irina give up and eat toast and cheddar cheese for dinner, and when she calls him out, he remembers, *actually remembers*, having done it, and can recall in great detail the nonexistent ingredients he used and how he prepared them). She fucks when he is horny. (And, increasingly, he comes too soon, which she now suspects is a by-product of his sexual distraction; and she herself is left unsatisfied and must take care of her own needs once he is asleep or out of sight. And of even this, he makes demands: "Why won't you let me watch you do it!" And she wants to take him by the shoulders and put her face up to his and scream, *It is not about you, Karl! It is, literally, masturbation!*)

And when he is a shitty father, and he is often a shitty (though, she admits, shittily loving) father, she is there to be a parent and a half, a parent and three-quarters, a parent and a parent point nine nine nine.

She is now prepared to admit to herself that Karl—not her mother, not her aunt, not anything her doctors told her or the fruits of her research—is the one true reason she didn't get the mastectomy. She kept her breasts to keep him. Because he wouldn't stay married to a titless woman. The decision was hers to make, but the doctors recommended the full double mastectomy. It was safest, they said. There are no guarantees, and you may be fine without it. And you may not be fine with it. But we recommend it.

My mother didn't have it. My aunt didn't have it.

You don't have the same cancers that they did.

You say they're discrete. That you can kill them all.

We think so.

You say there's no evidence of metastasis.

That's right.

But you want to remove the breasts.

It would be safest.

The understanding in her family was that mastectomy was over-recommended. That lumpectomy and radiation, in response to early-stage cancers, were as effective as full mastectomy in preventing recurrence.

She told the doctors this, and the doctors reiterated that, yes, that was true, but she had two different cancers, neither like her mother's or her aunt's, and they wanted to be sure.

The other understanding in her family, usually only spoken under the influence of drink, was that the over-recommended full mastectomy was an instrument of patriarchal domination, a means of controlling the sexual power of women. That in fact breast cancer itself was the world's response to its poisoning by masculine striving. Men wanted to blame the breasts for getting sick, instead of themselves for polluting them. The full mastectomy was a gendered act of violence, a cowardly expression of projected self-disgust.

Eleanor didn't impart this theory to the doctors. And she didn't mention any of it to Karl. Because maybe it was stupid. But she made her decision and moved ahead. She kept the breasts, and, until now, she has kept her dumbass husband.

When she confronts Karl, in her mind, about his Rachel, "to Irina" is the phrase that most often follows the words "How could you do this." Because if Eleanor is realizing this only now, Irina probably realized it months ago. She is brilliant, this child, and perhaps more significantly has little human contact outside of her parents. Irina's life is now sufficiently circumscribed that she has likely got both her parents figured out down to the molecular level, whether she knows it or not.

Of course Eleanor wouldn't have it any other way. She is not one of those parents who believes that her child must find a tribe, invest herself in society, hide her eccentricities in an effort to blend into the group—even though these are the lessons she herself was taught, and what she has historically done, and what, despite her engagement in ostensibly solitary pursuits, she is presently doing for a living. No, what she wants for her daughter is intellectual and creative self-actualization without compromise.

In other words: Don't be like me. Be like your father.

But if Irina knows? Knows that her father is a philanderer and that her mother is a sucker? Where does that leave the girl? Where does it leave their family, if everyone knows, and everyone knows that everyone knows?

If Eleanor's cancer is back, though, will any of it matter, or have mattered? Who will care? Rachel will replace her: another woman of means to supplant the dead one. Irina will learn new values and move back to New York. And Eleanor will have left behind a bunch of stories about . . . what? Attracting men, basically. Her work up until now has espoused a broken worldview, one that assumes the value, and plausibility, of a future wherein all problems have been overcome, all conflicts resolved, all uncertainties erased. When the truth of life, of middle-class American life, anyway, is that it is nothing but a handsome container for a bunch of feral, selfish, miraculously long-lived rutting, shitting beasts.

At this moment, Eleanor is wearing a maxi pad to protect herself against the mild urinary incontinence she has experienced three times in the past two weeks. Her legs have not stopped tingling for a month. Three days ago her hands began to feel cold and numb. Brisk walking makes the numbness and tingling better, but it increases the pain in her lower back. Which, in the wake of her scarecrow shamble to the car, has returned.

She is beginning to think that she is fucked.

....

Later she informs Irina that, despite her promise, she is going to have to go alone to New York.

"Nooooo!" Irina says, and, though she is amply justified in doing so, Eleanor endures a wave of uncharacteristic frustration and anger. Can't the kid see it in her eyes? That she is undergoing a personal and professional crisis?

"I'm sorry."

"Mother, you *promised*."

"I'm sorry, Irina. I will bring you after Christmas, okay? I need to go alone."

"I'm so *bored*."

"That's your problem." It is a philosophical tenet of their family that boredom is an ailment of a lazy mind and not the result of a lack of provided stimulation. It is the unsavory byproduct of bourgeois society.

"Right, go hunt a mastodon," Irina groans. It is something Karl says when Irina complains that she is bored.

"Won't your father be surprised when you catch one."

"And cook it."

They are sitting, as they often seem to be when they talk, on Irina's bed, a space they share with Irina's laptop, notebook, headphones, and guitar. It's late morning. Eleanor is planning to make herself an egg sandwich, then tell Karl she is leaving, and then leave. It's the middle bit that she is worried about. Irina says, "Mother, does this mean your novel is finished?"

"I suppose you could call it that."

"Is it good? Do you like it?"

Irina has read all three of Eleanor's novels. She doesn't know Eleanor knows. "Maybe. Yes."

"I want," Irina says, her face gaunt, taut, intense, "to see the look on your agent's face when he tells you that you are brilliant and then he hands you a check for a million dollars."

"That's not how it works," Eleanor says, and her heart is breaking.

But Irina just rolls her eyes. "I *know*, Mother," she says. "I didn't say it was real. I said it was what I *wanted*."

Well. She is not alone in wanting that, is she. Eleanor is leaning over for a kiss, thinking that this whole thing has gone much more smoothly than she anticipated, when Irina startles and makes a flurried motion at her side. It's her notebook, which has been lying open, half-concealed by a bony knee; Irina was trying to close it. She has succeeded, but not without dislodging an errant page: a streaky inkjet printout of a familiar image, which now half-peeks out from under the notebook's cover. Eleanor ignores it even as little pieces of what she didn't previously recognize as a puzzle are clicking into place, and she grips her daughter in an awkward little embrace. "I'll be back up later to say goodbye," she says.

"You don't have to," Irina counters, tucking the page back into the notebook and the notebook further under her knee.

Eleanor withdraws, reluctantly, too slowly. "But I want to."

"Well," her daughter says, not meeting her gaze. "Suit yourself." Eleanor can tell from Irina's expression—the mouth a taut bow, the cheeks flushed—that she wishes she hadn't said that, but it still hurts.

"I will do that," Eleanor tells her, but she won't.

....

Karl is not in the studio. He is sitting ten feet from its open door, upon a paint-splattered wooden chair between two skinny fir trees, smoking a cigarette. He doesn't smoke very often, but when he does, he treats it like a track and field event. His legs are spread, his feet planted firmly on the ground; if she pulled the chair out from under him, he would likely remain balanced there, in a crouch. After each drag he flings his arm out as though he's hailing a cab. He's wearing fingerless gloves, an oversized woolen cardigan pockmarked with burn holes, and, underneath that, an old hoodie with the hood up. Everything about this tableau—the placement of the chair, the bearish stance, the clumsily hand-rolled cigarette, the bulky clothes—would have charmed her just a few weeks ago. She would slide onto his lap, pluck the cigarette from his hand for a taste, kiss him on the mouth. Now, though, he's just pissing her off. He ought to have shaved, put on a suit. He should hand her a bouquet, beg her for forgiveness.

On the other hand, none of that would do any good. Which is probably why he isn't doing it.

"We have two things to talk about," she says.

"Yeah, okay."

"Because I'm leaving for New York."

He straightens a little. "With the kid?"

"No."

"I thought that was the plan?"

For a moment, Eleanor considers taking Irina after all. She's angry enough with Karl to want to keep their daughter away from him. But also to punish him with her presence. Just like that, she understands why divorcing couples use their children as weapons. They're so versatile and close at hand.

"The plan changed. I need to be alone. I'm going to talk with Springhill and do some other stuff."

Karl appears to experience a brief wave of disappointment, then one of calculation, then another of acceptance. He has his own plan. She has always envied him this—his ability to accept new circumstances and act accordingly, with barely a moment of transition. She has a mental image of him as a lumberjack—he's already got the beard— deftly, blithely hopping from log to log across a raging river. This image causes her to temporarily like him, so she puts it out of her mind.

"While I'm gone," she says, "call the contractor about the mold in the kitchen."

"I thought you took care of that."

"That was last time. The other mold."

They stare at each other. Neither wants to say what both are thinking: Maybe what we actually need is a lawyer. To sue the contractor. And maybe, when that's finished, to get divorced. But that is more than she can handle right now.

Karl nods. "Okay," he says. "That's one thing. What's the other?"

"That isn't either thing. It's an extra thing. Are you ready for the first thing?"

He drew another lungful of cigarette smoke before saying, "Sure."

"Rachel Rosen. In the Upstate. During Irina's art class."

If he says "Who?" or otherwise feigns ignorance, she thinks, she is going to kick him in the balls.

But he doesn't. He slumps a little, exhales smoke, mutters, "Hm. Okay."

"I don't especially want to talk about it right now," she says. "I have more important things on my mind. It should go without saying that you have to end it. *Again*. Either that, or just fucking go be with her." Dammit, she didn't mean to say *fucking*. She didn't mean to betray emotion. "I'm not even sure I'm willing to stay with you, to be honest."

"That's understandable."

"I'm going to be away for a week," she tells him, "performing the actual paying work that is now the only thing supporting your art hobby. Maybe, if I get bored, I'll try and have a talk with your girlfriend."

His only response is to slump further. The cigarette falls out of his hand and hisses itself out in the snow. He's gazing past her, into the woods. He looks as though he'd like to walk there, into the state forest, just walk forever. She knows the feeling.

"I honestly don't understand it," she can't resist saying. "She's not a serious person. She's a literary wannabe with family money. You shouldn't even be looking twice at somebody like that, let alone destroying our marriage with her."

She is immediately ashamed to have said it. This whole confrontation fills her with shame. Why? He's the one who should be feeling it.

He mutters something inaudible as he tries to rescue his dropped cigarette.

"What?" Preemptively angry, because it can't be anything good.

Karl is examining the wet stub with evident despair. "You don't know her," he repeats.

There are a thousand possible responses, many of them violent. She runs through a good number in her head before abandoning them all. "Jesus, Karl," she says.

"Sorry."

"I'm going to New York. Call the assholes about the thing."

"What was the second thing?" he says.

"What?"

His exhausted pink eyes are blinking like a rabbit's. "There were two things we had to discuss. What's the other one?"

I think I'm dying, she doesn't say.

"There is no other one," she says.

14

Karl is in the studio, pacing in circles, saying "Uh huh" into the phone over and over as he listens to what this client, this fucking guy, is saying to him. The client is some trust fund wanker from Santa Fe, and he is contemplating an order. Contemplating out loud. The thing the guy has said the most times is "Don't worry about money, man. I got plenty of money," and Karl is thinking that if the guy says it one more time, he's going to smash the phone on the cement floor.

His work table is piled high with books, some of them still nested in their shipping vestments, most of them on knives and swords. Japanese shit. *Chokutō, katana, kodachi*. People were fucking ruthless back in the day. He's been splitting glass, making blades like a fucking Comanche. Shards of the stuff are everywhere. He's so done with capital-A art. He wants to make things you can use. Instruments of change. The invention of the gun was the beginning of the end of human culture. Before then, nothing was not intimate. To kill an animal, to kill a man, you had to take it by surprise, seize it, penetrate it. To kill was to feel, in its desperate ebbing entirety, the life force of another being. A knife is an extension of the body. A gun is a plaything. It turns death into a remote-control toy. The knife guys he has been talking to think the glass idea is stupid. "It'll chip. It'll break when you use it." But that's not the point. The best edge comes from a barely controlled break. It is impossibly sharp and incredibly fragile.

Of course it will break. It is perfect, but only for the instant of its use, and then it is gone. The beauty of the knives comes from their limitations. Their utility is intense and focused. They are nothing more or less than what they are.

Which, admittedly, is maybe a little obscure for an eBay auction description. That's how this guy found him.

"So yeah, what I'm saying is," the guy is saying, "largely ceremonial use, so the decorative elements have to be perfect. Or else what's the point."

"Yeah, you said."

"I mean, what's your, like, do you have graphic design experience?"

"I went to art school."

"Okay but, like, *design?*"

"Look, man," Karl says, lifting one of his knives-in-progress from the work table and slashing it around in the air. "Enough with the exchange of bona fides. Just tell me what you want the thing to look like."

"Just so you understand, money isn't going to be—"

"Yeah, yeah, I get it, you're loaded, just tell me what you want," Karl says, clutching his phone harder, as though to protect it from himself. "Because I've got other clients waiting here and they know what they want and I can make the stuff and sell it to them *right now.* And so far I'm getting nothing but vague bullshit from you."

Of course this guy didn't buy the knife that was up for auction; he just contacted Karl through the site, asking for custom work. *hey your product is very interesting to me i would like to comision a number of pieces for specified use with my mens group money is not going to be aproblem my cell is 9293372281 if you can call me we can talk business thanks a lot.* This is now the third phone call, and if the guy doesn't move this conversation forward, it's going to be the last.

The guy does not respond, so Karl continues, parrying an invisible opponent, jabbing the knife in the air in front of him to punctuate his words. "If you would send me a *drawing*, I could work up a *prototype* and send you some *photos.* Okay? You there?"

A long silence.

"Yeah, man, the thing is, before anything like that happens, I'm gonna need you to sign a confidentiality agreement."

"What?"

"This design, it's strictly secret, right? So if I even show it to you, you know, you can't use the knives, like, to advertise or anything. Like, no one can see them but me. And you have to delete the drawings and everything. I mean, like, delete them totally from the computer. And if you print them out, you have to burn them."

Jesus effing Christ on a hovercraft. "Okay, yeah, sure, whatever."

"I'll email you the agreement first, okay? And send that back, and I'll send you the drawing."

"Fine."

"I just want to make sure you're taking this seriously, because—"

"Send it, man!"

Karl cuts off the call, swears, drops the knife on the table surface, heaves open his laptop, clicks the email app. Waits. Come on, man. Come on. While he waits, he opens up the pictures Rachel sent him back when they had just started fucking, the ones he keeps in a special folder marked TAXES 2008. His dick stirs, and he idly touches himself through his overalls.

What Nell said about Rachel wasn't true. She's not a wannabe. She's exactly what she is. She's a woman who is doing what she is capable of doing, and enjoying it. She isn't at war with her mother, or with her body, or with the company she keeps. She isn't ambitious. She likes sex so much. She likes him so much. She's straightforward. To be with her is to be in a place of confidence and calm and contentment. She takes nothing personally. She regrets nothing.

He loves Nell, but, Jesus, fuckin' Nell. They never should've gotten married. They should have brought up Irina in separate homes. The kid wouldn't have missed the nuclear family, they'd've been the only kind of family she knew. He thought he wanted somebody complicated! Maybe he did, once. But now he wants somebody simple.

Of course that's what he thought this whole knife thing was going to be, simple. Instead it's a constant negotiation. Knife people are fussy. *Men* are fussy. "You and your needs," a girl once said to him, or maybe that was lots of girls, and it's true, he's got a lot of them. Needs and girls both. But this guy—this fucker is the worst.

An email notification slides into view, and he stabs it with the cursor. Attached to it is a two-page document full of fake legalese. *pursuant to the verbal agreement entered into on this day 19th October 2017 . . . shall not distribute, disseminate, reveal, share, duplicate, summarize, paraphrase . . . the undersigned will be liable for any and all infractions of the right of copyright and confidentiality of the cosigner of . . .* For crap's sake. He prints the thing, signs and dates it, scans it with his phone, sends it back. Come on, man. Give it up. Let's see your fucking shaman guru Indian-chief bullshit.

While he waits, he takes a deep breath and calls Rachel.

"Heyyy, so, hey," he says.

"I was just packing," comes the reply, in a low growl that, a few hours ago, would have driven him crazy but right now just makes him feel like a dick. "Got something new here I think you'll like."

"Uh, yeah, so . . . change of plans, it looks like."

Silence.

"Turns out, she didn't bring the kid? She kinda . . . she looked at my phone and figured out you've been coming up here?"

"Oh, Karl," she says, and it sounds awfully familiar to him, and it sounds like she is getting tired of saying it.

"And she says . . . she told me she might . . . she might call you. Try to see you."

"Well, that's not going to happen."

"Not if you come up," he says. "You still could! You could stay at the Upstate, I could leave Irina at—"

"No, no."

"I need you."

She says, "I'm sorry. No, Karl. In fact—"

"Are you dumping me?" he says.

"I'm not doing anything. I'm just . . . this is getting ridiculous. We need to put the brakes on this thing."

"That's dumping me."

"It's not," she says. "It's just . . . let's take stock."

"Yeah, no, that's not . . . no."

"Karl," she says. "You're married. You have a child. This has been fun, but—"

"You love me! You're in love with me!"

Rachel sighs. "Yes. I mean—yes, sure. But—"

"Rachel. Rachel!"

"Look," she says, and he hates it when women say that to him, "I have to admit a lot of this, a lot of the intensity of this thing, it came from sticking it to your wife. Okay? I never liked her much. There, I said it."

"Hey, hey."

"But now that . . . I'm sorry. No, we need to rethink this, if she knows. It was reckless. You have to concentrate on Irina."

Karl's laptop pings. An email has come in.

"You said 'was'!" he shouts. "Don't say 'was'!"

"If she calls me, I'll talk to her."

"Rache, c'mon—"

"I'm going to hang up now. Okay, Karl? I'm saying goodbye for now."

"No! Dude! I love you!"

"Yeah, no, I know. Goodbye. I'll be in t— Well, I'll talk to you later, okay?"

"Don't hang up!"

"Bye."

"Don't!"

She hangs up. He screams, then slams the phone down on the workbench, making sure to slow down right at the end so that it actually lands sort of gently. He checks the phone for damage, confirms that there is none, and then slowly lowers his head to the wooden surface of the table. Okay. Okay. Set that aside for now. Get hold of yourself. Make some knives. Make some money.

With a growl, Karl hoists himself up, shakes the misery off his head like a bear bathing itself in a river (it feels that way, anyhow; lord only knows how it looks), turns to his laptop. The email. The guy actually sent it, and here it is. Karl clicks it open and clicks on the attached picture and at long last the guy's custom design unfolds upon the screen.

It's drawn in pencil on a piece of lined yellow legal paper, and it looks like a piece of adolescent comic-book fan art. The first page shows a dude with a loincloth over his junk and earrings in his nipples sitting in front of a primitive-looking rawhide sweat lodge drum and using a clear-bladed knife to slice the hand of another dude just like him. The blood from the guy's hand is dripping onto the drum head, and some kind of genie or ghost is rising up off it. And then the next page is a diagram of the knife.

The blade is just . . . it's stupid. It looks like a dildo with a point on it, some kind of Tolkien garbage. Beneath that is a crossguard that Karl thinks is supposed to look like a coiled dragon's tail with an arrowhead-shaped point on the end, but what it actually looks like is a pile of shit with a tortilla chip stuck in it. And then the grip is like . . . it's like a wooden dowel covered with a lot of symbols: Rosicrucian iconography, some Sanskrit or something, a Masonic square and compass, an ankh, a fucking *swastika*, for the love of Christ, and a bunch of crap that looks like Celtic runes and hobo codes.

It's complete nonsense, the whole package, and he is not going to make it. He's just not. Before he can decide how to say no to this guy, another email slides in. It says, *in case of your desire to not make a knife with a swastika on it, that is a very ancient symbol for buddhas and jains and it means auspicious or good luck it is only recently used by nazi germany which is not the meaning conveying here.* And before Karl can think of how to respond to *that*, another email arrives that reads, *I would like to order five of these pending approval of your prototype and I can offer you $150 a piece and also extra if you can fashion a velvet line wooden case.*

He's trying to get up a good head of anger, in the hope of just sweeping everything, including the laptop, onto the floor. He lays his arm down on the table like he's really going to do it; it would feel so great. But then he starts calculating the relative value of each object lying there, the knives and the books and the computer, and he thinks about having to live without a laptop until he can get it repaired or replaced, and how that would mean no video chat and no porn and no sensible way to alleviate his utter boredom with himself, and in the end all he does is emit a very calculated but still pretty satisfying wordless scream. He pushes himself away from the table, stops in the middle of the studio, and collapses, more earnestly this time, into a crouch on the floor. This feels good, so he elects to extend his self-debasing into a full-blown supine liedown. Now little bits of unswept glass are digging into his back. Well, that was stupid. If he stays perfectly still, the damage won't get worse.

He ought to get up and hang out with Irina. He knows that. But man, he just can't. He can't face these days alone with her. He loves her, for shit's sake, everybody knows that. But without Nell, the burden is too great. It's easy to talk to your kid when you know somebody is about to show up and take over for you—it doesn't even matter what you say, you just hang out, and then it's over and you can relax. But this open-ended shit . . . he seriously doesn't want to see her, or even leave the studio. Plus, and he tries not to think about this too much, but for real: Irina is a *girl* who's *part him.* How can he deal with that? How can anyone?

"Ugh," he says, and takes out his phone, the glass shards piercing his shoulder and upper arm. He scrolls through his email to the one Irina forwarded him. The one from the, the whatever, her friend. He taps the phone number she sent, and after a few rings the girl answers.

"Hey?"

"Is this . . . " Shit, he didn't catch her name. He pulls the phone away from his ear and squints at the screen.

"Hello?"

"Yeah, sorry, is this Sam? Sam Fike?"

"This is Sam."

"Yeah, I'm Karl. Um, Irina's dad. You know. Your friend, my kid."

She doesn't speak immediately; there's a bit of noise as a football game or something recedes into the background. "Yeah, hi. What's up?"

"Well, what's up is her mother and me need some help. Babysitting, I guess. Or whatever you call hanging around with a twelve-year-old. We can pay, I dunno, what do people pay?"

"Fifteen dollars an hour."

Jesus. "Seriously?" he says. "Okay. Ah . . . so . . . do you have a regular day job? Because I'm gonna . . . we're gonna need . . . things are a little chaotic around here. I mean, Irina's mother is out of town. So . . ."

"I work afternoons and nights at the moment. My mornings and some afternoons are free."

"Okay, okay, yeah. That's . . . that's cool for now."

"I don't have a car, though. Well—not reliably. Irina says you live in the country?"

"Yeah, no, shit, yeah, I guess you could call it that. Um, I can pick you up. I mostly want you to hang out with her when I'm working. On my stuff, in the studio."

"You're some kind of artist, she says?"

"Yeah, I'm an artist. So . . . how about I come get you and we try this out? Like, I'll interview you for a few m—or, I dunno, an hour? And just see if—you know, if—"

"That's fine," the girl says. Her voice is calming. It's deep and smooth. She sounds like a priest or somebody at the suicide hotline.

He agrees to meet her in the morning, 10 a.m., in front of the movie theater in downtown Broken River. He's a little miffed she didn't give him her address—what does she think he is, some kind of stalker? Anyway, it's fine. It's fine.

He's not sure how much time has passed when he is half-awakened by a timid knocking upon, then opening of, the studio door, and then fully awakened by a deafening shriek. He leaps up, lacerating both palms in the process, feels drool spraying doggily from his lips and beard. Even after he's crossed the room to take her by the shoulders, Irina won't stop screaming; she's like a car alarm. He has never seen her face like this before: it's terrifying.

"Dude! Dude!!" He wraps his arms around her, rocks her. "Dude, stop. It's okay. Stop."

"Daddy, there's blood!"

He is more alarmed by the word "Daddy" than he is by the word "blood." He peers over his shoulder. Jesus. It's all over the floor—wow, that will never come out of the cement. But then again, it'll be kind of cool. Bloodstains! Hell yeah! He releases his daughter, looks down at his bloody hands. "Oh man, Rinny. Sorry."

"What happened?" Clearly unsatisfied with the amount of hugging she has received, she wraps her arms around herself as far as they will go.

"I just . . . ah . . . I just laid down and forgot about the glass. And then I was too tired to get up."

Her dubious expression is understandable. "Okay," she says, very quietly.

"I think . . . I better . . . can you help me out with this, man?"

She nods.

Half an hour later Irina is still sitting behind him on a kitchen stool, picking bits of glass out of his back with tweezers and daubing the wounds with hydrogen peroxide and gauze. Karl is working on his hands and trying hard not to grunt or squeak. Irina is silent, businesslike, apparently glad to have a tedious project to take her mind off whatever is going on in her family. Which reminds him.

"So, yeah," he says. "Your mother."

Irina is quiet. She continues her ministrations as though she hasn't heard him speak.

"She's . . . I mean, she's out of town for her book, and . . ."

"I don't want to talk about it, Father."

"Okay, cool," he says, probably too quickly. "Um, yeah, so . . . I'm hiring your friend to, you know, look after you a little while I do stuff."

That gets her attention. "Sam?" she says.

"Yeah, her. I'm gonna go meet her tomorrow."

"She's coming here tomorrow?"

"Yeah, no. I don't know, really. Um. I guess I'm just going to meet her and see."

After a moment, she returns to her daubing. It's a minute or two before she says, very quietly, "It would be cool to hang out with Sam."

They drive into town in the Volvo. Karl hasn't tried starting the thing in a month and is secretly relieved that the engine turns over. The car smells richly chemical from the pile of studded tires in the back that he hasn't gotten around to installing. Anyway, it's warmer today, and the snow is melting, so no big deal. He's got Band-Aids all over his hands, and the pain as he steers feels good.

He parks at the public library, ushers Irina inside, says he'll be back in half an hour. That's how he wants to play it. After a few glances at his phone—no I-changed-my-mind texts from Rachel—he half-jogs over to the theater, his two-hundred-dollar Eccos splatting in the salty slush, and finds a girl who must be Sam leaning there against the empty movie-poster frames, hands shoved into her pockets. Unlike the Karl of several minutes ago, she is not looking at her phone. She's staring into the sky. He can't decide if this speaks well of her, or ill.

She's boyish, hunched inside a leather jacket; her jeans are torn, and she's wearing canvas sneakers and a longshoreman's cap. She doesn't look nineteen; she looks like a thirty-one-year-old who looks like a thirteen-year-old.

"Sam?"

"Hey."

They shake hands. She does this like a man, too (it hurts, but mostly because of all the lacerations). Is she a lesbian? A small shard of preemptive disappointment works itself into the already cluttered mess of his heart. Serves him right. He ought not start thinking about this child as a means of salvation. But it's in his nature. An escape from himself through women. See? He's not an idiot. This iota of self-knowledge, however, doesn't prevent his mind from leaping years into the future: Nell has left him, natch, and Sam charms Irina, becomes her mentor and his friend; they're a strange team, these three; people mistake Sam for his daughter all the time. And then one stormy night, Irina asleep, Sam comes to him in the studio . . . with the forge going it's hot as hell, so he's dressed only in boxers and welder's mask . . . et cetera et cetera.

With Herculean mental force, he pushes the fantasy aside. He says, "Yeah, so . . . you want to go talk someplace?"

She shrugs. "Frog and Toad's?"

"Which is what?"

"Coffee shop."

"Right."

It all seems pointless to him as they walk the three blocks (it turns out) to the place where, he now remembers, Nell hangs out, or used to hang out. They get a couple of coffees (Karl offers to buy, Sam declines) and sit down, and Sam folds her hands in front of her on the table and raises her eyebrows at him.

"So look, man," Karl finds himself saying, "I don't know what I'm supposed to ask you. You seem all right. Irina's into you."

"I'm not sure how. I've only talked with her for a minute or two."

"Yeah, well, she gets notions. So, I guess . . . you got any experience with kids?"

"Not really. I mean, I remember being Irina's age."

"Right, of course. You're, um, you're nineteen, she says?"

"Twenty, now."

"Okay, right." Relief. The imaginary affair seems slightly less improper. "Do you do drugs? Non-weed drugs, I mean."

"Not lately."

"Awesome. You got any references?"

"Denny's?"

"Right," Karl says, "howsabout you give me that?"

She pulls a pen and notebook out of her jacket pocket, writes a name and number on it, tears it out and gives it to him. He notices there's a lot of stuff in there, in her notebook—tight, spiky handwriting, lots of little drawings and diagrams. She's an aesthete. That's good. He's never going to even look at this piece of paper, let alone call the number on it. She sets the notebook on the table in front of her.

"Ummm . . . ," he says. "Anything you want to know? About me?"

She shrugs. "No. I mean, again, no car. That's okay?"

"Yeah, yeah."

"So you'd be picking me up, you know, mornings? And your place is where?"

"Oh—oh, yeah. It's out 94, like twenty minutes from here. Out by the state forest."

"And you'll bring me back into town after I . . . hang out with Irina."

"Yeah. Unless you stay over." Oh, for fuck's sake. "I mean, yeah, in the guest room. Or, office, I guess."

"I don't think I can do that," she says, drawing back a little.

"I didn't mean—"

"Yeah, no, it's cool."

"Just with her mother gone—not that—I mean, not that way. I mean, ah, shit."

Sam sips her coffee, says, "She runs the household. And she's out of town. So you need some help. I got it. You want me to cook for Irina? That kind of thing? Clean up a little?"

"Yeah, maybe."

"Maybe, you know, after you pick me up, we can stop at the supermarket on the way out. If you hire me."

"Yeah, good thinking. Actually, I might have another errand to do, too. Um, first. Or after. Whatever."

She's visibly less nervous now. "I'm not going to do your laundry and I'm not looking for a boyfriend, okay?"

"Ha! Yeah, no!" Karl idiotically half-shouts. Reel it in, there, buddy. "Hey," he says now, with a little casual nod of his head. "So, your notebook there. You like to draw?"

She gets that look they get when they're wary and flattered both: the head tilted a little forward to hide the face, the eyes turned up. The reflexive frown designed to suppress the smile. He grins just a little. Just a little one. Letting her know he's got her number but it's cool.

"Oh. Yeah, no. Just doodles."

"Sure, but seriously, you got something going on there."

"Uh huh," she says, but now the frown is losing out to the smile.

"Rinny told you I was an artist? A sculptor, actually. So, yeah . . . can I see?"

"See?" Sam says.

"The notebook. Your stuff." He waggles his fingers, inviting her to hand the notebook to him.

Wrong move. She snatches it off the table, pockets it. "Nah, not right now. So, the job?"

For a second he has no idea what she's talking about.

"Babysitting?"

"Oh, duh! Yeah, yeah, sure, you're hired, obviously!"

In the moments that follow, which Karl doesn't know how to fill, he suddenly remembers his cup of coffee and gulps half of it down. It's still hot—that's how little time has passed. He's relieved. Not just that the kid is cool, which, yeah, that is a relief, but he feels the way he always feels when he's met a new woman. She's in his life. She's not going to fuck him, it looks like, but she's still a project—somebody to get to know. Somebody with natural barriers to overcome. His restraint pleases him. See? He can do it!

"What now?" is what she says.

"Ahh . . . oh. Do you want to— I mean, can you start?"

She nods. "Night shift tonight, but I can work until then. Where's Irina?"

For a second, he doesn't know. At home? In the car? Where the fuck is Irina? Oh yeah: "Library. Also— But first I gotta— I have a quick phone call I gotta make. And then maybe an errand on the way home. Can you, like— How about you wait here? And then we'll go over and, you know—"

"Uh huh."

"Or, let's leave here together, and then you go meet Rinny at the library, and I'll make my phone call. And I'll meet you there?"

She appears nonplussed. "Um . . . okay, sure. Should I go do that now?"

"Well—finish your coffee."

"I'm done," she says, standing and gathering up her half-full mug. "I'll see you over there."

"Right, right."

He follows her out and then pulls his phone out of his pocket and leans against the window of Frog and Toad's. The thing is, he wants—

needs—some fucking weed. He has run out. And when, after Irina's last lesson, he asked Jasn Hubble to top him up, the old fucker got all google-eyed and backed off a step and said, Hey man, yeah man, no man, I'm not in that business anymore. Like, extra loud, as though the place was bugged. He wrote down a number on a scrap of paper and handed it to Karl with a little shove, as though to say, Here, take this and go.

Now Karl pats his pockets—where the hell did he put it?—and eventually finds the number in his hoodie pouch, along with a bunch of old kleenex and a uselessly small binder clip and the girl's Denny's reference. He brings it up to his face (Jesus, does he need fucking *bifocals* now?) and then thumbs the number into his phone, all the while thinking, That looks familiar, where have I seen that before? The phone starts ringing, and as it rings he watches Sam's narrow hips moving down the sidewalk in the distance, and then Sam stops and reaches into her pocket.

She raises a phone to her face, and a moment later a woman in Karl's ear says, "Hello?"

"Hello?" says Karl.

"Karl?"

"Hello?"

"What?"

A block and a half away, Sam turns to face him, squints, and then, after a moment, raises her hand in a little wave.

Sam directs them onto the rutted, unplowed streets that gird the town center, and eventually they stop in front of a doublewide surrounded by weird stone formations, as though somebody with pretensions got his hands on more rocks than he knew what to do with. Irina says, "This is where you live?" and Sam says, "For now." She gets out and hurries up the slushy flagstone walk.

"She's just gotta pick up a few things," Karl explains, unnecessarily. It occurs to him to worry that maybe Sam is not the ideal companion for Irina, if she's dealing. At least that's what the Nell in his head is telling him. But he shakes her off.

"It's a weird house," Irina says.

"It's a trailer."

"There's no wheels on it."

"It's not that kind of trailer. You haven't seen a trailer house before?"

"I guess, now that I think about it. But I haven't had a friend in one before." She pauses, then unbuckles her seat belt and scoots forward, wedging herself between the two front seats. "What are we going to do together? What if I'm boring? She's older! She's an *adult*. I can't entertain an adult!"

"It's cool, man. She's good with kids."

"Does she like music? We could talk about music."

"Yeah, I'm sure that'll be great."

Irina is bouncing up and down. The backseat springs creak. She's got the fingertips of both hands shoved in her mouth and she's moaning a little bit. Karl suddenly realizes that she's truly nervous.

"Hey, man, knock it off." The bouncing tapers off into a kind of rolling shudder. "I don't get it. You had sitters in New York. What's the big deal?"

"She's not a sitter. I'm too old for that."

"Hired companion."

"Father, *stop*."

"Okay, okay." He wonders if she's often like this around her mother—if she has to be like this a certain number of hours each day—and whether there are certain protocols he's supposed to be following. Shit. He wants to ask Nell, but of course he can't do that. Such an admission of incompetence would set him back even further in the marriage reclamation project he sort of hopes eventually to maybe be involved in.

Sam is emerging from the trailer now, carrying a small knapsack that could comfortably hold personal grooming products, a wallet, mace, and, glory be, an eighth of weed. He has already absorbed the coincidence of her being Broken River's hookup for the new hotness; weed has a way of finding those who need it. He's kind of bummed

out it'll probably be legal everywhere soon—its serendipitous manifestation is among the most charming things about it. Going to the
supermarket for it will be a drag. Sam climbs in and Irina dutifully
buckles herself back up.

"Got everything you need?" Karl asks as he throws the car into
gear.

"Yup. Hey, Irina," she says, "you ever played crazy eights before?"

Irina's response is exaggeratedly sprightly. "No, no, what is it, what
is it!!!"

Their conversation continues, but Karl's already in his private zone,
imagining himself alone in the studio without a single responsibility,
getting stoned and making glass knives.

Jesus. What a relief. What a fucking relief.

15

This morning, Irina took a break from her CyberSleuthing for a reality check vis-à-vis her impending friend arrangement in the form of a bulleted, word-processed list.

- Sam is a grownup and will probably not become your BEST friend
- Sam is being paid to be with you so it's kind of more like a therapist
- which is also cool when you think about it
- REALISTICALLY SPEAKING Sam is probably not Samantha Geary
- though it remains POSSIBLE that she has been brainwashed/reprogrammed
- or has amnesia
- so you should go into this with no expectations and have fun and enjoy being babysat

So far, Irina actually *has* enjoyed being babysat. Sam has been here for three hours, and they have done almost nothing except play card games, talk, and eat snacks. Sam knows a *ton* of card games. When she was growing up, her father was not around (which Irina is pretty sure means "dead" or, more likely, "ran off with another woman"), and her brother was often off committing crimes ("gentle crimes" is what Sam said, and she guesses that means not hitting, shooting, or stabbing anyone), so she and her mentally ill mother (that's what people are avoiding saying when they say "eccentric," as Sam did) spent a lot of time playing cards. Sam's mother knew how to play a huge number of obscure games, some of them nearly lost to history, and Sam has managed to remember most of them. Bezique. Knock-out whist. Turkish poker. Humbug.

On the one hand, the mentally ill mother seems to increase the chance that Sam really is Samantha; on the other, it's hard to imagine that somebody who remembers the rules to Egyptian ratscrew from childhood is likely to have forgotten her real parents' murder. Still, this afternoon has given Irina the overall impression that Sam is more complicated and mysterious than her rational self expected. Sam is *cool*. In fact she is an inspiration! She has *really short* hair and a *mysterious tattoo* of *interlocking triangles* on her arm. (When she went to deal cards to Irina, she rolled up her sleeves like a mechanic, and Irina instantly began plotting to get herself some button-down shirts so that she could do it, too.) Even if she isn't the only survivor of a brutal double murder in 2005, Sam has clearly mastered herself in the face of personality-disfiguring domestic troubles and has become this confident, serious, really nice person. Irina has yet to figure out what she *does*, if not in the physical world, then inside her head. Maybe nothing yet? But perhaps they will figure that out together! Maybe Irina is the therapist in this transaction!

Earlier, the three of them had fallen silent as they approached the turnoff to Nerd House, and Irina concentrated very hard on Sam's face, or the side of it, anyway, to see if the sight of the building and grounds were dredging up memories of the past. Much of the previous days' snow had melted and/or turned into gray-brown goo; the car heaved itself up the muddy drive, slipping this way and that while Father swore; first the turret was revealed, then the sharply pitched roof, then the rest of the cardboard-box pile that was their house.

Sam appeared curious, though, disappointingly, untraumatized. If anything, she seemed relieved—maybe she had worried that Father was crazy and criminal; a look at this house must have calmed her nerves. Their house is charming, of course! Irina is pleased to think this every time they come home. Father parked at his usual random diagonal in their weedy gravel lot (this bothers her, and sometimes, at her bedroom window, she squints through two fingers with one eye closed, trying to nudge it true with the Power of Imagination), and Sam stepped out and placed her hands on her hips. She drew a deep breath.

"Okay," she said. "Nice!"

"Wait till you see the inside!" Irina said, jumping out of the back, feeling very much as though she sounded a bit too eager. "There's a spiral staircase and Father's sculptures and the kitchen table is like four inches thick!"

Father hauled the groceries out of the back; they had stopped at Tops Friendly Markets on the way home and bought bananas, brownie mix, barbecue potato chips, fancy sodas. He led the way, and Irina backed in behind him, focusing once again on Sam's reaction to the place. Would she gasp? Would she drop her knapsack and fall to her knees, her face twisted by the terrible memories? But no: nothing. "This reminds me a little of the house I grew up in, except neat," she said.

"Yeah, neat's not my thing," Father said. "If Nell doesn't come back, it'll go to shit in no time. Rinny, man, how about you figure out how to do the brownies while I give Sam a studio tour."

"Sure, sure," Irina said, though she was annoyed. Why wasn't she being invited on the tour? She began to experience a familiar feeling that she only recently has managed to identify as disgust. "A man of impulses and passions," her mother once called her father in the tired wake of one fight or other, and Irina knows what that means. Girls like Father, and Father likes girls. That's just the way it is. It never occurred to her to judge him for this before, but now, with Mother gone for less than a day, it did *not* seem appropriate for him to be trying to get the babysitter alone. Besides, Sam was *hers*.

But, as it happened, the studio tour was brief. Like, a couple of minutes, tops. And Sam re-entered the house in a state of nonchalance, and everything has been great since then. They saw her father exactly once: he swept through the door; clunked around in the bathroom for a couple of minutes; snatched the bag of potato chips, a can of soda, and what looked like a book (that can't be right); and vamoosed. When he did, Irina experimentally rolled her eyes at Sam, and Sam responded with a conspiratorial smile. *Men!*

There are a couple of hours to go before Sam has to leave for her other job. Irina is a little bit sick of cards, and they've baked and eaten all the brownies they care to. She does not want to arrive at that awkward moment in a fun afternoon when you are all out of things to do and want to retreat into your room and be alone, and wish your friend would go home. Not that this would be a problem with her *hired pal*, it's just not a way she wishes to feel. And once she is alone, she will have to reflect upon the alarming words "If Nell doesn't come back." So she draws a breath and says, "Do you want to see where it happened?"

"Where what happened?"

"The *murders*?"

It takes a second before Sam appears to remember, and then something shifts in her face: nothing so definitive as a change of expression, really—more like another kind of light has been shined on her. She says, "My parents, you mean?"

Irina is dumbstruck; she can only nod. Oh wow, oh wow. They shrug on their coats and step outside. The clouds are wisps being torn apart by blinding blue sky, and it's warm enough not to zip up, although Irina does take her earflap hat out of her pocket and tugs it down over her head, because, you know, earflap hat. She takes Sam by the hand, and Sam squeezes back and doesn't let go. They walk down the driveway, Irina peering into the woods, looking for the familiar patterns.

"It's down a ways, on the right. The car went off the road. There's a tree that it hit. You can tell."

"How did you find this all out?"

"Internet, duh. But get this. I was at the library and actually looked up the *print* newspaper. Except it's on microfiche, so I had to learn how to use that." This is a white lie: or, rather, it's an incomplete truth.

In fact, smoking_jacket went to the library, found the microfiche machine, and discovered the newspaper articles and photos. Irina merely followed in her footsteps. She thought there might be additional information that smoking_jacket had overlooked (there wasn't), but mostly she wanted to feel what it was like to be this interesting person. She wondered if she had been in the library at the same time as smoking_jacket, if they had even seen each other. Irina has strained to remember every interaction with every rando she has come across in the months since they moved here. Maybe one of them was smoking_jacket. Maybe their gazes lingered as each recognized, in the other, a kindred soul? Maybe?

In any event, Irina has had to take a break from CyberSleuths. In fact, she has deleted her account. Her post about Samantha proved to be . . . controversial. The thread kind of exploded? Half the people demanded more information, requested additional photos, asked her to interview Samantha or lure her onto the board. The other half scolded her, told her she was wrong to interfere, that it was immoral to harass the victims of a crime, and against the rules of the forum to boot. Then those two groups of people started fighting with each other, and Irina's private-message inbox filled up with need and hate and hate-need, and she skedaddled.

"I don't think I know what a microfiche is," Sam says now.

"*Right?* It's like a giant sheet thing that you stick in this machine that magnifies it. It's obsolete technology. Which is something I'm into. There's a lot of it in my novel."

"Oh yeah. How's that coming?"

"Not awesome. Here!" They're roughly ten yards past the bend in the driveway, but Irina knows the place by a knot in a sapling that looks like (that she mistook for once, with deep disappointment) a little toad. They step off the drive and into the humusy slush. Sam makes a noise like she's not super happy about it but doesn't let go of Irina's hand.

"Sorry, I guess your shoes aren't ideal."

"It's okay."

The tree she's looking for is larger than the others. There it is: a

stout-trunked maple (or oak or sycamore or something, she honestly
has no idea) that's been rendered kind of lopsided by its proximity to
a bunch of pines or firs or whatever. She leads Sam to it and releases
her hand (with a small pang of regret: what if they never hold hands
again?) only to press it to the bark. "Here, touch it."

"Umm . . ."

"Check it out. Here's where the Volvo hit." Irina points at a barely
discernible scar, a crease, really, that might once have been an open
wound. It's at knee level, so she drags Sam's hand down to it. The rest
of her body follows. She's crouched there, white fingers against the
dark bark. It is so much like a movie, Irina can't stand it.

"Are you sure?" Sam says.

"Yup. There's crime scene pictures."

"Jesus. Really?"

"They didn't *show* anything, it was the newspaper. But yeah, with
the do-not-cross tape and all. Do you feel anything?"

"Just, well, I feel the bark."

"No, I mean—do you get any . . ."

"Ah." Sam tips her head back, blinks at the sky. Irina studies her,
hard. They stay like this for a long time—four, five, ten seconds. Then
Sam looks at her and says, "Maybe."

"Seriously?"

"Panic. Terror. Did they get . . . I mean . . . was it here? Were they
in the car?"

Irina shakes her head. She knows what happened. What happened
to the woman, before they killed her. She points.

"Over there somewhere."

Sam stands up, brushes her hands together. Gives Irina a serious look. Then she nods toward the little stand of trees where it was
all supposed to have taken place. Sam leads this time. It's like she
knows. Irina walks alongside her, shooting glances at her face. Sam
is determined now, somber. They stop walking and Sam turns a slow
circle.

"This is definitely not a good place."

"Right?" Irina says, very quietly.

Sam looks directly into Irina's eyes now. She says, "How did it happen?"

"They don't really know. But . . . the police figured . . . they tried to run."

No response. Sam wants her to continue.

"I don't want to say it," Irina says.

"I can take it."

Irina draws a deep breath. "They did . . . stuff . . . to the lady."

"My mother."

Irina nods. The whole thing has gotten very serious, and she is not sure how she feels about that. Sam is peering back toward the house. She says, "Where was the . . . I mean . . . where was I?"

"They don't know. You were out here, somewhere, hiding." Irina has said this *you* so many times—spoken it to the mirror, whispered it into her pillow at night—that it feels almost sacrilegious to be saying it now, to its true object. "At some point you went inside. You spent the night in the house, alone. Then in the morning you left, and the neighbor found you."

Sam appears to be thinking hard. Irina's not sure what's happening here—is this seriously real, or are they just playing? It should be awesome, and instead it's kind of scary. "Sam?" she says, quietly, trying to break the spell.

Instead of answering, Sam suddenly sets off into the trees, her wet sneakers squishing in the muck. She's determined—Irina has to run to catch up. Then she stops as abruptly as she started, at a place a third of the way back toward the house. There's a big old stump here, broken off raggedly at shoulder level, with a mossy half-frozen puddle inside it, like the bowl of a pipe. Irina holds her breath. This is the place she has imagined as Samantha Geary's hiding spot. This exact place. If Sam confirms it, she might just straight-up faint.

Sam says, "I think this is it. I think this is where I hid."

All Irina can manage is "Really?"

Sam is nodding, staring at the stump. "I could hear it. I put my hands over my ears. Later they came looking for me, but they gave up. I was down here, on the ground. When everything was quiet, I went inside."

"Were you afraid?"

"Yes. I didn't know what was happening. I thought I had to find them."

"You didn't know they were dead?"

Sam's face, when she turns to Irina, betrays a mild astonishment, as if this is the first time she's confronted the question. Maybe it really is. "No. Yes. No."

"No?"

"I knew and I didn't know. I was so little." And now something happens that utterly stuns Irina, that opens up a hole in her head and lets the cold air come howling in: Sam's eyes well up and overflow, and tears begin to creep down her perfect cheeks. "I was so little. Oh my god."

Irina has no idea what is happening or what to do. Or, rather, she does know what to do, she is just afraid to do it. But she has to. She does it. She takes a step forward and wraps both her arms around Sam's neck and holds her tightly. Irina can feel, through the leather jacket and tee shirt, Sam's collarbone against her face; the leather smells like smoke and Sam's neck smells like lavender and sweat. Sam's hands clutch Irina's back the way her mother's once did, after Irina slipped coming down the stairs of their old apartment and slid all the way to the bottom. It occurs to Irina that she has not been held, has not held another, in quite this way in quite some time. This is that thing desired by the characters in Mother's books: intimacy. A word whose definition she has known for a long time but whose actual meaning she has not understood. She is touching and being touched and getting cried on.

She thinks, Oh my god oh my god oh my god, and she doesn't know which of the many small shocks of the past five minutes this is her reaction to.

"I love you so much!" she blurts out, and before she can regret it, Sam clutches her harder.

It is at this point that Irina becomes aware of having heard something, a minute ago: an engine running down on the road, a conversation between two men. The slamming of a door. Ignorable sounds, as their little wide spot in Route 94 is a common place for hunters to pull over and tramp into the woods with their guns, in defiance of the POSTED signs posted everywhere.

But now there's another sound. One of the hunters is walking up their driveway. Irina hears his feet crunching on the gravel. Impulsively she whispers, "Hide!" and she and Sam shuffle, still clutching each other, behind the stump.

"What is it?" Sam whispers back.

"Someone's coming!"

They peer around the stump, and through the trees, a man can be seen, around Irina's father's age but smaller, skinnier, no beard, climbing up the drive. He's kind of tired-looking and his shoulders are hunched under an old ski parka. His wears a pair of acid-washed jeans and his balding head is bare. He stops, looks around. Stares at the house for a moment.

Irina holds Sam tighter, and she squeezes back. The man continues, all the way to the house, and the two of them adjust their position, keeping the stump between them and him.

"Do you know that guy?" Sam whispers.

"No. Do you?"

After a surprisingly long pause, she replies, "Maybe? He looks kinda familiar."

The man has knocked and now is waiting; he waits for a full minute, at least. Peeks in the windows accessible from the porch. Turns, gazes into the woods. He stares right at them! But they are still, and the man doesn't seem to notice them. He climbs down from the porch, returns to the driveway. Gazes back at Father's studio for a few seconds, as if thinking about checking it out. *Don't do it*, Irina tells him with her mind, and isn't sure why.

Anyway, he obeys. Turns, heads back down the hill. A minute later, they hear, once again, the thunk of a car door, and then the car emits a clank and a squeak and a roar and is gone.

Sam loosens her grip on Irina, and, reluctantly, Irina loosens hers on Sam.

"I think I know who *that* is," Irina says.

"Who?" Sam appears genuinely curious and surprised.

"Internet busybody. Wanting to see where *it* happened."

"Is that a thing?" Sam wants to know. "Like, people do that?" She holds out her hand for Irina to take, and they start trudging through the wet snow to the house.

"*Yes,*" Irina spits, surprised by her own bitterness. "Vultures!"

············

They end up slumped on opposite ends of the sofa, vaguely facing Huck and Jim and fitfully sleeping, until Sam jerks awake and says "Fuck me!" and rushes to the door. She hears Sam's footsteps on the porch and then crunching on the gravel path to the studio. "Bye, Sam," she says very quietly, or maybe doesn't actually say it out loud, and falls back to sleep until, presumably a few minutes later, Sam is back in the kitchen, this time with Father, and they are arguing.

"Don't worry about it, I'm cool."

"You're not cool. You're completely fucked up."

"I'm not that fucked up."

"You are. I'm taking your car."

"No, man, I need it."

"I'll bring it back tomorrow," Sam says. She is very mad. Irina isn't fully awake, but she is interested. "You shouldn't have smoked it until you dropped me off."

"Don't take the car!"

"Karl—seriously." There is a jingle of keys. "I have to go to work. Okay? It's not my fault you burned through half the fucking bag." There is a longish pause, and then Irina hears the keys change hands, the sound of a satchel being hoisted off a table. The front door opens and closes, the car starts and crunches down the drive.

For long minutes after she's gone, Irina is still with her, still with their car, hovering over it, watching it maneuver down the driveway, past the place where the Gearys ran off the road, left onto Route 94, and then away, toward Broken River and Denny's. But then she loses the thread. She's never been to a Denny's. She had a secret plan to persuade her father to go there for dinner, to surprise Sam at work. But now there's no car. Because her father can't drive. Because he seems to have smoked a lot of something. Something that, disappointingly, Sam seems to have supplied him with.

She is actually afraid as she stands and prepares to go into the kitchen. She doesn't want to see him. When she was a kid she had dreams about him—a version of him, monstrously transformed, a weredad. This creature, fanged and furred, was called Daddy Man. Such a silly name, but she trembles now, thinking the words. Daddy Man. In order to demonstrate her bravery to herself, she mouths them, soundlessly, and remembers waking with them on her lips, begging him not to hurt her. Mother's arrival in her bedroom, the lamp switched on, the hugs and kisses and reassurances. The eventual appearance, preceded by much weepy terror, of Father: the real father, Ape Dad, Mister Friendly. Which Father will be in the kitchen?

This is stupid. She draws a breath, takes a step, then five more, and there he is. Slumped over the kitchen table, head supported by a meaty hand. His eyes are red, but not with tears. "Rinny," he says.

"Hi, Daddy."

"Sorry about that."

"Are you stoned?"

"A little."

After a moment, Irina says, surprising herself, "Is this what life is going to be like now?"

It is into the chalice of his cupped hands that he mumbles the words "I sure as fuck hope not, dude."

16

Today (for this is something it understands now: that the humans conceive of their lives as enclosed by a series of discrete packages of time, defined by the turning of the Earth, that offer conceptual division for otherwise persistent events. "Tomorrow is another day," they say, as though the hours of darkness possess some kind of inherent power to alter factual reality. But the fascinating thing is that they do—that because the humans believe in the potential of the new day, the new day sometimes gives them what they want. Not, the Observer believes, this particular group of human beings, in this particular skein of motivation and action. But for some people, sometimes, tomorrow really is a new day) the Observer has watched the woman Sam and the girl Irina at play: the former serving as the latter's caretaker but also her collaborator, it seems, in an apparently innocent game of mutual fantasy and delusion. The girl, the Observer now understands, longs for connection with the former residents of this house, the ones now dead. The young woman, this Sam, is serving, for the girl, as a conduit to those people.

She is not the child who survived the killings. Yet she seems to value this role in the girl's personal mythology—a figure of mystery, a symbol of survival. Her playacting seems to give her a sense of self-worth, a narrative identity. But why does the girl Irina wish to meet this survivor-child, to be a part of that grim (and, set against the vast backdrop of human failure, unremarkable) story? Perhaps it is her natural curiosity, her penchant for confabulation. Perhaps her closeness to her parents and, thus, her premature exposure to their sexual foolishness, has instilled in her the desire to be part of something more consequential, more dramatic. The family's isolation and sense of itself as different from other humans, this illusory exceptionalism, is a dangerous thing, the Observer understands. But it is inevitable—a part of their makeup.

Broadly speaking, human accomplishment is a consequence of human folly. The two cannot be separated.

The young woman Sam is leaving. She has taken the car belonging to Karl, the man, who is slumped unconscious over the kitchen butcher's block as the girl Irina bustles around him, cooking herself a meal of spaghetti with red sauce. She is banging the pans and dishes as an ineffectual protest against his drugged state. Her body's movements resemble those of her mother at times when her mother channeled similar emotions, about similar disappointments, into similar household duties.

The Observer chooses to go with Sam now. Along with its discovery that the laws governing the physical world do not apply to it, that it can jump from place to place in an instant, has come the sensation, in the presence of the humans, that they refer to as impatience. Hurry, Sam. Sam returns to Broken River, to her uncle's trailer, where she rushes inside, changes her clothes, rushes out. She drives the car—it is a Volvo station wagon, similar to the one that ran off the road so long ago—to the outskirts of town, a complex of buildings just off the interstate highway, and she parks beneath the illuminated sign reading DENNY's and hurries into the building nearest to it.

The Observer follows her inside. Sam is arguing with a man—her situational leader, it seems, who expected her to arrive sooner. The Observer does not understand why it is significant to the humans that they should be in certain places at certain specific times, but it is clear that this is a perennial obsession of the species. Argument finished, the two part, and Sam begins what is apparently her temporary purpose, the conveying of food from one group of humans to a number of others in exchange for money. She does this for quite some time. The Observer grows bored. (What has happened to the Observer? Wasn't it once capable of watching cracks form in walls, vines creep in between window and sash?) It considers leaving—abandoning this group of humans entirely, finding some other collection of the things to pursue and ponder. Then two men enter.

One of them is the man in the windbreaker, the man called Joe. The other is a smaller man, stooped inside a ski parka, and balding, and bristling with nervous energy. Sam invites the men to sit, inquires about their desire for food, later returns with two plates.

Something has been visibly awakened in Joe. He is alert now, in a way that he was not before his ride with the Observer. His perpetual expression of near slumber has rearranged itself into a kind of slow concentration. His mouth hangs open; his forkful of fatty sustenance hangs in the air before him, forgotten. The Observer keeps its distance, hovering on the other side of the room, behind the salad bar.

Louis, Joe says.

Yeah, what, says the smaller man.

Girl, says the large man.

Girl what?

That's her. From the computer. Her brother is the guy with the weed. At the house.

The man called Louis squints, says, I don't get it.

She's the kid from the thing, Joe says. That's where the money went. The kid took it. They're using it. It's my money.

I'm not— I don't—

Louis pauses.

Oh, shit, Louis says.

What? says Joe.

That's the girl I saw at the house today.

What? says Joe.

Hiding in the woods with the other girl, you know, who lives there now. When you made me go up there before. I knew I knew her from someplace. She's the waitress, and she's the weed girl, and she's the internet girl.

The man named Joe is smiling. The Observer peers into his head, then pulls quickly away from the dark electric noise it finds there.

So what do we do? Louis says.

Maybe hurt her a little, says Joe.

The Observer watches the men's profiles as each contemplates the situation. Louis is stricken. Joe, on the other hand, does not appear troubled and has resumed eating. He does not seem to notice the Observer, even when his head tilts back and his eyes refocus and he scans the room, briefly, between bites.

The Observer experiences an urge. It senses the possibility of a shift in the narrative, of violent action. It would like to cause certain events to be averted, or perhaps compelled to occur. But it cannot, as far as it knows.

Or can it? Perhaps it has wrongly assumed a lack of agency. Perhaps it can, in fact, influence events and objects: but how? And what actions might result in which outcomes? The Observer understands this as a problem of equal import and difficulty for the humans: the unpredictability of cause and effect. Perhaps there would be consequences for the Observer should it interfere: but which? Administered by what, or whom? This question—that of whether there is some greater authority governing the Observer's thoughts and deeds—feels dangerous. As though, given over to the indulgence of contemplating it, the Observer might never be able to contemplate anything else again. It pulls back, both in its thoughts and its position relative to the table. It waits.

Is that really necessary? Louis says at last.

Joe shrugs.

If it's the money you want, I mean.

Joe has no visible reaction to this.

I don't wanna be around when you do things like that.

Joe's shoulders tense slightly, and a muscle on his cheek appears to twitch. Louis seems not to have noticed. The Observer believes that the likelihood of injury to Sam has temporarily ebbed but also that the likelihood of injury to Louis has increased.

The two men finish eating. They exit to the parking lot, climb into

Joe's long car, and sit in it, arguing. Rather, Louis argues while Joe sits in silence. The Observer elects to watch through the car windshield instead of from inside; it cannot make out the sense of the words. But the words aren't important. The Observer can see what Louis can't, that his argument is meeting with an immovable resistance and that Joe is growing angrier. An uncharacteristic sheen of sweat has appeared on his upper lip despite the cold, and one of his fleshy eyebrows twitches. The Observer can hear the dark static, harsh and deep, from here. Just as a new snow begins to fall, Joe initiates a series of actions. With his right hand, he reaches into his coat pocket and pulls out a set of keys; as he does so his left hand is curling into a fist. And as the right hand guides the car key into the slot designed to accept it, the left fist crosses over the extended right arm and makes violent contact with Louis's face. Louis's head bounces off the passenger-side window as the car's engine turns over and roars to life.

From outside the car, the Observer can make out the words *Jesus fuck!*

The car jerks violently out of its parking space, heaves and rocks as it heads for the exit. It is greeted on the access road by a chorus of honking horns and screeching tires. In less than a minute it is gone from view.

The Observer remains in the Denny's parking lot, bobbing up and down in the increasingly heavy falling snow. It doesn't have to bob. It doesn't have to do anything at all. It bobs because it wants to feel something. It wants to feel something akin to what the smaller man felt when the fist struck his face and his head struck the window. It wants to feel something like what Joe did when he noticed, and desired to hurt, the young woman Sam, and when that desire left him and was replaced by the desire to punch Louis in the face.

The Observer bobs in the snowy air, waiting for Sam to get off work, waiting to want.

17

For a while Louis was wondering why his phone wasn't ringing. If he's being honest with himself, he was hoping it would, hoping he could have the luxury of an argument with Pam during one of these horrific Joe errands, to inoculate himself with a dose of workaday familial disharmony. But then he realized he left it at home, on the kitchen counter, in the little basket where the garage key and checkbook are kept. This realization, which arrived an hour into the drive to Broken River, pitched Louis into a pit of such profound desolation that he thought he might throw himself out of the car and onto the highway. But no, of course he wimped out on that plan, too, and has survived to enjoy getting punched in the head in a Denny's parking lot.

Louis is pretty much straight-up crying right now, in the motel bed, just a few feet away from Joe, who is sleeping peacefully. Louis has taken the pillowcase off his pillow and filled it with ice from the machine down the hall; he is alternately pressing it against his cheekbone and cranium, dampening both, soothing neither. He is figuring he's doomed. He's been doomed for a long time, but now he's doomeder.

Joe has lost it. He came for Louis in the middle of the afternoon, no warning, Pam and the kids upstairs, football on the TV. And Louis could see that something had changed: Joe's ordinarily pale, expressionless face was pink and ticcing, and all afternoon he kept talking about *his* money: not Mr. Chet's money, *Joe's* money, how *these* people stole it and are using it, and how he's going to get it back. Plot twist: Joe is beginning to shit-talk Mr. Chet. In the car on the way here: "It's none of his fuckin' business what we do," Joe said. "I cleaned that job up good, and where's my reward?" Even though Louis remembers himself being the chief cleaner-upper on that job, and Joe the primary mess maker.

Reality check: there's no money, right? There never was. That's why those people got killed. They got in over their heads, doing whatever it was they did, involving themselves with whatever that fucking shit was all about. Anybody with a mortgage could tell you how it works. You think you're golden, then the roof springs a leak and the car needs brakes and junior gets conked in the head with a line drive and you end up in the emergency room paying your deductible out of pocket, borrowing from Peter to pay Paul.

People you have to go shake down are, by definition, up shit creek. Mr. Chet knew it was a lost cause; he was just maintaining brand integrity. It was Joe who couldn't help himself, Joe who got ideas into his head, even then. So, if there was ever money, those people spent it; thus, there is no money. And even if this girl is the girl who survived, she is not using the nonexistent money to fund that dude's weed operation.

None of it matters—the coincidences, the connections. Things look connected because everything is connected in a place like Broken River. That's why people want to leave small towns. Everything reminds them of some stupid shit they did or that was done to them. These people aren't part of some grand conspiracy. They're just some fucking losers living in a shit town, like pretty much everybody else on earth.

Which brings Louis to the thought he had right before Joe punched him. The thought that has been creeping up on him for weeks now, as this weird series of errands has made less and less sense: There is no Mr. Chet.

Not to say that the man who directed, unsuccessfully, their actions of twelve years ago does not exist. He was real: Louis met him! But, Louis now understands, a man like that is not likely to have much use for a man like Joe. In fact, after those killings, Mr. Chet is likely to have ceased relying on Joe for muscle: You're fired, effective immediately. Joe is probably lucky not to have been stuffed dead into the same hole they buried those poor fuckers in. And Louis himself is even luckier. That's what he expected at the time, wasn't it? Instead he never saw Mr. Chet again and heard of him only through the increasingly unreliable conduit of Joe. Joe whose last name he doesn't know. Joe who lives he doesn't know where.

Whoever Mr. Chet was, is gone. Louis is alone with Joe out here, and Joe is under orders from a ghost. All bets are off.

What Joe whispered to Louis in the car, as the blood poured out of Louis's nose and into his cupped hands: *Hey, buddy. This is real fun. But don't tell me not to hurt somebody. Okay? Or I'll hurt you instead.*

Yeah. Okay, Joe.

So. Short-term plan: stay alive. Long-term plan: protect himself and his family from Joe. No idea how to make that happen, short of killing him. But Louis doesn't have a gun, and he doesn't have a knife, and he isn't convinced either of these things would kill Joe even if he had it in him to kill. He's had nightmares: shooting Joe, stabbing Joe, but Joe keeps on coming, like a movie *T. rex*, like a fucking hurricane.

At some point during the night Louis manages to fall asleep. At another point he wakes up. His head is pounding. He takes a shower and crawls back into the same pants and shirt that he wore yesterday, complete with a salsa stain from the football game that now feels like it's ten thousand years in the past. When he gets out of the bathroom, Joe's standing there with his arms crossed, looking out the motel window. He says, "Let's go."

They stake out Denny's in Joe's ludicrously conspicuous car. It takes all day. Louis mostly sleeps—he's afraid Joe gave him a concussion last night. But he keeps waking up, so maybe not. Every now and then Joe half-turns the key in the ignition so that he can windshield-wipe their view free of snow, which is falling around them at a boringly steady pace. Louis gets a pang every time the snow disappears. He thinks he'd be content to watch it accumulate forever.

Eventually the girl shows up again. She's driving the Volvo wagon. And Joe says, "That's the car."

"What?"

Joe's pointing. The girl has gone inside; she doesn't seem to have noticed them sitting here. He's pointing to the car. "That's the car."

"No shit. She just got out of it." Louis winces preemptively, awaiting another punch, but it doesn't come.

"No," Joe says, with creepy gentleness, shaking his head. "The one from before. When we did that job."

It takes Louis a minute, because it doesn't make sense, what Joe's saying. His skin is crawling when he says, "We got rid of that car, remember? It was a Volvo, but it wasn't that one."

Joe says, "That's the one."

He shouldn't speak. He shouldn't. But he says, "So, what, it escaped from the chop shop?"

Joe shifts in his seat, grunts, farts. Now he's starting to get the face-punch look.

"No, yeah, sorry," Louis says, "you're right, I think you're right." And that seems to calm him down.

They sit in silence. Louis falls asleep for a while and wakes up to find Joe getting out of the Caddy and slamming the door shut behind him. It feels so good to be alone that Louis considers staying here, but he knows what's expected of him: Joe's crazy requires an audience. He opens the door and heaves himself out, then follows Joe's footprints into the Denny's.

The girl is their waitress again. There is no talk of hurting her. They eat. At one point Joe says to him, "You look like shit, buddy."

"Haha, yeah, thanks."

"Your face is fucked up."

Louis doesn't honor the comment with a response.

"What happened to you?" Joe asks.

Louis looks him in the eye. "Seriously?"

Joe's chuckling. "Wife get ya?"

After a couple of quiet moments, Joe resumes eating, and Louis says, quietly, "Yeah, she got me good."

Just when Louis thinks they're going to return to the car, a scraggly-looking white kid swaggers in, waving to the hostess and to the old men at the counter like he owns the place. He's wearing a long army surplus coat and a pair of expensive-looking work boots. He intercepts the girl and wraps his arms around her, picks her up off the ground. She squeals. "Daniel!" she says. "I'm at work!"

Joe says, "That's the guy."

"Who?"

"The grower. He's fucking her, see? She gave him the money."

The guy sits down at the counter, throws his arm around some toothless old geezer, strikes up a conversation. Then, a minute later, somebody Louis actually recognizes walks in. It's the dude from the guitar store. He walks over to this Daniel, sits down, chats for a couple of minutes. At some point Daniel pulls a baggie out of his coat pocket and slips it into the guitar-store man's coat pocket, easy peasy. Guitar-store man slaps some twenties on the counter, as though paying for dinner, and Daniel sweeps them away. Guitar-store man gets up to leave.

On the way out, his gaze lands upon Louis and Joe's table, and his smile falters and breaks. He turns away, beelines for the exit. A few minutes later the guy named Daniel stands up, leaving a near-full cup of coffee behind, and strides out with a cheerful wave to the girl.

Joe throws down a bill and heaves himself to his feet. Exhausted, Louis drags himself after. He says he has to go to the men's room and veers off toward it without waiting for a reply. He takes a piss, then spends a long time washing his hands with the faucet running, gazing at his hideously aged and bruised face in the dirty mirror. He stares and thinks.

Outside this men's room, at the end of the hallway, there's a side door, propped open with a brick, beyond which he saw some cooks having a smoke in the cold. Louis could exit, turn left instead of right, push through that door, say 'sup to the cooks, and stride through the falling snow into the night: past the dumpster, over the berm, across the access road, and into the Ponderosa, its illuminated fake A-frame like an arrow pointing to heaven, to salvation. He could walk in there and call Pam on the pay phone, if there's a pay phone, and ask her to please pack a couple of bags and pack the kids' bags and come get me, we have to go away for a while. Maybe she would do it. Whatever is about to go down here in Broken River can go down without him, if he walks out that door. Maybe Joe will get himself arrested or killed, who knows? and Louis will be able to forget about this shit once and for all. And if not, he'll figure something out. He needs to grow a pair and get himself and his family out from under Joe.

Louis turns around, drying his hands on a paper towel, and heads for the door. Fuck it, he thinks, I'm gonna do it. I'm turning left. He balls up the towel, throws it at the trash can in the corner. The ball ricochets off the heap of paper-towel balls already overflowing the can and falls onto the floor among the other paper-towel balls that have ricocheted off the heap. He says "Fuck it! What the fuck is wrong with people" and bends over and gathers up all the fucking paper-towel balls and shoves them deep into the can, squashing them so hard and so far down that he bangs his forehead on the metal lip and he shouts fuck one more time before leaving the men's room and turning right.

The car is there in the parking lot, the windshield newly wiped clean. Louis climbs in. He's full of eggs and meat and ineffective coffee and he wants to punch something, probably himself. Joe doesn't say anything about his having been missing for five minutes. Louis says, surprised by the anger in his voice, "Where are we going? What the fuck are we waiting for?"

Joe gestures out the windshield. The girl is getting off work. She climbs into the Volvo and the Volvo pulls out and they start following the Volvo. The Volvo maneuvers through the center of town and onto Route 94, and then there are trees on either side, and their headlights illuminate the falling snow. They follow her all the way to the house, the house in the woods where it happened, and she signals right and turns into, and disappears down, the driveway.

Joe brings the car to a halt at the side of the highway. They idle there in silence for a few seconds. Then Joe turns it around and heads back toward town.

The Cadillac speeds along, clinging implausibly to the snowy road, as though by some unfathomable black magic.

18

Eleanor wakes in the dark and decides to get up and shower, as though it's morning. And when she gets out of the shower and passes the window, gauzily half-covered by a thin curtain, she realizes that it actually is morning, though very early. The sun is up, barely. The streets are full of garbage and bakery trucks and the shouts of construction workers, audible only because the crush of humanity hasn't yet arrived to drown them out. The industry of these people depresses her, so she climbs, naked, back into bed and stares at the strangely wallpapered ceiling of Craig's girlfriend's apartment. This wallpaper has been mesmerizing her for two days. It is printed with a simple design of intersecting gilt lines that form a grid, set against a background of dark green. It is very seventies, as is the digital alarm clock on the bedside table that can be set to project the time onto the green-and-gold grid; the two seem of a piece. If she crosses her eyes, the gold grid seems to hover a few inches below the green field, and the projection of the time between the two. She reaches out and makes time appear: *4:56*, shuddering slightly with the trembling of the hand holding down the button.

She did not need a week to do the things she planned to do in New York, which consisted pretty much entirely of her meeting with Craig and an as-yet-unscheduled visit with her editor at Ballantine, who presumably would by now have heard the good news about the

existence of a new book. There was a third thing, a thing she had intermittently, and for weeks, been picking up her phone to do, and
then not doing, and that was scheduling an appointment at Sloan
Kettering. She's been lying to Karl about this for too long. That's the
danger, in her mind—that even the slightest dishonesty on her part
might be identified as comparable to his. She needs to get the marriage books in order, especially if the marriage is going to end. But she
didn't make the appointment, she still hasn't, and now it's probably
too late to get one.

Driving here a couple of days ago, she thought about everything
she could do, alone, to pass the many hours of solitude that she had
committed herself to. New York things, she decided: things that tourists do. Ellis Island, the Statue of Liberty. Central Park. MoMA and
the Met. The Empire State Building. Why haven't they taken Irina
there? She wants to go, Eleanor is sure of it. Irina would never admit
it, of course—she prefers to assume her father's stance of ironic de-
tachment and casual disdain: "Why don't we just hang out in Times
Square all afternoon?" she said once, with an eyeroll, in response to
the suggestion. But that merely makes it Eleanor's job to insist upon a
family outing there, to lead them into Manhattan and into the elevator some sunny day, and up to the top, where they will all have a lovely
time and thank her for making them go.

By hour three of her journey here, her lower back ached with a familiar, almost homey, pulsing intensity that bordered on nausea. She
had completed the decrepit-barn-and-speedway portion of the trip
and had entered the domain of inexplicable traffic lights, roadside
diners, and auto dealerships outlined in colorful flags and punctuated
by convulsing forced-air tube men. (She doesn't understand the tube
men. They catch the eye, yes, as only a madly flailing twenty-foot-
tall monster can; but who decided such a sight could make you buy a
car?) Sewn-on smile notwithstanding, the tube men appeared to her
earnestly, even violently, repulsive. *Turn back*, their frantic motions
seemed to say. *There's danger here. We're tall enough to see over the trees,
and only nightmares await.*

Town and country gave way to highway and tunnel, and to the

claustrophobic and clotted arteries of Midtown; by the time she arrived, her mind was tired of arguing with itself and had settled into its default state in times of uncertainty and doubt: mild depression and embarrassment and boredom. It couldn't be all bad, she reasoned, thudding over the speed hump of Shannon's apartment building's underground garage; maybe she'd have a posthumous bestseller.

The plan was to park, take the elevator upstairs, unpack, and hit the town. What happened instead was that she entered the apartment, put her bags down, climbed into bed, and, after a hallucinatory fifteen minutes alone with the golden grid, slept for fourteen hours. She awoke shivering in this spartan and largely unlived-in Midtown apartment. It belongs to Shannon, Craig's girlfriend, who has resided primarily at Craig's much larger, much hipper loft in the Village (family money, of course—you don't maintain a place like his on literary agent money, even if you're an uber-agent, and he is not) for more than five years. "A woman with my kind of luck doesn't give up her own apartment," Shannon is fond of saying, in an evident effort to ward off triple widowhood (a goal she will likely achieve, in fact, by not marrying again).

After that, what she ended up doing, instead of all the things she told herself she would do, was to read a couple of novels on her phone, sleep some more, and eat ibuprofen and Chinese takeout. She avoided calling home. She didn't have the energy to push through Karl, to get him to hand the phone to Irina. And really, she didn't want to talk to Irina, either. Instead, as a way of proving to herself that she was still capable of some sort of human contact, she impulsively emailed the author of the thrillers she was reading, saying that she was enjoying them, and thank you very much for writing them. And got a reply within the hour that read,

> Dear Eleanor, thank you so much for the kind words! My readers mean so much to me. Sincerely, Kelly

Which was unexpectedly depressing. What did she think, that the woman would recognize the name of a fellow novelist and indulge in some impromptu shop talk? Why would she assume this writer would have heard of her? Or worse, maybe the writer *had* heard of her but disrespects her, or perhaps her entire subgenre of literature, and this stock email was a not-so-subtle insult.

She figured the email would prevent her from enjoying the rest of the thriller, but no—after half a page, she forgot about her brief personal contact with the author and allowed herself to be absorbed by the protagonist's escape from a Slovenian prison cell, her choking murder of a potential rapist, and her confrontation of a mustachioed and sexually deviant human-trafficking kingpin. At least things fucking *happen* in these books, she thought: it's not just people lying in bed and thinking about their fucking *feelings*. This thought made her hate herself enough to actually call home. Tapping Karl's face in her contacts was physically painful. She limped through a meaningless exchange with him, and an exhausting one with Irina, and then fell asleep again.

And now, once again, she's awake. She doesn't really want to go to the Met or Ellis Island or anywhere else because she fears that it will be the last time she ever goes there. She doesn't want to go to Sloan Kettering because she doesn't want to see the truth written on the face of a doctor as she shuffles papers on the desk in front of her, papers covered with horrible facts that it is her job to convey to the doomed.

....

Eleanor wriggles into her favorite black wool dress and gray leggings, pulls on her Doc Marten boots and earflap hat, shrugs on her coat, and leaves the apartment with a pang of regret. Her back hurts. Her shoulders and neck hurt. The pain is not acute, but it's comprehensive. She is one big, exhausted throb. In a café she orders and doesn't eat a scone, drinks a coffee, reads a bit more, sits with her notebook open to a blank page that she fails to fill with words. When MoMA opens, she goes to it, in defiance of her desires. Even on an ordinary day she can't stand in front of a painting for more than a few seconds—she doesn't understand these people who linger, chin in hand, for ten minutes, gazing deeply at a work of art. She thinks they must be faking it. But today she can barely drag herself through the hushed and antiseptic rooms. When the time comes, she leaves the museum, gets on the train, and hauls herself into Craig's office building. The assistant is there, comely and bright, answering the phone and offering people bottled water. Eleanor doesn't have to wait long. She stands when Craig emerges, arms open; chooses not to judge the brief expression of dismay that darkens his face as he takes her in. Has she changed that much? (Not cancer, she reminds herself. Misery. I have been transformed by misery and self-doubt.)

He leads her into his office, and not, as she might have expected, out to lunch. This is the first piece of evidence.

If Eleanor has changed for the worse, Craig Springhill has changed for the better. Age suits him, as it often does for certain men of means. He is studiedly scruffy, his salt-and-pepper hair mussed, his wool cardigan askew over a designer tee shirt. He's very handsome. He slides behind the desk and says, "Nell. Nell."

She lowers herself into one of his slightly-too-low leather-upholstered armchairs, the ones that make him seem larger and more important than his clients, and her lower back, dozing until now, wakes up and begins to protest. "Hi, Craig."

"So glad you're back. So glad. Your upstate sojourn has taken you away from us too long."

She does not point out that it has been only six months since they've seen each other, a perfectly reasonable amount of time, even when she lived in Brooklyn. Which, to Craig Springhill, might as well have been upstate. Instead she says, "I've missed it here."

"And how is our budding genius."

For a second she thinks he means her. But no, he means Irina. "Adjusting. Obsessed with writing. Evidently being homeschooled?"

He laughs, though this isn't terribly funny. "You've embraced rurality in all its splendor. The shade of the pines. The old lady down the road sells you eggs. Cutting your own firewood. A kitchen garden, the song of the crickets." Craig likes clichés. In books and in life. She nods, smiling, feeling very uneasy.

Craig says, soberly now, "And Karl. Are you working out your differences?"

"Not really," she says, and now she remembers: she called him that night, called his cell after they decided to leave New York and Karl lumbered out, door slamming behind him, to stalk the streets with his shaggy head hanging low, presumably in order to appear sexily tortured to any woman who happened to be walking by. She called Craig in tears and he said "Just a moment, dear Nell" and held a whispered conversation with Shannon and sequestered himself inside his home office in order to receive her confession.

He shakes his head. "I was no better at forty than your husband. Men, Nell. We're weak. Weak in the face of our carnal nature, alas."

Does he not recall that it was she he was fucking at forty? He reaches across the desk, not far enough to pat her hand, as the desk is too large; but he pats the air eighteen inches away with apparently genuine feeling. "I'm very sorry," he continues. "You deserve better."

"I'm not here to talk about that."

He brings his hands together in a silent clap. "No, you are not. You are here to discuss this strange and compelling manuscript." He punctuates this statement with another pat, this one targeting, and actually connecting with, a neat pile of paper that must be her printed-out manuscript. Strange and compelling, she thinks. Oh dear.

"Why don't you tell me," Craig goes on, "what your thoughts are on this book. Where you wanted to take it. Where it actually went."

What the fuck, she thinks, kind of question is that? It's the kind of question you ask a condemned prisoner when you fervently wish she would just kill herself, to save everyone the trouble of an expensive and gruesome execution. "I have to admit I don't know," she says, though she does. She does know. She wanted to write something for herself, for once. She wanted to write something fucking depressing, something that her fans would email her angrily about. She wanted to not be a hero of the educated middle-aged middle-class woman of leisure, to not get invited onto any talk shows, to not bask in the adulation of fans at readings. She wanted to do something besides what Craig Springhill wanted her to do! For a decade he has perpetuated the idea that their interests are aligned, that it benefitted them both to go to bed together, to let him represent her, to give him editorial dominion over her novels, to let him run interference between herself and the marketing department over such trivial matters as her author photo, her book covers, her public appearances, her interviews and magazine pieces. It's all beneath her, he told her more than once, and of course that always felt good to hear. It was the dirty work that his 15 percent bought her freedom from. And she can't think of anything in particular from the past ten years that she would retroactively change if she could. But now, what she wants is for her agent to do what she tells him to, and for her husband to fall out of love with the other woman, and for her back to stop hurting, and for the umpteen hours of sleep her body just experienced to have been enough. She took the book exactly where she wanted it to go. Those are her thoughts. But she keeps them to herself, and Craig goes on talking, as men do.

"The writer's prerogative," he says with a chuckle, as if that notion is quaintly amusing. "The pleasure of not knowing. Giving the imagination free reign. The vagaries of the creative mind." Each phrase is like a match that fizzles out before it hits the puddle of gasoline.

"Maybe *you* can tell me what *you* think," Eleanor says. "That's why I'm here, I'm pretty sure." Her voice sounds thin to her, thin and ragged as a flailing tube man. Her back is spasming like one, too. She shifts in her chair to ease the pain, and it responds by galloping up into her neck and scalp. She tries not to wince.

"Yes, yes, yes. What I think." He leans back, makes a cage with his hands, taps his pursed lips with his two index fingers. "I think what we have here is a novel that shifts its focus. A novel that changes its identity midway, yes? On the one hand, it's, as I said, compelling. On the other hand, it's confused. It's uncertain of its aims."

"Okay," she says, but she stretches it out, turns it into a question. Because the novel is not uncertain of its aims. It is Craig, rather, who is uncertain of whether those are legitimate aims. Isn't that what's going on here?

Craig says, "I'm seeing a challenge for your audience. A conflict."

She doesn't speak.

"It begins . . . ," he goes on, pausing as though he doesn't know how to continue, but of course he does, ". . . quite splendidly, more in keeping with your established work, yes? with Paul and Nora trapped in their respective lives. Your evocation of marriage, the *ambiguities* of marriage, is, as always, peerless. These pages are very beautiful, of course. Very beautiful."

He hesitates as if awaiting gratitude for the compliments. As well he should, she thinks—this is how we talk to each other. These are the workings of our professional friendship. So why is it so hard to play her role? Even though she knows he's about to criticize her; he's done it before. Just smile. Say thanks.

She says, "Thank you, Craig."

But it comes across too sardonically. He doesn't like it, shifts in his seat, tugs his sweater sleeves up over his finely haired forearms, of which she can tell he is inordinately proud. But why think this about him? Why condemn his vanity in her mind, this man who has made her a success, who has given her a beautiful apartment to stay in?

Her back is killing her, it's taking her breath away. She would like to lie down on her back on the floor of this office right now. She is aware that she's panting a bit. She ought to be hungry, but she isn't, and the nonhunger gnaws at her. She says, "Go on."

"And then," Craig says, his voice rising in pitch, dropping in volume, as his fingers drum the desktop, "and then everything falls apart. Is that how you'd put it?"

"That's fair to say, yes."

"The child reads her email, asks her about it in front of Paul. They fight. And meanwhile, we learn in the next chapter, Paul has become deathly ill."

"Right."

"At this point I'd expect . . . that is . . ." He suddenly leans forward, folding his arms on the desk and looking intently into her face, though not her eyes. She surveys his idiotically organized, immaculate, dustless desk, with its little tray of fountain pens and its unobtrusive Scandinavian clamp lamp and its sleek black telephone. Her manuscript, even in its tidy little pile, is the only mess in the room. He says, "I'll put it this way. I don't mind an unhappy ending."

"Oh, goody," she can't resist saying.

"Don't mind at all," he says, more forcefully now. "Star-crossed lovers, heartbreak. Sadness and misery. Even death. Romeo and Juliet. That's a kind of book you can write . . ."

"Why, thank you, Craig."

But he's already talking again, before she has even finished speaking his name: ". . . but what you've done here is you've separated them halfway through, Paul and Nora, and their lives unravel . . . in parallel. Each without regard to the other."

"Correct."

"They never see each other again, after page . . . " His fingers find a sticky note, and he splits the pile of pages long enough to glance down at the page number she knows he has already memorized. "One hundred forty," he says, letting the pages fall, straightening them again with those delicate hands. "They never again speak to each other. They don't, if I remember correctly, even *think* about each other again. Ever."

"Yes."

"Your romance novel, if I may be so bold, splits and becomes two tragedies. Two unrelated tragedies."

"Not unrelated," she protests. Because they are not! They are two things she thought of all by herself and put in a book together, goddammit. And she is not happy with the words "romance novel." That is not what it is. That is not what *she* is.

"But separate. Utterly separate but equally bleak. Her suicide, his wasting away. Ruin. The affair no longer relevant."

"Of course it's relevant," she says.

"Yes, sure, of course," he replies, stepping on her words, talking quickly now, clearly annoyed by her reaction. "They die alone. The affair has ruined their marriages, and they die alone. Because of the affair."

"Not because of the affair," she says. "It isn't a morality tale."

"The affair is the thing that drives them apart, drives the narrative apart. Infidelity results in loneliness and death. That's the moral, if you will. The thesis."

"No," she says, "I won't."

He appears genuinely confused. "Pardon?"

"If you will, you said. And I'm saying I won't. It's not a moral. It's not a thesis."

His jaw works. His brow creases. She's annoying him. If this is a different Craig—and it's clear to her now that yes, he is, he's a new Craig, a Craig who says no—then it may also be true that she is a different Eleanor, as well. She is, of course. She can imagine how she must look to him right now—fatigued, depleted, disagreeable. Desperate. She doesn't want to be this way, and neither does he. But here they are.

"Nell—" he starts to say, and the flirty lilt is gone from his voice. She doesn't want to hear it. She doesn't want to hear this voice say anything at all. The pain has found her shoulders now, and it's sharp and deep, as though angel wings are trying to push themselves out through the flesh.

"It's an evocation of what life is like," Eleanor says, aware that she is making an ass of herself, that even she doesn't agree with a single word she's saying. "Things end. People become irrelevant. It's the kid's world now. The daughter's."

"But you don't even tell us what happens to the daughter."

"Of course I do," she says, and she notices that her hand is covering her eyes. She brought it to her face so that it could massage her temples, but it's still there, conveniently blotting out his face.

"You really don't. It ends with them. It ends with endings."

"The girl's going to be fine. It's obvious. She thinks about— There's the part where she—where she—"

Neither of them speaks for a minute. In the quiet, the noise from the street filters through the window, and she can hear breathing. Not Craig's, just hers. His breaths are as silent as a ghost's. She hears him settling back in his chair. In her mind's eye, his hands are laced together over his chest, and he gazes at the ceiling.

"I'm sure I wrote it," she says, less forcefully than she intends.

"Well, if you did, you didn't put it in the book."

"I meant to."

She takes her hand away from her eyes. His hands aren't folded. They're lying on the desk, pale and dry-looking, like elegantly carved marble paperweights. He isn't looking at the ceiling, he's looking right at her.

"I know you don't believe me, Nell," he says, "but I respect the choices you're making. If you don't want to write the kind of book you've been writing, I applaud you. When you have decided what book to write, it will be brilliant. And I will sell it for you, whether it's to Ballantine for three-quarters of a million dollars or to Ecco for five thousand. Because you are my writer."

She can't meet his gaze any longer and hangs her head. Her back pain isn't even back pain anymore; it's just generalized ache. Every part of her is breaking. I'm failing, she thinks, and I am also dying. What's going to happen to Irina? She'll be stuck upstate with a philandering child for a father; she will have to beg for the attention of a series of narcissistic sluts barely older than she is. Irina, I'm so sorry. She's trying not to cry.

"But this book isn't that book," Craig goes on, "not yet. This book is the work of a writer who is searching. I urge you not to perform this important work in public. Search, discover, then write. Show us what you've found, once you've found it."

With her fingernails, she tugs a long hair from her stocking. It doesn't want to let go. It makes a sound, a tick-tick, as the wool releases it. She lets it fall to the floor.

Craig says, "This book isn't finished. That's fine. There's no rush to find your new work, Nell."

He says, "You have all the time in the world."

....

Back at Shannon's apartment, sleep won't come. She finds some expired prescription painkillers in the medicine cabinet—nothing too heavy, just acetaminophen with codeine—and takes as many as she likes. She acquires a bottle of bourbon and drinks from it liberally, at least by her standards. But she's never really drunk and she's never fully asleep and she's never out of discomfort. She calls home again, wishing she had gotten Irina her own phone; Karl's voice is performing a reasonable approximation of despondence. "Let me talk to my daughter," she says, but once Irina's on the line, she doesn't know what to say. She has done nothing in New York; she has seen no friends, gone nowhere, made no amusing observations; and so she listens to Irina's tales of adventure and card games with her babysitter, the girl from the Dairy Queen. She finds herself reading between the lines, between the lines between the lines, for evidence that Karl is fucking the babysitter. She isn't sure why she cares. Eleanor does not want to be the kind of person who can become unhinged by jealousy, never imagined that she could be. But maybe when somebody is ready, any available stimulus will do to effect the unhinging.

When she's drunk enough to call Rachel, she calls Rachel. She uses Shannon's house phone. It's strange to hear someone say hello in that tone of gentle, expectant curiosity, tinged with worry, that used to be commonplace before phones let you know who was calling. Hearing it, Eleanor experiences a moment of rage—how dare she sound so innocent! How dare her voice express anything other than terror and self-disgust!—followed by another of pity as she realizes how unwelcome this call will be. She does not know where this sympathy is coming from and quashes it before she opens her mouth.

"It's Eleanor."

"Ah," Rachel says after a moment. "Hello."

"He told you I was coming?"

"He did."

"I intend to speak with you in person," Eleanor says. This line and the ones to follow have been revised and rehearsed many times and now feel stupid to say. "I don't want to make things difficult for you, but I will, if you won't meet me."

"No need for that," comes the prim reply. "I'll see you."

"Where?"

"Someplace convenient to you. When you like."

"Tomorrow," she says, though she doesn't know what day this is, what time. "Eight p.m. Do you know the Black Rose? In Greenpoint?"

Rachel says, "Sure. There might be live music up front. But the back room won't be crowded, I don't think."

Of course you know that, bitch.

"I'll see you there," Eleanor says, and hangs up.

She manages to sleep after that, once again until late the next morning. She tries and fails to read, tries and fails to watch TV, tries and fails to take a walk. Before she knows it, it's late afternoon, and she needs to make herself presentable—she needs to decide what variety of presentable she wants to present—and she needs to get to Brooklyn. In . . . how long? Two and a half hours. Why Brooklyn? Why at eight? No matter—less time to be nervous. She showers, dresses, applies and removes makeup, applies it again. Chooses severe over pretty—she doesn't need to prove to this woman that she's the more attractive of the two. Clearly she has already lost that battle. Into her satchel she throws phone, pain reliever, kleenex. She's dizzy and wants to vomit. The 7 to the G: riding the trains, she can't remember what she's eaten in the past two days. Since she's been in New York, really. There was the Chinese takeout, but then what? There were ice cream bars in Shannon's freezer, discolored and frosted over; she thinks she got some pretzels and tortilla chips at the bodega after she bought the whiskey. But she's not sure if she ate them. She falls asleep, misses the transfer; at Queensboro Plaza she climbs up the stairs, climbs down the stairs, heads south again. Gets it right this time. Off at Nassau. It's dark and cold but not cold enough for snow, so a light rain, a mist, really, stings her face; it feels like it's crawling under her clothes, soaking into them; her clothes feel heavy, her body feels heavy, even though she hasn't been eating. She is stumbling through the streets of Brooklyn. She feels herself missing the place but at the same time stands apart from emotion; she is standing five paces back, observing herself missing Brooklyn.

At some point she becomes extremely confused. None of the street names look familiar to her. She takes out her phone, locates the blue dot of herself, turns around in a circle. The map wheels with her, spokes around the dot. She asks a passing couple if they know where the Black Rose is. They don't—in fact they arc around her as though she's a crazy person. Finally she does something she's never done before—she activates the lady in the phone and speaks into it: "Give me directions to the Black Rose, please."

It shouldn't surprise her, but the phone tells her exactly what do to. This way, that way. One block, two. "The destination is on your right," says the phone, and there it is. It's only 8:12. That's fine. Her husband's lover can wait by herself for twelve minutes. She should have come even later, actually—late enough to make the woman sweat, not so late that she would just up and leave. Rachel was right— there's a jazz trio playing here, and Eleanor is forced to pay a cover. She takes a sharp right inside the door and moves down the hallway to the back room, a dark, close space illuminated by electric candles and, through the windows, streetlight. There are some disaffected-looking young professionals here, talking in low tones, but of course Rachel Rosen is not here yet.

Eleanor stands there, scanning the room for an empty table. Her entire body is trembling, quivering, really. She needs to sit down but would need to move in order to do it, and now that she has stopped moving, she is afraid to start again. Her jaw aches, and her head aches. A voice in her ear says "Excuse me" and she is gently brushed aside as a little crowd of overdressed millennials squeezes past. Her clothes grate her flesh and she leans heavily against the hall wall. She closes her eyes.

When she opens them again, Rachel Rosen's face is floating before hers. "Eleanor?"

She's older and fatter than Eleanor remembered; that's good. Her looping black curls are turning gray, and her face is fleshy and tired. But her expression is one of concern.

"I'm sorry I'm late," she says. "Do you want to sit down?"

Maybe it's the apology, or the inadvertent fasting, or the many, many pain relievers, or whatever it is that's eating her up from the in- side, but Eleanor thinks she can't even stand up anymore. Her knees begin to tremble, and she feels herself slide an inch down the wall.

The lacquered pine paneling catches on her coat, and she can hear the threads popping.

"Eleanor? Are you all right?"

She slumps a few inches more, then collapses. Her tailbone makes contact with something—a windowsill? an umbrella stand?—and pain radiates through her body, lighting up every distant part of her. She hears herself cry out and then she is falling onto the floor, and she is lying on her side, and her jaw clenches and she can't unclench it, and her head is screaming, and her legs won't move. She can't get up. She doesn't even know what up is anymore. Rachel Rosen's face is above her, and the faces of the young professionals, and her name is being spoken, and she thinks, Oh, fuck, oh, fuck, I've really done it now.

Part Three

19

Three nights before his phone lit up with a call from a Brooklyn hospital, Karl was sitting on the sofa, stoned, his laptop open on the cushion beside him, Huck and Jim standing before him. The room was dark save for the sculptures' dim underlighting, which illuminated, not quite strongly enough (by design), the skein of seams and planes and veins and cracks running through them. He didn't have to get up and walk around Huck and Jim to get the full effect; he'd memorized them a long time ago. He wished there were other people here to observe them along with him; he would like to see them trying to figure the pieces out.

Karl had, from time to time, stationed himself in one corporate lobby or another, in order to watch passersby interact with his sculpture. Which is to say that he typically watched them walk on by without even noticing, or anyway without betraying any obvious interest. But sometimes people stopped and looked. They followed the lines he'd made, the path the metal traced through the glass, obvious in some places, hidden in others. You could always follow it, he made sure of that; even when the steel was nearly invisible, when it plunged deep into the milky ice, you could hold its position in your head, walk around to the other side, watch it emerge. His sculptures were puzzles, really. Not puzzles you were supposed to solve but puzzles you were supposed to puzzle over.

Huck and Jim had been commissioned by a corporate client, but at the last minute Karl changed his mind about handing them over. He whipped up a couple of alternate pieces in record time, stupid-simple geometries, and nobody complained. But Huck and Jim, he couldn't let them go, couldn't unleash them on the world. Not that they'd blow anybody's mind, it was just that he would have known. People wouldn't get them, and he'd have *known*, and it would have broken his heart.

Because the lines didn't connect inside Huck and Jim, not all of them, not in the usual way. They veered off, faked you out. There were dead ends in there, intentional flaws in the glass, quirks and bends in the metal. And there were lines that seemed to terminate that actually connected the two together—vectors through the air between them. Facets of glass that jumped through space. The two had to be positioned just right—at the proper angles to each other, the proper distance apart. They were Karl's private joke at his own expense. His reminder that he could have made art like this all the time if he were serious enough. But he knew he wasn't. Huck and Jim were the only things he'd ever made solely for himself, not for money, not to get somebody into bed—that's why they were standing here, in the house, where most people would have put a fucking TV.

Maybe the knives were for himself, too. He proved this by selling all of five in the three months he'd been at it. The eBay adventure was kind of fun at first. But it was time to admit to himself that the whole thing was a bust. People just didn't get it. Two guys tried to cut up deer with theirs, and they broke, and another guy dropped his on the ground, and it broke, and they sent back the pieces and demanded refunds. He tried to explain, but of course that just made the dudes angrier, and he gave them their money back. He could have taken comfort in the likelihood that the other two guys had theirs on stands, in display cases, but somehow that was even worse.

Enemies. That's what the knives were meant to cut. They were made for warriors to use. Which is to say that they were made for a bygone era, a bygone culture—or maybe one yet to come. They were made for a time and culture that forged knives for the purpose of fucking *defeating foes*. The world that contained online auctions and digital payments and display cases and knife stands was not the world these knives were made for.

He was beginning to understand that he was losing it out here. Everything inside him that used to point outward, toward galleries and museums and lobbies and meeting rooms and women, had now grown in on itself. All the love, the lust, that used to emanate from him, through his dick, he'd had to aim at Nell alone, Nell and Rachel (because Nell alone was not working out), and now it was aimed nowhere and at no one. And there was nothing he could do about it. He hated to masturbate, it made him feel like a child. So now he didn't want to wank, he didn't want to proposition the babysitter, Nell wouldn't talk to him, and Rachel had cut him off, presumably for good. The daughter he suddenly realized he didn't really know was sitting cross-legged on the bed upstairs, making up stories and wishing her mother would come home.

Karl was now wishing the same thing. He wanted Nell to come home. On the laptop beside him, an animated GIF of a samurai chopped, again and again, the head from a foe's shoulders. A moment before, it had offered him comfort, what with its dynamism and reliability, the way the wind moving leaves in the trees must have been for whatshisname, the asshole who lived by that lake and wrote a fucking book about it. But now, suddenly, it was giving him a headache. Or maybe that was the weed. He snapped the laptop shut, revealing, behind it, on the bookshelf recessed into the triangle of wall the stairs formed, the little row of novels written by his wife.

They were demurely tucked in among other fiction titles, written by other people, that he had never read or even really looked at. Of course he'd spent time with Nell's books: turned them over in his hands and remarked disingenuously on their heft and visual appeal, usually at the moment when Nell removed them from the shipping box. (His mind, by this point, was typically focused on the celebratory fuck that was sure to follow.) Of course he'd promised to read them, but it was understood, at least by him, that this would not happen, because why the hell would he read any fiction at all, let alone fiction about boyfriends or shopping or mothers or whatever Nell spent her time obsessing over? These books weren't *for* him; he would no sooner read them than stick a tampon up his ass.

But now, there they were, and he was lonely and freaked out, and he didn't know how to talk to his daughter without her mother around, and suddenly the books called to him. He leaned over and tugged the first of them off the shelf, tried to remember. It was called *Maybe*. Was this always the title? The cover depicted a woman, a third of a woman, a stylishly dressed young woman not dissimilar in shape to Nell, facing the camera. She was cut in half by the edge of the cover, and cut off above the knee and below the eyes, and she was holding a half-finished whatsis—one of those knitting- or sewing-type things where you make pictures with thread on cloth in a wooden circle thing—with the needle hanging off it, and the stitching read, *My heart belongs to . . .* The woman's face was anxious and hopeful and composedly sexy; she was biting her red-lipsticked lip with preternaturally white straight teeth.

Karl heaved a sigh and again wondered how he and Nell had ended up together. In his bakedness he regarded this book, but any book, really, as a wildly implausible thing, mundane in form and hopelessly constrained, hardly an adequate vehicle for any kind of art. Every book propped up a table leg in the exact same way, he thought. Rectangles, rectangles, in rows and piles. Bricks. Slabs full of words.

Once, he had pretended to read this book, back when he figured her whole writing career was some kind of hobby that wouldn't pan out. He told her it was great, of course. Read some shit about it on the internet, regurgitated it for her over dinner one night. It didn't feel unfair at the time: after all, she could apprehend a piece of his in an instant: just a glance was all it took. But reading a book, man, that was work. Hours and hours, sitting in a chair or lying in bed, the eyeballs darting back and forth, line after line after line. It would have been an insane mental and physical endurance test.

He cracked it open, took a look at the dedication. *For Craig, who believed.*

For shit's sake, that guy. Karl threw the book down, annoyed.

Hadn't he, Karl, been in the picture at that point? And she dedicated it to *that* weenie? But the more he thought about it, the more he realized he couldn't really remember when she wrote it. The house suddenly seemed really, really quiet and empty around him, with Irina gone to bed and Sam at Denny's. Somehow Irina's presence upstairs, the possibility that she might wake up, need him, require attention, require emotional engagement, made the feeling worse. So he picked up the book and carried it out to the studio. He flopped down on the love seat, turned on the lamp. Stuffed a little more weed into his pipe and sparked it up. Opened *Maybe* again. *Chapter One*, he read, and thought, Does every fucking novel have to say chapter fucking one? But fine. He squinted some weariness out of his eyes and tried to focus.

The book was about this rich twentysomething girl in Boston, Andrea, the latest in a long line of lady overachievers—a suffragette, a pilot, a feminist, a CEO—who is brilliant and beautiful, yadda yadda, and everybody expects her to become president or something, but so far she hasn't done anything, and she isn't married, and everybody's kind of worried, or maybe hopes, that she's gay, but mostly they all just want her to get her shit together and become the new matriarch.

Which, okay, it was kind of interesting, but not Karl's cup of tea, and he figured he would give it a couple more pages and then drink himself to sleep. But pretty soon he was on page 10, and Andrea's little sister was getting married, and she meets this guy who's engaged to some dumb bitch, and she has an affair with the guy, who keeps promising to break off the engagement, and meanwhile this nerdy dude her brother works with becomes her sort of email bestie, and before long you realize the nerdy dude is hot for Andrea, and then there are like five more crazy reversals while meanwhile Andrea discovers that she is good, actually kind of fucking great, at ironic avant-garde dirty needlepoint (that's what the stitching thing turned out to be called) and ends up with a huge gallery show of the stuff and gives her grandmother a heart attack because one of the needlepoint things has a dick on it, and *where in the hell did this version of his wife come from because this shit is craaaazy!*

By now it was like two in the morning and he'd forgotten to eat and his vision was blurring. So he went to the kitchen and stuck a frozen pizza in the oven. The kitchen looked different: somebody had cleaned up. Sam? Irina? A plate, a glass, a fork were washed and now stood dry in the strainer. Did somebody break into his house and eat here? And clean it up?!?

No. No, it was Irina, she must have had dinner earlier, before Sam stole his car to go to work. Had she even asked if he wanted anything? Fuck, she didn't, did she. Or maybe she did? He couldn't remember. While the pizza heated he crept upstairs and knocked gently on Irina's door. No answer. He let himself in. She was asleep under the covers, her body curled awkwardly around her closed laptop, and, to his surprise, Sam lay beside her on her back, asleep on top of the covers in her work clothes. When did she come back? She looked like a child. The fuck: was she on the clock? Irina was gently snoring. He felt a sudden bubble of grief rising into his chest and bursting, for what, he didn't understand. He backed out and closed the door.

The fire he'd started in the woodstove was still going, albeit weakly. He threw another log into it. He stared at the glowing stove doors for fifteen minutes, nearly falling asleep. Then he took the pizza out of the oven and ate the entire thing off the kitchen counter, then finished *Maybe* before falling asleep for real, on the sofa.

In the morning Sam made Irina breakfast, and Karl took the second book off the shelf and went out to the studio and got high and read. This one was called *Seven Secrets of the Sarcastic Sisterhood*, and it was about a bunch of school friends who make a solemn vow to each other that one year into any relationship they ever have, the man in question must submit to a hearing before a panel of the other three friends, and the relationship will live or die based on their ruling. It goes pretty well for about ten years—a couple of the women use the pact to elaborately dump a couple of losers, and another one marries the man her friends have vetted. But then the protagonist, Lacey, meets a guy, thinks he's the one, and starts getting increasingly nervous about the hearing, because her friends have grown strange and distant and seem to know about the relationship even though she hasn't told them. In the end the novel turns into a kind of goofy psychological thriller parody and concludes with one wedding, one divorce, and one birth, and a moonlit séance in the woods.

At some point in the day Irina had actually brought him some lunch—a turkey sandwich on wheat bread and a mug of hot chocolate. "We made hot chocolate," she said by way of explanation, and it annoyed him that he had to interrupt his reading to accept the food. Irina looked weird—skinny and pale. He said, "Hey, man, you look weird, are you sick or something?"

"No. Are you?"

"No."

"But you're high, Father."

"Not really," he said, picking up a half sandwich and taking a bite, and then, largely involuntarily, devouring the entire thing in seconds, like an animal. The food reminded him that his body existed, and his body reminded him that other people existed, and he realized that he had just told his twelve-year-old daughter that she looked weird and sick.

But she didn't appear offended or self-conscious; she just looked confused. And less weird and sick, now that he had eaten something and his own body felt better. Irina said, "You're reading Mother's books."

"Yeah. Right."

"They're really good. She's a great writer." She was gazing at him, arms crossed over her chest, as though challenging him to disagree.

"You know, you're right. She is, totally," he said. He slurped the cocoa. Fuck, it was really good. "This is really fucking delicious, man."

"Thanks, Father. Sam made it. On the stove, out of whole milk in a pan."

"Yeah." He started on the second half of the sandwich, through which he mumbled the words, "Is she, like, spending the night?"

"I think she can, if you want. Also," Irina went on, high-and-mighty, "we are friends now, and sleepovers are appropriate."

"All right, cool," Karl said, gasping for breath between bites.

"Anyway," Irina said, "I'll let you get to it."

"Thanks, buddy. I'll be in eventually."

"Okay, Father."

"Okay."

He started the third book later in the day. Irina and Sam weren't around when he went into the house for it; maybe they were out taking a walk. The book was called *Stop Trying So Hard*. It was published two years ago. Eleanor had become famous enough by then that the author photo had migrated from the back flap to the back cover. The picture was black-and-white, intimate, sultry. She peered out from behind a curtain of gently curving hair; her gaze was piercing, understanding, full of humor and warmth. When was the last time she looked at him this way? Had she ever? Karl looked at the photo credit: some clown he had never heard of. Did she fuck him? She had to—how could you keep your hands off a woman who looked at you that way? Karl reached out with his mind for Rachel in a kind of panic, grabbing at the strands of his love for her, its marionette strings, trying to make it twitch and dance, trying to make it look like something alive. But he couldn't: now he just wanted Eleanor, he wanted the woman who wrote these books, who gazed out at him from this picture. Who in the hell was she? Was she even real?

He read the book all afternoon, finished late, stumbled into the house. Repeated the previous night's ritual of the pizza (and didn't he eat the last one the night before? Was Sam grocery shopping for them?), added a log to the fire Irina and Sam must have made, climbed the stairs to gaze at them as they slept. But this time, he could hear whispers, Irina's light was on, and a wedge of light extended across the hall from her door. He didn't dare step into it. He didn't want to risk discovery. He backed down the stairs, retired to the sofa to wait. He lay there, his body aching for food, his mind clouded by drugs, craving the wife who filled his head, the one he was finally listening to for the first time.

20

Irina lay awake after midnight. This was something she'd started last month—before that, midnight had always seemed like some kind of unbreachable barrier. To stay up past midnight was to violate some law of physics—if a kid was awake, the day couldn't change, the sun would stand still on the other side of the world, and Asia would be engulfed in flames in an endless high noon. But her novel (and, let's be honest, the internet) kept drawing her closer and closer to the line, until one night she lost track and didn't notice until quarter past twelve. She gasped. Her parents' footsteps climbed the stairs. Adrenaline coursed through her—there was still time to snap the laptop shut, switch off the lamp, dive under the covers. But then Mother's head was there, in the open door, and she was saying, placidly, "It's late, sweetie, go to sleep," and her father shouted good night from the hall, and she felt like rather a fool.

Now, though, the excitement of midnight was gone. It just felt lonely here, lying in bed, being awake for no reason when the rest of world was asleep. She wanted to go across the hall to Mother's office, where Sam was sleeping on the daybed, and wake her up and talk. But she knew that Sam would actually do it, would actually talk to her, because she was nice, but maybe also because she was being paid, and Irina didn't want to wonder which reason was the real one. She could call Mother, but her conversations with Mother-in-New-York had all been roughly the same: short and depressing. "Father is useless," Irina complained yesterday. "He isn't doing anything. Sam and I are doing *everything*. When are you coming *home*? Why didn't you bring me?" She was aware that this was hopelessly whiny and childish, but so what, she was a child.

"I'm sorry," her mother said, and of course this made Irina feel worse. "Soon, I hope. I'm sorry. I have to fix a couple of things here. It won't take long."

"Is it about Father? Is it about the other woman?"

A longish silence. "What do you know about that, buddy?"

"Ugh," Irina said, because it made her feel bad to play her hand like that. The adults needed to feel that you didn't notice things. They needed to feel like they had privacy and control, even though they didn't.

"I'm sorry," her mother said, a little strangled, and Irina was pretty sure she was trying not to cry. In bed!—Irina could hear the sheets and blankets moving. It was not good if Mother went all the way to New York City to cry in bed. "Work on your writing, baby," she said, her voice down to a whisper. "Fiction problems are better than life problems. They are easier to solve."

Irina's novel had changed a great deal in the past few months. Also, it kind of didn't make sense. This had become increasingly vexing to Irina—her incapacity to make the parts of the book work together. Last month, before this malaise settled over her family, she'd asked Mother about it—how to make it all make sense. "I had these ideas!" she cried; it was late and Father was out in the studio and Mother seemed uncharacteristically happy and relaxed there in her office, with a glass of wine. "And now I don't like them anymore!"

"That's because your book grew up while you were writing it."

"But what do I *do*?" Irina asked, drawing out the *ooooo* in dramatic fashion.

"You fix it in the rewrites."

"How long does that take?"

"Longer than the writing part, usually," Mother said. "For me."

Irina whispered, "But I worked so hard."

"You needed to work hard, to get to the good ideas. The old ideas weren't bad, they just weren't what the book wanted to be. It's okay to write a rough draft. That's why they're called that."

Irina held her mother for a while before saying, sort of into her armpit, "I don't like it."

"If you're going to be a writer," Mother replied, "you'll learn. Because the thing is, all of the stories we tell ourselves are wrong. All of them."

She'd heard her mother say that before. It was a shtick. She said it on television and on the radio and in the newspaper and on the internet. But it was quite another thing for Irina to hear it spoken especially for her, ear pressed to her mother's shoulder, directly through the flesh, like it would have sounded when she was still in the womb, that bassy hum of truth.

And so now she was trying to finish, and to enjoy finishing, even though she knew it was all wrong. Aiden was still called Aiden; she'd sent him and Kimmifer through a portal they'd found via a mysterious device given to them by Kimmifer's uncle, which enabled them to explore each other's worlds. Kimmifer's father turned out to have gotten sick and died, which Irina mostly did because she didn't like the missing father plot anymore. What she wanted now was to reunify New York City—to restore Quayside to its rightful place on the same plane of physical reality as Brooklyn and the other boroughs. "Just imagine," Aiden said, holding her hands (because they did that recreationally now, and also they'd kissed quite a great deal, by leaning as far as they possibly could over her bustle), "all the things our boroughs can give to each other. We need the magic in Uncle Johnseph's Millibeans Device! And your people need to see that some of your ways are rooted in fear of the unknown!" The ending was almost done—they'd found Uncle Johnseph and discovered a flooded abandoned subway tunnel where there were gondolas marked *To Quayside*, evidence of some former attempt at unification. Irina was going to make them all hold hands and pass through the membrane, and, "If my calculations are correct," Uncle Johnseph said, "the boroughs will unify, and all citizens of New York will be able to see each other, now and forever!"

Irina knew it was all just a big mess. Stuff kind of changed in the middle, because she had wanted it to. Everybody's personality was different now. Uncle Johnseph was less like the Wizard of Oz and more like Franklin Roosevelt. And Kimmifer was younger—she wasn't anything like Samantha Geary anymore. Irina didn't need a fictional Samantha Geary, because she had found the real one.

So, why didn't she feel any sense of triumph? Why didn't the mystery seem solved?

Because, as her mother had told her, all the stories we tell ourselves are wrong. She'd known for a long time, and she felt powerfully now, that Sam was never Samantha Geary. Samantha Geary was gone— on to a new life somewhere. She probably didn't even know that's who she used to be. Her story had grown up, and Irina didn't need her kid version anymore. It was nice of Sam to play along, but now Irina didn't know how to ask her to stop. Sam was playing *for* Irina, not with her. It wasn't like they were putting on a play together. It was a puppet show for a baby to watch. It was for the old Irina.

The problem she was grappling with now, though, was this: the Irina who started writing this novel was the old one. The Irina who was trying to finish it was the new. Was such a collaboration even possible? Did new Irina even want to share a .doc with old Irina? The situation felt hopeless.

But she was not ready to admit defeat. She was going to finish, and she was going to celebrate! And her mother was going to come home and help her fix it.

Right now, though, she had to eat something: she had stayed awake far enough into tomorrow for her body to start demanding breakfast. She had begun to fantasize about cereal: a bowl of honey O's, with the whole milk Irina liked to stash in the back corner of the fridge, where a chill descended from the freezer to make it ice cold.

So she threw back the covers and then thought she heard, against the quiet of the night, motion in the house: Father's heavy tread, filthily socked, climbing the stairs. If it was him, he was moving with uncharacteristic attempted stealth. His progress was slow; the old wood creaked. When the footsteps reached the top, they paused. Irina sat, momentarily terrified, her toes barely touching the bedroom floor.

Then she heard Father's familiar panting breaths and understood that he was considering coming in to say good night. She wanted to call out to him, but she held her tongue.

But what if Father had come upstairs to see Sam? Why, after all, would Sam otherwise be staying here tonight? The car, she'd said when she returned; Father was high, he couldn't drive her to town, and she was just going to have to come back tomorrow anyway. But what if it was something else?

Irina did not want this. She wanted Sam for herself, and she wanted her mother back. Suddenly she was afraid. She willed her father to stop at her door and to go no farther. Please, she whispered, I don't want to hear you laughing down the hall. Please come to *me*.

But, in the end, he didn't do anything. He retreated back down the stairs. She heard him settle onto the sofa, in front of the wood-stove and Huck and Jim. She heard him begin to snore.

What was that all about?

....

Father was still snoring five minutes later, when Irina finally decided she'd waited long enough and crept down to the kitchen. She snapped on the dim stove-top light and in its glow prepared her cereal. Father's phone was sitting on the kitchen table, so she keyed it open and idly played a word game while she ate. When the cereal was gone, she washed and dried the bowl and spoon and put them away, and she picked up the phone and played the game for a few more minutes, waiting to be tired again.

It was not working. She was not tired. Instead, she was lonely. She closed the game app and opened up the phone app. Her mother was there, in the list of favorites, and her thumb hovered over the screen.

Mother, it's Irina, she would say when her mother sleepily answered. *Irina?*

Mother, I'm lonely. Come home. I need help with my book.

It's one in the morning.

I can't sleep.

I'll be home next week, honey, her mother would say, and Irina would be able to hear the exasperation in her voice, her wish that she could be left alone, just for a week.

I need you, Irina might say. And her mother might say . . .

What? How could this conversation end? With her mother getting in the car and coming home, days early and in the middle of the night, to make Irina a second breakfast and apologize for leaving in the first place? No. She would tell Irina she would have to wait. That she was a big girl now and would have to make do with her father until Wednesday. Irina would hang up feeling ashamed and immature.

So instead, impulsively, Irina brought her thumb down onto the unidentified number that she knew corresponded to the Famous Rachel and raised the phone to her ear.

She changed her mind immediately. Why was she doing this? What would she even say? But before she could pull the phone away from her ear, there was a click, and a woman's voice said, "I told you."

Irina didn't speak. In the background of the call, a fire engine siren sounded, cars honked. It was New York! New York was on the other end!

"Karl?" said the voice.

There was still time to hang up, but now she couldn't resist: "It's Irina."

Now Rachel was the silent one. What could she hear in the background of the call? Nothing. Maybe Father's snoring, if she was listening hard enough.

Then Rachel said, "Hi there. Is everything all right?"

That did it. Irina began to cry. "No, it's not!"

"Baby," Rachel said. "I know. I know."

"Everything's different. I don't know what real life is supposed to be anymore. And my novel is bad."

"How old are you?" Rachel asked after a moment.

"Twelve."

"You're writing a novel?" She didn't wait for an answer. "Honey, it doesn't have to be good. Not yet. Nothing's good when you're twelve."

Her voice was low and gentle. Irina heard ice clinking in a glass. The siren was gone now. Irina was trying not to sob, but the tears were coming anyway. She got up, crossed the room, wiped her face and nose with a paper towel.

"Does your father know you're calling me?" Rachel asked her, the words a little slurred.

"He's asleep."

"Don't tell him. Why don't you go wake up your mother and talk to her?"

"She's in New York."

"Hmm, that's right." Rachel drew breath. "Well. Maybe I'll see her, then." There was a long pause, more clinking of ice. Irina tore off an extra paper towel and sat down again. "Irina," she went on, "you and I have something in common. Our families are very strange. They don't follow the rules. People come and go and do things impulsively, and they hurt each other and themselves. The outside world doesn't understand. Do you get that?"

Irina thought of her friend's mother, the one who didn't want to let her ride on the subway alone. She said, "I guess."

"Life is very messy," Rachel said, "and sometimes it is lonely and painful, but sometimes it is exciting and beautiful. You're in a lonely part." She paused. "Your mother is a good person."

Hearing this from Famous Rachel gave Irina a strange feeling, half-pride, half-irritation: I don't need *you* to tell me that!

"I will tell you the truth, Irina: I didn't used to like your mother. But I was just jealous of her. I wish I could be as good at something as she is at writing. Sometimes I wish I'd had a child like you, too."

Irina now understood that Rachel was drunk. "Thank you," she said, quietly. The tears had stopped now. She was getting sleepy. She thought, You are dumb for not liking my mother right away. "I think I should go."

"I agree. Good night, Irina. I won't tell your mother you called."

Irina hadn't even thought of that. "Thank you."

"She'll be home soon. But it's okay to be alone. Don't forget that, whenever you're feeling lonely."

"I won't," Irina thought, and then thought: But really, I won't. That is good to know.

The call was over. Irina said goodbye, but Rachel was already gone: back to her loneliness and drinking and the pleasure of living in New York. Irina watched as her thumb led her to the phone's call log and deleted the call to Rachel. She put the phone to sleep and replaced it on the kitchen table. Turned out the lights and climbed the stairs to bed.

Another secret to keep from Mother and Father, she thought, closing her eyes against the black early morning. Soon there would be more. Pretty soon she would be made almost entirely of secrets. In her imagination, as sleep began to pull her down, Irina pictured each secret like it was a little translucent ball, like one of those scented bath globes you might find in some fancy person's bathroom, piled up in a little china dish on the tub's edge. In her dream (for it was a dream now), the camera pulled back to reveal how many secrets there were, and how small: red ones for her blood, pink for the muscles, cream for the skin and brown for the hair and blue for the eyes. Like atoms, they were, the secrets, and they made her what she was: a real girl, a real person, alive in the world, right now.

21

It had begun to snow in earnest. Louis could tell this one was the real thing—the temperature had dropped to below twenty degrees, the flakes were big and fuzzy edged, and the stuff didn't melt when it hit the windshield. Louis and Joe were staking out the supposed weed house, the place where Daniel lived, directly under a streetlight in Joe's enormous fucking car. Louis was shivering. Meanwhile the heat was rolling off Joe like he was a boiler in some basement—some midwestern torture basement, Louis imagined, with a clothesline for drying out all the flaps of human skin and a dirt floor all the leftovers were buried under. Every few minutes Joe turned the key to run the wipers, and the snow was swept away to reveal a party in progress—raggedy-looking people, arriving at the house in groups, every one of them glancing over their shoulder at the car where Louis and Joe were sitting.

"Big party," Louis said.

Joe only grunted in reply. He had been grunting often, more often than usual. Louis regarded this as ominous. Everything seemed ominous now that Joe's insane worldview had been validated, including the revelation that Joe had actually brought a change of clothes, as though he'd understood they would be spending time here, three nights so far, with another impending, some kind of sick foreplay to violent action. Louis was forced, yesterday morning, to wash his own unmentionables in the motel sink, roll them up in a towel to wick out the moisture, and put them back on still mostly wet.

That was a mistake. They were still wet, and he smelled no better than he had. By now Pam had probably called him and heard his phone ringing on the bedside table or wherever the hell he'd left it. Maybe she figured he'd taken up with somebody else. At this point he may have lost his job. But no—it had been only three nights. Louis could still perform damage control, if he could find a way out from under Joe.

For now, though, he was in, all the way. He was here for the big show, whatever the hell it was supposed to be.

Joe grunted, turned the key, ran the wipers, grunted. The kid, Daniel, was there, framed by the door of his house. Behind him, bright rooms were crowded with people, holding drinks, smoking smokes. Daniel was peering out at Louis and Joe.

Joe snickered. This was worse than the grunting. They watched as Daniel receded into the house. The door closed.

"Wanna go to a party," Joe said. He opened the driver's door and heaved himself out onto the street.

"All right," Louis said, mostly to himself, and followed. His boxer shorts unstuck and restuck themselves from and to his ass and balls. His socks squelched inside his frozen shoes. He had no idea what was going to happen inside that house, but at this point he'd take anything besides the Eldorado. Fuck: incandescent lighting? Heat? Beer? Bring it. Maybe Joe would have a heart attack or something? Louis almost didn't care that it was tantamount to breaking and entering.

He mentioned this to Joe on the way to the door. "They're gonna notice us, you know. They could call the cops."

Another chuckle. "Nobody's calling the cops. The weed's here."

"Huh," Louis said. He couldn't imagine how the kid could've been growing here—there was no evidence of it. For a second, though, he considered calling the cops himself. Borrowing a phone from somebody and just straight-up confessing. Throwing himself on the mercy of the court and all that. He was an accessory to murder, at worst—how long would they put him away for, really? Maybe he could just get time served and parole, for cooperating. Joe would probably die in jail and Louis's wife and kids would live long, happy lives.

Well, they would live, anyway. Happiness was likely to elude all of them regardless. Anyway, he knew he wasn't going to call the cops. He was a fucking coward, was the reason.

They didn't knock, of course—Joe flung open the screen door with ludicrously excessive force, and it slammed against the clapboards as though in a hurricane. They pushed through, into the party.

It was hot and loud. Everyone was stripped down to their under-shirts and the air was heavy with smoke from their cigarettes and joints. Louis remembered this kind of party with genuine fondness, though he didn't really like them at the time. They always gave him a headache, made him long for his own sofa, a little TV or a golf maga-zine. Now, though, he felt nostalgic. Why didn't he have any kind of social life these days? He and Pam could go out if they wanted— Janine was plenty old enough to look after the boy. Hell, they'd pay her, even. Years ago they used to fantasize about the day Janine turned thirteen and they could fly the coop every now and then. But thir-teen had come and gone, and neither of them had mentioned going on a date.

Joe bulldozed forward, through the crowd, creating a slipstream for Louis to follow in. A few people got jostled; Louis apologized on the big man's behalf. Heads were turning. So far nobody had chal-lenged them—the place was pretty full, surely everybody couldn't know everybody. They moved through a living room, a dining room; they moved down a hallway. Joe was alert, checking out every door and wall, poking his head into the bathroom, bedroom, linen closet. Louis didn't know what he expected to find. Some stash of drugs or cash? A sign that read WEED IN HERE? They ended up in the kitchen, the most crowded, loudest, hottest, and closest space in the house, and Joe's eyes narrowed. He peeled off, moved rudely around the edge of the room, examined the walls and floor.

Louis hung back, found himself in front of a beer keg. Again con-sidered bolting. Then imagined being caught, murdered, by Joe. Nah. For now, stay still. Your moment will come, you miserable pussy. He took a red Solo cup from a stack on the counter and pumped himself a nice full heady serving. The beer was warm and sweet.

"Hey there, friend."

Louis looked up, over the lip of his cup. It was the kid, Daniel, standing there. The tone was jovial. The gaze was serious. Louis's initial impression: prick.

"Don't believe I know you guys." He was peering over Louis's shoulder, presumably at where Joe was still rummaging around like a foraging ape.

Louis took a big swig of beer, said, "Yeah, we're here with Valerie."

"Don't know any Valerie, friend."

"Mike's girl?"

"Don't know Mike." He sure was interested in whatever Joe was up to. Louis turned to take a look. The big man had become absorbed in a floor-to-ceiling shelving unit covered with cans and jars. He moved some of these aside, peered behind them.

"Everybody knows a Mike."

"Look, this is my house, and my party, and I don't know you. So maybe you and your pal should leave."

"Yeah, well," Louis said, "whaddya gonna do, call the cops?" He took another swig of beer, half-emptying the cup, and looked Daniel right in the eye and mouthed the words *Call the cops.*

The kid stared, hard. Louis stared back, sending him mind bullets. *Please? Please call the cops?* "Look, friend," Daniel said, "don't fuck with me. What the fuck is your pal doing right now?"

Louis turned again. Joe had unscrewed the lid off a jar and was poking around in it with a meaty finger.

"I guess he wants some lentils?"

"Shit," said Daniel. "Did Barney have somebody send you fuckers? Because fuck Barney."

"I told you, man—Valerie." Wait, or was it Vanessa?

"Fuck!"

Joe had evidently hit pay dirt, because he was pulling something out of one of the jars. It was a key. He dropped the open jar onto the floor—Louis could barely make out the sound of breaking glass over the din—and bent over, as though to fit the key into a lock. Louis had the presence of mind to block Daniel, who was trying to get past him.

"Friend, I wouldn't." Though Louis wanted him to. Wanted somebody to roll the dice for him.

Joe tugged on the shelving unit, and the whole thing came away from the wall, smoothly, on hinges. A door. The other partygoers didn't seem to notice, or maybe they didn't care, or they already knew about the secret door. Daniel, on the other hand, was suddenly transformed into a writhing, flailing muscle of rage.

"Fucking move it!" he spat, and Louis was shouldered aside by a flurry of skinny, taut limbs. He stumbled backward, bumped into somebody. He felt somebody's beer splattering all over the back of his already filthy coat.

"Whoops!" Louis said. "Sorry!"

"No worries, chief!" came a voice, and Louis turned. He knew this guy—it was the old stoner from the guitar shop and from Denny's.

To Louis's surprise, the man blanched and dropped his cup of beer on the floor. For a second he was immobilized by the sight of Louis—Louis! The manager of Carpet Universe and World of Window Treatments! And then, in a kind of insectile spasm, the man turned around and ploughed through the kids behind him, as though hightailing it away from the devil incarnate.

Wait for me, Louis said to himself, but didn't move. Instead he took a deep breath and replenished his beer from the tap.

Some goth chick, moderately hot, was giving him the stink eye from the other side of the keg. "Hey," she said, "who are you again?"

Louis was starting to feel a little drunk. "Vanessa and Mike's friend," he replied, "again. Who are you?"

"This is my house."

"It's a lot of people's houses tonight, sounds like. Anyway, thanks for the party." He raised his cup in an unrequited toast, then peered over to see what was going on with the secret door. Joe, it seemed, had disappeared behind it, with Daniel in pursuit, because neither was anywhere to be seen.

And just like that, for the first time in many days—in many months, really—Louis felt pretty all right. He was warm and drowsy and a little bit drunk; Joe was out of sight. The goth chick was more than moderately hot, actually; she was clearly pissed at him, and that made her even hotter. He suddenly wished he could freeze time, just stand here drinking warm beer and arguing with her.

As though in response to this thought, the girl spun around and drilled into the crowd, as though in search of someone. Daniel, Louis figured, but she wasn't going to find him. She elbowed her way out into the hall: wrong direction. It was probably for the best.

And then the kitchen suddenly got kind of uncomfortable. Louis's presence appeared finally to be having some small effect. People were peering over at him, whispering to each other. They sensed that something was up. He elbowed his way to the can-and-jar rack, pardoning himself as he went, trying not to spill his beer. He tugged on the shelves, and nothing happened. Where was Joe looking, before? There—at waist height, a little latch behind the creamed corn, above a keyhole. He squeezed, the door popped open, and Louis slipped in, pulling it shut behind him.

A narrow staircase, leading down. Weird light—almost like it was full daylight down there, impossible daylight. "Hello?" he stage-whispered. He could hear heavy breathing. "Hey!" A few steps later, he peeked under the handrail.

Here's the tableau he saw: Daniel and Joe, standing before a massive, glowing, cellar-filling apparatus of ducts, pipes, fans, and translucent, glowing sheet plastic, behind which loomed hummocks of thick, hazy green. The two men faced each other, about six feet apart, about ten feet from the staircase. Both of them held handguns. Daniel appeared bewildered by the arrival of Louis. His armed hand swung from Joe to Louis to Joe to Louis.

"Whoa, fuck," Louis said, and this seemed to make up Daniel's mind. He pointed the weapon at Louis and steadied himself as if to shoot.

"Whoa, whoa!!" Louis shouted, because it was all happening too fast, and he didn't think there would actually be shooting, he figured threats, or beatings at worst, but it was clear now that that was stupid and of course there was going to be shooting. This all started with shooting. It was a thing that Joe liked to do. Louis's hands flew up, his Solo cup fell to the stairs, and beer splashed over his shoes, and he continued to shout whoa as Joe shot Daniel in the chest, and Daniel stumbled backward, striking and distending a wall of daylight-corrected plastic, and slumped to the floor. He still held his pistol but no longer seemed motivated to use it, or to do anything at all, for that matter.

Louis was still saying whoa when Joe took a few steps forward and shot Daniel again, this time in the head. What was left of Daniel tore through the plastic, and the smell of marijuana joined, then quickly overwhelmed, odors of gunfire and blood.

Louis felt like he was having a fucking coronary. His ears rang and he gulped air. He sat down now, four or five stairs from the top, and above him the hidden door rattled.

Joe was chuckling again. "Told ya so," he said.

"What?" It was hard to hear, what with his ears blown out.

"Told ya." Joe gestured with his gun at the weed operation. The room was stuffed with it, like a fungus.

"Yeah. Yeah."

"It's fuckin' mine."

"Yeah, sure." Louis stayed silent for a second. The rattling upstairs was growing more urgent, and people were talking right behind the door. They'd heard the shooting, no doubt. "Hey, Joe," Louis said, quietly, "what do you want to do now?"

Joe shrugged, secreting the gun in his jacket somewhere. "Dunno. Gotta be money down here." He glanced around for a second, then ripped through the nearest panel of plastic, revealing the plants, the grow lights, the irrigation system that was spraying a fine mist over the crop. Joe stepped in, started thrashing wildly around, knocking shit over, tearing shit down. It felt to Louis like a desecration, some-how even more so than the murder he had just witnessed. Jesus fuck: he just witnessed a murder. Sorry, *another* murder. With like a million fucking witnesses. His ears were ringing, and his jaw was clicking as he moved it back and forth.

"Hey, Joe—hey, buddy," he said, trying not to sound panicked. "Maybe we ought to try to get out of here, what do you say?" He was trying not to look at Daniel's body, which was lying in a spreading puddle of its blood. Louis was shivering, even though it was warm, too warm, really, and he was still wearing his coat. The rattling upstairs had ceased, but people were talking urgently at the door. The party seemed to have given way to intense discussion about what had been going on in the basement.

"What?" Joe said amid the sounds of crashing metal and splintering wood. Didn't he understand that the plants were the valuable thing here? If there was money, it was probably in a safe upstairs. And there was no time for that.

"We gotta go, man. You killed a guy. They heard it upstairs."

This got Joe's attention. He emerged from the wreckage, backlit by the artificial daylight. He looked like an avenging angel, a fat one, an evil one. Louis could sort of make out his facial expression, and it was one of annoyance.

"We killed a guy," Louis corrected, and Jesus fuck, it was actually true, he was again accessory to madness, and they were both going to go to jail very soon. "We gotta go."

The commotion upstairs finally seemed to register on Joe's consciousness. He grunted. Started glancing around the room for an alternate way out, but there wasn't one. It was back upstairs or nothing.

The secret door crashed open. It sounded exactly like a hundred cans and jars rattling in unison. Louis jumped to his feet.

"Pick it up," Joe said, pointing. He was pointing to Daniel—to his gun, which was still tangled up with his dead hand, a finger hooked through the trigger guard. The gun, the hand, the whole forearm, were lying in the pool of now-congealing, blackening blood.

Louis scrambled down the stairs, lunged for the gun, grabbed it. In the process he made brief contact with the dead hand and was nauseated. His foot unstuck from the blood puddle with a wet crackle, as though from a movie theater floor. The gun was bloody, and now his hand was bloody. The stuff was viscous, sticky, an awful syrup.

He turned to the stairs in time to watch the goth chick, lady of the house, gallop halfway down, stop, take it all in. She screamed with her whole body, really digging into it, like an opera singer.

"Lady, please," Louis started to say when she paused between breaths, but then Joe stepped up and shot her, too, right in the chest. The shot was loud, so fucking loud; it filled the space like a new, toxic kind of light. She sat down, hard. Her mouth seemed to be saying *ohgodohgodohgod* but Louis couldn't hear anything. A second tone had been added to the ringing in his ears; it was a chord now, persistent and bothersome, as if somewhere in his head a cat was standing on the keys of a church organ.

But he heard Joe when he said "C'mon," grumpily, and walked past Louis and onto the stairs. He stomped past the dying woman, who didn't even look up at him. She was just staring into space, blinking, with her hand pointlessly clutching the wound. Upstairs, Joe was greeted by screams. "Everybody shut the fuck up and back off!" he shouted, and in response a stampede of feet rumbled across the basement ceiling.

Louis briefly entertained the notion of putting the gun in his mouth and ending it all right now. But he couldn't imagine letting this bloody object anywhere near his face. Funny, that—he'd be dead in seconds, who gave a shit what was in his mouth? But no, it was already bad enough the stuff was on his hand and shoe—and now, somehow, on his coat and pants.

Upstairs, the screen door slammed. Bus was leaving. Louis made a run for it, taking the steps two at a time, but something tripped him up, and he went down, breaking his fall with his unarmed arm. It fucking hurt. He hazarded a glance back: the girl had gotten her gray-white hand wrapped around his ankle. Her sweater and other hand were soaked in blood now, and her eyes were crazed. She was licking pink foam off her lips and she coughed a Pepto-Bismol mist.

When she started to whine—to keen, really, a high, shrill sound that was getting louder by the second and that Louis was certain would drive him out of his mind if he had to endure it for even one second more—he came to his senses and kicked free, knocking her onto her side. His ankle was freed, but he felt a sudden, vertiginous lurch, as though the floor had collapsed beneath him, as though there had been an earthquake. It wasn't an earthquake. It was his soul. It was his soul leaving his body. Nevertheless he clambered to his feet and crab-walked to the still-open and unoccupied jar door.

Nobody up here had moved. They were pressed to the edges of the kitchen and gasped when Louis appeared. Some girl was crying. Louis had to look fucking horrifying, even aside from the gun in his hand.

There was the front door, wide open. Cold air rushed in. Across the street, the Caddy's headlights illuminated vertically blowing snow. Joe was trying to execute a K-turn in the street, but he was sliding all over the place. He nicked another parked car, backed fully into another one.

Fuck. Fuck! Louis said a little wordless prayer in his head to the god he didn't believe in until just now, when he kicked the dying girl over, and he dashed out the door. He nearly wiped out on the stoop, stumbling in the snow like a child. Joe had completed the turn and for a moment Louis was certain he was going to be left behind, here at the scene of the crime, literally with blood on his hands. And it really did appear that this was what Joe was trying to do—the tires spun freely in the snow, and the big man's face, lit by the dashboard, was intent only upon the road ahead. But before he could downshift, Louis reached the car, flung open the passenger door, and jumped in.

Joe gave him a sideways glare, and then the car was in motion. They gathered speed on the empty street.

"Fuckin' idiot," said Joe.

"What? Me?" Louis was still shaking. He couldn't catch his breath; the words were more like gasps.

"Fuckin' idiot."

Joe's breaths were low and fast and the air smelled like sweat. He turned left, then right, then left. They moved through downtown Broken River. The streets were quiet. The world didn't yet know about the thing they just did.

Louis said, "What are we doing, Joe?"

"Driving."

"Where?"

"House," Joe said.

"What house?"

"The house."

Louis didn't get it. They'd just left the house. Then Joe jerked right at the Route 94 sign and the car slid around untethered for a couple of seconds and Louis understood.

"We're going to the house?" he said.

"Yeah."

The silence deepened, lengthened, and they moved inexorably through the snow in pursuit of god knows what. Louis accepted for the first time that he might not get through this night alive. His mind was working all the angles, or trying to—the conceivable modes of escape, the possible endgames. Then, as the road emptied onto the highway and the Caddy gathered speed, he remembered that there was still a gun in his hand—stuck to his hand, in fact—and he slowly, nonchalantly slipped it into his inside jacket pocket. He had to wiggle it a little to detach it from his fingers. He zipped up the jacket and reached over his shoulder for the seat belt and pulled the belt tight and clicked it home. He closed his eyes and waited.

And here we are.

22

It has been happening for some time now: the Observer is coming to understand that it does not need to "be" in one place at any one time. It doesn't need, even, to be at one time at one time. It can be everywhere and anytime: and as the threads of cause and effect, real and imagined, that give the humans' lives meaning become increasingly intertwined (inextricably so, at this point), it *must* be. It cannot properly observe the humans—and the acts they perform and compel others to perform—without pulling apart, or perhaps expanding, or doubling and trebling, or creating an all-encompassing manifestation of itself.

The Observer's growing reach makes it feel more powerful. It can see and know all in this world (and what, it wonders, of other worlds? other consciousnesses? other phenomena, unfathomable to the humans, that it might study?), more than any single human can know about itself or its society. Indeed, it can know, if it wishes, more about humanity than all of humanity can ever hope to learn.

Yet the Observer feels less powerful than ever before: the immensity of its arena of observation throws into ever-sharper relief the fact of its incapacity to change the things it sees.

Unless—

Unless the humans' own awareness of their stories—that is, their understanding of their own lives as manifestations of, engines of, narrative lines—can be regarded as the domain of the Observer. In which case, the Observer is a part of them.

Or perhaps the Observer is something they have made: another god in the pantheon of invisible and powerful forces they have fashioned in their image.

And if it is so—if the humans have made the Observer—does this mean that it is beholden to them? Are their powers of self-determination, of ambition, of artful untruth and strategic misdirection, dependent upon the proximity and attention of the Observer? Or may the Observer go off on its own, test its skills and their limits, explore the totality of existence as any god might?

It doesn't know. Right now, it is certain only of its desire—and its responsibility—to see these narrative lines to their ragged ends. And of course these lines are only a few among a great many. New lines have already presented themselves, at least for most of these humans, but the humans are too absorbed in the imperatives of the moment to have yet perceived them. For unfortunate others, not many lines remain. For the equally unfortunate few, all lines have already come to an end. In truth, the Observer already knows all the outcomes, or something close to them; at this late hour, most alternate paths have been closed off.

In the wine bar in Brooklyn, New York, the woman named Rachel kneels on the floor over the woman named Eleanor. At first, she thought the woman had merely fainted, and her immediate response was annoyance. It took a lot out of her to open with an apology: to speak Eleanor's name, look her in the eye, and say *I'm sorry.*

She *is* sorry. It took her a while to get here, but here she is. She is sorry. Not just for hurting Eleanor, but for hurting herself. Acting like a child with Karl has made her feel old. Being in his company has made her feel lonely. Irina's call made her feel lonely, too. Watching Karl try to love the girl has caused her to remember her own father's failures at love. It is time to change her life.

"She's coming," Karl told her, as though his wife were an occupying force or weather event. Rachel now understands that their move was not, as he claimed, for the benefit of Eleanor's writing and his art, a bid for peace and quiet, but an escape from her, and punishment for his offenses against his marriage, of which she herself is one.

Rachel doesn't like Eleanor, despite what she told Irina. She was happy to believe Karl's insinuations (never actual lies that could be disproven) that she was cold and lifeless and uninterested in sex, and that their union was a sham, a convenience, a misguided effort to give their daughter some semblance of an orderly home. But Karl, of course, is both a bullshitter and his own principal bullshittee. His wife, she believed, deserved better than him. And better than Rachel, for that matter.

And when Rachel walked into the bar's back room and found the woman slouching and staggering, eyes underscored with purple-gray, Rachel could see that she'd been suffering. She had barely met Eleanor's eyes, barely begun to speak, before something seemed to set the woman's body into twisting motion; it began to fall, glitching like a scrambled TV signal. Eleanor half-collapsed, and her eyes rolled back in her head, and all solidity abandoned her. She slid down the wood-paneled wall, knocked over a stack of folding chairs, and tumbled with them to the floor.

A body hitting the floor in a crowded bar does not go unnoticed. All conversation stopped, all heads turned. For shit's sake, lady, Rachel thought, get hold of yourself. And then she thought better of it when she crouched beside Eleanor's prone, unmoving form and saw the whites of her eyes and the nightmare-twitching of her hands, and smelled urine.

"Eleanor," she says now, gently smacking her clammy cheek. "Eleanor!"

The Observer takes note of this behavior with interest. This woman, Rachel, rival to Eleanor, competitor for her husband's attention, has shifted now to the role of helper, of nurse, of friend. Rachel takes Eleanor's hand in hers, strokes her pallid face. The eyes focus with excruciating slowness upon her unlikely rescuer. The eyelids flutter. Something like a belch emerges from the throat. Rachel moves a strand of hair from Eleanor's eyes.

"Can you hear me? Eleanor?"

Is this, could this be, a form of love? Can the enemy in need become, suddenly, a friend? Or is Rachel's compassion merely an expression of projected selfishness, what she wishes Eleanor might feel were it Rachel herself doubling over in agony, folding to the ground, falling unconscious?

The woman can't speak, but she seems to understand. A waiter arrives at Rachel's shoulder, says, "What happened, did the chair break?" and Rachel says, "No, no, she passed out or something." This appears to alarm the waiter. He pulls out a phone and calls for an ambulance. People have resumed talking, seeing that this event is under the control of others, has nothing to do with them; but it is clear from the tone of their voices that their evening of levity and inebriation is ruined.

Eleanor's body is lying at a strange angle, one that a healthy human in repose would never assume. Her legs are folded up half-underneath her; one arm is flung out over her head, as though in an effort to catch something; the other arm clutches at her midriff. She seems somewhat more alert now, panicked, and little shocks travel across her face, dispatches from the malfunctioning machinery. Rachel says, "Can you move?"

If Eleanor understands the question, she doesn't reply. But the Observer notes that her hand squeezes Rachel's.

"Hold on," Rachel says, and pushes the chair out of the way and rearranges Eleanor's body—the legs out straight, the wayward arm down at her side. Rachel balls up her scarf and places it under Eleanor's head. Eleanor has no visible reaction. Her mouth and eyelids are twitching again; the eyes reel. The waiter is still standing there, staring in evident terror, phone still in his hand.

"Why don't you go find a blanket," Rachel tells him.

The man looks confused for a moment, then snaps to and hurries away.

That's the last Rachel will see of him. She holds Eleanor's hand and waits. The Observer waits with them. Whatever just happened has taken the air out of the room; people have gathered their things and are edging awkwardly past this strange tableau, one woman on her knees, holding another's hand.

Over the next twenty minutes—as the two paramedics arrive, entering the bar with disturbing nonchalance, like they came here for after-work drinks and just happened to find a woman lying on the floor; as they load Eleanor, roughly, onto a stretcher and into the ambulance; as they try to prevent Rachel from riding along until she tells them, with an inspired fierceness that surprises all three of them, that Eleanor is her wife and she will not be treated this way; as they ride to the hospital, sluicing through red lights with a vertiginous, dreamlike frictionlessness—Rachel begins a series of thoughts that she will later come to regard as transformative, the first being how wonderful it is, how selfless, that she is doing this thing, cleaving herself to the woman she has wronged in her moment of crisis, and how pleasurable it will be in the days to come, recalling what a mensch she was on this cold and miserable night on the cusp of the winter of 2017. The second thought, which comes hot on the heels of the first one, is that wow, is she ever a narcissistic whore.

There are more thoughts along these lines: about the nature of her cruel and unfeeling father, her weak-willed mother, their wealth and privilege, her own failings as their daughter and as an adult. Indeed, it takes almost no time at all, the complete unraveling of the illusions out of which Rachel has assembled her life. Watching it happen—watching this sudden shattering of barriers, opening of doors, mingling of previously confined and sequestered truths—the Observer is struck by how liberating it is for the humans to accept blame for their own misfortunes, to forgive those who have hurt them. They are capable of such anger, such violent fury, such resentment! And yet, it can all be dispelled in an instant. Rachel, as the Observer watches, is being rewarded with a feeling of bodily lightness and a surprising visual clarity, the details of the world taking on an almost surreal specificity as they assert themselves, for the first time, as entities without any relationship to her at all. Not only is Rachel no longer the center of the universe; she isn't even the center of her own reality. Rachel is an object in the world dedicated to its own gratification and the reciprocal gratification of a small number of other, equally unimportant objects. It is as though she sees herself from outside, from above and behind, as in a near-death story; she is both observed and observer. It is not necessary to be the way I've been, she thinks, as the nurses and doctors swarm and confer, as they ask her questions she hasn't the slightest idea how to answer. I can be different.

Rachel is standing in the emergency room, and Karl's wife is being rolled into a slot and attached to machines. The light is bright and dirty and the air smells like bandages and truck exhaust. She takes a breath, approaches a doctor. Touches her arm. Says, That's my friend. What can I do to help?

....

Meanwhile, in the kitchen of the house in Broken River, the young woman called Sam (and what, the Observer wonders, might have happened had she gone by some other name? Would the girl, Irina, still have chosen to believe she was the adult incarnation of the lost child Samantha? What if the man, Karl, had not found her appealing, had not held out some faint hope of sexual congress with her? Would he have declined to engage her services as a babysitter? What if she had stayed in Buffalo with her mentally ill mother? What if she had held more tightly to the hand she found in the pile of coats? The narrative lines that radiate from these plausible events and choices are distantly visible to the Observer but, upon closer examination, bifurcate, sprout tributaries, diffuse into a cloud of possibility too complicated even for the Observer to comprehend. No, Sam's present story is its focus, and she has reached a bottleneck: there is suffering she must now endure in order to move forward. That suffering has just now begun) closes her phone and sets it down on the kitchen table, then lays her two hands on either side and wills them to stop shaking. Nothing that she has just been told makes any sense. (But it does, the Observer thinks: everything that has ever happened, and everything yet to happen, makes sense.) The voice on the phone was someone's, some girl's. Janet, she thinks is the name? An occasional boarder at Yetta's, a friend, a hanger-on. Sam remembers her, sort of. On the phone just now, she was screaming and crying, and their conversation was interrupted several times, but the gist of it was that something has happened, some men came to the house, they crashed a party Yetta and Daniel were throwing, and they found the weed door and went down there, they killed Daniel and Yetta. Sam, the girl said, where the fuck are you, it was a big guy and a little guy, they took off down the street in an old car, and lock the door, Sam, because they're out there.

Sam is sitting very still now. She's processing the information. A big guy and a little guy came to the party. They shot her brother and they shot Yetta, both of whom are now dead.

An old car, she thinks. A Cadillac. A light-blue Cadillac.

Why does she know this? An immaculately preserved powder-blue Cadillac. She can see it in her mind's eye, idling in the dark somewhere, with snow falling on it. She can see it parked across the street from the old theater in the bright daylight, two men emerging from it and onto the dirty sidewalk, the big one in a windbreaker a little too small for him, the little one in a ski parka and a pair of acid-washed jeans. Passing it on the road out to the trailer park, in the shotgun seat of Uncle Bobby's car, she can hear him saying, "Look at that rig, it's right out of a time capsule, just look at it."

Sam has seen the men at Denny's. She served them. They were there, watching Daniel. Of course it's them. The big one gazed intently at her. Not the way other men do. Not with longing.

She saw the Cadillac when she was exiting Karl and Irina's driveway in Karl's Volvo. She saw the Cadillac pulling away from the shoulder of Route 94 at the bottom of the hill, as though it had been sitting there, watching and waiting.

She saw the man in the ski parka while she hid in the woods with Irina. She watched him climb onto the porch and knock on the door that Sam now must suppress an impulse to turn and stare at.

She doesn't entirely understand what is happening. She only knows that Daniel is dead, that he has been murdered, how will she ever tell her mother? She doesn't know what it has to do with her—is it the weed? that Daniel was growing, that she was dealing?—but it hardly matters. She fears that they are coming here. They have, after all, been here before.

From the outside, to the Observer, Sam merely appears, hunched over the table with her hands palms-down on the table, to be deep in thought, as though trying to solve a difficult problem. Her expression is one not of grief or shock but of concentration. But the Observer knows that she is about to act. Her narrative line is clear now. The next half hour she will later remember as a kind of infinitude, a sealed but borderless chamber in her life. At times, looking back, she'll believe her brain must have shut down, gone into cold storage, for all she can recall. At other times she'll remember it as a box of memories—her life up until then not flashing before her eyes, like a film flickering by at high speed, but rather a whirling storm of fragments, spinning all around her, revealing themselves only in brief, static images, bursts of speech. Rightly or not, these minutes will serve as a gravity well of her past and future life—a collapsed star of memory, a black hole, all lines bending toward it. (Yes, the Observer tells itself, yes.)

The man named Karl is approaching now, around the side of the house. He's holding an empty coffee mug and is about to step onto the porch. He does it—he climbs the porch steps, stamps snow off his boots, comes in the door. The girl Sam starts, stands up fast, and the chair clatters to the floor behind her. "Karl," she says. "Get Irina. Turn out the lights. Go to the studio."

"What?" he says. He seems dazed, puzzled. The Observer, and Sam as well, know that this is because he has been smoking to excess, out in the studio. To him, events are unfolding slowly, mysteriously, disconnected from one another and from their causes. The redness of his eyes, the dilation of his pupils, are driving Sam to irrational anger.

"Take Irina to the studio," she says in a near shout, "and turn out the lights!"

A small smile appears on his face. "Hey . . . ," he says. "What's going on?"

"Karl!" Sam screams now. "These guys killed my brother! They are coming here!"

He looks down into his coffee mug, as though an explanation might be hidden there. He says, "Wait. Wait."

"Fuck," Sam says, then she runs up the stairs two at a time.

Irina is sitting cross-legged on her bed, surrounded by books and papers, holding her guitar. She says to Sam, "Did you just yell at Father?"

"Buddy, you have to come with us now. We're going out to your dad's studio."

Her mouth is a perfect O. She blinks. "Why?"

"Some people are coming, I think. Bad people. It'll be fine, we just have to go out there and . . . lay low."

There is a moment of silence, which, in its new incarnation as an entity of nearly limitless knowledge, the Observer finds shockingly long. The future of these people is clearer now than ever. Everything that will happen in the next thirty minutes is now almost certain to happen, regardless of how long any of the humans spends contemplating his or her potential actions. Lay down your guitar, Irina, and follow.

Irina is paralyzed by doubt. She doubts the reality of this moment, and her trust in Sam, and her faith that there is even a correct choice to be made. For a surprising instant, the Observer actually thinks it might be mistaken: Irina might not go with Sam, and the narrative lines might tremble, flex, and shatter. But then, at last, Irina lays the guitar down before her and scrambles off the bed.

Downstairs, Karl has barely moved. The coffee mug is on the table now. He stares at them, confused. He says, "Okay, what?"

"Your studio," Sam says. "Come on."

And like that, he believes. He shakes himself, like an animal coming up from sleep, and says, "Okay, then." He digs in his pocket for the keys, holds them out. "I'm going to call the cops. Take her."

"Father?" Irina says quietly.

Sam leads her across the kitchen, takes the keys from Karl as he draws his phone from his pocket. The three hurry to the door and set off running through yesterday's snow. It has begun to snow again, and the air has the hushed, protected quality that implies much more to come. Then, "Wait," Karl says suddenly. He points behind them, toward the porch. "Footprints."

The three of them look at each other. Then Irina says "This way" and grabs Sam's hand. She leads her back, past the steps, then circles them around the house the other way, clockwise, keeping them close to the shrub line. Their trail disappears in the shadows of the bushes—there is not much moon behind the storm, and the only light is the inside light from the living room.

"Good thinking," says Sam.

"I always knew this would happen," Irina says, with no evident fear in her voice.

The Observer feels now, more than sees, a convergence of thoughts in the minds of Irina and Sam; it is true that Irina has renewed her recently dismissed fantasies of involvement with the crimes of the past; her dalliance with CyberSleuths, which not so long ago seemed childish, now seems preordained, consequential, and she believes that her doom is sealed. And as for Sam: she has never imagined herself as old and content, surrounded by loved ones, in some comfortable and uneventful future life. She has always felt hunted. By whom, or what, she has never understood, but tonight it seems right that these men are hunting her. Crazy murderers. They were always going to come for her.

The Observer recognizes that both young women are wrong but cannot see precisely how. It cannot project that far into the future.

Karl is muttering into his phone now, talking to the police. "Tell them it's the guys from the killings on Gauss Lane," Sam says. Irina has led them far into the trees, evidently intending to double back from behind the studio. She whispers, "Sam? Is your brother . . . did they hurt your brother?"

"Yes," Sam says.

"It's not your fault," Irina tells her, with absolute seriousness.

Sam gathers her closer, and the girl throws her arms around her waist. They walk in tandem, awkwardly, moving along the studio wall. Karl is repeating the address into his phone. He seems to be having trouble making himself understood. "No," he says, "after the entrance to the state forest. Before the church with the reader board." The snow is blowing gently into their faces.

And then they're at the studio door. Lights are blazing through the windows above, but no headlights shine from the drive. No sound. As though channeling the Observer's thoughts, Sam is suddenly confident that she is completely, embarrassingly wrong. The men aren't coming here. The killings have nothing to do with her, or with Karl and Irina, or with this house, or with the murders of the past. She wants to tell them, Wait, stop, it's a false alarm. There's nothing to fear.

Karl unlocks the door, slips in. Darkness arrives with a snap.

Inside, it is hot and close and muggy with marijuana smoke. Sam hears the click of the lock behind them, and then Karl's phone illuminates the floor. "Other side of the forge." He leads them there, and they wedge themselves into the corner, between the forge and the wall, and sit cross-legged in a row, with Irina in the middle.

Karl whispers, "The call you got. It said they're coming here?"

"Not exactly."

He's poking at the phone. His head is a black, furry ball. Finally the little rectangle of light disappears. The windows along the ceiling glow faintly with the light from the house; Sam feels a hand on her arm, Irina's, and the hand travels down and interlocks its fingers with hers. The Observer occupies the corner with them, impatient for events to unfold. It wonders if it will be right; or, rather, it wonders how right it will be.

"The police will be here soon," Sam says. "Then we can go back inside."

"Okay," Irina whispers back. "Sam."

"Yeah?"

"It's not your fault," she says again. But this time she adds, "It's my fault. I told Jasn and the art teacher about the house and the murders and everything."

"Who?"

"I told them about how your parents died. Or who I thought was your parents. It's those men that killed them, isn't it."

"Irina—"

"It's them," Irina says. "I'm sorry. They found out." There are tears in her voice.

"Shsh."

"Sam," she says, very quietly now. "I put your picture on the internet. I'm sorry. I told those people, and I put your picture on the internet. Saying you were Samantha."

Sam says, "My . . . you have my picture?"

"I took it outside Dairy Queen. I put it on a messageboard. About crimes. I said you were her."

"Jesus," Sam whispers involuntarily, and Irina begins to cry. So Sam holds her tighter, says, "It's not your fault, either. Bad things don't need reasons to happen."

A hand brushes Sam's shoulder; it's Karl's. She almost forgot he was here. He was putting his arm around his daughter and then, almost as an afterthought, has extended it to Sam as well. Sam leans into it; she can feel the nearness of Karl's head to hers, with Irina's soft hair underneath. The three of them sit there, listening to each other breathe.

They wait. Minutes tick by, or hours. (The Observer is aware that, for these humans, time has slowed to an excruciating degree, and it experiences a moment of irritation at the pettiness of their impatience. They have not, after all, floated for a decade inside an abandoned house. But then it remembers that they fear the imminent arrival of death, and it chastens itself for this lapse in compassion.) Sam is restless; she is on the verge of apologizing for scaring them and for putting them through this. And then, faintly, the sound of footsteps striking wood—specifically, the wooden front porch of the house— drifts through the night and into the dark studio.

"Did you hear that?" Irina whispers.

"It must be the police," Karl croaks.

But they don't move. Irina's hand grips Sam's tighter. Karl leans in harder. Their heads bump together. His breathing is audible in the room, deep and resonant and hoarse.

The time has come for the Observer to leave its charges here, in the dark studio that is gradually growing colder, and return to the place of its origins. It is time to go back to the house. It gathers itself, contracting, identifying its now-disparate and diffuse parts and pulling them in close. It tries to remember what it was like to move slowly, to confine itself to rooms, to see only one thing at a time, to be blind to the future. It tries to remember what it was like to be more human.

Only an instant passes in human time, but the process feels laborious to the Observer. To limit itself is no longer in its nature. When it has shrunk to a point, the Observer makes its way through the crack between the doorframe and door; drifts through the falling snow to the kitchen wall; flits into a tunnel in the cedar shakes made years before by a carpenter bee; and enters the kitchen through the screwhole of an electrical-outlet faceplate. (The Observer remembers, now, the contractor's workman who dropped the missing screw and watched it roll into a crack between two floorboards. "Fuck it," the man said, and left the hole empty.) Soon it is hovering, gently bobbing in the kitchen as it did for much of a decade, enduring the interminable fractions of a second it takes for the men on the porch to push open the door. (The door isn't even latched. The people left in haste and didn't pull it closed all the way. If all the humans disappeared right now—and for a moment the Observer wishes they all would, so that it could enjoy, as it once did, the complexity of unpeopled silence—the wind would soon blow the door open, and leaves and rain would coat the kitchen floor.)

At last the door flies open, and the men enter, the big one and the small one, each with a gun drawn. So primitive, these devices made for killing at a distance; the Observer doesn't understand why the humans have not designed more efficient and precise tools for this simple task. Their technology is certainly capable enough. Perhaps they enjoy the sensation of an explosion in the hand, the noise and smoke. Perhaps they don't really want to kill and wish to introduce an element of uncertainty into the process.

In any event, the Observer is bored now as the two men creep through the house, seeking the inhabitants who are not there. It draws what would be a breath if breathing were something it needed to do and explodes itself back into its full scope and articulation; it leaves the house now and is instantly with its people in the studio, as they await the conclusions of their narratives.

The girl named Sam has admitted to herself, at last, that it is not the police who have arrived at the house; they would be calling out now if these people were the police. They would shout Karl's name and tell him it was safe to emerge from hiding. So it must be them—the men. All three of them know it because none of them speaks or moves. They wait a long time for the next thing to happen. It feels to Sam like an hour, though it can't be more than five minutes—how long does it take two men to determine that a house is empty? Or is it money they're looking for now? None of it makes any sense. If it is all true, if Daniel is dead, if these men kill Sam as well, it will confirm their mother's every misapprehension about the world. Everything is exquisitely interconnected, malevolent, and dangerous. They are, in fact, out to get you.

Her thoughts are interrupted by the sound of a door slamming shut. Again, footsteps on the porch, down the stairs. Low voices. Then the voices quiet, and there is silence. But a fuller silence, a more expectant one. Irina shivers, and Karl pulls her closer. Sam leans into them both. Minutes pass, and then the thudding of boots reaches them from outside the studio door. Somebody jiggles the knob, then pounds, violently. "Hey!" a man shouts. Irina lets out the tiniest peep, barely audible even to Sam.

The men are talking. They walk around the exterior of the studio, looking for a way in. Will they notice the footprints? It was dark where Irina led them, and the snow has continued to fall. Perhaps it filled their prints. The men don't hesitate as they circle the studio, and they don't speak. Sam can hear their shoes crunching in the snow, their coats dragging along the shrubs. At one moment, the men are mere inches from where the three of them are huddled, separated only by the wall. But the men continue their circumnavigation, confer again at the door.

And then, incredibly, they seem to give up. Their voices recede. Sam hears the words "in the woods," "fuckin' freeze to death."

They have decided to leave. They're leaving.

(Wait, says the Observer.)

Karl's phone rings.

It is approximately the loudest noise Sam has ever heard—a grating electric chirp like a motel alarm clock, accompanied by the sudden illumination of their corner as the screen switches itself on. Before Karl can silence it, it rings again. Then it stops. Karl has apparently hit ANSWER. He's holding the phone in his lap and a woman's voice is coming out of it, a tiny beacon from the world of safety and freedom, small but distinct. "Karl?" it says, with some urgency. "Karl?" A long pause. "Are you there? Karl, please pick up."

Surely the men outside can hear. What in the hell is he doing?

"Karl! Please!" the woman says, and then his thumb occludes the display and the call is ended. The screen goes black.

"I'm so sorry," he says, and a moment later the pounding on the door resumes, the sound of pure, unfettered rage. It sounds like they have found a heavy branch and they are bringing it down over and over on the knob.

"Open!" a man is bellowing, as though this will work, "open it!," followed by more pounding. It's a heavy door—Sam noticed this coming in—but if they want it to open, it will be opened.

(The Observer is aware that a nexus of narrative possibility, the last in this skein of cause and effect, is now approaching: choices that can be made, outcomes that will result. As the seconds go by, paths pass in and out of existence; probabilities shift from one path to another. If these were visual phenomena, they might register as flickers, jumps, as in the completion of a high-voltage electrical circuit or, slowed a thousandfold, the movement of floodwater through a landscape that both guides the water's movement and is altered by its force. If it were aural, this dynamism might manifest as crackles that give way to a rumble or hum, like the cascading action of an earthquake, or the starting of an engine, or the illusion, to the human ear, of repeated unpitched pulses resolving into a musical note.

But,) "Stay here," Karl says in a normal, disconcertingly calm speaking voice, and he gets up from the floor.

"Daddy!" Irina stage-whispers. Sam has never heard her utter this word.

"Stay!" is the stern response. Sam feels him stepping over them; he moves a few feet away, to where Sam thinks she remembers a work table. Irina throws both arms around her, squeezes her tightly. The pounding continues, then gives way to muttered conversation.

What is Karl doing? She hears metal scrape against wood. Something hard and heavy falls to the floor. His faint shadow, cast by light through the high windows, crosses the room, an indeterminate distance away.

Even Sam screams when the shooting starts. At first she thinks they're firing through the walls, trying to kill them that way. Then she realizes that they're shooting the lock. Between shots, the men are shouting at each other. Sam envelops Irina with her body; she cannot get her arms far enough around the girl.

There is one more shot, and then all the noise stops. Sam hazards a peek around the corner of the forge.

The door has fallen open: a two-inch slice of dim light extends from ceiling to floor. A coatsleeve is visible through it, two bare hands clutching something. A gun.

Sam grips Irina tighter, willing her to silence. There's a click, and the lights come on. Sam closes her eyes. The door creaks, three slow footsteps sound, and a man's voice says, "Where the fuck—"

Then there's a gunshot, but it is so huge in the room, it seems to come from everywhere at once. Sam is deafened; then the silence gives way to a high, pure sine wave, a test tone. Through it she can she hear something soft and heavy hitting the floor, and a metallic clatter against the concrete. Sam opens her eyes. She can see past the corner of the forge to where a massive human arm the size of an entire child is flung out on the cement, and a few feet beyond it, a pistol. Beyond that is the work table, and Karl is visible behind it, his dark eyes, frightened and determined and bloodshot, peeking over the top.

Through the ringing in her ears, Sam hears Irina's quiet weeping. She is trying to be quiet, but she just can't. Against the concrete sounds a footstep, and then another. "Hey," says a man's voice she thinks she recognizes, gentler this time. She can't see him. But she can still see Karl behind the table, and she realizes, with growing horror, that he is about to do something.

....

It is now clear to the Observer that one narrative line, that of the man Karl, is about to come to an end. It wonders when, exactly, this outcome—the one that is imminent—became inevitable: was it when he read his wife's books, here in the studio, and in so doing rekindled, or perhaps kindled for the first time, feelings of familial responsibility? Or was it when he bought the bag of herbal intoxicants from the girl Sam, which have now aroused, in his racing mind, a heightened sense of paranoia and an inflated confidence in his own physical prowess? Or was it when he hired Sam as Irina's babysitter? Or was the die cast earlier than all that: when Karl selected this house as the future site of his marriage and career rehabilitation, or when he chose the path of faithlessness in his union with Eleanor, or when he compelled her to enjoy sexual intercourse with him without the use of a birth control apparatus, or when he decided to attend art school, or when he fell in, at the age of seventeen, with the adult woman of twenty-five who would teach him how to have sex, or when he learned to masturbate, at the age of thirteen, or when he drew his first picture, at the age of one, with a crayon on a piece of butcher paper at the table in his parents' apartment?

Perhaps, in the future, these are questions that, in other circumstances involving other human beings, the Observer will be able to answer. For now, though, it cannot; for now it can only watch the man Karl prepare to blunder toward the completion of his story. He is trembling now, crouched behind his work table, clutching a glass-bladed knife in his hand; he draws silent breaths and his jaw twitches as his pupils constrict against the sudden light, and he thinks:

Because of course this was always what you were going to do. Because one minute you're gooned on grass and reading your wife's unfinished novel you scammed from her backup drive; and the next you're crouched in the dark with the weapon you forged, gripped in your cold hand; and the cuts healing on your back are itching like mad, pushing you forward; and you have no fucking idea what is going on except that there are ene-mies and they have found you and shots have been fired. Because you're a shitty father and because you had a shitty father. Because being a sculptor is, in retrospect, fucking stupid. Because you didn't defend yourself when you were six and the neighbor twins stole your bike. Because you didn't defend yourself when you were eight and Pete Nagel pissed on you on the school bus. Because you didn't defend yourself when you were eleven and Todd Clark pushed you into the lockers and told you that you were forbid-den from using the first-floor boys' room ever again, and you never used the first-floor boys' room ever again. Because you tried to defend yourself when you were twelve and Kevin Drangle pushed you over and emptied your backpack into the mud and you didn't get in even a single punch be-cause he pushed you back down laughing and said if you got up he'd shoot you with a bow and arrow through your bedroom window. Because you didn't defend Heather Giselson when you were both fifteen and Nathan Johnson spat on her, and though she said that wasn't the reason when she dumped you a week later, of course it was the fucking reason. Because you didn't defend your mother when you were twenty and your father called her that crazy bitch at a celebratory dinner for his third wife who had just gotten a PhD in semantics and everybody laughed as though getting a fucking PhD in semantics was less crazy than anything your mother ever did in her life. Because you thought your wife was a hack until the other day. Because you are a fucking pussy, and your moment has come. Because you are an animal, and before you stands an animal, and you were both brought here to kill. That is why you stand up, joints cracking, and scream, and lunge forward screaming with the knife out in front of you like a blazing torch to light the way toward life or death, and that is why the guy takes one step back, then another, his face inhuman with what you belatedly recognize as terror, and you manage to think that maybe none of this had to happen as you collide with him, sink the knife in until it strikes bone, then feel the hot bite of metal on your scalp and the world explodes and the hand of god comes from out of nowhere to stop you in your tracks and grip you in its fingers made of sky and lay you gently, firmly, on the ground where you belong.

....

It is baffling to the Observer, the things they do, the patterns they create that they inhabit and re-create again and again. They find one another so irresistible, even when enmity is the form their affinity takes. Over and over they come together, and if they fail to derive pleasure from these encounters, they find satisfaction in suffering. They are more attached, perhaps, to their suffering than to their pleasure.

This stands in direct contradiction to their stated goals, which are those of comity, happiness, calm. But it is pain that gives their lives meaning.

Pain is not something the Observer understands. It has not experienced corporeality, but it sees that conceptual disharmony can lead, eventually, to physical harm and deformation. The body reacts to mental disturbance—it shapes itself according to the mind's instructions. And of course the humans can inflict bodily harm upon one another, sometimes reluctantly or even accidentally, sometimes with great eagerness. A penchant for inflicting bodily harm invites harm done to the self—and thus the hunger for pain is satisfied.

Four of them are here, in this room: the three who concealed themselves, locked themselves away and out of sight, and the one who pursued them. The man called Joe is dead. He was shot by the one called Louis, who has fled through the open door, clutching his arm where the knife went in, and disappeared into the cold night. Joe's body is like a sleeping infant's blown up to gargantuan proportions. His left hand is trapped beneath the ruined head from which blood is still emerging, and his gun lies on the cement, inches from his splayed right arm.

The man named Karl is also dead, killed in much the same way as Joe, and his body, too, lies facedown on the cement, emptying itself of blood.

The young woman Sam is doubled over with grief, or nausea, or both, and her eyes are squeezed shut. The Observer does not wish to intrude upon her thoughts now. Better simply to watch. Sam clutches herself, emits a high, quiet sound, takes in breath in great, ragged gasps. But then she straightens; her arms fall to her sides, her eyes open. An expression of resolve hardens on her face. She crouches beside the girl, Irina, who has made herself small on the floor in much the manner of the child who, more than a decade ago, survived the killings Joe performed. Sam tells the girl not to look, to keep her hand, both hands, over her eyes, and Irina agrees with a nod. The blood from Joe's body is encroaching into their shared space behind the forge; it is time to move. Sam pulls Irina to her feet, adds her hand to the mask of Irina's own, and guides the girl around the bodies, out the door, and into the falling snow.

Now the Observer drifts out of the room and into the woods, where the man Louis is running blindly, tripping over roots and fallen branches, whimpering, trying to suppress, with his inadequate fingers, the hemorrhaging of blood from his wounded arm. His teeth chatter; his body shakes. He is holding the knife, dark with his own blood, which he had the presence of mind to remove from the crime scene. He appears both to be in shock and extremely cold. The heavy snow is already filling his footprints. The Observer rises above the trees, charting Louis's likely trajectory, teasing out the strongest (and growing ever stronger) vector of probability: he will cross that creek, dropping the knife into it on the way. He will break into that house on the other side of the rise and bind his wound with rags; he will walk along the road, ducking into the trees whenever a car passes, until he reaches the closed gas station, to which he will gain access through a weak panel in the rotting garage door. There, he will sleep for a few furtive hours, and in the morning he will manage to hitchhike to the bus station with a drunk woman in flight from the abusive husband she will return to days later. The woman won't think to alert police to the passage through her life of a shivering man bleeding through a bundle of rags. Such events are not remarkable, or even memorable, in her world. She won't ever hear of the killings. She will die of a heart attack before long. The gas station owner, similarly, will discover the hole in his garage door, attribute it to junkies or kids, repair it with a square of plywood, and forget all about it. He'll learn of the killings in the house over the rise but won't connect them with his break-in, or feel much concern about them at all. Some people get themselves killed. That's their own business.

The Observer moves down the hill, to where the police officers have arrived, one man and one woman. They are young and uncertain. They stand beside the empty powder-blue car, which has indeed been parked at the bottom of the drive, blocking it, for some time. Nearly an inch of snow has fallen upon it; the hood, still radiating heat, remains clear, but not for long. The officers have been told to wait for reinforcements. They are waiting for reinforcements. It doesn't matter anymore, though their inaction may eventually have some consequences, ones the Observer cannot predict. Internal punishments inside the police organization. Feelings of guilt—pointless ones, because there is nothing they could have done upon arriving to prevent the two deaths.

The Observer no longer cares. It feels the lightness of not having to pay attention to events and people that no longer interest it. The earth recedes beneath it as it rises up into the snowstorm, in much the way that the events inside the studio, which just moments ago aroused such intense interest, have now receded from its attention. The Observer returns to the house where the young man and woman were shot in the cellar. The house is surrounded by police cars, lights flashing. Police surround, mark, and photograph the bodies downstairs, in the room filled with artificial light and living vegetation. Other police, upstairs, interrogate the bereaved partygoers, writing down their statements in notebooks. To the humans, these deaths represent instances of chaos that must be investigated, explained, understood. The Observer has no such obligation now. It turns now to the city to the south. The wife of Karl, the woman named Eleanor, is here, lying in a quiet white room, in a building of a hundred other rooms like it. She is unconscious. Another woman sits beside her, holding her hand—it is Karl's lover, Rachel. The lover does not belong here, she feels—she barely knows the dying woman. She has tried to contact Karl but couldn't reach him. The situation, however, brings her a sad kind of satisfaction. She is fulfilling a need. A social need, at this point, more than a personal one; for the woman, Eleanor, has no awareness of the other woman's presence here, nor any sense of how she arrived here, or even where she is. Inside Eleanor's mind, dreams are unfolding, or perhaps memories. The difference between the two is unclear to the Observer; they are so similar. The Observer can sense the mind trying to ascribe meaning, to create it and contextualize it. Even unconscious, the mind is burdened by this imperative. Eleanor is sitting on a wooden bench near a fountain in a city. The fountain is in front of her—it seems enormous, like a public swimming pool, though she has been instructed not to climb into it, or even to drag her hand through it, because it's filled with bacteria. Other children are running around it, splashing one another, and she feels pity for them, for the illnesses they're likely to contract as a result of this play. Between the fountain and her bench, a large number of pigeons are clustered; they are pecking at the ground where a passing old man has scattered seeds. On a nearby bench, her mother and aunt are sitting, talking. They're speaking in low tones, as though privately, but she can hear their voices very clearly, above the noise of the children and splashing water and traffic on the street that runs past this plaza. The conversation they're having is about Eleanor and her husband, or rather her fiancé, for they are not yet married, though Eleanor is pregnant with his child. This can't be so, because in this scene Eleanor is still a child herself, and she hasn't met her husband yet, or ever even yet conceived of having sex with a man; she's barely five. Yet she hears them saying:

"I don't think she's strong enough."

"Strong how?"

"Not physically I mean, not her body—I'm afraid having a child will break her mentally. She's not ready."

"You weren't much older."

"I was different. It was a different time. I was married. She's fragile."

"He could be a good father. You never know."

"He's useless, of course. He's a philanderer—I overheard her talking to her friend."

"He's charming, I'll give him that."

"You can't charm a clean diaper onto a baby."

"Ha!"

"This will sound terribly narcissistic, but I feel as though it's all a repudiation. It's her way of showing us."

"There's some truth to that, I'd imagine."

"She's always been headstrong. She'll do it her way, even if it isn't the best way, or any way at all."

"Look at her now," Eleanor's aunt says, "she's afraid of the pigeons."

As her aunt speaks these words, Eleanor realizes that it's true—the pigeons have eaten the seeds they were given and have approached her bench, expecting more. They surround her, milling about, bobbing their heads, rarely looking directly at her. But their expectations are clear, and she fears that they will hop up onto the bench with her, then onto her lap. They, too, carry disease, according to her mother. Eleanor pulls her legs up, crosses them under her skirt, and the birds fill the space her feet occupied; they're under and behind and around the bench now. The plaza's masonry is a strange color, a dark green arranged in a pattern of diamonds, mortared by thick lines of gold. The pigeons make a sound, a low burbling; their feathers rustle against each other. The rustling is strangely amplified, displaced; it's like it is happening right beside her head, right there at her ear.

But no, that sound isn't coming from the pigeons but from Irina's hands, moving in her sleep—they're in bed together in Brooklyn, it's a Saturday morning. Irina is lying on her side, half-curled like a cat; her arms are crossed at the wrist, and the hands lie on the pillow between their faces, writhing in a constant, evolving motion. She is two. Karl is off somewhere. Not in the bed, anyway. Eleanor is fully awake now, perceiving the strange spectacle of her daughter's hands. It's like a sign language—the motions aren't jerky, they're fluid, practiced—and she wonders if they mean something, if each movement is a word or letter or idea, if Irina is expressing something from her dream, in a form her mind has devised specifically for this occasion and will permanently forget when the dream has ended. There is something about this experience that is too rich, too frightening and beautiful, and Eleanor closes her eyes and rolls onto her back, and when she opens them Craig is there above her, she's in his bed in Manhattan where he has brought her for sex, and she focuses on the soft gray and blond hairs on his chest as he moves into and through her. She recognizes that he is a sad man, lonely, though he is beautiful and moneyed and would be the first to admit few human beings born to this earth are luckier. And yet it's his sadness that attracts her, probably attracts most of the assistants he sleeps with, it's something that makes her feel grown-up to recognize and appreciate. It feels good to give a man something that he wants that won't turn into an obligation. The beauty of Craig was that he appreciated everything that happened as it was happening and never betrayed any disappointment when it ended, whether it was a good meal or a professional relationship with one of his writers or half an hour in bed with a woman half his age.

She leans forward, bringing her mouth close to the microphone, and half-turns her head to the man twice her age at the other end of the table, who has just spoken, and she says, "There's nothing wrong with giving people what they want." A titter ripples through the crowd, and a few people gently applaud, but the most prominent sound in the room is the man's snort—it's a phlegmy, resonant snuffle, as from an animal many times his size, and he makes sure it carries over the PA and through the room; it's obnoxious and deafening, but it silences the audience, and he says, "Well, then, that's the difference between you and me." There's no tittering this time, but there's applause, she guesses it's different people applauding this time. The man is a writer, comparable to her in sales but valued by other men and by the academy. They are panelists at a conference. Later that night, in the hotel bar, he says to her, "A pleasure sparring with you," and instead of saying "likewise" and turning her back, she says, "Suck my cock," and then feints at him as though to knock him over. He starts, takes a step back, and then a mask of murderous rage falls down over his face and he says "You fucking bitch!" and a young woman steps between them like a fight is about to break out. Eleanor goes back to her hotel room, clenches her jaw in the bed half the night, weeps with rage. Don't engage. Don't engage. She's in a bed now, again, somebody is holding her hand, she wants to pull them closer to see who it is, but she can't. The pigeons are burbling around and beneath her, they're minding their own business. But they're death. They're death without even knowing it! Death is everywhere and alive, but it is motivated by nothing. It can't be reasoned with, it can't be persuaded away from its dispassionate aims. It rises all around you with its mottled gray wings, envelops you in a cloud of noise and dust, and takes you.

....

Except of course that it doesn't, not yet. If the Observer were able to convey this kind of information to Eleanor, it would have by now. It has known for some time that her worries—some of them, not all— were for nothing. But it has understood for some time the folly of wishing to soothe the humans; they are built to feel, and there are feelings they crave, and no amount of information can suppress the emotions they torment themselves with. Sometimes, the Observer has discovered, these emotions can warp and corrupt the body itself, in some cases flinging it headlong into the path of external danger—as in the case of the man, Karl—and in others, harming it from the inside, in ways even its inhabitant can't fully comprehend.

The woman Eleanor falls into this latter category. Her emotions have driven her, at long last, into a hospital. It's daytime—late afternoon, the light seems to suggest—and someone is holding her hand. She blinks. It's her—that woman. Rachel. Eleanor can feel her own body now. She can move her toes.

Rachel says, "Hello."

"I'm alive."

"Yes." Rachel reaches out, moves a strand of hair off her forehead that Eleanor didn't even realize was bothering her. There's an IV in her arm and another one, she gathers with a twitch of the lower muscles, shoved up into her urethra. She's achy and itchy.

"What happened?"

"Anemia, malnutrition, dehydration. Stress. You collapsed. In a bar."

"I remember." She has to gulp—her mouth is dry. "I have cancer. I was dying of cancer."

Rachel scowls. "They didn't say anything about that."

Eleanor tries to think, can't. "I'm dying. I'm sure of it."

(She isn't.)

"They said you would make a full recovery."

"I don't— that's not—"

They're both silent for a minute. Then Rachel says, "I think you were planning on telling me to fuck off last night, before you collapsed. I just want you to know that you are still welcome to do that, once you're feeling better. I don't expect any of this changes anything."

Eleanor closes her eyes.

"I tried to call Karl," Rachel says. "He isn't answering."

"Is my bag here? Can you find my phone?"

Eleanor hears Rachel rummaging at the foot of the bed. She says, "Here you go." Eleanor opens her eyes, takes the phone from the outstretched hand. Presses the power button.

"It's out of charge. My charger— It's— I left it where I'm staying."

Rachel gets up. "I'll find one." She strides bossily out of the room. Eleanor can see the appeal of this woman, suddenly. The woman thinks she can make things happen, so she does. It's not even the money. It's the shadow the money casts. She walks back into the room with the white cable bunched in her fist and says, "Nurses had one." She crouches down with a grunt and plugs the charger into a wall outlet beneath the side table. She takes the phone from Eleanor, inserts the connector into it, and hands it back. The boot logo appears on the screen.

"Is there water?" Eleanor asks.

Rachel crosses the room, pulls a paper cup from the dispenser, fills it in the sink. "Would you like me to hold it for you?" she says, with evident earnestness, at the bedside.

"No." Eleanor heaves herself to a sitting position, takes the cup, gulps the water.

Then the phone winks on and finds a signal and the screen explodes with notifications, one after the other, in a stack. All from an unfamiliar number.

> PLEASE CALL IMMEDIATELY EMERGENCY
> LEFT VOICEMAIL
> SOMETHING HAS HAPPENED IRINA IS FINE
> MY NAME IS SAM PLEASE CALL AS SOON AS YOU CAN

"Oh my god," Eleanor says, and dismisses the texts, and opens the phone app. Nine calls, all from the same number. One voicemail. She pokes it and presses the phone to her ear and listens to the sound of her world falling apart.

....

The Observer understands that it is free now. It can go where it wants, pursue whatever connections it desires; it has that power. It isn't certain what it is supposed to do, or whether anything is expected of it, now that the vectors of these lives have converged; it isn't aware of who or what might be doing the expecting. If it has been, for a time, the manifestation of the humans' need to see themselves in a certain light, and in the context of certain entities and situations, then this need is no longer so strong. For some, particularly for the girl Irina, the need has been supplanted by an equally strong repellent force, a powerful craving not to observe the self and to regard cause and effect with suspicion.

The desire, in other words, for narrative has abandoned these people. They no longer wish to be governed by events, to set events into motion. They will not be inclined to notice the Observer, to *invoke* it.

And yet the Observer's interest in them has not yet quite been exhausted. It is still curious.

To the south, the wife of the man named Louis is drunk and angry. She is on the phone, telling her friend he's really done it this time. She's going to contact a divorce lawyer first thing tomorrow. Upstairs in the house where this conversation is taking place, the girl Janine is composing a text message to Duane, the man from the carpet warehouse. He has sent her a photo of his aroused genitals, and she has reacted, inwardly, with a mixture of disgust and fear and interest. She can't see him again, that's for sure. She is trying to think of a way to put him off without accidentally intensifying his interest. She doesn't know how she knows this is a danger, but she does. As soon as she sends the text, she's going to delete the message thread, delete the photo. But she has been working on the text for almost an hour and feels no closer to completing it. Across the hall, her brother is playing a computer video game. In it, he assumes the identity of a man roaming endless hallways, seeking aliens to kill. Evidence of previous violence passes through his field of vision, whetting his appetite for the dangers that lie ahead. His absorption in this task is total.

Louis will arrive home at midday of the next afternoon, his arm numb and lifeless at his side inside its stolen coat. His wife will scream, first in anger, then relief, and then horror at her husband's appearance: he is a wreck. His children will come home from school to an empty house; a bag of chocolate chip cookies on the kitchen table will bear a sticky note that reads, FATHER HOME. AT HOSPITAL. EAT THESE. Louis will attribute the wound, in conversation with the doctors who try and fail to save the arm, to a workshop accident. The doctors won't believe him. Eventually they will have to amputate, but for now he will return home after a few days, heavily bandaged, to a family who see him differently: a figure of mystery and slightly frightened respect. When his daughter notes that the CyberSleuths thread about the Broken River murders has been updated to include information about two new killings, including a description of an escaped perpetrator who is believed to have been wounded, she will spend an entire night awake, mind racing. During this time she will text Duane back. In the morning she will delete her CyberSleuths account and remove the bookmark from her browser. She will also find the paperback about the murders and burn it in the backyard and bury the ashes in the cold ground behind the shed.

Louis will not be able to believe that he hasn't been caught. The possibility will remain real, both to him and to the engines of fate. The Observer doesn't know what will happen; maybe some future sleuth, official or avocational, will discover the clue that cracks the case open and leads the police to his door. But until then, Louis will return to work at the carpet warehouse with his new prosthetic arm, and will rejoin Duane, who will vanish from Argos around the same time Janine announces that she is pregnant. Louis will declare this turn of events to have been inevitable and will tell his daughter that he loves her. He will learn to wank lefty. He will wait for arrest, either until he is arrested or until he is dead.

Miles away, the trailer where the man Joe lived sits quietly among others like it, in a tidy arrangement of unpaved streets. It will be some time before police arrive to search for evidence of his previous crimes, and, unexpectedly, to free the near-starving cat that has been trapped there without food or water for days. The cat will dart past the officers as they pop open the door with their crowbar; it will not be long before it finds shelter in some other trailer.

And out of the chaos of the crime scene there will eventually emerge a kind of order. Police will investigate and question; a silent ambulance will arrive to take the bodies away. Sam and Irina will spend twenty-four hours alone together in the house, under the protection of police and in constant telephone contact with Eleanor and Rachel. Rachel will bully the hospital into releasing Eleanor and will drive her north to be with her daughter. By the time they arrive, the grandparents will have converged as well: Karl's father and stepmother, Eleanor's mother and aunt. Together this group will move around the house in Broken River like ghosts; and the house, too, will be like a ghost, for none of these people will wish to stay there, and they will soon abandon it, and it will once again stand empty, this time for good. (One double murder is a fluke; two is a curse. Even the hobos won't roost here anymore, and someday teenagers will burn the place to the ground.)

Eventually Eleanor and Irina will return to New York, where they belong. They will bring Sam with them because Sam needs somewhere to go, and the three will live in a Brooklyn apartment owned by Rachel Rosen's family, who will eventually rent it to them on a permanent basis at a reasonable but, of course, not ridiculously inexpensive rate. (The Rosens did not acquire their money, after all, through acts of generosity.) Eleanor will revise and complete her novel, and Irina will abandon her near-complete draft. She will have lost interest in writing and developed, before long, an equally powerful desire to make art.

And farther north, across a border that is meaningless to the Observer, in a town called Brandon, a teenaged girl lies on her back, upon a filthy rag rug, in the basement of a gray-and-yellow bungalow. She wears thin black canvas shoes stylized with three white leather stripes; the girl has used a black marker to color the stripes black as well, though much of the ink has since worn away. Her torn jeans are black and tight against wide hips. A fold of pale belly is exposed between a studded black leather belt and a loose-fitting tee shirt, also torn, that depicts a fierce, white-eyed tiger head surrounded by orange horror-movie text spelling out the words *PIERCE THE VEIL*. Thick powder has rendered the girl's face a stark white; black lipstick and eyeliner throw her features into sharp relief. A trail of shapes descends from her left eye, drawn in black eyebrow pencil; the first is a teardrop that, several iterations later, has evolved into a dagger that seems to threaten her left ear. Her hair is cut unevenly at around shoulder length and is dyed purple save for an orange streak that hangs over her eyes. Her eyes are closed, and her hands drum a rhythm on the rug; her mouth forms words, a chant:

> . . . I hate my *mo*ther
> I hate my *fa*ther
> I hate my *birth* pa*rents*
> I hate Ca*n*ada
> I hate the *day*time
> I hate my *bod*-dayyy
> I hate Thanks*giv*ing
> I hate the *liv*ing . . .

The girl is aware that she was adopted, from America, in 2005. She knows nothing else about the time before she was taken in by Mr. and Mrs. Gerald Fucking Murray and given a new life in Mani-fucking-toba. She knows herself only by the name her parents gave her, which is Jenny Murray, but she likes to tell people she's an American and that someday she's going to go back there and find out what she came from. Also she is going to get a fucking job so that she can get a fucking apartment and her own drum set and then she can have an actual band of her own instead of just sitting around like an idiot getting high while her boyfriend's shitty band practices their shitty songs.

She will be seventeen in three days. One more year and she is free. Her chant goes on and on as her mother's footsteps make their nervous way across the kitchen floor, to the dining room, to the foyer. "Jenny!" she's calling up the stairs, evidently convinced Jenny is up in her bedroom with headphones on. Which is why she has come down here, on the little nest beside the hot-water heater, where the dog used to sleep before the dog died. Her old stuffed frog is here—at some point it became the dog's, and now, lying just a few inches from her head, it reeks of him, his terrible breath and rank fur. "Jenny!" Her mother wants her to go to bed. It's late. Jenny isn't tired. The Observer is in her mind and above her. The water heater kicks on with a whoosh. She chants, faster and faster, until she can't take it anymore, and then she laughs until she can barely breathe.

Acknowledgments

I'd like to thank everyone who helped me to revise and publish *Broken River*, particularly Rhian Ellis, Laurel Lathrop, Ethan Nosowsky, Adam Price, Jim Rutman, Lauren Schenkman, Sharma Shields, and Ed Skoog. My colleagues at Cornell University were very supportive during the writing of this book, and I'm grateful to them as well. And I continue to feel honored by the enthusiasm, goodwill, and tireless energy of Fiona McCrae and the entire staff of Graywolf Press.